# INDIGENOUS TOURISM:
# THE COMMODIFICATION AND
# MANAGEMENT OF CULTURE

# ADVANCES IN TOURISM RESEARCH

**Series Editor: Professor Stephen J. Page**
University of Stirling, U.K.
s.j.page@stir.ac.uk

Advances in Tourism Research series publishes monographs and edited volumes that comprise state-of-the-art research findings, written and edited by leading researchers working in the wider field of tourism studies. The series has been designed to provide a cutting edge focus for researchers interested in tourism, particularly the management issues now facing decision-makers, policy analysts and the public sector. The audience is much wider than just academics and each book seeks to make a significant contribution to the literature in the field of study by not only reviewing the state of knowledge relating to each topic but also questioning some of the prevailing assumptions and research paradigms which currently exist in tourism research. The series also aims to provide a platform for further studies in each area by highlighting key research agendas which will stimulate further debate and interest in the expanding area of tourism research. The series is always willing to consider new ideas for innovative and scholarly books, inquiries should be made directly to the Series Editor.

Published:

PIKE
Bridging Theory and Practice

THOMAS
Small Firms in Tourism: International Perspectives

LUMSDON & PAGE
Tourism and Transport

KERR
Tourism Public Policy and the Strategic Management of Failure

WILKS & PAGE
Managing Tourist Health and Safety in the New Millennium

BAUM & LUNDTORP
Seasonality in Tourism

TEO, CHANG & HO
Interconnected Worlds: Tourism in Southeast Asia

ASHWORTH & TUNBRIDGE
The Tourist-Historic City: Retrospect and Prospect of Managing the Heritage City

SONG & WITT
Tourism Demand Modelling and Forecasting: Modern Econometric Approaches

RYAN & PAGE
Tourism Management: Towards the New Millennium

Forthcoming titles include:

SIMPSON
Back to the Future: In Search of an Effective Tourism Planning Model

**Related Elsevier Journals - sample copies available on request**
*Air(line) Transport journal*
*Annals of Tourism Research*
*International Journal of Hospitality Management*
*International Journal of Intercultural Relations*
*Tourism Management*
*World Development*

# INDIGENOUS TOURISM: THE COMMODIFICATION AND MANAGEMENT OF CULTURE

EDITED BY

## CHRIS RYAN

*University of Waikato, Hamilton, New Zealand*

## MICHELLE AICKEN

*Horwath Asia Pacific Ltd, Auckland, New Zealand*

2005

ELSEVIER

Amsterdam – Boston – Heidelberg – London – New York – Oxford
Paris – San Diego – San Francisco – Singapore – Sydney – Tokyo

Elsevier
The Boulevard, Langford Lane, Kidlington, Oxford OX5 1GB, UK
Radarweg 29, PO Box 211, 1000 AE Amsterdam, The Netherlands

First edition 2005
Reprinted 2006

**British Library Cataloguing in Publication Data**
A catalogue record for this book is available from the British Library

**Library of Congress Cataloging-in-Publication Data**
A catalog record for this book is available from the Library of Congress

ISBN–13: 978-0-08-044620-2
ISBN–10: 0-08-044620-5

For information on all Elsevier publications
visit our website at books.elsevier.com

Printed and bound in *The Netherlands*

06 07 08 09 10   10 9 8 7 6 5 4 3 2

Working together to grow
libraries in developing countries

www.elsevier.com | www.bookaid.org | www.sabre.org

ELSEVIER    BOOK AID International    Sabre Foundation

*With thanks to Alison, Anne, Asad, Charlie, Jenny and Tim.*
*Your help by taking on other tasks helped to make this book possible.*

# Contents

# List of Figures

# List of Photographs

# List of Tables

# Contributors

**Michelle Aicken** graduated from the University of Otago and subsequently worked in Japan and the United Kingdom in a variety of posts. Currently she is completing her doctoral studies at the University of Waikato, New Zealand. She was a co-organiser of the conference, *Taking Tourism to the Limits* hosted by the Department of Tourism Management. Michelle is able to claim affiliation with Ngai Tahu of the South Island of New Zealand.

**Jeremy Buultjens** lectures at Southern Cross University and is the course administrator of the Degree of Bachelor in Indigenous Tourism Management offered by the University in conjunction with the College of Australian Indigenous Peoples. He holds a doctorate from Griffith University. His research interests include indigenous tourism, tourism in protected areas and regional tourism.

**Dean Carson** is the Head of the Centre for Regional Tourism Research, Southern Cross University. His research interests include managing regional tourism for economic and social gains and the use of information and communications technology in tourism product distribution. Dean has degrees in history, communications, tourism and science. He has worked in rural and regional Australia researching topics as varied as: infrastructure and housing needs in remote Indigenous communities; health workforce retention in rural areas; and the role of Local Government in tourism management.

**Jenny Cave** lectures in special interest and cultural tourism at the University of Waikato. She had a distinguished career in Museums, having served for many years with the Canadian Museum services before being "head-hunted" back to the land of her birth, New Zealand, to establish Capital Discovery Place, Wellington. She was then subsequently Director of Library and Museum Services for the City of Hamilton. Having a Master's degree from the University of Ottawa, she is currently completing her doctorate at the University of Waikato.

**Johan R. Edelheim** lectures at the International College of Tourism and Hospitality, Manly, Australia, and is completing his doctorate at Macquarie University, Australia. Johan is a member of the Cultural Studies Association of Australasia and his research interests relate to imagery, identity and culture. His Ph.D. is entitled "Special Interest Tourism as a Contributor to Cultural Identity Formation" and the methodology he is using is a triangulation of Narrative analysis, Sociological deconstruction and Hermeneutic Phenomenology.

**Maribeth Erb** is Associate Professor in the Department of Sociology of the University of Singapore. She obtained doctorate from the State University of New York. Her research interests lie in anthropology, kinship relationships and social anthropology, and urban anthropology. She has published research relating to tourism and Indonesia including work published in the *Annals of Tourism Research*.

**Vicky Gerbich** grew up in Western Springs, Illinois, a suburb outside of Chicago and obtained a Bachelor of Science degree in Geography from the University of Illinois and a M.Sc. in Geography (Environmental Planning and Policy) from Southern Illinois University. She began to research and study the environmental land ethics of Native Americans and reservation development for her undergraduate thesis, and throughout her education and professional experience, continued to be interested in sustainable development within different socio-cultural contexts. After working for an open-space county agency outside of Chicago, she moved to American Samoa in the South Pacific. There she is trying to establish a system whereby the public sees the value of preserving the natural resources and implementing a land use system that adopts more enforceable regulations to promote economic and cultural development through environmental stewardship.

**Sasha Graham** is a research assistant with the School of Tourism and Hospitality Management, Southern Cross University. She is currently completing a Bachelor of Social Science at Southern Cross University.

**Freya Higgins-Desbiolles** lectures at the School of International Business in the University of South Australia. She served on the Management Committee of the Responsible Tourism Network in Adelaide and was the Coordinator of the Global Education Centre for a number of years. She is now on the Management Committee of the International Institute for Peace through Tourism (Australia). She has worked with the Ngarrindjeri community of South Australia for over seven years.

**Jeremy Huyton** spent several years in the hotel industry holding various managerial positions before resuming his education and gaining a doctorate from the University of Birmingham in the UK. He currently lectures at the University of Canberra after holding posts at Hong Kong Polytechnic University, Charles Darwin University and the Australian International Hotel School. In addition to his teaching Jeremy has sought to establish training schemes for Australian Aboriginals, has business interests in China, and still finds time to develop his olive trees outside Canberra.

**Gloria Ingram** is currently completing her doctoral studies at Edith Cowan University, Western Australia. She has long had an interest in Aboriginal Affairs having previously undertaken research and also has a sustained interest in phenomenology as a research process. Consequently she has contributed to the *Indo-Pacific Journal of Phenomenology* including research on farm stay tourism.

**Henare Johnson** is Postgraduate Researcher in the Centre for Maori and Indigenous Planning and Development, Lincoln University, New Zealand. His main research interest is Maori tourism and Maori economic development.

**Joseph E. Mbaiwa** is a Research Fellow in Tourism Management at the Harry Oppenheimer Okavango Research Centre, University of Botswana. He has a BA (Environmental Science), Post Graduate Diploma in Education and an M.Sc. (Environmental Science), all of which qualifications were obtained at the University of Botswana in 1992, 1993 and 1999 respectively. He is presently pursuing a doctorate degree in the Department of Recreation, Park and Tourism Sciences at Texas A&M University, United States. His research interests centre on sustainable tourism development in the Okavango Delta, Botswana, and he has contributed to projects relating to local people participation in the tourism industry and the implementation of the Community-Based Natural Resource Management programme in the Okavango Delta.

**Alison McIntosh** is Associate Professor at the Department of Tourism Management, University of Waikato Management School. She obtained her doctorate in the United Kingdom, and migrated to New Zealand in 1997. Her main research interests are in tourists' experiences of heritage and culture, and the sustainable development of indigenous tourism. Some of this latter research has been funded by the New Zealand Foundation for Research, Science and Technology, and by the New Zealand Ministry for Maori Development, Te Puni Kôkiri. She has obtained publications in leading journals such as *Annals of Tourism Research* and *Tourism Management*.

**Dieter K. Müller** lectures at the University of Umeå in Sweden in the Department of Social and Economic Geography. He has a number of interests pertaining to tourism and its use of space, and recently completed research into patterns of holiday home ownership in addition to work completed with Robert Pettersson on Sami culture and its role in Swedish tourism.

**Sanjay Nepal** is Assistant Professor at the Department of Recreation, Park and Tourism Sciences at Texas A&M University. He holds a doctoral degree from the University of Bern, Switzerland. He is currently researching the involvement of local communities in tourism planning in British Columbia, Canada and in several protected areas in Nepal. He is also a co-author of *Great Himalaya: Tourism and Dynamics of Change in Nepal* and is a recognized expert relating to the impacts of tourism and environmental impacts in the Himalayas. In Canada he has obtained grants from the Canadian Social Sciences and Humanities Research Council for research on biodiversity, human impacts and conservation.

**Robert Pettersson** gained his doctorate in Human Geography from Umeå University in Sweden. His thesis related to the development of Sami tourism in Northern Europe, which is also the subject of his book *Sami Tourism in Northern Sweden – Supply, Demand and Interaction*, published in 2004. He works as a researcher at the European Tourism Research Institute, ETOUR, in Östersund, Sweden. His research interests are currently centred on indigenous tourism, tourism in peripheral areas, attitudes, accessibility and cultural events. He has published various papers on this issue, and has also published papers on second home ownership in Sweden for the Cerum Research Institute.

**Chris Ryan** holds a doctoral degree from the Aston Business School, United Kingdom. He is the editor of *Tourism Management*, an elected member of the International Academy for the Study of Tourism and Professor of Tourism at the University of Waikato Management School and Visiting Professor at the Centre of Travel and Tourism, the University of Northumbria.

Currently he is completing an audit of New Zealand's tourism research strategy for the New Zealand Ministry of Tourism.

**Birgit Trauer** is completing her doctoral studies at the University of Queensland having graduated from Griffith University with a BA and the University of Waikato with a Post Graduate Diploma in Tourism Management. She has worked for a variety of businesses including Air India and other airlines, and as a consultant. Her teaching experience includes work at Lakehead and Queensland Universities.

**Iain Waller** spent several years as a manager of properties and businesses before returning to do some post-graduate study where he accidentally ended up as an academic for a decade. After about 30 publications and a lot of fun with various research partners and topic areas, he has now returned to the business world and is enjoying the challenges of starting his own business and putting his theories into practice.

**Takayoshi Yamamura** gained his doctorate in urban engineering from the Department of Urban Engineering, University of Tokyo, Japan. He is currently Associate Professor in Heritage Tourism Planning and Management at Kyoto Saga University of Arts, Japan and is a researcher at the National Museum of Ethnology in Osaka. Additionally he is a member of the ICOMOS International Committee on Historic Towns and Villages. His research interests pertain to culture, heritage, historic towns and for several years, since 1998, he has been monitoring changes in Lijiang, China; the subject of his contribution in this book. Other contributions on the same topic include his chapter entitled *Authenticity, ethnicity and social transformation at World Heritage Sites: tourism, retailing and cultural change in Lijiang, China* In Derek Hall's book, *Tourism and Transition: Political, Economic and Social Issues*, while he has also published various other papers relating to the same topic in journals such as *Tourism — an interdisciplinary journal* and *Acta Scientiarum Naturalium*.

# Preface

At the time of writing, May 2004, the issue of the rights of indigenous peoples remains salient. In the editors' country, New Zealand, a debate over Maori claims to the foreshore under the Treaty of Waitangi has sparked a national debate about the constitutional position of Maori in an increasingly multi-cultural society. The then current Government was tending toward the establishment of a Royal Commission to assess these issues and their constitutional implications, but even as we write in early May 2004, the issues remain unsolved and contentious. Further, but a matter of months prior to our completion of the text, in March 2004, Australia again faced the problem of the marginalization of Australian Aboriginal peoples and more particularly an urban-based, economically-deprived grouping, as Aboriginal people rioted in the streets of the Sydney suburb of Redfern following the death of Thomas Hickey in a police car chase. In Kuala Lumpur, in February 2004, indigenous peoples made representations calling for a full recognition of indigenous rights to their traditional territories, genetic resources and traditional knowledge at the Seventh Conference of the Parties (COP-7) of the Convention on Biological Diversity (CBD) held under the auspices of the United Nations. In Canada, in February 2003, the British Columbia Court of Appeal, in what has come to be known as the Haida Decision, upheld the right of indigenous peoples to be involved in and give free prior informed consent to developments initiated by governments and private corporations as they affect traditional territories.

It thus seems that a world of turmoil exists with reference to the rights of indigenous peoples; and yet it exists in face of a curiously indifferent and unknowing population given that generally so little of the issues emerge in the news on occasions other than those of riots or specific conclaves that initiate public exhibitions of dissent. Thus, on many occasions, the public face of indigenous peoples is one of anger and of claims that to many seem extreme. Rarely do the media seek to rationalize such sentiments and at times it appears that debate comprises the utterance of slogans on both sides of the issue. That this need not be so was exhibited by the *New Zealand Herald's* examination of New Zealand's foreshore debate, the customary title of Maori to coastal waters and the nature of the Treaty of Waitangi in many long articles in February and March 2004. Given that the media help shape perceptions of place and peoples, the role of not simply the news media, but that media associated with tourism promotion might deserve examination, particularly if the relationship of tourism to the wider social issues is to be understood.

There then exists a paradox. On the one hand there appears little public concern over such issues as indigenous peoples' claims to rights over biological diversities and DNA that emanate from their traditional lands until some "news-worthy event" usually based on discord occurs. However, on the other hand, tourism promotional bodies both: (a) exhort the importance of tourism based on indigenous people's cultures in the portfolio mix of tourism product that a country has to offer as meeting a growing demand in "cultural tourism"; while (b) simultaneously holding out a promise that tourism can generate income and employment for communities traditionally marginalized from the economic mainstream.

Therefore there appears little reason to doubt the importance of tourism based on indigenous peoples' cultures, either as part of tourism itself or as part of a wider social movement, and that in itself would justify a book looking at these issues. That this specific book emerged was due to a much more prosaic reason. In December 2003 the University of Waikato Management School's Department of Tourism Management hosted a conference entitled *Taking Tourism to the Limits*. One of the approaches suggested to potential delegates was to consider issues pertaining to liminality, especially with reference to indigenous tourism. This topic was selected for a number of reasons, including the interests of the conference convenors and the University's location and tradition. For example, the University is a leasee of land awarded to the Tanui tribe under a land settlement, while one of the evening events was a visit to the Rotowhio Marae where delegates were hosted by representatives of the Te Arawa people at the New Zealand Institute for Maori Arts and Crafts. This evening proved both enjoyable and interesting, particularly as our hosts patiently dealt with questions from 100 or more academics about what it meant to be Maori in contemporary society. Essentially the answer that emerged was that it was a personally enriching experience as those concerned enjoyed the advantages of living in both Maori and non-Maori societies.

For whatever reasons, one of the best subscribed themes in the conference was that dealing with indigenous peoples and tourism, and thus for the most part the book comprises chapters derived from those papers. Additionally papers have been included based on published works, and the due recognitions are formally recounted in the acknowledgements.

The purpose of the book is therefore to complement earlier collections edited by colleagues and friends, notably those of Dick Butler and Tom Hinch (*Tourism and Indigenous Peoples*, 1996) and Mike Robinson and Priscilla Boniface (*Tourism and Cultural Conflicts*, 1999). In doing so it represents an update of research while perhaps illustrating that the same themes of control and presentation still exist. This book perhaps differs from the others by endorsing a strict definition of indigenous peoples as defined by the United Nations. By reason of the location of the conference the book is slanted toward experiences in Australasia, if only because of the experiences and research of the editors; but cognizance of a wider global phenomenon is provided with reference to research in China, Scandinavia and Canada. In an attempt to provide some coherence to what might otherwise appear to be a disparate group of papers, the editors have provided some linking text seeking to contextualize the individual chapters, and it is hoped that contributors will not look askance at such attempts. Finally, the book would not have come into being were it not for the kindness of immediate colleagues both during the conference itself and subsequent to that event as the editors "escaped" the rigors of daily office attendance. The support of Stephen Page as editor of the Elsevier series must also be noted as he smoothed the path toward publication, of Tom Clark at Elsevier for trusting in the project, and finally to the co-ordinating editor at Elsevier, Hannah Collet. For their support, the editors are truly thankful!

Chris Ryan and Michelle Aicken
*Editors*

Chapter 1

# Introduction: Tourist-Host Nexus — Research Considerations

Chris Ryan

## Introduction

The purpose of this introductory chapter is to examine the nexus of researcher and researched within the context of the relationship between tourism and indigenous peoples. It will be argued that three dimensions exist in this relationship, namely academia, the indigenous perspective and the imperatives of tourism. Subsequent to this there will be a definition of what constitutes an indigenous people derived from the United Nations. Finally the contributions of the different authors will be introduced, highlighting their subject matter and the ways in which they relate to each other and the themes identified in this introduction.

From an academic perspective there has been a growing interest in tourism and indigenous peoples, symbolised in part by the books edited by Butler & Hinch (1996) and Robinson & Boniface (1999). As will be noted from the bibliographic listing at the end of this book, of the total number of references approximately 40% date from the year 2000. It is also true to state that the perceptions of meanings associated with cultural tourism have changed considerably. One example of this is provided by Greenwood who, in 2004, reviewed his earlier writings of Hondarribia's festival, the Alarde using the words "Fourteen years later, I find myself not only more troubled by my own judgments but also by the professional stance that they imply. It is not that my critique of tourism's cultural impacts seems wrong, but I have now experienced the way I've researched and deliver this judgment to be professionally self-serving"(Greenwood 2004: 167). Similarly, one turn of the academic gaze is from the impacts of tourists to one that scrutinizes the perceptions of tourists. Bruner (1996: 171) tells the story of how tourists viewed two equally "legitimate" performances of the Indonesian Ramayana, but assessed each differently, and rating the second as being "like Miami Beach" because of the location of performance — a Hyatt Hotel. In short, perception of performance had little to do with the nature of the performers, but to a sense of staging. In the experience of the author the same comments are made of Maori performances by tourists at the Maori Arts and Crafts Centre in Rotorua, even whilst the performances

**Indigenous Tourism: The Commodification and Management of Culture**
Copyright © 2005 by Elsevier Ltd.
ISBN: 0-08-044620-5

may be akin to those performed at the Aotearoa Maori Performing Arts Festival (Richards & Ryan 2004).

Consequently the modeling of the relationship between native peoples and tourism has passed through several refinements, but for the most part remains dominated by an academic parameter based upon traditional European perspectives. Therein lays a potential problem in any analysis of this subject. In the European/North American tradition, universities exist to generate and disseminate data, information and knowledge to and for all who can benefit from that process. Public funding of universities is predicated on that understanding, and it is because of that premise that concerns are expressed about possible departures from objectivity and open peer assessment in systems where private industry sponsors research, particularly perhaps in the field of drugs and medicine, but in other arenas also. Consequently, the researcher trained in an American/European tradition who works in the field of indigenous tourism is continually reminded, if not mindful of, the fact that many indigenous societies are exclusive and not inclusive. Knowledge is transmitted to those who are initiated, and indeed, in some instances, only those from certain families may be potential initiates. The researcher is ever the outsider.

On the other hand, this role of the researcher is not unique to tourism, and has been the matter of long debate in the field of anthropology. The conventional response of the anthropologist or ethnographic researcher is to seek means of immersion into a host people's society through various means, including marriage in some instances, so as to become an honored member of a cultural group. That status involves the role of interpreter and intermediary as the researcher writes about and explains a cosmology different to that of the dominant culture. This perspective is amply illustrated by the late T. G. H. Strehlow and his role of both recorder and advocate of Australian Aboriginals (Rowse 1999). Strehlow recognized this debt and role many times, for example writing:

> [I] must . . . [acknowledge] what is by far my greatest debt — that which I owe to my old native friends who supplied me so liberally with their secret lore and admitted me to so many of their totemic rites.

> Though born at Hermannsburg and thus "conceived" into the ratapa totem, I was only a very young newly-fledged University graduate when I returned to Central Australia in 1932. I was watched for 12 months before . . . the ceremonial chief finally decided to reveal to me his . . . ceremonies and to entrust his sacred myth and his song verses to my keeping . . . From that point onwards I was sure of the confidence of the remaining Aranda and Loritja totemic clan elders. — Songs of Central Australia (TGH Strehlow 1971: xiv).

Strehlow worked among the Arrernte and subsequently other Aboriginal peoples of Central Australia from the 1930s at a time when traditional ways were still strong, but under such threat that native peoples themselves feared for their extinction. The contemporary tourism researcher works under a different imperative of an emergence of, and new confidence among, such peoples, as is evidenced in land claims and statements of rights. Nonetheless, in many senses this, it is argued, creates a more complex research environment. Ryan

(1997b, 1999a) is of the view that, in New Zealand, Maori occupy three worlds, the world of Maoridom, of Pakeha (New Zealanders of European descent) and the world where the two worlds interact, while at the same time Maori society is traditionally tribal and not wholly homogenous in Maori eyes. Not to understand this is to fail to appreciate the importance of tribal, family, genealogy and attachment to place that exists not simply at an emotional level but within the very core of a person's being. The non-indigenous academic researcher thus has to immerse themselves in such worlds, but does so from an academic system where increasingly research assessment exercises require publication more frequently than was once the case. In cultures where time possesses the characteristics of seasonality and an awaiting of when time and circumstance are "right," the regime of research funding born of perceived needs of transparency and accountability of and for research monies sits badly because of its constant demand for "output."

The consequence is that there is a potential for indigenous peoples to be treated poorly by academic researchers; not necessarily through ill-intent on the part of researchers, but because of systemic differences between worlds. The indigenous person might well view the enquiry of the academic tourism researcher with a degree of cynicism, as the publication of a paper progresses career, but not necessarily promotes benefit for the host. Such a relationship fits poorly with the concept of gift giving in many indigenous societies where gifts are an exchange of mutual obligations and not simply the bestowing of a favour that seeks nothing in return. That progress is made, is because a series of mitigating circumstances exist with three domains; namely those of academia, the society of indigenous peoples and the imperatives of tourism. Briefly these circumstances can be described thus.

## The Frame of Academia

A traditional role of universities is that of being a critic of society, and in the search for knowledge there lays an inherent questioning of why are things the way they are, and an inclusiveness of sources of information and knowledge. Consequently around the world universities have established centres, departments and/or faculties that are devoted to the study of marginalised groups, including those of indigenous peoples. Increasingly these are being staffed by members of those groups themselves. This is not always a comfortable process for either organisations or individuals as evidenced by New Zealand's Performance Based Research Funding exercise, where Maori and Pacific Island concerns and students were specifically itemised for mention in documentation released by the Tertiary Education Council with a re-affirmation that research in these areas could equal world best practice. The very specificity of such mention hints at a debate within academic circles relating to Indigenous People's interests and concerns within a traditional European academic domain of objectivity and measurement. How does that fit with traditional wisdom or an oral tradition? On the other hand parallels exist with other debates about the nature of empiricism, such as those pertaining to feminism as an example of a critical tradition, and in the application of post-modern analyses to contemporary society.

One facet of this process has been the emergence of sensitivities toward indigenous communities with the publication of guidelines and codes of ethics pertaining to academic research. One example of this is the guideline produced by the Australian Institute of

Aboriginal and Torres Straits Islanders Studies (AIATSIS). This identifies a requirement for consultation, mutual understanding, respect of individuals and cultural property, involvement, benefits to communities, good faith and informed consent. Szynklarz & Firth (2004) illustrate the practicalities involved in implementing these principles in a paper describing research at Manyallaluk in Australia's Northern Territory. Foremost, among respondents, were issues of shyness, poor English and a reluctance to discuss what is deemed to be private and cultural issues, the nature of which might determine who can speak about what. The conclusion drawn is that extensive planning and preparation is required before conducting research. Again, however, it is possible to overstress this requirement with reference to indigenous peoples — a requirement that appears to demarcate indigenous people as possessing difference that poses problems. The same issues exist within other marginal groupings in Western societies. Ryan & Martin (2001) discuss issues pertaining to research among strippers and it is noted that immersion into the world of strip bars was a pre-requisite to obtaining confidences, that even then, emerged partly by chance. Ethnographic work with homosexuals, football hooligans, gang members and others groups deemed "marginal" illustrate the same issues of not only trust but problems for the position of the researcher and the researcher's role as confidant, information source and reporter. Indeed Ryan (2004) even goes so far as to argue that these situations pose problems for ethics committees within academia that proceed on Weberian lines and the reality for many academic researchers is that these procedures potentially inhibit research.

Consequently, and perhaps specifically within tourism with its emphasis upon the importance of the experience as the core of the "product" and its embracing of "gazes," there is an acceptance of complex understandings of issues pertaining to indigenous tourism. Researchers perhaps no longer seek for a meta-narrative, but rather embrace specificities that relate to time, place and context comprising host, tourist and location. The nature of the debate abounds with terms such as "commodification," "hegemonies," "politicisation," "authenticity" and "authorisation." Tourism is increasingly viewed not simply as a force for the creation of a stereotypical image of a marginalised people, but a means by which those peoples aspire to economic and political power for self advancement, and as a place of dialogue between and within differing world views. Thus, for example, native American Indian peoples can use casino revenues to reinforce systems of cultural integrity, Sami peoples achieve markets for traditional goods through events such as the festival at Jokkmokk and Australian Aboriginal people tell stories of the dream time as a counter story to colonial histories. At the same time, on governmental tourism boards and working parties, indigenous peoples claim a voice to secure greater or smaller degrees of political power as tourism acquires an increasing importance through its economic growth.

Again, all is not lost for the conventional academic researcher. Although it is not a complete picture and is one-sided, research into the attitude of visitors to sites of Indigenous people's culture is more accessible. Additionally such research may be important as an antidote to the optimism that seems to be expressed among many politicians that international visitors are "very interested" in the culture of others. Just what is the nature of that interest, and the level of that interest are important determinants in establishing the feasibility of possible tourism products based on the culture of Indigenous peoples.

## The Society of Indigenous Peoples

First, a caveat! It is evident that any writing of the "society of indigenous peoples" represents a classification of homogeneity that fails to recognise differences important to peoples; be they differences of language, cosmology, culture, arts and heritage. Yet there are commonalities; one of which is the wish by those responsible for tourism promotion to capitalise upon the culture of people unique to a place and the images thus created. For example, National Tourism Organisations seek to identify assets specific to their own country, and while good hotels, restaurants, beautiful scenery and McDonalds might be found in any country, the Navajo, Larrakia and Te Arawa peoples are specific to a place; thereby in marketing terms, generating a unique selling proposition and images that support branding of that place. As will be discussed within the following selection of papers (e.g. Yamamura) this might be said to pose problems of commodification of art and culture, giving rise to what has been termed "airport art" as facsimiles of traditional art are shrunk to fit the suitcase of the international tourist. For indigenous peoples, however, contrary to much of what was initially written by academic researchers (e.g. as indicated by Greenwood in 2004), the issue is not so much an issue of a debasement of art, but who is undertaking the "copying" and the rights of that person. As Daniel (1996) has pointed out with reference to dance performances, dance, and indeed other arts, are exercises in creativity, of an expression of a performer's, painter's or carver's skill, inspiration and art. The multiple replication of, for example, a print, does not inherently diminish the original thoughts and designs. This is, of course, a complex question with many nuances. To what extent do the numerous reproductions of the "Mona Lisa" enhance or diminish the original, and people's reactions when perhaps they finally see the painting in the Louvre's art gallery?

From the perspective of an indigenous person, such arguments are perhaps even more complex. Art is not wholly an individualistic act, but the continuance of a tradition bequeathed by ancestors for social purpose, as is demonstrated by the panels in Maori meeting houses. Equally, art may possess something of the sacred; it is an expression of a person's being, of his or her life, and thus the aesthetic criteria used within Western tradition to critique a piece of art is not appropriate. What is appropriate within the eyes of some indigenous peoples, particularly those of Australasia, is whether the person has the "right" to use that art style. Consequently the reports of the Aotearoa Maori Tourism Federation (1994, 1995) define Maori art as essentially work by Maori inspired by being Maori, and hence the use of Maori designs by non-Maori persons is an appropriation of Maori "mana" or authority. The issue of authenticity as discussed in the academic tourism literature is perceived as being subsumed within a more important argument of "authorisation" — who authorises and for what purpose?

This issue is expressly shown by The Dumbartung Aboriginal Corporation — Wall of Shame web site that specifically rejects: (a) eco-tourism because it does impact on sacred sites; (b) tourist commodities based on Australian Aboriginal designs that are made by non-Aboriginal peoples; and (c) the appropriation of Aboriginal designs by non-Aboriginal graphic artists. The Dumbartung have taken their resistance even further by, for example, demonstrating at locations where the author of "*Mutant Message Down Under*," Marla Morgan, gives promotional talks on the premise that she has not simply misinformed audiences about Aboriginal culture and rites but has done so for personal gain.

Yet there is another side to this coin. From this perspective of the indigenous belonging solely to native peoples, it would almost be impossible for non-indigenous researchers to write about the affairs of indigenous peoples. But such writing does appear, and is made possible only through the active co-operation of the societies being reported upon. Complex nuances are at work in these processes. First, most indigenous peoples retain strong concepts of hospitality, and, as with gift giving, hospitality often entails an acceptance of mutual and reciprocal responsibilities. Indeed, in the tribal histories of many Maori tribes, the breaking of the protocols of hospitality legitimises acts of *utu* or revenge. The academic researcher can and does utilise such a tradition and one pre-requisite of this is that due recognition of information sources must be given. It is thus essential to both parties, the researcher and researched, that due acknowledgement must be given in any academic writing, and hence any author must establish the policies of the tourism journals in which he or she wishes to place their writing prior to submission in this respect. Second, increasingly the intermediaries through which a researcher may make contact with those he or she wishes to study are increasingly better educated and indeed may be tertiary educated. Hence there is a better understanding of the role of the academic researcher and the wish to acquire and disseminate information and knowledge. Two consequences flow from this. First, there is a respect among many indigenous peoples for "knowledge," which might be said to acquire its own patina of sanctity. There is respect for the process of knowledge acquisition, which is perceived as requiring its own sacrifices. The role of academic researcher can thus be appreciated from this perspective, particularly if the researcher shows respect for informants. Second, indigenous societies are, to state the obvious, societies in a process of change. Impacted by dominant societies within which they have been, for the most part, dislodged and marginalised, the need for adaptation through which they retain core values but work out a *modus operandi* in a new world is an imperative important for their longer term survival. It is also the way in which they can contribute to an enrichment of the wider society, providing for it alternative voices and perspectives that challenge and cause reflection. This author lives in an Australasian context where the relationship between a dominant society (that is itself emerging from a past colonial subservience by which it no longer calls itself European) and its own indigenous peoples is complex, tense but notably enriching, particularly perhaps in the case of New Zealand. Australian Aboriginal peoples from different tribes and their Maori counterparts have recognised that tourism and the advocacy platform it provides is important in achieving recognition for both culture and claims. The danger of "cultural" tourism is that it classifies and categorises product into an entertainment where the entertainers are captives of the impresarios. On the other hand the promise of cultural tourism is that it creates dialogue, provides access to economic levers of income and job creation, and perhaps even more importantly, to the mainstream of economic activities. The difficulties of this should not be under-estimated. For example, many of the communities of indigenous people are not only socially marginal, but also spatially so. Access routes are limited. The communities may exist peripheral to the main tourist flows. It is true that many indigenous peoples have migrated from native homelands to cities in a search for work, but more often than not live in communities characterised by higher than average levels of unemployment and lower than average incomes for those who are employed, due primarily to their employment in lower skill level occupations. While these communities can be artistically creative, their ability to reach out to tourism through urban based initiatives has often been limited by finite resources, and in consequence patronage is often required. A key source of such patronage has been the public purse, and it is not uncommon for academic researchers to find themselves acting in a consultancy or liaison role. Doing so is part of the process of reciprocation involved in accepting hospitality.

It can thus been seen the networks of relationships that are built up are based upon senses of reciprocal and mutual interests. Like any network, the effectiveness of these relationships tends upon directions of communication flow, density of networks, frequency of communications, attitudes of those occupying nodal points, clarity of objectives and homogeneity of purpose. Additionally the very existence of such networks normalises the existence of the indigenous group and minimises their existence as an "other" that potentially stands as a group demarcated by such difference that no dialogue exists. Indigenous communities are sensitive to these issues and negotiate their way through problems motivated by a wish to retain their own sense of integrity and to acquire a sounder economic footing for, at least, its younger people.

## The Imperatives of Tourism — The Tourist-Indigenous Interface

In the early years of the twenty-first century tourism exists as a growing industry increasingly characterised by a process where it is subsumed into a wider world of entertainment. Travel programmes on television, holiday pages in newspapers and specialist magazines exist to provide advice. Tourists themselves are the subject of reality television, whether in series like *Airport* or *Greece Uncovered* which record the idiosyncrasies of product, producer and consumer alike. Documentaries provide models of roles that tourists hope to emulate, whether swimming with dolphins or whales, or gazing upon gorillas. Entertainment centres commodify the carnivalesque to create tourist product, whether it is theme parks or the provision of buskers in waterfront developments like Darling Harbour and elsewhere (Ryan, Trauer & Pendergast 2004). Tourism increasingly offers its consumers a series of roles from which they might select any, based upon whim or serious purpose.

Thus one role is that of the lay anthropologist seeking to acquire a patina of culture from attending a performance of Indigenous people's art, dance or song. While, as McKercher & Du Cros (2002) have shown, visitation to places of cultural and heritage interest have continued to grow in popularity, such visits can be motivated by a range of desires. These can extend from the mildly curious or simply accompanying a partner or friend who has an interest in such sites to, at the other extreme, visits motivated by significant levels of interest in the culture or heritage symbolised by the site. Their work indicates that perhaps as few as 12% of visitors can be designated as purposeful cultural seekers. This same phenomenon has been evidenced in studies pertaining to sites of Indigenous peoples' tourism. Ryan & Huyton (2002b) have argued that as few as 2% might actually wish to spend nights at an Australian Aboriginal tourism community as the product is currently constructed, while Ryan has also noted that even in such a successful Maori tourism product as the Tamaki Village outside Rotorua, only 21 visitors in 2002 took advantage of the opportunity to stay overnight at a Marae. McIntosh (2004) also finds that levels of interest in Maori culture might be characterised as being "moderate" at best. Similarly subsequent work commissioned by

Tourism New Zealand indicated that Maori culture was a secondary rather than prime motivation for visits to New Zealand. Ryan & Huyton (2000c) in a paper that is reproduced in this volume have argued that one reason that might explain this is that current product is heavily oriented toward a representation of Indigenous peoples that represents their culture as being in the past; as possessing perhaps an unchanging nature that gives it a curiousity value but which fails to show a contemporary image and expression of a living culture. It is perhaps not without reason that one of the most popular of representation of Aboriginal culture is that of Tjapukai Dance Theatre where a multi-media presentation of dance, visual effects and music are combined to form an artistic whole; yet it is also controversial in being criticised by commentators like Dyer, Aberdeen & Schuler (2003) as neither being "authentic" nor creating the benefits that might otherwise accrue to local Aboriginal people by reason of contractually limiting the opportunities of those people to capitalise on their culture as a tourism product.

In a previously unpublished paper Ryan has drawn upon data collected by Pitcher (1997) to develop the model shown in Figure 1.1 to indicate the role of tourism intermediaries. Two key continua are the degree to which the community is aware of the nature of tourists visiting their community and their needs, and second, the nature of the tourists. These tourists are defined as "the questing tourist" and the "accepting tourist" based upon their degree of knowledge of the culture of the hosts and the degree to which they wish to participate in the life of the community. The questing tourist has a high degree of knowledge and wishes to acquire insight into the culture based on that knowledge, while at the other extreme the "accepting tourist" has little knowledge and wishes to perhaps dabble and/or be entertained.

It is argued that four possible situations result with reference to the ways in which the tourist product might be structured. If the community is not tourist aware, when faced with the questing tourist a tension can result between the cultural inhibitions on knowledge

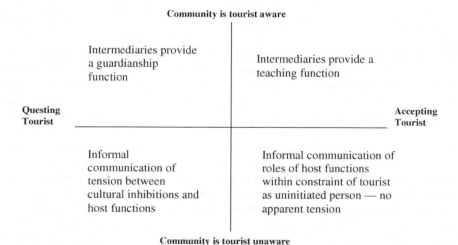

Figure 1.1: Model of community-tourist intermediaries in indigenous tourism.

transfer to un-initiated people and the need to show hospitality. In the case of the "accepting tourist," although the community may not be fully aware of tourist needs, the lack of curiousity and a willingness to accept things at face value means that the tourist is satisfied with that hospitality shown to the un-initiated person. When the community is more tourist aware it might then nominate people as intermediaries to play primarily either a guardianship or teaching role. The former involves a revelation of knowledge appropriate to that possessed by the guest, while the latter is a more general teaching role of awareness generation.

While therefore the imperatives of tourism might generally be said to be those of creating satisfactory tourist experiences in order to sustain economic structures of income and employment generation apart from other considerations pertaining to the assimilation of marginal groups into political, social and economic mainstreams while permitting them a separate identity, it is organised that the organisation of the product at site or destination level requires consideration of the dimensions identified in the model and resultant categories. Successful indigenous peoples' tourism products require awareness and exercise of a guardianship and/or teaching role. The model implies that successful product is therefore not simply a question of presentation to tourists and the requirement that tourists respond in culturally approved ways, as is perhaps indicated by various models and codes of "responsible tourism," but that the purveyors of the product also need to be aware of the nature of tourism and of tourists as consumers of culture. Edelheim, in this volume, pursues a similar theme with reference to concepts of what is "the real Australia" as represented by tourism imagery, and concludes that for the most part it is "roos, the rock, the roof and the reef" with consequently the original inhabitants being secondary in contemporary imagery. Nonetheless, given the importance in the early twenty-first century of generating a *modus operandi* between on the one hand minority indigenous peoples and their inheritance from the colonisations of the nineteenth century and, on the other, majority populations that comprise both beneficiaries of that colonisation and newer migrants in an emergent multi-cultural as distinct from bi-cultural society, Higgins-Desboilles, again in this work, argues that tourism has an important role as a means of bridging such societal gaps.

## Defining Indigeneity

As is evidenced in discussions over land rights in various countries, the terms "indigenous," or "native peoples" are contested political assertions. Nonetheless international organis-ations such as the United Nations Development Program and the International Labour Organisation provide definitions that may be accessed via the web pages http://www. undp.org/csopp/NewFiles/ipaboutdef.html (as at March 2004). The UNDP notes two starting characteristics, these being descent from groups present in a given area and occupied by them prior to the creation of modern states and definition of modern borders and who have maintained cultural and social identities, and institutions separate from the dominant or mainstream society. The UNDP goes on to note that:

> Additional characteristics often ascribed to indigenous peoples include: (i) self-identification and identification by others as being part of a distinct indigenous cultural group, and the display of desire to preserve that cultural

identity; (ii) a linguistic identity different from that of the dominant society; (iii) social, cultural, economic, and political traditions and institutions distinct from the dominant culture; (iv) economic systems oriented more toward traditional systems of production than mainstream systems; and (v) unique ties and attachments to traditional habitats and ancestral territories and natural resources in these habitats and territories (United Nations Development Program 2004).

It is these definitions that have been adopted in this text by the various authors and commentators. Consequently it might be stated that the degree to which an attraction, activity or destination exists as an indigenous tourism product exists along three dimensions, namely the degree to which the culture of the indigenous peoples pervade the product, the duration and or intensity to which the visitor becomes immersed in the cultural "production" and the degree to which the activity, site or performance is owned by indigenous people (Ryan 1999). This approach helps explain Bruner's (1996) dilemma in considering the authenticity of performance of the Indonesian Ramayana. The immersion of the tourists into the occasion was inhibited by the presence of two to three hundred other tourists in a Hyatt Hotel — and it was this circumstance rather than the authenticity and ownership of the performance that inhibited the perception of "indigeneity."

## The Contributions

The contributions offered in this book indicate a number of the issues and problems identified in this introduction. Yamamura shows some of the positive aspects of tourism with reference to traditional design of *Dongba* art in Lijiang in China, yet at the same time noting the implications of how success has generated imitation by non-Naxis people hoping to also gain from tourist expenditures. Nepal provides a study of the Tl'azt'en people of Northern British Columbia and the means by which they hope to obtain benefits from tourism as the local forestry industry seems no longer able to support gainful employment. He notes that the growth of eco-tourism is both a help and a hindrance, in that while eco-tourism might be said to incorporate an interest in indigenous peoples, their comparative lack of capital and knowledge places them at a disadvantage with other operators who also have access to the wilderness regions. Similarly, in a study of the Okavango Delta Mbaiwa argues that the Basarwa people have also suffered from marginalisation and that as a consequence some communities have become dependent upon safari companies owned by overseas interests, while additionally issues of governance common to many developing countries also impose problems. Buultjens, Waller, Graham and Carson argue that, equally, all is not always efficiently organised in more economically advanced nations in their paper which analyses support provision made for Australian Aboriginal people in their tourism endeavours. It highlights a mismatch between Federal and State government initiatives and the very difficulty of accessing information about some of those schemes. For their part Ryan and Huyton question the nature of interest shown by visitors to Australia in Australian Aboriginal culture to conclude that for the most part the prosaic truth is that tourists are holidaytakers, not lay anthropologists. Finally, the editors drawing upon past research undertaken in Australia and New Zealand seek to contextualise the contributions and locate them in the burgeoning literature pertaining to tourism, culture, heritage and identity by introducing the text within two sections of the book. The first relates to the experience of consumption while the second refers to the impacts and wider social significance of that consumption. Finally a short section identifies the silences within the text.

# Section A

**Visitor Experiences of Indigenous Tourism**

Chapter 2

# Visitor Experiences of Indigenous Tourism — Introduction

## Chris Ryan and Birgit Trauer

Section A of this book is concerned with the tourist experience obtained when visiting sites of indigenous peoples culture. The section includes chapters by Alison McIntosh and Henare Johnson, and Gloria Ingram, that are based on interviews at specific sites, whereas Chris Ryan and Jeremy Huyton undertook a different, quantitative, approach based on the premise that the potential nature of the demand for such visits can only be assessed by contextualizing demand within the entirety of holiday product offerings.

The purpose of this introduction is to offer a suggested framework of analysis of visitor experiences as a context for the work of researchers such as McIntosh, Johnson, Ingram and others. In many instances the experiences of visitors are place and time specific, but arguably the motives that prompt such visits can be generalised. Hence the success of the tourist visit and the intensity of emotion that might be felt with such visits are explicable with reference to such motives. One problem with research in this area of visitor experience of indigenous peoples' sites and cultures is that the research design either concentrates on visitor statements which, as Ingram shows in her contribution, are of varying degrees of reflective depth, or they are tied to particular product attributes, as evidence by the other chapters in this collection. The question arises as to whether it is possible to identify a more general model that can inform future research design and offer a common base for comparison.

It can be argued that the academic study of tourism has conventionally adopted a multi-disciplinary approach in its analysis of the structures of tourism, the respective impacts that the travel experience has had upon participants and the contexts within which touristic behavior occurs. At the heart of these structures and impacts lies the nature of tourism experiences. The industry is characterized by high levels of repeat purchases, implying that these experiences are special and meaningful to its consumers. It is commonplace to observe that the purchase is of intangibles, of places unseen, and that even when returning to a place, experiences are never entirely replicated. Given its centrality in the tourism phenomenon it is not surprising that researchers have attempted to better understand the nature of tourism experiences (Ryan 2002; Wang 2000). From a more pragmatic perspective, research into the experience of a place or product is justified on the grounds that better understanding of the tourist experience aids management to more ably promote the destination or activity, mitigate negative impacts by behavior modification or better design a product.

In attempting to analyze such experiences the researcher is, to simplify, and as noted above, often impaled upon the dilemmas of either reporting the specific or seeking to generalize. The former leads to qualitative research whereby respondents provide rich data sets, generally in a textual form arising from conversations or interviews, but often contextualized within a specific time and/or place. Such approaches are often within an interpretative/constructionist research ontology which recognizes a shifting framework of truth dependent upon factors such as the nature of place, the past experience and skills of the participant, the structure of product supply and a potentially endless number of other variables including mood of both service provider and consumer, and, it might be said, the motives and location of the researcher him or herself. An alternative approach can include the derivation of scales from psychological concepts, conceptual frameworks or modeling of tourist motives and/or behaviors. These might be subjected to psychometric testing in an attempt to generalize models pertaining to tourist motives, behaviors, attitudes or experiences. These models and frameworks are commonplace in the academic literature and arguably include the Leisure Motivation Scale (Beard & Ragheb 1980, 1982, 1983), Pearce's (1988) Travel Career Ladder, Servqual (Parasuraman, Zeithaml & Berry 1988, 1991, 1994a, b, c) and its variants such as HostQual (Christou & Sigala 2002) and the Involvement Scales of Havitz & Dimanche (1999). These may be justified by the use of factor analysis and used to describe psychological states of visitors through the use of cluster analysis, multidimensional scaling or similar techniques.

While these latter models have been and continue to retain undoubted importance, for many researchers various doubts arise about their efficacy in understanding the nature of the touristic experience in all its richness, nuances and abilities to elicit a range of emotions from boredom to spine chilling excitement. Trauer & Ryan (2005) have alluded to intimacy theory in tourism, arguing that tourism has parallels with intimacy and romance in terms of acquaintance (engagement), build up (emotion), continuation and dissolution (disengagement). While not necessarily fully committed to such a thesis (which was offered as a speculation), the present authors are inclined to the notion that tourism engages a "sensescape" of touch, sound, smell, taste as well as the visual — all of which add to the intensity of experience — and which individually possess an ability to evoke memory of an experience if the sense is subsequently engaged. For example, the sound of a song might evoke memories of a bar used on holiday, or the smell of a food might remind one of a memorable meal. While such "sensescapes" are not limited to holiday experiences, people are arguably more attuned to such "sensescapes" in the process of relaxation associated with vacations.

If, therefore, holidays are subject to rich stimuli, interpreted through complex neural nets of remembered experience, but are also time and place specific, then how much more might this be when the tourist is engaged with peoples who possess a totally different cultural perspective that shapes their world view.

This text adapts a framework proposed by Ryan & Trauer (2004) with reference to adventure tourism possessing two linking systems. The first operates at a macro system and is based upon Leiper's (1990) tourism system of tourism generating (demand) and tourism receiving (supply) locations. To this they add a further dimension of media — arguing that it possesses importance because: (a) it creates image of place and activity; (b) it stimulates demand; (c) it advertises place; and (d) it creates familiarity with the unfamiliar and casts the tourist in the role of "actor." This last component links with a micro system that is developed around the themes of flow (Csikszentmihalyi 1990), involvement (Havitz & Dimanche 1999; Zaichkowsky 1985), and the hard vs. soft dimensions of adventure tourism. It can be contended that the same dimensions are applicable to tourism involving indigenous peoples, even to the extent that such contacts can be "adventurous."

For the purposes of this book emphasis is laid on the micro-components of the model as they lie nearer to the issue of "indigenous tourism experiences." That framework is shown in Figure 2.1. The main cells are formed by a horizontal axis that traces the level of interest/involvement; a continuum that ranges from high levels of interest/involvement in an activity, to low levels of such commitment. The vertical axis presents a second continuum, from products, places or destinations that possess differing degrees of cultural familiarity that range from the unfamiliar to the familiar.

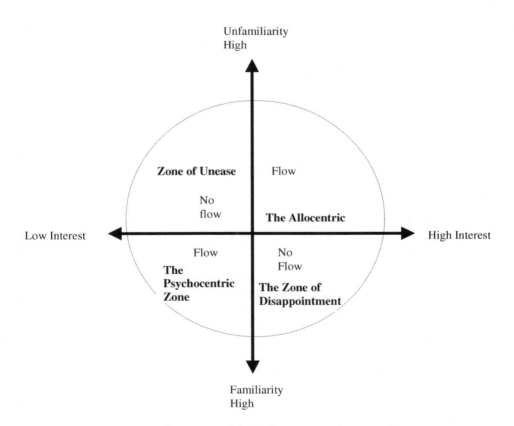

Figure 2.1: The nature of the indigenous tourism experience.

It will also be noted that reference to Csikszentmihalyi's (1990) concept of flow is made — but not in the usual linear fashion. Rather in this instance it is circular. In the top right hand cell the allocentric seeking difference potentially possesses "flow" as does the psychocentric in the bottom left hand cell — given that in both situations there exists a match between desired familiarity/unfamiliarity of the location and the level of interest of the tourist in such locations. Flow is, on the other hand, absent in the remaining two cells. Four cells can therefore be identified, these being:

*The zone of unease* — this exists where a tourist with little interest in experiencing cultural difference finds him or herself in such a location of unfamiliar culture. The location possesses little to interest the person and degrees of boredom at best might result, but equally the tourist may feel threatened by the strangeness of the place and the nature of the interactions. From the perspective of "flow" this is not only lacking but may give rise to elements of disabling arousal in the neural system.

*The allocentric zone.* In this location can be found the tourist possessing high levels of interest in the unfamiliar or the new culture who has those interests matched by the nature of the location/destination. In many senses this resembles the situation described by Plog (1977) as a match between destination and the allocentric personality, or indeed more recently by McKercher & du Cros (2002) as the "purposeful cultural tourist." It is this type of tourist that may stay overnight in the communities of indigenous people.

*The zone of disappointment.* This represents a zone where the person possessing high levels of interest in cultural difference finds him or herself in a location of little cultural difference and high degrees of familiarity, defined as possessing features common to the culture of the normal place of residence or home of the tourist. Consequently a lack of flow attends this experience and disappointment may result.

*The Psychocentric Zone.* In this location the tourist having little desire for viewing different cultures and wishing for a place that possesses a culture familiar to them will be duly satisfied. There is a sense of flow in the sense of an absence of duress or boredom. This type of visitor will happily attend "cultural performance" shows.

## Deriving Questions

Having developed a conceptualization of cultural tourism the question is whether the framework identifies possible ways of aiding future research. Given constraints of space this section will identify groupings of "sets" rather than specific items. The concept of flow lends itself to measures of boredom vs. excitement or exhilaration, sense of discomfort vs. a sense of wholeness with the activity, a sense of threat vs. achievement. From the viewpoint of statistical transformation it might be of use to point out that a conventional mode of transformation is to set the mean score at zero with a standard deviation of one, which technique fits well with measures of continua.

Interest may be defined as possessing attributes of importance, the derivation of interest, a wish to pursue a given activity, and the significance and importance of the activity to the person. Indeed Ryan & Huyton (2002) have argued that importance attributed to an activity is a key determinant of satisfaction with indigenous people's product in the instance of Australian Aboriginal tourism. Overlaps with the concept of flow as advanced by Csikszentmihalyi (1990) are neither surprising nor accidental given the common psychological theorisation. The authors would wish to more specifically distinguish a distinction between situational and enduring involvement which necessitates differentiating between what might be termed "life style importance" associated with "sign" and the activity specific feelings of pleasure, risk, etc. The third component of the framework becomes situational specific when respondents perceive their activity consumption on the continuum of familiar vs. unfamiliar. This is where a technique such as "fuzzy sets" possess an obvious advantage inasmuch as one person's familiar may be another's unfamiliar — and hence the continuum of familiar vs. unfamiliar is as much a perceptual as an objective differentiation. Indeed the fuzzy set can potentially cope with nuances of the unfamiliar vs. familiar in the instance of the purposeful cultural tourist (McKercher & du Cros 2002) seeking to repeat experiences in a culture different to his or her own, but with which previous contact has been made and where therefore some degree of familiarity exists.

From this framework it becomes possible to identify factors that might be important for better understanding the dimension of visitor experience when faced with different cultures, particularly those of indigenous peoples. These items are listed in Table 2.1. One aspect that distinguishes the specificity of indigenous peoples culture as a tourism product from a more general cultural tourism is the inclusion of the item "distinguishing between reality and fantasy." In unpublished work, Ryan has noted the nature of readings undertaken by visitors and the presence of what is termed a "new age" romanticism of indigenous peoples as guardians of a "sacred" knowledge lost to urbanised societies. Just as past western generations portrayed native peoples in images designed to meet their conscious or unconscious needs (e.g. the exotic "other" female, the "noble savage") so some in a current generation impose their own uncertainties onto new stereotypes of "exotic others."

If the proposed framework is to possess any validity it needs to at least not be inconsistent with the research reported in the chapters included in this collection of research findings. Arguably this is the case. Ingram's findings, it is argued, possess the aspects of a tension between attraction and inhibition. Senses of personal difficulties emerge, as do instances of personal insights on both cognitive and affective learning. McIntosh (2004) also describes the emergent dimensions of her study as being those of education, authenticity, personal interaction, sincere hospitality and emotion which are not inconsistent with the sense of the proposed framework.

From this approach a series of pertinent linking "what if" questions can be identified. Examples include:

> What is the impact upon longer-term interest if the 'language intense' cultural product is purchased by less linguistically skilled tourists seeking minor cultural displacement?

> What is the impact upon senses of fulfillment if 'proposed high unfamiliar' cultural product are found insufficiently challenging?

There is, however, one further observation that might be made. In the chapters that follow in part A, it is notable that the research concentrates upon the visitor, but essentially adopts a passive stance toward the host as an actor in the interaction that creates the experience.

Table 2.1:  Possible attributes within cultural tourism with reference to indigenous cultures.

| Dimension | Attribute |
| --- | --- |
| Product | Linguistic skills required/not required |
| | Protocol skills required/not required |
| | Remote location |
| | Initiation required/not required |
| | Anthropological experience offered |
| | Strong sense of personal challenge |
| Interest/Involvement | |
| Situational | Emotionally intense |
| | Personally difficult |
| | Skill enhancing |
| | Status enhancing |
| | Social (group) bonding |
| Enduring | Sense of self worth enhanced |
| | Sign (life style) enhancing |
| | Time consuming |
| | High prioritisation in expenditure |
| Flow | Loss of self in activity |
| | Feelings of intense awareness/being |
| | Balance (between challenge and competency) |
| | Sense of creativity/achievement |
| | Sense of fulfilment |
| | Pleasure |
| | Discovering "reality" vs fantasy. |

McIntosh, Johnson and Ingram adopt a qualitative approach and elicit responses through generally indirect means of questioning. Ingram's work shows the ambiguities that exist — yes — there is a sense of the sacred at various sites, and a sense of awe, but there is also a sense of not being able to bridge differences, of tourists being hesitate about being involved with a host group who are perceived as being drunk or possessing no direction. The lack of penetrating the host group to establish one to one relationships are revealed. McIntosh and Johnson interpret interviews of visitors to a Maori *marae* or meeting place and while identifying personal interaction as being important to visitors, it can be argued that the interaction exists within constraints of inequality where the visitor as the uninitiated person has either yet to learn a language that truly permits insights into Maori culture, or is inhibited by the role of tourist as being time constrained. In short, there exists still a comparative lack within the academic literature (albeit with some notable exceptions such as those of Tahana & Oppermann 1998) about the direct experience of the host in the visitor-host interaction.

Chapter 3

# A Phenomenological Investigation of Tourists' Experience of Australian Indigenous Culture

Gloria Ingram

## Introduction

My research findings are based on tourists' experience of desert Aboriginal culture in Central Australia and no assumptions should be made with regard to the applicability of my findings to any other region. I acknowledge and respect the diversity of Indigenous culture across Australia and in particular, within my study region, the diversity of language and culture of the Arrernte, Anmatjere, Kayteje, Walpiri, Pintupi, Lluritja, Pitjantjatjara, Yankunytjatjara and Ngaanyatjarra peoples as well as people from other central desert language groups who may have contributed to my study.

An important question for the future of Australia's tourism industry that has remained largely unanswered by research is "What is the nature of tourists' experience of Australian Indigenous culture?" Associated with this are the sub-questions "What do tourists know about Australian Indigenous culture?" and "What impressions of Australia's Indigenous people do tourists take home with them?" Answers to these questions are at the heart of my research. I have chosen to explore tourists' experience of Indigenous culture using phenomenology, a very appropriate methodology for uncovering essences of human experience. My study takes phenomenological findings from a small group of respondents interviewed in-depth and translates them into a questionnaire enabling data of experience of Australian Indigenous culture to be obtained from large numbers of visitors using a traditional quantitative survey method. By using these combined methodologies, experiential data will become available to assist Indigenous tour operators and other stakeholders in Australia's Indigenous tourism industry.

This chapter describes the methodology and findings for the first stage of my research, consisting of phenomenological interviews with 17 tourists recruited in Alice Springs. The interview transcripts have been taken through a rigorous process of phenomenological analysis to extract interpretive themes of each person's experience of Indigenous culture.

The interpretive themes showed great diversity in how different people experienced the Indigenous tourism product. Some examples of the interpretive themes revealed include:

Indigenous Tourism: The Commodification and Management of Culture
Copyright © 2005 by Elsevier Ltd.
All rights of reproduction in any form reserved
ISBN: 0-08-044620-5

the power and spirituality of Uluru; admiration for the survival skills of Aboriginal people in the harsh desert environment; fascination with various aspects of culture — painting, dance and language; meaningful interaction with individual Aboriginal people; disappointment at the absence of Aboriginal tour guides at tourist attractions; quality of cultural information supplied by non-Indigenous bus drivers and tour guides; negative perceptions of Aboriginal people as social misfits and victims of Western society; and feelings that some aspects of Aboriginal culture were missing from their cultural experience.

It is hoped that this study of the nature of tourists' cultural experience in Central Australia will provide new insights for Australia's Indigenous tourism industry, complementing previous research in this area of a more quantitative nature (see e.g. Ryan & Huyton 2000a, b, 2002).

## The Context of the Study

In the decade to 1999, inbound tourism to Australia increased from 2.1 million to 4.5 million (Boyle 2001: 19) reflecting a world-wide trend reported by the World Tourism Organisation (WTO 1998). During this period, the Indigenous cultural experience was high on the list of attractions sought by overseas visitors to Australia (Boyle 2001; ONT 1998) and many new Indigenous tourism businesses were established. One of the consequences of the rapid growth in Indigenous tourism is that it has not been supported by a solid research base, leaving the important topics of visitor satisfaction and visitors' perceptions, virtually unexplored. Research of this type, which informs Indigenous tourism operators and planners of the impact of their product is even more important in the current climate as the tourism industry recovers from the effects of world terrorism, the threat of SARS and the sudden changes to Australia's airlines, and as operators struggle to recover business and maintain their competitiveness in the global marketplace. The need for more qualitative research in this area has been recognised by Ryan & Huyton (2002), prominent researchers in the field of Indigenous cultural tourism, who recommended a phenomenological approach to research into visitors' perceptions. The current study responds to these identified needs by undertaking a phenomenological investigation of tourists' experience of Indigenous culture to attempt to discover what tourists really think about Aboriginal culture and what kinds of impressions they take home with them.

This research is conducted in two stages, of which stage 1 is nearing completion and is the subject of this text. For the purposes of this chapter the term *tourist* refers to either *domestic* or *international* tourists; *Aboriginal people* refers to people who are recognised and identified by the Aboriginal community as Aboriginal; and in the Australian context, *Indigenous (people)* refers to Aboriginal people.

As previously stated, stage 1 consists of phenomenological interviews with a small number of tourists, but sufficient in total to gain a viable range of experience. Stage 2 of the research (which is being conducted at the time of writing in early 2004) is the development and implementation of a cultural experience survey based on the themes described in this text, and it is hoped that the questionnaire will be completed by approximately 1,200–1,500 tourists. In this way, experiential data will be obtained across a large enough sample to be of value in assessing whether any changes or improvements could be made in the industry.

The study area is the Central Australian desert region, centred on Alice Springs and the Uluru-Kata Tjuta National Park. Participants for the phenomenological study were recruited in Alice Springs. For continuity and to provide the opportunity to compare statistical data with the findings of Ryan & Huyton's (2002) quantitative study, the Cultural Experience Surveys will be administered in the same locations used by these researchers, namely Uluru-Kata Tjuta National Park Cultural Centre and Alice Springs Desert Park.

## Phenomenology

The aim of my research into tourists' experience is to understand what emotions and feelings are stirred by the human experience of Indigenous culture in the desert environment. For this reason I have chosen phenomenology as the theoretical framework for my research. Phenomenology provides strong methodological underpinnings for the investigation of human experience through the phenomenological analysis of the expression of that experience. Phenomenology is the study of lived experience as applied to a particular phenomenon or, as Schweitzer (1998a: 14) states, "the study of the lived world and our experience of it." Phenomenology seeks to reveal the *essences* or *structures* of experience of the phenomenon under investigation (Van Manen 1990: 184). It is not constrained by pre-determined categories so has the potential to uncover elements of experience which cannot be captured using quantitative research methods. Crotty (1996) makes a distinction between "mainstream" phenomenology (aligned with the earlier Husserlian traditions) as the study the objects of human experience to elucidate what people "are making sense of", and "new" phenomenology (empirical models) which "gathers people's subjective meanings, the sense they make of things" (*ibid*: 3). This "new" or empirical existential phenomenology has been applied in a range of fields including psychology (Edwards 2001; Giorgi 1997; Schweitzer 1998b), education (Van Manen 1990), nursing (Benner 1994; Crotty 1996) and different forms of counselling and therapy (Holroyd 2001; Sherwood 2001).

Phenomenology as an applied method has rarely been employed in tourism research (Ingram 2001, 2002; Ryan 2000b). Its usage in tourism has been almost entirely adapted to phenomenological or phenomenographical approaches such as Masberg & Silverman's (1996) study of visitors' experience at a heritage site.

In the process of phenomenological research, interviews are conducted with a number of participants who have agreed to participate in a process that can potentially generate in-depth reflection. The interviews are semi-structured, being guided only by a small number of base questions in which, in an atmosphere of empathy, the phenomenological researcher casts aside all biases and prior knowledge of the phenomenon (using a technique known as *bracketing*) in order to enter the world of the participant's recall of lived experience. The interviews are meticulously transcribed and taken through a rigorous process of explication (phenomenological reduction) to enable the core interpretive themes of experience to be uncovered.

In this study, the interviews were transcribed and explicated according to the combined phenomenological model tested in my recent Masters research (Ingram 2001) with adaptations as necessary to accommodate the diversity of the data. This model is based on the work of Schweitzer (1998b) expanded from Giorgi, Moustakas' (1994) adaptation of Keen-Colaizzi-Stevick models, Sherwood (2001) and Devenish (2002) and contains the following steps with two categories of analysis; the ideographic and nomothetic. These are described below.

### The Ideographic

- Reading and re-reading of transcripts to gain an intuitive feeling for the data.
- Separation of the text into discreet sections of text (natural meaning units — NMUs).
- Development of a research key into likely categories suggested by the data.
- Transformation of the categories to individual themes by elimination of excess material.
- Construction of a textural description of the experience based on the central (individual) themes (four texts only).[1]
- Composition of a structural description of the researcher's understanding of the participant's experience using a process of imaginative variation (four texts only).[1]
- Derivation of major interpretive themes from the textural descriptions using the original text as a referent (four texts only).[1]
- Composition of short descriptions of each participant's experience intuited from the data.
- Explication of short descriptions using the original text as a referent.

### The Nomothetic

- Integration of all individual themes under major interpretive themes.
- Explication of major interpretive themes drawing on the lived experience of the participant as experienced by the researcher.[1]
- Synthesis of explicated themes to a single unified statement or synthesised extended description of the experience.[1]

## Data Collection

The criteria for selection of tourists for participation in my research were that they be *bona fide* tourists, over 18 years of age and native speakers of English. The English language restriction was introduced to eliminate the possibility of cross-cultural misinterpretation of their experience of Australian Indigenous culture. A minimum of 15 persons was set as a large enough group from which to extract a comprehensive set of themes of experience, given the complexities of the topic, on which to base the second stage of the research. Approximately 35 people were approached initially of whom half declined for various reasons, the most frequent that they had only just arrived in Central Australia so were not prepared to commit to speaking about their experience of Indigenous culture. A few were not native speakers of English so were not eligible. From these, 17 were recruited in case

---

[1] Denotes elements of the study not included in this chapter.

any difficulties arose in contacting them by telephone for the interviews. Minor difficulties occurred but these were overcome, and all 17 tourists were interviewed.

The sample included nine overseas participants from four English-speaking countries (New Zealand, Britain, Scotland and Canada) and eight domestic tourists from four Australian States (NSW, Victoria, Queensland and South Australia). Their estimated ages ranged from under 30 through to over 50 years of age with six members of the older group being from overseas and four from Australia. In the 30–50 years old group there was one from overseas and three from Australia and in the youngest group, two from overseas and one from Australia. Of the international tourists, five were male and four were female, and the domestic tourists included one male and seven females, giving a total of six males and 11 females in the total sample.

One Australian tourist had visited Central Australia 18 years ago. For the remainder of the group, this was their first visit. Most people had had some brief exposure to Aboriginal culture through advertising media, film and television. All the participants had stayed in Alice Springs and had visited a similar range of Indigenous tourism and Central Desert attractions, thus lending cohesiveness to the data and enabling experience of the same phenomena by different types of people to be explored.

## The Phenomenological Interviews

Of the 17 tourists who agreed to participate in the research, 14 opted for a telephone interview shortly after returning to their homes while the remaining three were interviewed in Alice Springs at their accommodation. The interviews were guided by the following set of simple open-ended questions:

(1) Please describe your (most) recent experience of Aboriginal culture.
(2) Was this any different from what you expected? If yes, in what ways?
(3) What did you like best about your experience of Aboriginal culture?
(4) How did this make you feel?
(5) What was the least enjoyable aspect of your experience of Aboriginal culture? and why?
(6) Did you experience any similarities between your own cultural background and Australian Indigenous culture?
(7) Did you experience any differences between your own cultural background and Australian Indigenous culture?
(8) If you have seen another Indigenous culture from another country, how would you compare this with your experience of Australian Indigenous culture?

## The Research Findings

This chapter presents two sets of findings. These are first, the individual experience of Australian Indigenous culture and second, interpretive themes derived from the experience of the whole group. In order to get a sense of each person's experience without taking the data through to the extended description stage (complete phenomenological reduction),

Schweitzer's technique of intuitive reading of the data was applied, together with my own experience of entering into each person's life-world to briefly articulate the essence of their experience in a short descriptive statement illustrated by relevant passages from the original transcripts. The descriptions show that for eight of the group this was a predominantly positive experience and for the nine others this was a predominantly negative experience. As the limitations of this chapter preclude the full explication of each descriptive statement, only two or three passages have been included for each person. These are set out below. The names of the participants have been changed.

## Individual Responses

### Part 1: Predominantly Positive Experience

#### ALAN (New South Wales)

*Alan found the trip very interesting and educational and enhanced by learning about the culture through an Aboriginal presenter.*

"I learned so many new things from the dance."

". . . all the implements he [the Aboriginal presenter] showed us he'd made himself . . . to us that was important because he related to the implements and what they were used for on a first-hand basis."

#### BRAD (Canada)

*The most prominent features of Brad's trip were his positive experience of Uluru and his understanding of Aboriginal culture based on his own knowledge of native Canadian culture.*

[about Uluru] ". . . you really felt small in its presence . . . it certainly was the highlight of the trip, definitely!"

". . . the Aboriginal culture . . . similar to North America where the native Americans only took what they needed, never more than they needed."

#### GEORGE (New Zealand)

*Although lacking in contact with Aboriginal people, the holiday was enjoyable for George, with the highlight being the opportunity to purchase authentic souvenirs.*

"We . . . had no contact culturally with the Aboriginals . . . I didn't personally speak to any."

". . . up at Ti Tree . . . that would probably be the pick of everything we saw in the whole trip . . . they seemed to be the genuine items . . . that's very important if you want to bring something home with you that's truly reflective of their artistic abilities."

#### HARRIET (South Australia)

*Even though Harriet was not able to connect with any Aboriginal people, her visit to Uluru-Kata Tjuta made her holiday a very positive experience.*

"We did go to Uluṟu and we were taken around part of the Rock by an extremely informative and a very delightful person . . . she's a white girl . . . we didn't actually meet any of the Indigenous people there at all."

"I saw the change of light, both at Uluṟu and at the Olgas . . . that is a very impressive sight and enough to send a chill up your spine."

*INGRID (United Kingdom)*

*Ingrid enjoyed learning about Aboriginal culture which was a positive experience, but would have liked to have felt she could speak to Aboriginal people.*

"We didn't meet any Aboriginal people — we did feel that we shouldn't actually make contact with them on an ad hoc basis."

"[Uluṟu] . . . it was awe-inspiring and . . . I found the . . . Dreamtime stories . . . fascinating . . . I think the art is tremendous, it's not like any art that I've ever seen anywhere else . . . it's vibrant, it's bright and it's just lovely, I really loved it."

*LAURA (South Australia)*

*Laura was so impressed with the hospitality and friendliness of Aboriginal people that she completely changed her view of them. She felt the presence of Aboriginal people throughout the Northern Territory and felt a strong spiritual connection with Aboriginal culture at Uluṟu.*

"[Aboriginal people invited us to dance in a corroboree with them] . . . I thought it was quite moving really . . . I almost felt a little bit honoured that they wanted us to do this with them . . . it just gave me a different perspective on the Aboriginal people . . . it changed my entire view of how they see things . . ."

"[At Uluṟu] I felt that there was something sacred . . . just something special, and I had climbed it 20 years ago and I thought my God I don't want to climb it any more, it's got to be looked after, and I don't even know where that came from."

*MARJORIE (Queensland)*

*Marjorie's holiday was better than she expected, particularly Uluṟu and the Aboriginal Dreaming stories.*

"At Uluṟu I was overcome by the sheer immensity of the rock itself, a little bit of awe I suppose at the size of it, and with the Olgas they were just so beautiful . . ."

"[The cultural experience] was far better than I expected . . . when I actually saw what they were talking about, it made so much more sense than just reading the tales . . . I did enjoy it very much."

*RACHEL (Victoria)*

*Rachel came home from her holiday with enthusiasm for Kata Tjuṯa and Aboriginal art, although she was disappointed at not having an Aboriginal guide at Uluṟu.*

"At Uluṟu we walked around the base with a guided tour led by a park ranger — it was a white ranger. I was a bit disappointed, I would rather have had an Aboriginal park ranger."

"I felt the Olgas . . . gave me a feeling more of . . . a spiritual feeling than Uluṟu . . . it made me feel how small we are and made me think we're here [on the Earth] for such a short time."

"Now I've seen the . . . landscape . . . how it was formed . . . I now have feeling for Aboriginal art."

## Part 2: Predominantly Negative Experience

### CAROL (United Kingdom)

*What Carol saw of Aboriginal culture did not measure up to her expectations.*

"I thought they [the rock paintings] were very primitive and they reminded me of children's scribbling — very, very primitive . . . I was expecting something a bit more intricate I guess and was shocked at how primitive they were."

"The Cultural Centre was very disappointing because it was laid out not very well . . . it needs a lot of work on it . . . you wouldn't spend a lot of time there because it's just not that interesting, it doesn't grab you."

### DELIA (New South Wales)

*Although Delia had a connecting experience through didgeridoo healing and felt the power of Uluṟu and Kata Tju̲ta, she did not feel that she could get close to Aboriginal people.*

"The best part of my experience was the didgeridoo healing . . . there was a real connection there with the Earth."

"[at Uluṟu] you could just feel the whole thing as a being . . . the Olgas were just amazing . . . you're just sort of awestruck . . . you can feel the presence."

"We actually ended up avoiding the Aboriginals to be honest because they were often dirty or loud . . . yelling to each other up the street — it was an eye-opener for all of us."

### EMMA (United Kingdom)

*Emma's holiday experience was spoiled by visions of Aboriginal people drinking in Alice Springs. She was unaware of the Aboriginal custom of getting together in groups in town and saw this as a negative aspect.*

"I was quite shocked to see this, especially in Alice Springs . . . it was quite an ugly sight to see them just sitting and drinking and wandering about in herds and they just didn't seem to have any purpose at all to what life was all about."

"It just wasn't something that the tourists want to remember about Australia . . . it was not what I expected to see."

*FRED (New Zealand)*

*Fred was disappointed that there wasn't more contact with Aboriginal people on the tour and the landscape of the desert didn't appeal to him.*

"We had very little actual contact with the Aboriginal people, I found. Even at Uluru, we went to the cultural centre but we found that most of the people there were European that were handling things, or appeared to be."

"I'm afraid the open plains, the stuntedness of that centre of Australia didn't have a great deal of feeling to me, other than being a rather flat, boring looking sort of a land."

*JOAN (New Zealand)*

*A major disappointment of Joan's holiday was not being able to meet with more Aboriginal people.*

"[I went to] the Ayers Rock Cultural Centre. I decided it was very good but personally not enough time or contact with the native Aborigines."

"At Ti Tree Point . . . again I was disappointed . . . it belongs to the Aboriginal community but there's no doubt about it, the staff are definitely European . . . there were a lot of Aboriginal artefacts on sale but no Aboriginals themselves."

*KEITH (United Kingdom)*

*The most significant part of Keith's holiday was his experience of open spaces which evoked in him a sense of admiration for those who survived the harsh desert environment, both Aboriginal people and settlers but he was also quite dissatisfied with and sceptical about many aspects of culture and critical of what he saw as a "dissonance between culture and behaviour of people in the streets of Alice Springs."*

"It's the scale of things that is impressive . . . that's what got to me . . . it made you feel respectful of the people who had tracked across that space, and survived in it."

"You hear descriptions of a cultural lifestyle which is interesting and perfectly respectable as a lifestyle and then you find groups of people blind drunk lying around the streets."

"I think Uluru is disgracefully commercialised . . . it's a question of who's being exploited, is this over commercial, is this a sanitized version for the benefit of the tourist?"

"The designation of cultural sites, we did wonder whether that was being manipulated . . . we kept coming across "oh no you can't go in there because this is a designated site of cultural significance," well why? What for? And nobody could tell you."

*NANCY (Victoria)*

*For Nancy, the experience was predominantly negative due to undesirable behaviour of young Aboriginal people in Alice Springs, and stories she heard at Uluru-Kata Tjuta National Park.*

"When we got to Alice Springs . . . you can't help but see the Aborigines . . . they . . . were a bit harassing and a bit confronting . . . a whole lot of young kids came up behind us and were very rowdy, very loud, their language was quite disgusting and they were shouting right behind us."

"We went out to Uluru and the next thing that absolutely destroyed me was the incredible amount of fire that was around . . . one of the tour guides . . . said it had been deliberately lit, by Aboriginals . . . that was a hell of a shock to our system."

"[a] story I've been told was, when I asked why aren't they telling us the stories and greeting us — 'they don't want to, they just want the money.' "

*OLIVER (New Zealand)*

*Oliver took a negative view of Aboriginal people's behaviour as well as doubting whether rock art and people were genuine and also questioned Aboriginal people's motivations concerning tourists.*

". . . up north in the Kakadu . . . there was . . . an Abo family on the riverbank. I think we wondered if they were a plant. We weren't sure whether they were genuine wild Aborigines, we thought they had been put there for . . . the entertainment of the tourists, that was my impression."

"We saw rock paintings and I wondered and so did our driver, how recent they were. . . . we saw some in other places which looked very recent to me, they hadn't faded at all."

"I thought it was very sad . . . to see the degradation of the Aborigines. All they seemed to do in town was shuffle into town in the morning and sit down under the trees and spend the day sitting under the trees . . . absolutely nothing to do and seeming to have no interest in what was going on around them."

*PAM (New South Wales)*

*While appreciating connections with the land at Uluru-Kata Tjuta and identifying unique abilities of Aboriginal people, Pam was disappointed by a number of aspects of her holiday which failed to present a meaningful, authentic cultural experience.*

"We went to the bush medicines . . . I found that a little bit disappointing because you actually had an Aboriginal person talking to you but he was referring to Aboriginal people as others . . . as if he wasn't immersed in his own culture."

". . . and what I found with bus trips . . . we had so-called white people talking about Aboriginal culture and just giving us little bits of information, so it's second hand, it's been through the sieve of the person whose giving it, it's already been Westernised if you like, by their perception of it, then it's dished up to you as factual."

"My experience of my visit to Uluru and Kata Tjuta, was really quite different . . . wherever you were going there was quite spiritual . . . at the Olgas . . . you felt you could sit there and be quiet, and it pervaded you as a person . . . I just felt that . . . we did come from the land."

## The Interpretive Themes

Given the absence of limitations placed on each participant and the potential variety of their experience, the themes are many and varied, representing diverse views and impressions expressed by a diverse group of tourists from vastly different backgrounds, each with their own different worldview. After eliminating duplications, 107 different themes remained, falling into four distinct categories. These are

- Culture.
- Contact with Aboriginal people.
- Effects of Uluru and Kata Tjuta on tourists.
- Perceptions of Aboriginal people.

## Overview of Interpretive Themes

Since the limitations of this chapter do not permit the inclusion of all of the themes, I have selected from within each category some of the themes which represent some shared perceptions across the group.

## Culture

### Tourists Appreciate Indigenous Culture

Tourists experienced the culture or specific aspects of culture as being meaningful, interesting, fascinating and educational.

### Tourists Find Aboriginal Culture Basic and Primitive

Tourists found rock art very primitive, like children's scrawls, and dot painting to be very basic.

### Tourists Experience Connections with Aboriginal Culture

Tourists experienced feelings of connectedness with Aboriginal culture and feelings for the land that they felt had been eroded by Western civilisation. Tourists perceived similarities between European myths and legends and the Aboriginal Dreaming.

## Contact with Aboriginal People

### Tourists are Disappointed at not Being Able to Meet More Aboriginal People

Tourists said they either didn't see any Aboriginal people at all, there were no Aboriginal people at tourism sites, or they felt they couldn't approach Aboriginal people for a number of reasons. These included not wanting to appear patronising, being told that Aboriginal people were very private and didn't like to be approached, being told they were "shunned and not to be approached," and being put off by observed behaviour of some Aboriginal people drinking in Alice Springs.

### Tourists Find that the Majority of Tour Guides, Bus Drivers, and Presenters of Cultural Information are Not Aboriginal People

Tourists learned of Aboriginal culture from white tour guides, rangers and bus drivers, and noticed that tourism attractions seemed to be run by Europeans with no Aboriginal people in sight. Tourists felt they were getting "second-hand" information from white tour guides. Tourists thought Western tour guides were "good" and had "done their homework."

### Tourists Prefer Aboriginal Guides and Presenters

Tourists said they would have preferred to have an Aboriginal guide. Where there were Aboriginal guides and presenters, tourists felt the information was more meaningful.

## Effects of Uluṟu and Kata Tjuṯa on Tourists

### Tourists Experience Uluṟu and Kata Tjuṯa as Impressive

Tourists found Uluṟu to be impressive, majestic and spectacular. Tourists experienced Kata Tjuṯa as a place of great beauty.

### Tourists Have Feelings of Spirituality at Uluṟu and Kata Tjuṯa

Tourists experienced Uluṟu as a spiritual place, powerful, a place that made them feel small, a being, intimidating, and felt a need to protect it.

### Tourists Show Respect for Aboriginal People's Wishes by Not Climbing Uluṟu

Tourists did not climb Uluṟu out of respect for the wishes of Aboriginal people. Tourists also strongly disapproved of others climbing, particularly Japanese tourists and Australian schoolgirls. One tourist felt the need to protect it from being climbed.

### Tourists Expecting to Climb are Disappointed that Uluṟu is Closed

Tourists expecting to climb Uluṟu were disappointed to find it closed and wanted it to be permanently open or permanently closed to climb.

## Tourists' Perceptions of Aboriginal People

### *Tourists Complain About Behaviour of Aboriginal People in Alice Springs*

Tourists experienced as negative the behaviour of Aboriginal people in Alice Springs, including Aboriginal people drinking in the streets of Alice Springs, Aboriginal people especially youth "yelling at each other down the street" and experienced Aboriginal people as "shabby," "dirty" and "smelly." Tourists felt threatened by Aboriginal people, especially young Aboriginal people and at night.

### *Tourists See Aboriginal People as Having No Purpose in Life*

Tourists perceived people sitting in groups around the town and walking about the town as shuffling around, sitting around with nothing to do, wandering about and having no purpose to their life.

### *Tourists Appreciate the Friendliness of Aboriginal People*

Tourists saw Aboriginal people as friendly and positive towards tourists. They were impressed by their entrepreneurial skills in tourism and admired the way they "cared for each other."

### *Tourists Have Limited Knowledge of the Recent History and Situation of Aboriginal People*

Tourists expected Aboriginal people to still be living a traditional hunter-gatherer lifestyle. Tourists perceived Aboriginal people to have no education and understanding of how to use money, to be unable to fit into a Western lifestyle and to have been abandoned by the Australian Government.

### *Tourists Experience Doubts About the Authenticity of Some Aspects of Culture Presented*

Tourists questioned the authenticity of rock paintings and of people representing the culture, and wondered whether sacred sites were being manipulated.

### *Tourists Fear They May Be Exploited*

Tourists saw Uluru as over commercialised and wondered about the motivations of Aboriginal people selling artefacts rather than sharing culture. They expressed a desire to know more of the culture than they felt was being offered.

## Other Issues Arising from the Data to be Investigated

The research has raised many issues impacting on the future of Indigenous tourism, which need further exploration. Briefly these are: cultural information and misinformation; cross-cultural misunderstandings; climbing Uluru; lack of appreciation and understanding of cultural differences; lack of awareness of cultural and linguistic diversity; perceptions of the stolen generation; the impressions given by Western tour guides; level of contact with Aboriginal people; perceived lack of involvement of Aboriginal people in tourism; Western influence on Indigenous culture; Aboriginal views on being approached by tourists; and the connection that many people feel their Ancestors used to have with the land and that is still possessed by Aboriginal people.

The current chapter has two purposes. First, to provide a phenomenological description of tourists' experience of Australian Indigenous culture. While the full phenomenological reduction to be applied to four of the transcripts is beyond the scope of this chapter, short descriptions encapsulating the essence of each person's experience have been presented to provide an overview of the diversity of the Indigenous tourism experience, both positive and negative. The second objective was to explicate an inclusive set of interpretive themes of the experience of the phenomenon as a basis for developing a Cultural Experience Survey for the next stage of the research. It was found that the 107 themes extracted from the data fall naturally into four main categories: (a) Culture; (b) Contact with Aboriginal people; (c) Effects of Uluru and Kata Tjuta on tourists; and (d) Perceptions of Aboriginal people. These themes formed the basis for the development of a "Cultural Experience Survey" that is the instrument for the second stage of the research, and interested readers are invited to contact the author for details.

Chapter 4

# Understanding the Nature of the Marae Experience: Views from Hosts and Visitors at the Nga Hau E Wha National Marae, Christchurch, New Zealand

Alison J. McIntosh and Henare Johnson

## Introduction

Within the range of Maori attractions available in New Zealand, *marae* or Maori village visits are popular among tourists and represent settings for cultural understanding and the experience of cultural authenticity. Conversely, the *marae* can be a setting for commodification or even cultural misunderstanding. This chapter reports the findings of in-depth interviews conducted during the summer season of 2003 with three hosts and twenty visitors at the Nga Hau E Wha national *marae* in Christchurch, New Zealand to explore the key attributes or dimensions of a *marae* visit from the perspectives of hosts and tourists visiting the *marae*. Findings revealed five common dimensions of the *marae* experience: namely, *education, authenticity, personal interaction, sincere hospitality* and *emotion*. The chapter concludes that some similarities can be drawn with tourists' experiences of non-indigenous contexts whereby cultural understanding and cultural authenticity are experienced as inherently *experiential* in nature. Whilst authenticity, therefore, lies in the nature of interaction between host and guest in a *marae* setting, this chapter argues that further attention needs to be directed at the complex factors and readings of authenticity in cross-cultural encounters.

## Context of the Study

Tourists are said to be increasingly demanding experiences of other cultures that are different to their own, motivated by their desire for an authentic experience (MacCannell 1976). The Maori people of New Zealand have had a long history of involvement in tourism and a

Indigenous Tourism: The Commodification and Management of Culture
Copyright © 2005 by Elsevier Ltd.
All rights of reproduction in any form reserved
ISBN: 0-08-044620-5

new wave of Maori operators are seen to have emerged over the last two decades to provide experiences to meet this demand (Taylor 2001). Much of the tourism product in which Maori have been involved, to date, is cultural performance, such as cultural experience evenings (Maori Tourism Taskforce Report 1992). The cultural experiences offered are commonly promoted by tour operators as "traditional" or "authentic" experiences of Maori culture. This may be termed "staged authenticity" as it involves the commercial performance and presentation of traditions to a contemporary audience (Cohen 1988; MacCannell 1973).

The performances are commonly conducted out of their cultural context, for example, in hotel environments, in museums, or at specially constructed *marae* (Zeppel 1998d). The performances are normally part of a structured tour itinerary that involve only a brief visit to the performance venue. As such, the cultural experiences offered for mass tourists allow little time and opportunity for personal contact and sharing between tourists and their Maori hosts. Furthermore, such performances have been viewed as a threat to cultural values as they tend to rely on caricature and stereotype (Keelan 1996; Taylor 2001). Indeed, much critique has been afforded in the published literature to the so-called "homogenizing" or "stereo-typing" effect of tourism on indigenous culture (see for example, Douglas & Douglas 1996; Mathieson & Wall 1982; Te Awekotuku 1981). Thus, within the published literature on Maori tourism, the importance of the integrity, ownership, participation and control of the promotion and presentation of Maori culture is recognised (Barnett 1997; Keelen 1996; Ryan 1997; Ryan & Crotts 1997; Walsh 1996; Zeppel 1997b, 1998d).

Within the range of Maori tourism products available in New Zealand, *marae* (Maori village) visits are now popular among tourists. Taylor (2001) has argued that in contrast to the staged performances, a visit to a Maori *marae* is an opportunity for "cultural exchange" or "interaction experiences" rather than an experience that is overtly staged as an experience of the "authentic Other." In this way, the experience provided for tourists within the setting of a *marae* is, "significantly more 'genuine' and educational than those more commonly provided by tourism" (p. 22). Taylor relates this to a "so-called 'staged back-region' approach" in which the point of tourist-host interaction is made to revolve around issues of "sincerity" as well as authenticity (p. 16). A *marae* visit is therefore said to meet tourists' increasing demand for "meaningful" experiences (McIntosh 2004; Zeppel 1995) or to become more "absorbed" within the cultural experience (Taylor 2001), as well as providing Maori people with the opportunity for cultural integrity whilst also providing economic benefits to the Maori community. An exploration of the notions of sincerity and authenticity within the context of a *marae* visit is an objective of the present study.

There has been considerable debate in the published literature about the concept of authenticity regarding questions about what it is, who owns it and where authenticity can be found (see for example, Cohen 1988; MacCannell 1976; Trilling 1972; Wang 1999). For example, notions of authenticity can be defined according to emergent, contextual, material, conceptual and historical measures (Lengkeek 2001; Ryan & Crotts 1997; Tahana & Oppermann 1998). However, it is only recently that it has been suggested that the audience of Maori performances on a *marae* is not merely observing staged authenticity but are actually experiencing an *authentic* Maori experience (see Taylor 2001). In this way, the tourist is not merely the observer as the host culture is observed (Urry 1990), but the nature of authenticity is *experiential* (Daniel 1996; McIntosh & Prentice 1999; Taylor 2001). Rather than *observing* host values, tourists *experience* them. This moves beyond searching for authenticity in the past to experiencing it at the present time of the tourist-host encounter. Taylor (2001) has argued that, within this context, the notion of "sincerity" is a more appropriate term for authenticity's present applications and understandings from both the host and visitor, as it implies an exchange of values shared in the tourist-host relationship. Through a "sincere" experience, tourists are incorporated into certain cultural aspects of the host community, as determined by their hosts, although this inclusion is for a short amount of time and linked with the immediate cultural performance. The nature of sincerity gained by tourists is also likely to vary according to the extent of tourists' interest in indigenous cultures and their previous interaction(s) with different cultural groups (Moscardo & Pearce 1999; Zeppel 2002).

An implication of this perspective is that the provision and presentation of cultural authenticity, or the cultural experience for tourists, must be defined and delivered in a manner that is culturally-acceptable, that is, defined by the hosts themselves according to their unique cultural values (Keelan 1996; McIntosh *et al.* 2002, 2004; Ryan 1997; Taylor 2001). In this way, a "sincere" interaction influenced by hosts' values creates an understanding and an authentic experience for why certain traditional cultural aspects are best kept for the host culture's viewing or experience only, or, alternatively, why some traditions may be commodified for tourism. However, whilst the performance remains a staged concert for tourists, it is based on values acceptable to the hosts. The unique cultural values presented will also define the nature of sincerity exchanged between host and guest, although cultural expressions evolve over time (Tahana & Oppermann 1998). In particular, it is important to note that many indigenous peoples share value and belief systems that are difficult for outsiders to understand. For example, the New Zealand Maori have a spiritual and symbolic bond with the environment based on a belief that humankind is not separate from the environment but part of an indivisible whole that is bound by *mauri* (a spiritual life force). This may effect the extent to which tourists are able to gain cultural understanding and respect for the values held by their indigenous hosts. In particular, if tourists misunderstand or fail to appreciate the valued belief systems shared with them in an exchange experience with their indigenous hosts, possible instances of cultural offence may occur.

Of importance to understanding the nature of cultural experiences provided within a *marae* setting are the Maori concepts of *tikanga* and *kawa*. *Tikanga* and *kawa* guide the behaviour of both visitor and host. *Tikanga* are values (Barlow 1994) that establish and set *kawa*. *Kawa* are protocols or rules in which one or a group is expected to behave. Although these two concepts cannot truly be understood without other key values of the Maori culture, they are nonetheless the more significant Maori values with regards to visitor management within the *marae*. It should however be noted that *tikanga* (values) and *kawa* (protocols) are not universal in their application throughout the Maori culture. That is, they differ with each tribal area. This is of particular relevance when the cultural experience is *marae*-based and is important to tourists' experiences and understanding gained from the cross-cultural encounter, as well as to the potential impacts on the host culture arising from that interaction.

In addition to attention to the hosts' perspectives of cultural exchange, tourists' perspectives are also important. Tourists' perspectives of their experiences of indigenous host cultures are less understood. Although, exceptions to this include studies by McIntosh (2004), Moscardo & Pearce (1999), Ryan & Huyton (2002) and Zeppel (2002). Primarily, the focus of the published literature on tourists' perspectives of indigenous tourism, however, has been the market potential for indigenous products rather than a conceptualisation of the key attributes of the cross-cultural experience from tourists' perspectives. The literature on heritage tourism, more generally, has provided an increasing number of studies that have examined the nature of experiences consumed by tourists in experiential terms (for example, Moscardo 1996; Prentice *et al*. 1994; Schanzel & McIntosh 2000). From an experiential perspective, the consumption of heritage tourism is influenced by tourists' subjective experiences and the personal backgrounds and agendas that they bring to a tourism encounter (McIntosh 1998; McIntosh & Prentice 1999). However, previous studies of tourists' experiences have been restricted to contexts of comparatively lesser cultural distance, for example, evaluations of British tourists' experiences of museums interpreting British social and industrial history (see for example, Beeho & Prentice 1997; McIntosh & Prentice 1999).

It has been suggested in previous studies, however, that the cross-cultural experience is particularly effected by the extent to which tourists are culturally motivated and by the extent of cultural difference between tourist and their hosts (McIntosh 2004; Prentice *et al*. 1994). In this sense, the most "meaningful" experiences for tourists may occur through informal personal contact with indigenous people, as in the process of feeling "endearment" towards local people (Prentice *et al*. 1994), rather than through staged cultural events. Through informal contact with an indigenous host, tourists may pose questions that are pertinent to them, potentially on a one-on-one basis or through a guide or interpreter, in order to help them to personally understand and appreciate the cultural lifestyle and values of their indigenous hosts. Or, other specialist-interest tourists may seek more in-depth experiences of indigenous cultures (Zeppel 1995, 1997b, 2002). However, it should be questioned whether tourists can ever truly gain cultural understanding where the belief system is significantly different to their own.

In addition, some scholars have noted that tourist motivations for experiences of indigenous culture appear to be generalist in nature (McIntosh 2004; McKercher & Du Cros 2002; Ryan & Huyton 2002). In view of tourists' generalist motivations and the fact that the most accessible opportunities for experiences of Maori culture in New Zealand remain centred around a staged cultural performance, the nature of the experiences that tourists gain of Maori (indigenous) culture may, arguably, be more superficial, more formal (cognitive) and less affective than has been reported in tourists' experiences of more familiar (non-indigenous) cultural contexts (see McIntosh & Prentice 1999; Prentice *et al*. 1994). Or conversely, if tourists' experiences of Maori (indigenous) culture are more superficial, they may be less cognitive and more emotional in nature. It might therefore be argued that the cultural exchange or experience of "sincerity" may be more superficial and therefore less authentic in the context of a *marae* setting than Taylor (2001) has advocated because tourists' experiences are based on partial understanding, spectacle and a sense of hospitality without reciprocity.

Fewer studies have recorded the experiential and authentic nature of tourist-host interaction from both host and guest perspectives. Yet, attention to visitor and host experiences of a *marae* visit raises important issues for product development and strategies for the sustainable development and cultural enhancement of Maori communities. In particular, the nature of authentic interaction between host and guest is likely to be a complex, dynamic, fluid and creative process involving various negotiations of identity, meaning, understanding; also involving spatial, socio-political and temporal influences (Lengkeek 2001; Murray 2000). In a study of tourists' experiences at Iban longhouses in Sarawak, Zeppel (1995, 1997c) identified authenticity in tourists' responses to the physical setting (situational authenticity) and in relation to the fulfilment of tourists' personal needs (behavioural authenticity). For hosts, authenticity may, conversely, exist in the extent of control they exhibit over the cultural experience presented to tourists (Walsh 1996).

To date, however, there has been minimal attention in the published literature to the nature of the *marae* experience, particularly with regards to an empirical investigation exploring the nature and meaning of a *marae* visit to visitors *and* their Maori hosts. To this end, this chapter aims to explore the key attributes or dimensions of the *marae* experience as reported by visitors and Maori hosts at Nga Hau E Wha national *marae* in Christchurch, a case study *marae* in the South Island of New Zealand. In an exploration of the key attributes of a *marae* visit during the main summer season of 2003, issues relating to the experiential nature and authenticity or sincerity of the cultural interaction are examined. This chapter therefore contributes to current thinking on cultural tourism through the provision of insights from hosts' and tourists' perspectives into the meaning and experiential nature of the cultural authenticity experienced within a *marae* setting. As an examination of the actual extent of understanding gained in the host-tourist encounter is outside the scope of the exploratory nature of this study, further research is called for into issues of cross-cultural understanding to build on the dimensions of experience in the *marae* setting described here.

## Case Study — Nga Hau E Wha National Marae

As a context for an investigation of cross-cultural exchange and understanding, a brief description of the *marae* selected as a case study and the function and cultural importance of *marae* is required to inform the present study. Whilst the word *marae* is commonly used to describe the complex of buildings and land that form the nucleus of a tribal Maori village, the *marae* is, essentially, an institution from classical Maori society that is central to Maori values and way of life and the tribal cultural identity (both in a contemporary and traditional sense). The function of the *marae* is as a place for welcoming visitors, a centre for informal and formal meetings, for debate and decision-making and a place of deep significance to Maori people (Tauroa & Tauroa 1986). The *marae* is an expression of Maori autonomy and authority and is often the most authentic centre in terms of Maori cultural values and symbolism (Durie 1998). As such, all visitors to a *marae* must be welcomed on to the *marae* by the *powhiri* (welcoming) process according to traditional Maori *tikanga* (values) and *kawa* (protocols), (see Harawira 1997).

Nga Hau E Wha national *marae* (NHEW) was established in 1990. It is located in the city of Christchurch in the South Island of New Zealand and is perceived among Maori as an urban *marae* (Tau 2000). Many urban *marae* differ from tribal *marae* in that their purpose is to facilitate and accommodate for all Maori rather than just one specific tribal or religious group. NHEW translates as "the four winds" and is a metaphor for combining people from different areas and ethnic backgrounds. As such, the *marae* represents Maori on a "national" level. NHEW was established, in particular, to provide for the increasing numbers of North Island Maori people migrating south to Christchurch. Since 1995, NHEW has offered a tourism product to generate financial income and employment for local Maori. The tourism product is promoted as "The Night of Maori Magic" and offers, for a minimum of fifteen people, a traditional Maori welcome (*powhiri*), a traditional feast (*hangi*) and concert performance (*kapahaka*). NHEW is perceived among some Maori groups to have defied many issues of Maori *tikanga* (values), and therefore provides an interesting case study for examining the key attributes of cross-cultural experiences and issues of authenticity in a *marae* setting. Indeed, this perception is founded in the wider debate about the extent to which *marae* have become sites no longer for the symbolisation of kin-group unity and local identity, but for the display of a generalised "Maori" tradition, mainly through their communication of cultural identity to outsiders (Sissons 1993, 1998).

For example, in terms of design, NHEW is reflective of a North Island style *marae* with carved ancestral houses that are rarely seen in a *Ngai Tahu* (the main Maori tribe of the South Island) *marae*. In effect, it is perceived to impose North Island Maori values on to the tribal area of the South Island Maori. However, for North Island migrants, this is a representation of their unique values as they may feel marginalized in a *Ngai Tahu marae*. Furthermore, in contrast with many *marae* that only portray carved images of great Maori ancestors, NHEW also portrays two European ancestors (James Cook and Abel Tasman). Thus, NHEW has a multi-cultural focus, thereby also representing non-Maori in *marae* activities. In terms of its tourism product, the *powhiri* (traditional welcoming ceremony) has been adapted at NHEW to accommodate visitors. As is customary, and in accordance with Maori *tikanga* (values), all visitors must first complete the *powhiri* (welcoming) process prior to entering the *marae*. However, for tourist comfort, the experience provided for visitors at NHEW allows people to walk on to the *marae* before the *powhiri*. The reason for this, according to *marae* staff, relates to the lack of facilities to accommodate tourists outside the gate of the *marae*. The significance of the *powhiri* process is therefore explained to visitors once they are inside the *wharenui* (ancestral meeting house). A further example relates to conflict over the use of the *marae*. For example, *tangi* (funerals) become the sole purpose of the *marae* until the grieving period has ended. Tourist bookings that occur at the same time as *tangi* therefore represent a further example of the compromise of *tikanga* at NHEW. The unpredictability of *tangi* and the inability of the *marae* to cancel bookings impact not only on the operation of NHEW but also the family of the deceased. Despite these compromises to Maori *tikanga* (values), the tourism product offered at NHEW is viewed as a vehicle through which visitors can become educated on Maori customs and *tikanga* (value).

## Study Method

In-depth interviews were conducted with three hosts and twenty visitors at the Nga Hau E Wha national *marae* in the summer of 2003. Specifically, the key attributes or dimensions of a *marae* visit were explored from the perspectives of both hosts and tourists. Issues relating to the experiential nature of the cross-cultural experience and the authenticity and sincerity of the interaction were also examined. Face-to-face in-depth interviews were conducted with twenty international tourists aged over 18 years. The tourists interviewed represented a range of nationalities and different types (i.e. age, gender, package tourists, free and independent travellers). The number and design of the in-depth interviews conducted was consistent with other inductive studies of the tourist experience (Beeho & Prentice 1997; Schanzel & McIntosh 2000). However, as the sample size was small, findings of the study should be treated as indicative, not substantive.

Each visitor interview lasted approximately 20–30 minutes. Due to the in-depth nature of the interviews, interviews were conducted with English-speaking tourists only. Respondents were approached randomly at the end of the evening's entertainment following the Maori concert performance whilst they were seated in the dining hall. Open-ended questions were employed to elicit as accurately as possible tourists' experiences at the *marae*, as described by them in their own words and in relation to key attributes identified by them. Consistent with other experiential studies of the tourist experience (for example, McIntosh & Prentice 1999), respondents were asked to describe the experiences they had gained at the *marae*, particularly in terms of how it had made them *feel* and what *thoughts* had come into their mind. Visitors were also asked their motives for visiting NHEW, what they thought was important to experience when visiting a *marae* and to relate their experiences at NHEW to their general experiences of Maori culture in New Zealand and other Maori attractions they may have visited. Further questions related to visitors' satisfaction with their visit, their perceptions of authenticity and how they might have preferred to experience Maori culture. To elicit the meaning of the *marae* visit to visitors, the in-depth interviews incorporated the principles of the "laddering" technique into the interview design (see Reynolds & Gutman 1988). As such, respondents were asked to think on a more emotional level and about the importance of their underlying motivations and reported experiences gained (see McIntosh 1998). As such, an aim of the study was to provide an inductive exploration of the nature of the *marae* visit, as reported by tourists in their own words and in relation to attributes expressed as being of personal importance to them.

In addition to the in-depth interviews with international tourists, in-depth interviews were conducted with three staff members at NHEW. Attention to both hosts' and guests' perspectives of a *marae* visit can provide insights into whether a potential mismatch is apparent between the experiences gained by visitors and the experiences that managers and interpreters at the attraction think they are providing (see Beeho & Prentice 1997). However, this is not an objective of the findings presented here. All the staff interviewed were Maori by descent and included one manager and two cultural performers. The staff interviewed were selected on the basis of their knowledge of management strategy, their direct involvement in the tourist experience and their willingness to participate in the study. Each staff interview lasted approximately 30–45 minutes. In order to explore the key attributes of a *marae* visit and examine issues of authenticity and sincerity within the experience provided at the *marae*, the in-depth interviews with the *marae* staff included open-ended questions relating to the perceived benefits of hosting visitors at the *marae*, the nature of the experience that is provided for visitors at the *marae*, the key messages that they want visitors to take away from their *marae* visit and what changes, if any, had been made to the cultural experience or knowledge that is shared with visitors at the *marae*. Staff at the *marae* were also asked to describe how they feel about hosting visitors and whether they have ever experienced difficulties with visitors, including occurrences of cultural offence or potential misunderstandings shown by visitors relating to the nature or function of the *marae*.

The staff and visitor interviews were tape recorded and then transcribed to ensure the accuracy of respondents' responses. The data obtained from the interviews was content analysed to elicit consistency of response (Patton 1990). Both the present authors analysed the data. The Maori co-researcher ensured accuracy of the interpretation of findings and was able to elaborate the cultural meanings of responses that may have been missed by the present non-Maori author. As such, outsider and insider perspectives were facilitated in data analysis (see McIntosh *et al.* 2002).

## Dimensions of the Marae Experience

Findings of the in-depth interviews revealed that the key attributes associated with a visit to NHEW were similar as reported by both hosts and tourists. Specifically, these dimensions related to reported experiences of *education, authenticity, personal interaction, sincere hospitality* and *emotion*. These dimensions are discussed below in the context of the views of both hosts and tourists, as emerged from the interview data. The nature of the visit at NHEW was therefore found to be meaningful to both hosts and tourists as it provided an exchange that was authentic, sincere, educational and often affective in nature, although further research is needed to validate these findings.

## Views of the Hosts

The in-depth interviews with staff members at NHEW revealed four key dimensions of the *marae* experience, as perceived by them. These included *education, authenticity, personal interaction* and *staged* elements. These dimensions were reported by the Maori hosts to represent the nature of the experience they provided for visitors at NHEW.

Indeed, the staff members interviewed reported that the main experience provided at the *marae* was one of, "Education and the chance to get involved; as it's hands-on, lots of people learn better that way, and that way the information will stay with them"; or, "An understanding of a *marae*. Also an understanding of some contemporary aspects of Maori culture such as NHEW being an urban *marae*"; and, "A better understanding of Maori culture and people from what they had previously." An important part of delivering an educational experience for tourists visiting the *marae*, according to the staff members interviewed, was the requirement for visitors to gain an *interactive* experience through, "Incorporating the visitor in to the experience rather than observing it"; "Tourists always like the *interactive* elements; some have asked about stay-overs at the *marae* and more hands-on things like trying the short sticks (hand-eye coordination game)." That tourists demand personal interaction with indigenous people is a conclusion shared by previous studies of tourists' perspectives of indigenous tourism (McIntosh 2004; Notzke 1999; Ryan & Huyton 2002; Zeppel 2002).

The staff members interviewed described how the setting of the *marae* inherently makes the experience *authentic* for visitors. However, it was also reported to be important to offer visitors a traditional Maori welcome and to ensure that the performers have a basic level of knowledge of Maori traditions so that delivery of the experience is authentic. As such, *authenticity* was seen to be evident in the physical setting as well as in the nature of the shared interaction between host and visitor. Comments made by respondents included, "Visitors should feel what it is like to be welcomed on to a *marae*; see an authentic aspect of Maori culture other than just the cultural performance"; "There is a lot of authentic stuff in the package; the singing, dancing, the fact that they are on a *marae*, the *whare* (ancestral meeting houses), the participation we make them do, the *kai* (food). But the most authentic things we have are the *whare tipuna* (ancestral meeting house) and *whare wananga* (house of learning), for the simple fact that they portray the traditional carvings and the *tuktuku* (traditional weaving patterns)"; "The way tourists are welcomed and incorporated to the *marae* and the *tangata whenua* (host people), is, with the exception of the *powhiri* (welcoming ceremony), exactly the way Maori people are welcomed"; "Much of the enjoyment and authenticity comes from the enjoyment on the performers' faces; showing that we enjoy performing and sharing our culture with them." That tourists are incorporated into a sincere interaction with their hosts is argued to be an *authentic* experience of Maori culture, according to Taylor (2001). However, if authenticity is perceived, in this instance, as the moment of interaction between host and guest, some recognition of the complexity of factors that may come into play in this interaction must be given (see Lengkeek 2001; Murray 2000; Ryan 1999). In particular, whilst the focus of Taylor's notion of sincerity focuses on the *experience* of authenticity, many hosts' comments also alluded to authenticity being presented in authentic things, or objects, or the enjoyment of performers. Furthermore, whilst hosts' views on authenticity tend to relate predominantly to issues relating to the control of the content and presentation of a performance (Walsh 1996), tourists' perceptions of and preferences for authenticity may be different.

The fourth dimension of the *marae* experience reported by the staff related to the *staged* aspects of the visit. Although, as described above, the staff members interviewed felt that the experience provided for visitors was authentic, it was recognised that, "Some of the things we do are specifically for the tourist's wants, or our perceptions of their wants." As such, some aspects of the *marae* experience have been *staged* or altered to cater to perceived tourist demands. Comments made by the respondents included, "I don't think tourists are getting educated properly about our *tikanga* (values) and our culture; NHEW is about all tribes in New Zealand, not just about one tribe, it is portrayed as a national *marae*; our tour guides need to have *all* the knowledge"; "I think what we do for tourists could be a bit more authentic; not so much contemporary stuff like using the guitar in our performances."

Respondents further described how the changes that had been made to the cultural experience mainly related to the *powhiri* (welcoming ceremony) and to the performance itself. One respondent reported that, "Visitors are explained the *powhiri* on the *marae*. It's funny to see a welcoming ceremony to welcome people onto a *marae* when they have actually been on the *marae* for about half an hour sitting inside the main meeting house, but that is only because of a lack of facilities outside the *marae*." "Other than that, the only difference between tourists and Maori coming on to the *marae* is that we explain the whole process to tourists bit by bit, right down to teaching them the songs. So we nurture their learning from the beginning to the end." Confirming these comments, one other respondent mentioned that, "The only other change is mainly to the performance itself. We've had additional performers that have brought their own spark to the show." That indigenous involvement in tourism potentially entails continually having to reassess what is, and what is not permissible in the delivery of a cultural experience for tourists is a comment raised elsewhere (Ryan 1997). Furthermore, cultural authenticity should be seen in the context of the dynamic culture and commercial opportunity it represents (Murray 2000; Ryan & Crotts 1997).

Although there were some aspects of the experience that were seen to compromise Maori *tikanga* (values), respondents alluded to the overall authenticity of the *marae* experience, as perceived by them, in terms of the traditional functions ascribed to the *marae*. For instance, one staff member described how, "I think, despite those compromises, the *marae* is brought to life with its everyday use as a place where the community can benefit from an activity that is utilised by the *marae*; the *marae* is not dormant because of the life that running a business like tourism brings to it." Another respondent stated that, "I think that of all the places that I've actually performed and hosted people on, this is probably one of the best because of the set up that it has and it *is* a *marae*; and because of the number of *whare* (ancestral meeting houses) it has to offer, and just the whole span of information and history. We're not performing in a theatre; the place is just over-loaded with information and experiences for people to have." As such, hosting tourists at the *marae* was seen to maintain the authenticity of the traditional functions of the marae, including, being a place of education and a place from which to serve the community. Indeed, it has been similarly noted in previous studies that cultural identity may be consciously and/or purposefully commodified through tourism but the integrity of that identity is maintained among members of the host culture (see for example, McIntosh *et al.* 2002; Walsh 1996).

Overall, the in-depth interviews with the *marae* staff revealed positive attitudes towards hosting tourists at NHEW. Whilst the experiencing of hosting tourists on the *marae* was generally seen to be positive, all three of the staff interviewed did comment that they had experienced difficulties with tourists at the *marae* due to occurrences of cultural misunderstandings. For example, one respondent described how, "Once at the *marae*, one of the tourists had purchased a *patu pounamu* (short hand club made out of greenstone). He was the representative for the group and he brought the *patu* along with him to the *marae*. During the performance he had no place to put it, so he sat on it. To me, it was hard to witness that something such as a *patu pounamu*, or any type of weapon, be sat on." "Another time, one of the tourists grabbed one of our *rakau* (wooden sticks) and started mimicking the various movements of the weaponry in a degrading manner. That was a bit hard to take. Following that, some of the performers were waiting for an opportunity where that particular tourist had no attention drawn to him so they could give him a quick reminder of being culturally disrespectful." The need to adhere to traditional protocol to ensure the cultural significance of the *marae* is preserved and respected has been similarly noted by McIntosh *et al.* (2002) and Walsh (1996).

## Views of the Tourists

As might be expected, most of the international tourists interviewed commented that they had never previously visited a *marae* and most reported very little previous experience or knowledge of Maori culture. Among the main motivations reported by tourists for choosing to visit NHEW, respondents reported that the *marae* had been recommended to them as one of the "must-sees" during a visit to New Zealand and was perceived to provide an "educational" experience and an experience that represented a "truer" experience of Maori culture. As such, a particular interest in Maori culture did not appear to represent a primary motivating factor for visiting. Indeed, previous studies of tourists' perspectives of indigenous tourism have similarly alluded to the generalist nature of the experiences sought by mass tourists (McIntosh 2004; McKercher & Du Cros 2002; Ryan & Huyton 2002). The tourists interviewed reported that they had enjoyed their visit and described the nature of the experiences they had gained at NHEW in terms of five main dimensions; namely, *educational, sincere hospitality, authenticity, personal interaction* and *emotional*. These dimensions are elaborated below.

## *Educational*

The *marae* visit was described by the majority of the tourists interviewed as *educational* or "an experience of cultural exchange." In particular, respondents commented that learning the protocols and cultural significance relating to the *marae* was the most important educational component. Comments made by respondents included, "You need to learn and follow the rules and regulations, out of respect for the culture and their religions; you also need to have explained all the things that happen here and also what all the carvings stand for; it's spiritual; and the importance of ancestors; you learn that family is very important"; "It's very important because we're coming in to experience their culture and we shouldn't offend, so it's important to have an overview telling us what to expect and how we should react"; "it's important to know what to do, especially when you are visiting another culture; that's the reason I came here." Indeed, the protocols associated with a *marae* visit are seen as an essential educational and cultural element of the experience provided for tourists within a *marae* (see McIntosh *et al.* 2002; Sissons 1993). Learning about indigenous culture and history has also been found to be a key part of the experiences reported by tourists visiting other indigenous tourism centres (McIntosh 2004; Zeppel 2002).

## *Authenticity*

Most of the tourists described the nature of their experience as "authentic," or, "as authentic as possible." The main authentic aspects mentioned by respondents included the "dress," "costumes," "tattoos," "dance," "*marae* setting," "welcome process" (*powhiri*), "sculptures," "food," "meanings behind objects or activities," "the involvement of the audience" and the "sincerity" of the Maori hosts. As such, authenticity was perceived in the setting, audience participation and sincerity of the hospitality provided at the *marae*. Whilst respondents did comment that the cultural experience had been modified for tourism, they still perceived the nature of the "interaction" to be authentic. This finding was articulated by one respondent who described the experience he had gained as, "Definitely authentic; the welcome was genuine but there were some things that had been compromised because we were tourists and this is a tourist thing; but I don't think you should change your customs, like allowing us to keep our shoes on in the meeting house. We wanted to *experience* Maori culture and we got that, although it seemed it had been modified for us."

Further comments made by respondents that described the authentic nature of the experiences they had gained included, "It was authentic, as far as you can portray your ancestors on stage, and the involvement of the audience; but I think it's easy to see we are in a city and not in the setting of an authentic tribe"; "It's hard to be authentic because of the cross-cultural things that are happening, electricity, technology, but if this is as close as they can get to it, then that's fine; if they provided an authentic experience, they might frighten a few people"; "I would say it's as close as possible; most of it was very moving and emotional; it's very genuine and from the heart"; "It's authentic because you are living your culture; I don't know how it cannot be authentic if you are the one doing it." The fact that NHEW is located within an urban setting was reported by respondents to have made the *marae* visit, in their opinion, a "truer" or more authentic experience. As one respondent summarised, "You cannot get away from urban now; you expect people to want to continue their traditions and it's a culture within a culture; I think if you put it away out in the sticks, it would lose its meaning and importance to the culture; it's part of what is going on in the real world; this is where Maori live now, so why pretend otherwise; it also makes it more accessible to tourists." Cultural authenticity was therefore reported by tourists to be found in cultural markers of the setting and performance, as well as through personal interaction with the hosts (Zeppel 1995, 1997b, 2002). As such, the findings of the in-depth interviews provided some support for the conclusions made by McIntosh *et al.* (2002), Taylor (2001) and Zeppel (1995, 1997b), namely, that *authentic* Maori culture can be found through the communication of honesty, integrity, accessibility, acceptability and cultural dynamism, rather than merely through the historical accuracy of dance performances. Although, the complex range of factors that come into play in this communication must be acknowledged, as noted above.

### Sincere Hospitality

With further reference to the authentic nature of the experience gained, many respondents alluded to the *sincere hospitality* or sincere welcome that they had experienced. For instance, respondents described how, "You could see emotion in the music and that was a very vivid way of expressing themselves; it showed the personality of the culture; I enjoyed the dancing very much because I could see that the performers are really into it; they're not just doing a performance, they are really showing you with passion"; "Just the moments when the performers seemed to be really into what they were doing"; "The movement and spirit were authentic; because I could feel it"; "To feel welcomed is the most important thing to experience; I think in every culture, greeting is the most important part; and the *powhiri* (welcome ceremony) is the first impression we have of Maori culture"; "It is important to receive a sincere welcome and to know that it's something you clearly wanted us tourists to know about." As such, authenticity may be more apparent and important to tourists in the nature of the sincerity or genuine hospitality shared with the hosts, as similarly noted by Taylor (2001) and Zeppel (1995, 1997b).

## Personal Interaction

The nature of the *marae* visit was also described by most of the respondents as "hands-on" or "interactive." Respondents described the experience they had gained as the opportunity, "To be able to participate and get up on stage; it's important to be more involved"; "We were integrated into the whole experience; we were able to come in as a tribe, get up on stage and experience the things they do; that's special; they don't have to share their culture and the meaning of everything with everybody." Many of the respondents also responded that they would have liked more opportunities to interact with Maori people, including the chance to "ask questions one-on-one." Furthermore, many respondents stated that they would have liked to stay overnight at the *marae*. Previous studies have similarly found that tourists demand personal interaction with indigenous people and the chance to meet indigenous people in a genuine manner (see for example, McIntosh 2004; Milne *et al.* 1998; Ryan & Huyton 2002; Zeppel 1995, 1997b, 2002).

## *Emotion*

Whilst some previous studies have argued that tourists' experiences of indigenous culture may be less affective (emotional) in nature than tourists' experiences of more familiar cultural contexts (see for example, McIntosh 2004), there was some evidence to suggest that this was not the case in the present study. The nature of the experiences reported by tourists at NHEW was therefore somewhat consistent with previous studies that have examined tourists' experiences in contexts of comparatively lesser cultural distance and have similarly recorded the affective and emotional nature of heritage experiences (see Beeho & Prentice 1997; Daniel 1996; McIntosh & Prentice 1999). Many of the tourists interviewed in the present study commented, unprompted, that their experience at the *marae* had been "emotional." Emotions experienced by respondents included reported feelings of "privilege," "spirituality," "awe" and "excitement." For example, respondents described how they had felt, "The feeling of tradition; how special the place is; how sacred it is; I felt privileged that I could experience that"; "I was in awe; I was very subdued; from the *marae* itself, it was the beauty of it and obviously the skill of the people that built it; I was wondering the reasoning behind it all; obviously for that level of detail, it wouldn't be meaningless; it creates some kind of internal feeling"; "It was spiritual; I find it really brings me down to earth; I go away with a real sense of understanding about what the Maori people believe in; it's very touching to visit a place like this to find out more in the world than what we say or believe or do"; "It was very exciting, very expressive, you could feel the energy and the vibe; all the shouting, all the vocals and shaking; I felt really moved"; "It was certainly spiritual; the feeling you get when you just struggle to explain what exactly you are feeling; that's probably, for me, when you are closer to something spiritual and when there aren't any words for it; you know, your hair stands on end; I experienced that several times during the performance and the songs." However, the affective nature of the *marae* experience, as reported at NHEW, is likely to be immediate and short term, although a longer stay on a *marae* may represent a greater emotional involvement for the tourist (Ryan 1999).

## Conclusions

Drawing on recent debates about the authenticity and experiential nature of cultural encounters, this chapter has explored the notions of sincerity and authenticity in the context of a *marae* visit. Specifically, it identified the key attributes of a *marae* visit, or, the nature of the experiences provided at Nga Hau E Wha (NHEW) national *marae* in Christchurch, New Zealand, as reported by both hosts and tourists. Previous studies of tourists' perspectives of indigenous tourism have been predominantly marketing focused and have not considered the salient dimensions of the cross-cultural experiences shared between hosts and tourists. Furthermore, previous studies of tourists' experiences from an experiential perspective have been restricted to contexts of comparatively lesser cultural distance. And few studies have explored the experiential and authentic nature of tourist-host interaction from the perspectives of both tourists and their indigenous hosts. As such, this chapter has contributed insights into the nature of the experiences gained by tourists in a cultural setting that represents significantly different valued belief systems from their own, and the key attributes of the cultural experience as identified by the Maori hosts.

From in-depth interviews with staff and tourists visiting NHEW, five common dimensions of the *marae* experience were revealed. These were experiences of: *education, authenticity, personal interaction, sincere hospitality* and *emotion*. These experiences provided the sharing of cultural traditions and protocol within the authentic cultural context of the *marae* and through the sincerity of the hospitality shown by the Maori hosts. Of particular note from the study findings was the reported affective nature of the experience among tourists. Indeed, whilst tourists visiting Maori attractions, including *marae*, have been found to hold predominantly generalist motivations, the nature of the cultural experiences gained by tourists at NHEW was found to be affective (emotional) as well as cognitive (educational) in nature. Although, the actual extent of connectivity felt or understanding gained by tourists from their experiences remains an area for further research.

The findings of the exploratory study also provided some evidence to show that the dimensions of the *marae* experience were somewhat consistent with some previous studies that have explored tourists' experiences in more familiar cultural contexts (see in particular, Beeho & Prentice 1997; McIntosh & Prentice 1999). That is, the experiences gained by tourists from their visit to NHEW were *emotionally-imbued, interactive* and *educational*. If these findings are validated by further research, it could be argued that tourists may experience cultural attractions of lesser or greater cultural distance in similar ways, although this is perhaps not surprising given that most heritage attractions involve a constructed experience centred on cultural or temporal distance of which the visitor is potentially unfamiliar. The findings reported here may, thus, have relevance to other cultural contexts, including tourists' experiences at other indigenous attractions.

Findings of the present study showed that authenticity was, reportedly, an important aspect of the experience provided at NHEW *marae*. Although, previous research has raised debate about whether a Maori product can ever have real "authenticity" in a situation where adjustments to the cultural experience provided for paying customers may need to be made (Ryan 1997; Walsh 1996). Specifically, an experience of authenticity at NHEW was found, as reported by the hosts and tourists interviewed, in the nature of interaction or "sincerity" communicated between hosts and tourists, and experienced within the physical setting of a *marae*, rather than in interpretations of historical accuracy that may be presented out of the original context. This finding thereby provides some support for Zeppel's (1995, 1997b) conclusion that tourists' responses to authenticity in indigenous culture may relate to aspects of the setting (situational authenticity), and to tourists' fulfilling personal needs through experiencing indigenous culture such as through the enjoyment of a personal and genuine encounter with a host (behavioural authenticity). Inherent in this conclusion is the notion that tourists differ in how they conceive "authenticity" and how they personally respond to the cross-cultural encounter. Indeed, the influence of tourists' personal agendas on their subjective experiences of heritage has been noted elsewhere (see for example, McIntosh & Prentice 1999).

Also inherent in this conclusion is the notion that the Maori hosts are in control of the nature of cultural authenticity presented to tourists in the physical setting and nature of genuine interaction experienced by tourists at the *marae* (Walsh 1996). For example, it may appear from the findings of the present research that Maori hosts at the *marae* are potentially more concerned about the delivery of authentic "understanding," as it serves to validate their culture. This may not be so directly counter-posed with the view of tourists visiting the *marae*, for whom personal "interaction" appears paramount. Both hosts and guests therefore bring their own agendas into the cross-cultural encounter. In a broader sense, hosts' control and presentation of cultural authenticity should also be seen in the context of a dynamic and evolving culture (Ryan 1999; Ryan & Crotts 1997), of the systematisation of *marae* (Sissons 1993), and the socio-political influences on indigenous communities, among other things. The factors that come into play in the nature of authenticity experienced in the cross-cultural encounter involving hosts and guests of comparatively different cultural (indigenous versus non-indigenous) backgrounds are therefore complex. As Lengkeek (2001) has noted, notions of authenticity potentially involve emergent, contextual, conceptual, material and historical measures.

This chapter serves to highlight the importance of *experiential* authenticity, or, *sincerity*, to the examination of cultural understanding and experiences. As such, authenticity is potentially evident in the (albeit brief) moments of shared experience and genuine hospitality that make authenticity an interactive experience and an experience of a present (as opposed to a past) reality. However, notions of authenticity are more complex than a focus on one experience or moment of interaction may describe, as noted above. Furthermore, an authentic cultural experience may be reportedly gained despite compromises to cultural values or modifications to the cultural activities presented to tourists. However, it is important to note that there is still the possibility that, from an experiential perspective, cultural authenticity may be misinterpreted by tourists due to the influence of tourists' own agendas and experience (see McIntosh & Prentice 1999), or conversely, may be misread by hosts in terms of what they perceive tourists to want. Such misinterpretation may cause instances of cultural offence or misunderstandings to occur (McIntosh *et al.* 2002). As such, further research is required to examine how tourists experience and interpret their encounters with indigenous people so that notions of cultural authenticity, cross-cultural understanding and the potential impacts of tourism on host culture, may be more fully understood in experiential terms, thereby building on the exploratory knowledge presented here.

## Acknowledgments

The authors wish to acknowledge the grant funding received from the Tourism Research and Education Centre, Lincoln University, New Zealand.

Chapter 5

# Balanda Tourists and Aboriginal People

Chris Ryan and Jeremy Huyton

## Introduction

Although this research project was grounded in a positivistic, quantitative tradition, it is about visitor perceptions of tourism products based upon a culture very different to that derived from European Judeo-Christian roots. Arnold (1999: 275) cites the Aboriginal poet George Tinamin as writing:

> One land, One Law, One People,
> Ngangatja apu wiya, ngakyuku tjamu—
> This is not rock, it is my grandfather.
> This is a place where the dreaming
> comes up, right up from inside the ground.

Therefore, like other chapters in this book, this text is about the ways in which Balanda (non-Aboriginal) visitors attach importance to sites of cultural difference; where the visitor for the most part comes from cultures traditionally located in scientific rationalism to view the artifacts and places of societies adopting more holistic and intuitive perspectives.

Consequently this chapter initially describes the context of the research in terms of: (a) current initiatives in promoting Australian Aboriginal culture as a tourist product; (b) the type of debate that has been engendered in academic and wider literature about such products; and (c) briefly indicating concerns about the effectiveness of such tourism products in generating desired returns to Aboriginal communities, citing Tjapukai Dance Theatre as one such example. It is noted that tourists see little of what is a developing Aboriginal cultural revival. It further queries to what degree tourists have an interest in Aboriginal culture. The research reported here concentrates on this last issue. Reference is also made to other aspects of the research project not fully reported in the chapter. The chapter is thus based within a positivistic rationale that is applied to the visitors and not to the hosts.

Indigenous Tourism: The Commodification and Management of Culture
Copyright © 2005 by Elsevier Ltd.
All rights of reproduction in any form reserved
ISBN: 0-08-044620-5

## The Context of the Study

That Aboriginal culture is used for tourism promotional purposes in both a general as well as product specific manner can be illustrated with reference to the 1999 brochure, "Central Australia Holiday Guide." In it the Northern Territory Tourist Commission (NTTC) copywriters write:

> This region holds not only one of the most culturally significant icons of Aboriginal and Australian culture, Ayers Rock/Uluru; it holds onto the true Outback spirit that made this country great . . .
>
> Nature overwhelms you in The Center. The skyscrapers are made out of rock, not steel, and one of the best shows in town is the million-star display at night. The largest population of unique animals, birds and reptiles proves that this arid climate is more than hospitable . . .
>
> The Aboriginal presence here is strong; their cultural and spiritual connection to this region echoes in every rock and landmark. You'll have numerous opportunities to learn about and understand Aboriginal culture when you visit The Center.
>
> . . . you'll have a fantastic time, but it will leave you wanting to come back to:
>
> The Heart. The Soul. The Center
>
> (Northern Territory Tourist Commission 1999: 1)

What is of significance within this copy is the linkage between "Outback" and "Aboriginal culture" and it will subsequently be argued that the copywriters have identified a key relationship within visitor perceptions of this part of Australia.

Zeppel (1999a) notes that in the 1990s Aboriginal culture was increasingly promoted as a tourist attraction. Additionally, Ryan (2000) identifies indigenous peoples, their role within tourism, the nature of indigenous peoples' culture as a tourist product and the associated issues of authorization as one of the growth topics within tourism research literature. Be this as it may, problems accompany this topic. Academic research undertaken by non-Indigenous academics raises issues as to the ontological perspective of the research. Indeed, confusion seemingly exists within academia as to what constitutes "Indigenous" (see Ryan's 1997 review of the work by Butler & Hinch 1996) even though such definitions are internationally recognized through UNESCO's declarations on such peoples.

For the purpose of this chapter, Zeppel's (1999a: 124) definition of Aboriginal tourism products has been adopted, that is the attraction features: (1) Aboriginal People; (2) Aboriginal Spirituality or the Dreaming; (3) Aboriginal Bushcraft Skills; (4) Aboriginal Cultural Practices; and (5) Aboriginal Artifacts. It has been argued that there exists a gap between the premise behind the promotional effort noted by Zeppel (1999a), and the reality of visitor interest (Ryan & Huyton 2000a; b). For example, while Aboriginal people at Manyallaluk offer an award winning tourist experience partially based upon a stay within their community, the actual numbers of visitors remain small (about 2,000 to 2,500 per annum). There is thus a paradox. On the one hand, research findings indicate a wish expressed by tourists for a greater interaction with Aboriginal people, but where a product offers precisely that opportunity, it attracts far smaller attendances than those overtly staged events where such wishes are revealed (for example see the work of Moscardo & Pearce at Tjapukai 1999). Additionally researchers like Finlayson (1992) and (Altman 1987) demonstrate that receipts from tourism at Uluru-Kata Tjuta have not significantly benefited the local Australian Aboriginal Anungu people. It would also appear that much of the academic literature has been oriented towards issues of image, authenticity, discussions of ownership or simply descriptions of product (e.g. Dow 1999; Zeppel 1999a). Alternatively there has been a past emphasis upon social and economic impact research, but comparatively few results have been published in the tourism journals and thus been subject to review (see Zeppel 1999b). It would appear that the impacts of tourism depend on factors like ownership and management of attractions (Altman & Finlayson 1992; Gillespie 1988). However, such an approach implies that tourist demand is a given, and the nature of that demand is not analyzed.

Ryan & Huyton (2000a, b) argue that tourist attractions based upon Aboriginal culture may not be as popular as is generally thought, and that one of their major functions within tourism promotion is that their presence helps an evocation of "the outback," of which Aboriginal culture is part. The linkages between Aboriginal people and tourism have also been examined in other ways. In an examination of 689 brochures relating to wildlife attractions, Higginbottom, Muloin & Zeppel (1999) found that only 32 sought to establish any relationship with Australian Indigenous people. Current work being undertaken by the Office of National Tourism in Australia is also generating data, which, it is understood, show that only a small minority of people have a strong interest in Aboriginal cultural tourism products and that for a larger proportion of visitors Aboriginal peoples are part of an image of Australian landscapes (Pitterlee 1999). On the other hand, Moscardo & Pearce's (1999) study of the Tjapukai Dance Theatre in North Queensland makes clear the popularity of dance performances.

### *Tjapukai Dance Theatre — a Case Study*

Yet even this success story is problematic. For example, the website http://www. tjapukai.com cites the fact that the Tjapukai Aboriginal Cultural Park is the largest private employer of Aboriginal people in Australia. About 85% of the 80 or so employees are Aboriginal, and the park is a partnership with "Tjapukai, Yirrgandyji and Djabugay people." However, Tjapukai Aboriginal Cultural Park (1997) notes that Djabugay actually own 15.8% of the equity, Tirrganydji, 10%, Nganydjin, 3.6% and the remaining Aboriginal ownership is made up of ATSIC and indirect Aboriginal interests through their shareholding in Skyrail. Thus the ability of local Aboriginal people to influence the Park through their share holding is diffused. Schuler (1999: 111) comments that:

The Djabugay employees themselves believe that what is portrayed at the Park is unauthentic. They are taught how to dance to accommodate the Park managers' requirements although the Park managers explained that such dances are adjusted periodically to take into account comments from tourist surveys. Therefore the Djabugay performances are adjusted according to the need of the market, resulting in the commodization of Djabugay culture.

It is also to be noted that on its web site the Park notes that:

The Tjapukai communities . . . own the land the Park is situated on, and have a substantial equity interest in the venture. There is no other presentation of Aboriginal culture in the area which provides any benefit to our community or which has requested or received the authority to present our culture for profit (http://www.tjapukai.com.au/welcome.htm April 6th 1999).

However, Clause 17.1 of the Deed of Agreement for the Park Management and the Djabugay Corporation restrains competition by any of the parties to the Agreement. If any party:

whether as owner, manager, shareholder, trustee, beneficiary, licensee, lessee or otherwise howsoever, conduct or be involved in any business or other activity which materially involves Indigenous dance or culture for tourist purposes which is in competition with the business of the Partnership

then the Deed is in effect negated. Thus the reason why "There is no other presentation of Aboriginal culture in the area" is because this agreement restricts Djabugay from establishing other similar businesses while maintaining the current arrangements at the Park.

## Contemporary Issues

Issues relating to Aboriginal tourism are important within contemporary Australian society as it seeks to address issues relating to Aboriginal poverty, unemployment, over-representation in prisons and mortality rates. For some commentators there exists a danger that the image of Aboriginal people presented through tourism promotion reinforces existing stereotypes. Clendinnen (1999) commented:

I suspect that the hidden springs behind what is often taken to be white racism is a fixed image of the vanished tribal Aborigine, the nomadic hunter with spear and throwing-stick and body-paint, and therefore the denial of Aboriginality to anyone not fitting that model. This artificially narrow notion of culture combines with a passionate egalitarianism to oppose any extension of benefits to the Aboriginal poor beyond those available to impoverished whites. Simultaneously, perhaps perversely, growing acceptance of multiculturalism also tends to work against Aborigines. We

> say, 'Let them have their culture: let Aboriginal dance troupes perform, let didgeridoos roar, even give them first place in the procession — they are, after all, our indigenous culture. But do not give them anything more'.

Yet any wider view of contemporary culture and the Aboriginal place within it will quickly show that this view is a partial perspective. In the world of contemporary pop music the bands of Arnhemland have a tradition of pop music since at least the 1960s. Not only have *Yothu Yindi* achieved international recognition but contemporary groups like *Letterstick Band* from Maningrida achieved some coverage for their blend of traditional and rock. For example in *An Barra Clan*, they combine reggae with yidaki (didgeridu) playing. For their part *Yothu Yindi* have established a foundation for the development of music training, and from this base have sought to both aid traditional culture and make non-Aboriginal Australia more aware of the diversity and strength of Aboriginal culture — for example in the Garma Festival of Culture at Gulkula in July 1999 (Yothu Yindi Foundation 1999). These examples indicate the vibrant nature of contemporary Aboriginal culture as it blends themes together. Thus far the tourist seems unaware of these trends, and from the perspective of tourism marketing there is an apparent divorce between the images and products used by tourism organizations and the flowering of contemporary Aboriginal music, drama, dance, writing, theatre and political action as is now being expressed in the clubs, theatres, and art galleries of Australia.

It appears that the academic literature about Aboriginal culture is primarily one of describing product development from a marketing perspective, discussing authenticity and analyzing economic impact. Two major omissions can be identified. The first is the Aboriginal perspective itself. The second, paradoxically, is the voice of the visitor. This is only recently being addressed (see Moscardo & Pearce 1999; Ryan & Huyton 2000a, b). This chapter continues examining this voice.

## The Attitudes of Visitors

### Research Design and Implementation

The research was conducted among visitors to Central Australia at two locations. These were the Desert Park in Alice Springs and the visitor center at Uluru-Kata Tjuta National Park. It sought to identify how important to such visitors was exposure to Aboriginal culture. It was decided to replicate the approach adopted by Ryan & Huyton (2000a; b) whereby items relating to Aboriginal culture are located within a questionnaire containing a list of other attractions, thereby making it possible to compare rankings.

The questionnaire comprised sections covering travel patterns, the importance and evaluation of various attributes of the Northern Territory as tourist attractions and socio-demographic characteristics. It utilized an importance-evaluation approach and the items were based on the Beard and Ragheb Leisure Motivation Scale applied to the context of the Northern Territory. Defined as being a model of reasoned action by Sheppard, Hartwick & Warshaw (1988), importance-evaluation matrices have been used in a number of studies reported in the tourism literature (see Duke & Persia 1996; Go & Zhang 1997; Hudson

& Shephard 1998; Novatorov 1997). Manstead (1996: 16) has argued that the model "has performed quite well in terms of the ability of the constructs in the model to predict behavior and behavioral intention."

The importance scale was based on a Juster Scale because of the linkage between it and subsequent behavior (Gendall, Esslemont & Day 1991; Gruber 1970; Juster 1966) while a non-response option was also used. This mode of questioning overcomes the problem of visitors having to assess importance when, within the sample, some will have undertaken an activity and have experience of it, while others have yet to do it. It adopts the alternative of assessing importance by revealed behavior or intention (For a discussion of the issues see, for example, Foxall 1990). The correlations between intent and places visited were high and measures of respondent consistency were high. For example the Guttman Split half-test coefficient of correlation was 0.81. The Kaiser-Myer-Olkin test for sampling adequacy equated 0.84, which is deemed to be "meritorious" (Norusis 1990).

The sample consisted of 358 people. The self-completion questionnaires were administered in cafeterias at the two parks on the basis of every visitor being approached in the hours of 10.00 a.m.–12.00 a.m. and 2.30 p.m.–3.30 p.m. that corresponded to the busiest periods. Only if the party was a coach party was this not done, with only about 2–4 people per party being approached under these circumstances. This was to avoid over-representation of groups like school parties, but it means that the sample is biased towards independent travelers.

Of the sample about one-third was below the age of 30 years, 29% were between 31 and 50 years of age and remainder were over 50 years old. Fifty-six percent were married. Forty-six percent were female, 43% were male and the remainder did not provide information on their gender.

## Results

Table 5.1 sets out the importance and satisfaction scores. Pearce (1993) has lamented the lack of comparative research in tourism, and thus to partially address this, the table also shows the importance scores derived by Ryan & Huyton (2000b) in their study of visitors at Katherine, which lies approximately 1000 kilometers north of Alice Springs.

The similarities between the two samples are striking. First, among the attributes thought important is the desire to visit "places that are different to anywhere else" (means of 8.06 and 7.93, $p > 0.05$). The nature, culture and recent frontier history of the Northern Territory means that it offers a terrain different to much else of Australia, not to mention other parts of the world. Its national parks and memorable sunsets also feature as attractions for both the current and Katherine samples. However the heat of Central and North Australia inhibits more sustained physical activity and in consequence bush walking is ranked about half way in both samples in terms of importance scores (6.25 cf. 5.88) with no significant difference in scores. It does appear that the current sample seems more predisposed "to camp under the stars," but a complicating factor for this item is that a popular, award winning attraction offered by the "Sails in the Desert Hotel" at Yulara is an attraction where visitors are taken for a meal served under the stars in the middle of the desert — the Sounds of Silence Dinner (see web site

Table 5.1: Mean score on importance and satisfaction scores.

| Item | Kath. Sample | | Central Sample | | | |
|---|---|---|---|---|---|---|
| | **Rank Impt** | **Mean Impt** ($n = 471$) | **Rank** | **Mean Impt** ($n = 358$) | **Mean Satis.** | **No.** |
| Visit places that are different | 1 | 8.06 | 1 | 7.93 | 7.93 | 311 |
| Visit National Parks | 2 | 8.04 | 4 | 7.37 | 7.68 | 306 |
| See Katherine Gorge | 3 | 7.54 | 19 | 5.37 | 7.77 | 76 |
| The warm sunny climate | 4 | 7.30 | 8 | 6.47 | 7.06 | 327 |
| Visit Yellow Waters/Kakadu | 5 | 7.04 | 12 | 5.93 | 7.76 | 68 |
| See memorable sunsets | 6 | 7.11 | 3 | 7.56 | 7.10 | 257 |
| Experience vastness of space | 7 | 6.73 | 6 | 6.76 | 7.79 | 314 |
| Satisfy sense of adventure | 8 | 6.70 | 7 | 6.48 | 7.20 | 283 |
| Swim in fresh water pools/swimming pools | 9 | 6.70 | 15 | 5.77 | 7.06 | 79 |
| See crocodiles | 10 | 6.08 | 22 | 5.15 | 7.00 | 91 |
| See Uluṟu (Ayers Rock) | 11 | 6.01 | 2 | 7.59 | 7.84 | 261 |
| Go bush walking | 12 | 6.25 | 13 | 5.88 | 6.93 | 198 |
| Bathe in hot springs | 13 | 6.04 | 16 | 5.75 | 7.34 | 56 |
| Make new friends | 14 | 6.04 | 9 | 6.42 | NA | |
| *View Aboriginal Rock Art* | 15 | 5.94 | 14 | 5.84 | 6.39 | 234 |
| Learn about fauna | 16 | 5.83 | 11 | 6.15 | 6.94 | 280 |
| Visit Alice Springs | 17 | 5.63 | 5 | 7.29 | 6.74 | 265 |
| See Kangaroos | 18 | 5.52 | 10 | 6.39 | 6.62 | 227 |
| Camp under the stars | 19 | 5.08 | 21 | 5.16 | 7.74 | 144 |
| *Go on aboriginal guided tours* | 20 | 4.42 | 20 | 5.30 | 6.94 | 56 |
| *See aboriginal music and dance performance* | 21 | 4.36 | 23 | 5.00 | 6.38 | 83 |
| Go on an outback tour | 22 | 4.21 | 18 | 5.47 | 7.44 | 169 |

Table 5.1: (*Continued*)

| Item | Kath. Sample | | Central Sample | | | |
|------|------|------|------|------|------|------|
| | Rank Impt | Mean Impt (*n* = 471) | Rank | Mean Impt (*n* = 358) | Mean Satis. | No. |
| Have good hotel/motel accommodation | 23 | 4.08 | 17 | 5.73 | 6.67 | 246 |
| Canoeing/kayaking | 24 | 3.76 | 25 | 3.01 | 6.27 | 26 |
| *Buy authentic aboriginal souvenirs* | 25 | 3.57 | 24 | 4.14 | 6.04 | 181 |
| Visit friends and family | 26 | 2.36 | 27 | 2.44 | 8.19 | 87 |
| Go hunting | 27 | 0.92 | 28 | 1.10 | 5.14 | 14 |
| Conduct business | 28 | 0.77 | 29 | 0.92 | 5.90 | 29 |
| Go Fishing | 29 | NA | 26 | 2.60 | 6.31 | 34 |
| Overall satisfaction with holiday | | | | 7.89 | | 331 |
| Had value for price paid | | | | 6.66 | | 317 |

http://www.ayersrock.aust.com/AyersRockResort/Sounds_of_Silence/sounds_of_silence. html). This is a popular and long established component of many tours to "the Rock."

Given the unique nature of the Northern Territory with its fauna, flora and Aboriginal culture, what emerges quite strongly from both of these samples is just how unimportant are those attractions that meet the intellectual motive for travel. McKercher & du Cros (1998) have specifically written of the iconic nature of tourism to Uluru, while commentators like MacCannell (1992) and Rojek & Urry (1997) among many others have explored themes of spectacle, role-play, hedonism and directed gaze. Indeed, with specific reference to a Northern Territory site, Ryan, Hughes & Chirgwin (2000) argued that a particular form of nature, namely bird life, was enhanced to the point where, as a spectacle, visitors gained an affective experience of nature which expressed wonder, yet were comparatively oblivious to other aspects of the natural and cultural heritage of the site. Thus in an area which pitches many of its appeals to the eco-tourist, one finds that some specific intellectual motives are not valued highly by the sample. Thus, while the NTTC specifically draws our attention to "the large population of unique animals" and "The Aboriginal presence" the items on the scale that refer to learning about flora and fauna and Aboriginal culture perform poorly in terms of their ranking. In the current study the item on learning about flora and fauna ranks 11th compared to 16th in the Katherine study, while the items on Aboriginal culture rank 14th, 20th, 23rd, and 24th in the current study. In short they equate with the rankings found in the past Katherine study. However, one mitigating factor is that in the current sample, the scores allocated to these aspects of Aboriginal culture are higher. One possible interpretation is because of the iconic nature of the "Red Center" respondents may tend to higher ratings of importance. In short, it is a possible example of "I am told this place is important, therefore I rank it as being important."

Table 5.1 also shows that the number of respondents indicating satisfaction with tourist attractions based on Aboriginal culture is reduced in number when compared to other items. Thus, only 56 of the 358 respondents score satisfaction with an "Aboriginal guided tour" and only 83 for an Aboriginal dance performance. Ryan & Huyton (2000a; b) argue that only about one-third of visitors to the Northern Territory actually possessed any interest in Aboriginal culture, and that for many of these it was but one part of a conceptualization of "The Outback." Consequently attractions based on Aboriginal culture had to compete in a crowded market place. These figures seem to support that contention with about 23% of the

Table 5.2: Visitor origin and responses to Aboriginal items.

| | North Americans | | Irish | | UK/Euro | | Other Australians | | *F*-Ratio |
|---|---|---|---|---|---|---|---|---|---|
| | **Mean** | **nr%** | **Mean** | **nr%** | **Mean** | **nr%** | **Mean** | **nr%** | |
| See Ayers rock | 8.21 | 32 | 8.02 | 20 | 7.79 | 15 | 7.76 | 29 | 0.91 |
| *View Aboriginal Rock Art* | 7.37 | 27 | 6.17 | 26 | 6.04 | 23 | 6.35 | 41 | 2.87* |
| Go on Aboriginal Guided Tours | 6.43 | 73 | 5.96 | 85 | 7.71 | 98 | 6.88 | 83 | 0.58 |
| *See Aboriginal music and dance performance* | 7.03 | 64 | 6.51 | 78 | 6.42 | 72 | 5.96 | 77 | 0.82 |
| *Buy authentic Aboriginal souvenirs* | 6.84 | 46 | 5.42 | 43 | 5.84 | 44 | 6.12 | 63 | 2.29 |
| Satisfied with value for money | 6.46 | | 6.45 | | 5.32 | | 5.32 | | 2.95* |
| Overall satisfaction | 7.83 | | 8.05 | | 7.81 | | 7.81 | | 0.47 |
| Number in sub-sample | 41 | | 73 | | 39 | | 169 | | |

*Note:* nr% = non-response rate.

*p < 0.05.

sample experiencing an Aboriginal music and dance performance, and about 50% buying Aboriginal souvenirs. It can be objected that the figures for seeing rock art present a counter view. Thus 338 respondents provided a rating of the importance of rock art, and 234 indicated a satisfaction rating. What is significant about this figure is that rock art can be viewed by simply walking around the base of the "The Rock." Even under these circumstances it appears that some respondents had very little interest in this easily accessible aspect of Aboriginal culture.

Looking at the nationality of those expressing an opinion it was found that some specific patterns emerged. The normal way of looking at differences between national groupings would be to undertake an analysis of variance, and this is done in Table 5.2. But in addition the table shows the pattern of non-response to the items specific to Aboriginal culture as a tourism product. Logically, it can be argued that the main reason for non-response is that the respondent has not experienced the event, and indeed respondents were directed to specifically use the non-response option if this was the case. Other reasons can also be proposed — for example the tourist may have experienced the event, was disappointed, and does not wish for various reasons to express this. Whatever the reason, a specific pattern of non-response exists whereby Australians are much less likely to reply to the items listed in Table 5.2. Also, there is a high rate of non-response by "Other Europeans" (i.e. non-British/Irish) to the item "Go on aboriginal guided tours," while North Americans are more likely than others to attend a dance or music performance. Does this indicate a higher predisposition towards entertainment or to viewing such a performance as another means of gaining knowledge of another culture? Or is it that Americans simply have a higher predisposition to pre-book packages that include such things? That this is the case is evidenced by work undertaken by Pitterlee (1999), which showed that of those Americans visiting places associated with Aboriginal culture, 48% were on pre-booked tours.

*Analysis*

The data were then examined to assess whether any relationships existed between the various items and socio-demographic variables that might explain levels of satisfaction with specific reference to those items based on or related to Aboriginal culture. First coefficients of correlation were calculated between the items shown in Table 5.1 with the three measures of overall satisfaction used in the questionnaire. These were ratings of "overall satisfaction," "value for money" and whether respondents had felt the price they had paid was a "fair" price for the experience they had gained. Various combinations were used but overall the following items emerged as having a strong correlation with overall satisfaction; a sense of visiting a place that was different ($r = 0.81$), having a sense of adventure (0.90), and satisfaction derived from visiting national parks (0.63). With specific reference to Aboriginal based products, one item, "going on a tour with an Aboriginal guide" correlated at a value of $r = 0.87$ with "overall satisfaction," but unfortunately this was based on only 51 respondents' scores due to non-response on the former item. What this may imply is that, while for the majority of visitors, Aboriginal culture is comparatively unimportant as a tourist attraction, for those to whom it is important; a strong linkage between the act of participation and satisfaction might exist. This is consistent with anecdotal evidence derived from the site and from New Zealand where Ryan (1998: 298) writes of the "emotional experience of great intensity" shown by such visitors after a trek with Marae guides.

Various hypotheses can be advanced. First, it can be argued that interest in Aboriginal culture is greatest among younger, female, better educated visitors from North America, the United Kingdom and Germany than among other visitors. Such a thesis would be consistent with data derived from the International Visitor Monitor maintained in Australia (Blamey 1998). Second, following the thesis advanced in the ServQual debate that satisfaction with a customer service is partly determined by levels of previous satisfaction experience (Taylor 1997), it can be argued that a higher order, re-iterative process exists between importance attributed to a feature and the satisfaction derived from it. Hence a model can be developed whereby

$$A^{1-n}_{sat} = f(A^{1-n}_{imp}, \text{ Nat, Age, Gender, Income, Educ, Occup})$$

where $A^{1-n}_{sat}$ = Level of satisfaction expressed with Aboriginal tourism components; $A^{1-n}_{imp}$ = Level of importance attributed to Aboriginal tourism component $1-n$; Nat = Nationality of respondent; Age = Age of respondent; Gender = sex of respondent; Income = level of income of respondent; Educ = level of education of respondent; Occup = Occupation of respondent.

At first it appeared that linkages between importance and satisfaction ratings were weak. For example the coefficient of correlation between satisfaction with, and the importance of Aboriginal dance and music performances was 0.24, while with an Aboriginal guided tour $r = 0.39$. However, the implication of the above model is that importance *per se* is not sufficient as a variable — it is the importance *to whom* that is at issue. Thus, for example, if the better educated, younger female from Germany has ascribed an importance to a variable, then for that person the relationship between importance and satisfaction will be linked. On the other hand, an older Australian male may ascribe a relatively high level of importance to the same product, but might not even bother to attend such a performance. As has been noted in the literature, importance, salience and determination are not the same and not to make the distinction can mislead (Lego & Shaw 1992). To paraphrase their findings, salient variables are those that are present and contextual, important factors are those that form part of a decision set (but may be inhibited from creating attitudinal-behavioral links) while determining variables lead to behavior. Thus, it can be argued, to the Australian male Aboriginal performance is salient in that it impinges on consciousness but is not a determinant of tourist behavior. Given these relationships, the interactive relationship proposed in the above model will only be weakly caught in a measure of correlation between importance of, and satisfaction with, an individual item. Thus, when the "cut off" point of eight is selected on an item like the importance of aboriginal dance and music performances, and an analysis of the socio-demographics is undertaken of those who score eight or more, specific biases are found. First, the sample becomes significantly skewed toward females (65% of this sub-sample as against 51% of the total sample). Second, the sample becomes skewed towards three national groupings — British, North Americans and Germanic speakers — 48% of this sub-sample as against 32% in the total sample).

As a consequence, an attempt was made to model the above relationships. For the purpose of analysis the scores on importance and satisfaction were divided into three groups, scores one to three were designated to be "low," four to six were "medium" and seven to nine were labeled "high." This is a convenience and obviously is not related to the standard deviation, but by definition if "high" was designated as values in excess of the mean plus one standard deviation it would have meant that the sub-sample was restricted to but 16.5% of respondents, assuming a normal distribution. The development of these categories meant that the whole of the data were categorical in nature thereby permitting analysis based on differences between observed and expected distributions in cells of tables. The data were analyzed in two ways. First it was possible to simply define categories and assess the distribution of scores on items related to Aboriginal culture. Second, it was possible to use hierarchical log linear analysis as a mode of regression analysis suitable to categorical data (Norusis 1990). Problems quickly emerged with the former method. For example, while $r = 0.88$ between the importance of aboriginal guided tours and the satisfaction derived from such tours for young females from Australia, the sub-sample was but 12, and this was one of the larger sub-samples. Hierarchical log-linear analysis offered the opportunity to work with larger sample sizes by utilizing all categories simultaneously.

To summarize the results of this approach the item "to see Aboriginal music and dance performance" is provided as an example. The first step was to assess whether a higher order interaction including the variables of "importance of aboriginal dance and music" and "levels of satisfaction with aboriginal dance and music" was pertinent. Utilized with the variables age, gender and occupation for the sample of North Americans, British and Europeans alone, the likelihood-ratio chi-squared value was zero with $p = 1.00$, whereas when $k = 1$ (that is when all variables are included in a saturated model) the likelihood-ratio chi-squared value (which is a goodness of fit statistic) was 303.03 with $p = 1.00$. Testing for $k$-way effects reconfirmed the importance of both age and "importance of dance and music" to the respondent as determinants of satisfaction with aboriginal music and dance performances. Basically a number of permutations were run through the software with assessments being made of the sensitivity of the model to the variables listed. Generally speaking nationality, age and importance of the item emerged as the main determinants but some problems were presented by small sample sizes in some instances. For example, while in the case of aboriginal dance performances satisfaction 80 respondents provided ratings, because of missing data in other cells of the model the results cited above were derived from a smaller sample of just 55 respondents. Similar tests were undertaken with other items and in almost every case the variables of age, nationality and importance emerged as being significant.

## Conclusion

It appears that these findings provide an antidote to the past exhortations of various public sector pronouncements that have tended to a view that tourism is one, if not the main answer, to problems of unemployment and low income among Aboriginal communities. They confirm the wisdom of the report by the Aboriginal and Torres Strait Islanders Commission (ATSIC 1997) that drew attention of researchers and policy makers to the lack of data about visitor perceptions, expectations and wants with reference to Aboriginal peoples, and strongly expressed the view that there was a need for further research. But if the interest of visitors is not as large as that previously thought, does this matter? From one perspective it may mean that if Aboriginal communities are unsure about tourism, and wish to solely maintain a presence through the sale of artifacts and Aboriginal art, such actions may be appropriate. While critics have voiced concerns about authenticity and commodization, new processes of authentication set in motion in November 1999 will in part protect Aboriginal interests. It certainly means that Aboriginal people can provide a souvenir market without having visitors intrude upon their communities. The findings also identify the need to avoid too many new businesses coming onto the market, as such businesses may adversely affect the financial viability of those that currently exist.

From a Northern Territory perspective, the emergence of new urban-based Aboriginal businesses that tap into the tourist markets in locations like Sydney and Melbourne must create some concern. If interest is limited, and characterized by a "been there, done that, tick it off" mentality, then when combined by direct flights from places like Sydney into Yulara, the question arises, why should the tourist visit other locations in the Northern Territory that offer apparently similar experiences based on Aboriginal culture? The attractions in the urban areas of the more populated south east of Australia are, at least potentially, no less authentic in the telling of Aboriginal stories than those in the "Top End" or in Arnhemland, no matter how much the Territory may perceive itself as the true heart of Australia. Ryan and Huyton (2000b) argue that one way forward for those Aboriginal communities who wish to be involved in tourism is to seek means of providing "added value" to more mainstream products. Perhaps one way is to locate Aboriginal interests within the context of the landscape if that is how it is perceived by many tourists. Schuler (1999) and Finlayson (1991) have suggested that one reason why Aboriginal communities have looked to culturally based products is because they have little business experience and tend therefore to repeat known successful products.

In addition to these conclusions, it can also be added that the data independently confirms statistics being co-ordinated by the Office of National Tourism (ONT) derived from a survey undertaken by the various State and Territory Tourist Commissions in 1998/1999. The actual proportion of visitors with a strong interest in Aboriginal culture is small. Ryan & Huyton (2000b) indicated that it was 3%, although a further 30% had an interest that linked National Parks, Aboriginal culture and landscape. Pitterlee (1999) reports that only 2% of visitors to the Northern Territory actually visit an Aboriginal Community.

From this research it appears that:

> Interest in Aboriginal culture is evidenced at a number of levels. First, only a small minority has high levels of interest. In this study, of the respondents only 29% scored above eight on a nine point scale for the importance of the items 'aboriginal dance', 28% for 'aboriginal guided tours' and 18% for 'authentic aboriginal souvenirs'. This compares with 60% for 'National Parks' and 75% for 'seeing somewhere different'.

> Second, this research confirms the view (although not here analyzed) that a sizeable, although still a minority percentage have an interest, but it is contained within a larger perspective of landscape.

Third, even much of this interest is confined to certain groups based on age and nationality. North Americans, British and German nationals are found to have such an interest. Young females show a higher proclivity to high levels of interest. It was found though that older Americans have a propensity to book organized tours including Aboriginal products prior to departure, while younger British and German tourists are more likely to book such tours upon arrival in Australia.

Fourth, there is a self-confirming relationship between importance and satisfaction. Simply put, if something is important to a person, they derive satisfaction from meeting the need to achieve the important thing. Importance is a goal when importance is akin to determining subsequent behavior as distinct from salience. From a tourism marketing perspective this might imply that an emphasis on product is not misplaced; for a self-selecting consumer is easier to satisfy than one attracted through problematic appeals to tourist motives.

Fifth, it needs to be re-stated and emphasized, Aboriginal communities have rights not to be involved in tourism if they do not wish.

Sixth, given the limited interest of the market, it is important that if Aboriginal people do wish to be involved, they should seek product placing within the mainstream. For example, Torres Strait Islanders successfully run retail and garage businesses serving the tourist traffic on the Cape York Peninsular, North Queensland.

From an academic perspective, the authors query whether the emphasis on authenticity in tourism product is not in fact misplaced when considering the tourist search for "reality." It would appear that few tourists actively search for that reality. It might be said that their view is "it's nice when it happens, but essentially I wish to enjoy myself." Thus:

The indigenous holiday concept is less likely than other traditional holidays to be considered on its own because of its close association to learning and education. Because most holidaymakers desire rest and relaxation from a vacation they consider that they would need to incorporate the indigenous day trip into their another more relaxing holiday experience. Further to this, there are many holiday ideas and concepts on the "shopping lists" of holidaymakers, and most consider that they would have to have done most other things before taking a 'dedicated' indigenous holiday experience (Tourism Queensland 2000: 75).

The post-modern, post-tourist knows that he or she is a tourist, orientated towards a hedonism that allows escape from the daily world — they are not, for the most part, anthropologists. If tourists do not really expect authenticity, then does it really matter that the tourist attractions are superficial? The host cultures are able to distinguish between the superficiality of a "cultural park" and the realities of their own lives. If this distinction is perpetuated then it is unlikely that the host culture will be negatively impacted by the tourist attraction. Perhaps the danger exists whereby promotion of cultural attractions sustains a promise of authenticity where at least some tourists actually believe that they gain insights into a complex culture through these parks, and thereby come to conclusions based upon their experience. Perhaps promoters should be more honest and simply say — there is no way in a short time we can deliver authenticity, but "we can offer an entertainment based upon some aspects of another culture." It is suggested that the term "authorization" may be a better term than "authenticity" as it redirects attention to *who* authorizes and *what* is authorized. Future research needs to involve itself in a more phenomenological approach using questions that distinguish between importance, salience and determinance. Qualitative research that examines motive and locates cultural products within a touristic-infotainment context as well as the authentic-inauthentic/authorized-non-authorized dimension might provide more of an insight than that provided thus far. Other considerations involve further examination of the use of such sites by tourists — are they sites of acceptance or ritual sites of rejection (Kirshenblatt-Gimblett 1998). In 1984 Hamilton noted that to the tourist "the Aboriginal is an object of his or her vacation gaze, something to be photographed and taken away as a souvenir of 'the real thing' in the Great Outback" (184: 377). This appears to still be true.

## Acknowledgments

The authors are Balanda (non-Indigenous) scholars and would thus like to thank colleagues from Aboriginal and Maori backgrounds for their help in aiding us in trying to establish a wider context for this study. The help of the Northern Territory Tourist Commission (particularly Sara Pitterlee) and Glen Miller from Tourism Queensland is acknowledged. The authors wish to thank the Northern Territory University for providing a grant derived from ARC Quantum monies. However, any interpretation of data is that of the authors alone and do not represent policies of any of the above individuals or organizations.

Additionally, the permission granted by Jafar Jafari and Pergamon to reproduce an original text submitted to *Annals of Tourism Research* is acknowledged. An amended version of that text was finally published as Tourists and Aboriginal people, *Annals of Tourism Research*, *29*(3), 631–647.

# Section B

**Who Manages Indigenous Cultural Tourism Product — Aspiration and Legitimization**

Chapter 6

# Who Manages Indigenous Cultural Tourism Product — Aspiration and Legitimization

Chris Ryan

The previous section dealt with the nature of the visitor experience at sites where the cultures of indigenous peoples are presented to the tourist as objects to be purchased. The cases presented by the different researchers are indicative, if not fully representative, of the type of products that exist. A whole gamut of experiences exist, ranging from the potentially highly emotional where visitors have stayed over night in the company of Indigenous peoples as described by Ryan (1998, 2005) to the show performed in a hotel lounge. In part it might be said that the tourism industry provides different products for different market segments, which range from those simply wishing for an entertaining evening as part of a package holiday organized by a tour operator, to those, on the other hand, designated by McKercher & du Cros (2002), as serious, purposeful cultural tourists. Yet even these latter remain primarily tourists, and are holidaymakers and not, as Ryan & Huyton (2002c) observe, lay anthropologists.

Nonetheless, although commodified and produced as commercial packages for consumption by holidaytakers, the wider social implications of the interest of the tourist, no matter how detailed their interest, is significant. That significance arises from a number of factors including:

(a) The value and distribution of economic revenues associated this tourism to sites of Indigenous peoples.
(b) Where does the organizational power lie?
(c) The perception by governments and National Tourism Organisations that tourism has an ability to generate jobs and income for otherwise marginalized groups.
(d) The presentation and images presented of Indigenous Peoples and their cultures.
(e) The attribution of monetary value to symbols of normative values, religion and possible sacred objects.
(f) How do societies on the margin of the mainstream cope with expectations and demands of tourists?
(g) How do such societies utilize the monies gained and for what purpose?

Indigenous Tourism: The Commodification and Management of Culture
ISBN: 0-08-044620-5

(h) How do marginal societies access the power structures within mainstream economic and political life?

(i) Why is there a surge of interest in the culture of peoples previously perceived as "primitive?"

Tourism is an industry and its structures exist solely because profit can be generated. It can be objected that for many smaller enterprises the profits being recorded do not necessarily represent a high rate of return on capital, and that for many the main return is an emotional one wherein the entrepreneurs are able to sustain a desired life style. From a cost benefit analysis perspective however, that emotional return can also be ascribed a monetary value, and simply put, people stay in a business so long as total returns, tangible and intangible, outweigh the costs. But what happens when a stakeholder in this process is not motivated by the capitalist system, as might be the case in products based on non-western cultures? The response may that the motives for participating in a commercialized product are more of an intangible rather than tangible nature. Why should an indigenous group, whose culture may not necessarily engage in entrepreneurialism as understood by capitalist cultures, engage in tourism?

A number of responses may be suggested. First, having been marginalized to a point where real threats exist to the perpetuation of a culture, the opportunity to have that culture recognized and honoured as possessing value to the mainstream of society is one that restores a sense of pride and ownership to a subordinate group. The issue facing indigenous peoples in many parts of the world is not simply one of low income and unemployment, but of low self esteem as characterized by high rates of alcoholism and dysfunctional family life. With low esteem comes a loss of ownership of self and one's own culture. However, tourism offers a paradox because by offering employment and income by capitalizing upon and giving value to arts and crafts previously thought unimportant, it then threatens to gain ownership of those designs and the ways of thought of which they are an expression. Indigenous people are manipulated into positions whereby tourist producers and tourists desire that which the peoples have; tourist producers and tourist each have their own purposes, and the manipulation is also clothed, whether intentionally or not, in a mantra of providing income for the marginalised. Different cultures respond in different ways, but the harsh reality of the early twenty-first century is that the interconnection of globalization makes it difficult for any group to turn their backs on mainstream economic structures. Indigenous societies require income for their future generations to survive, even if it means that the modes of survival are such that those generations will increasingly, in all likelihood, acquire life-styles unrecognizable to their parents and ancestors. For societies where inter-generational relationships are seamless senses of identity tied to a land made sacred because it is the place of their ancestors and their way of life, the absorption into and of the ways of mainstream society represent real psychological challenges. The Indigenous person occupies a world of tradition in a sense that is generally unknown to a western generation that itself occupies a hybrid culture of post-modern de-differentiation of history, present and future, of fact and fantasy, where the image is the thing. It is the clash between a sense of eternal relationship of self and place versus the culture of the 15 second sound bite. Ironically, for some of the latter, the answers to a sense of disengagement with that seemingly superficial culture lies not in the traditions of their own literary, musical and philosophical antecedents but in an acquisition of seemingly simpler "truths" thought to be associated with more traditional cultures. Thus Edwards (1993: 4) could write:

> As this new wave of spirituality began, something remarkable was happening, but behind the scenes. The wise ones of many cultures — from Native American Indians to aborigines — were receiving a series of visions. The message to them was clear: it is time to release your ancient wisdom to the outside world. It is time for humanity to wake up.

> As a result, countless shamans, yogis and spiritual teachers began to spread their wisdom to the Western world. Ideas and practices which had been closely guarded secrets, passed on only to apprentices and initiates, became available to thousands and thousands of ordinary people. Many westerners became keepers of the flame, and began to spread the light to others-and new methods began to emerge from the synergy of the old.

It is thus being suggested here that the commercial success of books like Morgan's *Mutant Message Down Under* represents an unease in contemporary society that leads at least for some, like Morgan & Edwards, to represent Indigenous peoples as possessing some secret of a mystical nature that will provide meaning to lives. Some of these peoples are sufficiently commercially minded to provide what is wanted!

Thus indigenous peoples receive income from tourism, and may well use that income to not only address the lack of physical possessions that hamper their lives (for example, even having access to reliable transport can revitalize a community) but to educate their children so that they will not have to face the problems of not knowing the laws, business protocols and ways of life of the dominate cultures in their surrounding worlds. Thus it might be stated that tourism offers a means of escape from the economic deprivation associated with tourism for future generations if not a current generation. The potential problem is that this is a process of assimilation whereas perhaps, in marketing terms, what is required is the development of a uniqueness that bestows advantage.

There are many parallels between the position of indigenous peoples and those of other marginalized groups in that marginality creates economic deficits and the addressing of those deficiencies creates a tension between absorbing advantages bestowed by liberal interventions and the maintenance of unique identities. Yet this is a problem experienced by any tourism destination as is evidenced by the debate surrounding Butler's destination life cycle model. As places attract tourists, revenues and recapitalize, so they change.

The position of indigenous peoples might be represented as shown in Figure 6.1. The diagram indicates four main players, the Indigenous peoples themselves, the tourism industry, the government (representing the wider public sector of both local and national government) and tourists. Indigenous peoples offer their culture to the market place and in return tourists offer money. The product is distributed by a tourism industry, which in many cases of cultural tourism is sponsored by governmental actions through, for example, National Tourism Organisations (NTOs). These may offer advisory services and support for product development, as indicated by Buultjens *et al.* in their chapter. Such policies may well be drafted not only in accordance with a simple tourism promotion policy but

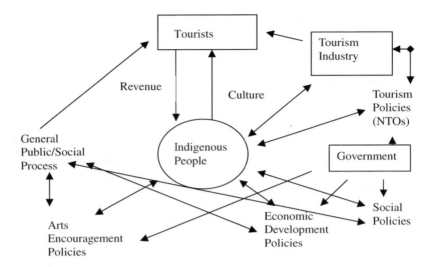

Figure 6.1: The network of indigenous tourism — a framework.

within a wider framework of social, artistic and economic development. Governments accept responsibilities for corrections of market failure and for the benefit of not only the disadvantaged but for the wider public good and so seek to promote policies that generate economic and social well being. These are often undertaken in consultation with the affected groups, who therefore experience a changed status. They become formally recognized and legitimized stakeholders in a process of distribution of public funds, and thus have an input into the formulation of policies. Thus in Australasia the establishment of the Aboriginal and Torres Straits Islanders Commission and Te Puni Kōkiri have become influential determinants of public spending even while being critical of government policies.

The outcome of these policies is a formation of public images and views, particularly perhaps through the creation of images developed through arts encouragement policies. Nor must it be forgotten that the non-tourism industry private sector has a role to play; which it does through sponsorship and other programmes. As the cause of indigenous peoples is legitimized through this process, it is better able to attract corporate funding. For example Qantas commissioned Aboriginal artist John Moriarty and his design studio, Balarinji Design, for its aircraft livery *Wanuala Dreaming* while Telstra (Australia's major telecommunications company) is the principal sponsor of Bangarra Dance Company, a contemporary Aboriginal theatre group. Telstra support Bangarra through provision of technological and internet support as a means of promoting Australian arts and linking itself to the creative life of Australia. A reciprocity exists between sponsors and sponsored in promoting positive images of each other.

Figure 6.1 thus represents a network, and like any network its strength lies in the numbers and frequencies of communication and the facilitation of that communication by key players in nodal positions. The issue that faces indigenous peoples is that while now occupying positions in the network, do they as yet occupy those key nodes wherein they begin to own the messages and direct the information and other flows?

The following papers address these issues. Joseph Mbaiwa's text is also of importance in indicating not only the way the Basarwa in the Okavango Delta have dealt with and changed governmental initiatives but have also had to cope with the emergence of new power elites within their own communities as a result of tourism promotional policies. Sanjay Nepal also addresses a key issue in his chapter, namely that of how do peoples with limited capital resources develop a product that can capitalize on an emergent interest in eco- and cultural tourism. Jeremy Buultjens, Iain Waller, Sasha Graham and Dean Carson present an analysis of where good intention meets the reality of administrative, political and resource constraints in their analysis of Australian governmental support policies for community based tourism with reference to Australian Aboriginals.

Together these and the other papers present a number of facets of the issues identified in Figure 6.1. But they also illustrate the diversity and dynamics of this aspect of tourism it is not passive, it is evolving and is perhaps one area of tourism where a social ethic is continuously addressed. That in itself makes the subject both interesting and important.

Chapter 7

# An Evaluation of Sustainable American Indian Tourism

Victoria L. Gerberich

## Introduction

American Indians have had to endure decades of economic deterioration due to inappropriate federal economic development strategies. While tourism has been cited as a potentially destructive activity to a region's cultural and natural resources, there has been an emerging concept of sustainable tourism. Understanding the factors and practicing the concepts that contribute to sustainable tourism has become an integral component in the management of some reservation-based tourism developments. Many reservations are incorporating sustainable tourism factors into their developments, giving them the ability to manage their resources according to their tribal beliefs and avoiding the poor management practices that were applied to their lands by the federal government.

This chapter evaluates several case studies of sustainable tourism developments that have been established on reservations as a means of cultural, environmental, socio-economic and political sovereignty. The case study analysis highlights the factors of sustainable tourism and how incorporation of certain elements into reservation development is essential to the sustainable development and management of American Indian reservations. This work helps fill a gap in the existing knowledge about contemporary American Indian tourism through this review which leads to an assessment of those factors which create successful, sustainable tourism developments. By understanding these factors, other American Indian reservations could adopt more sustainable tourism policies. Sustainable development is essential for all communities, especially those who have perceived themselves as victims of exploitation in the past. Therefore, it is important to implement culturally appropriate, sustainable developments into tribal communities.

## American Indian Socio-Economic Condition

American Indian tribes currently own approximately 52 million acres of federally recognized reservation land. Reservation lands are held in trust by the United States government for the tribes' occupancy and benefit. Many American Indian reservations, however, lack the bare necessities of modern life, such as running water, indoor plumbing, electricity, or telephones, not to mention the basic infrastructure components of police, fire, sanitation and health and education. Expanding population bases, limited land space, destructive economic developments, diminishing water resources, deteriorating infrastructures and many social ills are the reasons why the American Indians especially need to develop sustainable land uses which do not jeopardize their community and environment.

## Reservation Tourism Development

Given the socio-economic status of American Indian reservations, it has become apparent that some type of economic development is needed for the revitalization of tribal communities. While the U.S. government has attempted to develop reservations through resource extraction, most of these strategies have failed. Many studies indicate that tourism has been widely accepted by American Indian reservations as an economic development tool (Hill 1992; Lew 1996; Rudner 1994; Sweet 1991; White 1993). Lew (1996) stated that an increasing number of American Indian communities have developed or are in the process of developing some form of tourism on their reservation lands. According to this study, 55.8% of tribal governments are involved in some type of tourist activity. This study also indicated that another 10% are interested in future tourism promotions.

However, several tourism developments surrounding nationally protected areas have jeopardized American Indian religious rights and land ethics. Since the founding of the first national park, many American Indians have been barred from their traditional lands. While setting aside these lands and providing the public with tourism destinations, parks also prohibited many American Indians from either the use or the benefits of their traditional lands. More than 70 American Indian religious sites on federally owned land have been threatened by development and tourism (Buchsbaum 1995).

Protection of Federal lands denies American Indians religious access, but provides others unhindered access. The *Badoni vs. Higginson* case involved the Navajo and their disapproval of the construction of the Glen Canyon Dam which would flood Rainbow Bridge, a sacred site to the Navajo (Haynes 1997). The Navajo and Hopi have also lost sacred lands to the expansion of the Arizona Snow Bowl Ski area on the San Francisco Peaks in Arizona, which is of spiritual significance to the Navajo and Hopi religion.

Another case involving the disrespect of tour operations includes *Fools Crow vs. Gullet*. The state of South Dakota made a tourist attraction out of Bear Butte, destroying the pristine quality of the site. The Lakota and Cheyenne stated that the construction of roads and parking lots disturbed the natural features of Bear Butte, located in the Black Hills of South Dakota, which are sacred to the Lakota and Cheyenne. The Indian tribes also claimed that the state had neglected to control visitors' behavior by allowing them to camp on Bear Butte during tribal ceremonies. The courts claimed that the occasional misbehavior by tourists did not impair the religious practice of Indian vision seekers.

These examples illustrate that American Indian reservation lands are becoming some of the more sought out tourist destination sites in North America (Lew 1998). They also illustrate the importance of establishing sustainable projects which take into consideration all of the cultures and communities within the region. The development of tourism could alleviate tribal economic problems, or it could cause increased stress on the economies, environments, and cultures of the tribes.

With the increased adoption of tourism on reservations and the increased interest in visiting reservations, there is a need to ensure that policies are in place that will mitigate the negative impacts that tourism development could have on reservations. Therefore, the identification of examples of successful developments of tourism on American Indian reservations is critical. The advancement of appropriate tourism developments may facilitate the protection or enhancement of the natural, built and cultural resources, providing an environmentally conscious means of generating economic growth and enhancing the quality of life of the tribal communities. However, an understanding of tourism and what factors produce more sustainable forms of tourism is essential to the successful implementation of tourism on American Indian reservations.

## Tourism

Tourism has been argued to be the largest global industry (Boo 1990; Brohman 1996; Wall 1997). The tourism industry affects the lives of millions of people worldwide, both positively and negatively. Tourism development and the opening of areas to unguided and uneducated visitors, creates concern for the welfare of the people and their cultural and natural resources. According to McKercher (1993), there are certain consequences of establishing a tourism development in a region. Tourism is an industry, and as an industrial activity, tourism consumes and relies on resources from the natural, built, and cultural environment. Tourism can also lead to excessive consumption of these resources on which it relies. Tourist destinations under stress exhibit a wide range of social, environmental, and cultural impacts that can be directly linked to the over use of the resource base (McKercher 1993).

Tourism began as a private sector dominated industry and was driven predominantly by profit maximization. This type of mass tourism often creates a lack of environmental concern and a disregard for the types of impacts the industry has been creating in the region. Tour operators are trying to get as many people to their destination as possible regardless of the consequences to the local population or its resources. Mass tourism consumes enormous quantities of water, power, and natural resources such as coastal, forest and mountain terrain. Furthermore, it generates more waste on average than the local residents of the communities (Cater 1995).

However, people have become increasingly aware of the need to protect and conserve the earth's natural resources as well as the living species and cultures around the world. History and culture, the environment, and the outdoors are the top three travel interests among the U.S. population (The Ecotourism Society 1997). The growing concern for the global resources and the effects that tourism can have on a society has encouraged the tourism industry to move towards establishing alternatives to mass tourism. Unlike mass tourism, alternative forms of tourism have been acknowledged as a solution to economic, social and environmental problems that many communities face. Table 7.1 indicates factors that need to be considered when planning tourism.

Table 7.1: Factors impinging on tourism planning.

| Factors | Indicators |
| --- | --- |
| Cultural | Educational activities, guided tours, availability of information |
| Environmental | Group size, regulations, biological degradation, resource use |
| Socio-economic | Community and infrastructure improvements, economic diversity |
| Political | Who participates in development, level of outside assistance |

## Factor 1: Cultural Sustainability

The cultural impact that the tourism development has on the community must always be considered. In order to be sustainable, the development should increase the awareness and understanding of the tribe's cultural beliefs and traditions. Learning about the host culture is of primary importance to the sustainability of tourism (Place 1995). Visitors should be able to experience representative communities that have not been manipulated by outside interests. The tourism should also minimize negative cultural impacts on local people, respecting the cultural traditions and activities. The integrity of the tribal cultures must be protected, either minimizing the chance for acculturation or permitting local people control over those forms and speed of acculturation that are acceptable to them.

### Indicators for Cultural Sustainability

The level of involvement in educational and interpretive experiences for visitors, the type and amount of information given and materials available to visitors before and during visits must be adequate so as to provide visitors the opportunity to learn more about host cultural traditions while developing a reciprocal sensitivity between cultures. The tourists must understand and respect the tribal rules and regulation and be unobtrusive while they experience the culture and environment.

## Factor 2: Environmental Sustainability

The impact that the tourism development has on the region's natural resources is a key determinant to whether or not the tourism will or can be sustainable. It is essential to ensure that sustainable tourism minimizes negative impacts to soil, wildlife, vegetation, water, and air quality. Efforts should be made to be less consumptive, travel lighter, produce less waste and be conscious of the surrounding environment and people (Boo 1990; Cater 1995; Goodall 1995; Nelson 1994; Orams 1995; Place 1995).

*Indicators for Environmental Sustainability*

Indicators that suggest minimal environmental impacts include small group size, strict rules and regulations, high quality of training given to guides, accurate and appropriate information given to visitors before and during visits, high level and amount of interpretive materials and activities available. It is also important to look at the change in resource consumption rates and the type of economic developments which tourism has possibly replaced. Measures of ecological change such as vegetation, erosion, water quality and wildlife existence are also primary indicators of the level of environmental impacts. Finally, if the community or development supports conservation projects and e tourism increases the level of environmental commitment and activism of the region, then tourism can be seen as successful in minimizing negative environmental impacts.

## Factor 3: Socio-Economic Sustainability

Tourism development should direct economic and other benefits to local people that complement rather than overwhelm or replace traditional practices such as agriculture, fishing, and traditional social systems. Sustainable tour operations are of smaller scale and more susceptible to changes in season, weather, access, economic and political events and therefore yield irregular and modest returns when compared to mass tourism. Thus, local economies should not rely completely on tourism or else the economy could fall apart if conditions in the tourism industry change. Economies will be healthier if they are diversified and the communities are not asked to make dramatic shifts in their way of life (Hill 1992; Kinsley 1994; Lew 1998). Also, the economic benefits which are gained should be used to improve the needs of the community and not make only a few wealthier.

*Indicators for Socio-economic Sustainability*

An increase in the diversity of economic activity, the number and level of tour employees, and the number of programs that train or assist with the development of locally owned businesses are all indicators of socio-economic benefits. Another important indicator of the positive impact on the socio-economic component of tribal lands is the reinvestment of revenues into community development projects and the continual distribution of benefits among the community members.

## Factor 4: Political Sustainability

The tourism development needs to maximize the early and long-term participation of local people in the decision-making process that determines the kind and amount of tourism that should take place. The key is the early establishment and continued functioning of committees, partnerships and other tools that provide local input to public and private interests that operate in the area (Brandon 1993; Place 1995). Throughout the literature on tourism development, local control and citizen participation are keys to success. This holds true for any community and regional planning efforts. Many developments have been slowed or stopped due to unhappy citizens who felt abused by the political system. Efforts need to be made to ensure that all of the community is informed and educated on planning proposals for their region, and if, when and where public meetings are going to be held. Giving the people a voice provides a much smoother road to development for all participants.

### Indicators for Political Sustainability

The strength and duration of local advisory and planning groups, the incorporation and implementation of local ideas in area management plans and tour activities, the development of local tour itineraries that accommodate to local needs and schedules; and the attitudes that the local tribal communities have towards tourism are key indicators of appropriate tourism resource development. Cornell (1990) and Smith (1994a, b) also indicate that tribal sovereignty and ownership of the development are pivotal components for the successful implementation of economic development strategies.

## The Sustainable Tourism Market

Countries around the world have been faced with the dilemma of either economic or environmental poverty. Poor people often have no choice but to choose immediate economic benefits at the expense of the long-term sustainability of their livelihoods and there is no point in appealing under these circumstances to idealism or altruism to protect the environment, when the individual and household are forced to behave selfishly in their struggle to survive. Sustainable tourism now allows communities to develop the economy without compromising their natural resource base. While ecotourism has been developed as a conservation tool many communities have adopted tourism activities as an economic tool. The primary reason for developing tourism activities may be more likely linked to economic development, however, the sustainability and preservation of cultural and environmental systems should remain just as important.

American Indian nations and tribes across North America have begun to recognize the economic benefits of tourism, but still feel the need to protect their cultural and environmental resources. The literature on American Indian tourism (Hill 1992; Lew 1996; Lew & Van Otten 1998; Snipp 1986; Sweet 1991; White 1993) has contributed to the knowledge about the progression towards more sustainable forms of tourism on reservations. An examination of current tourism developments that have been identified as sustainable indicate that beneficial development strategies can be successfully implemented on American Indian reservations and will have minimal negative impacts on tribal cultural, environmental, socio-economic and political resources.

# Methods

The emerging self-determined tribal governments have attempted to find ways to balance their cultural identity with economic development opportunities (Smith 1994a, b). American Indians offer a rich heritage and culture that can provide visitors with authentic and stimulating experiences during their travels. However, the negative consequences of some tourism, such as that which has been seen in and around many national parks, have become more apparent. Some of these problems associated with tourism include the decline in tradition, increased crime rate, social and religious conflicts and environmental and cultural deterioration. This has led to the recognition that tourism development is not always for the general good of the local communities. Coupled with rising concern for the environment, debate has grown as to whether tourism is sustainable on American Indian reservations and how it can be developed without adding to the many economic, social, cultural and environmental problems that the reservations have already had to face in the past.

Case studies were used to analyze information about specific examples of development in order to better understand the potential for beneficial tourism implementation. Table 7.2 summarizes the cases and tourism activities. The case studies represent a variety of activity types and geographical location as to refrain from the suggestion or interpretation that sustainable tourism has spatial or activity-based restrictions. This proved to be false and inaccurate within the case study analysis completed. The evaluation of the American Indian tourism case studies was based on the four factors of cultural, environmental, socio-economic and political sustainability. The degree to which the tourism projects have impacted, both positively and negatively, on the populations vary from case to case as is outlined.

# Results

The sustainability of tourism is acknowledged as a balance between the local economy and the physical and cultural environment. In order to achieve the goals of sustainable tourism, all four factors of cultural, environmental, socio-economic and political sustainability must be established within the development. The case study analysis revealed the sustainability factors found in each tourism development.

### *Cultural Factors*

In each case study, the cultural integrity of the developments remained the primary objective. Many of the cases had very specific rules and regulations and all forbade tourism during certain rituals or during certain times of the year. The cultural component was in no way jeopardized in the case studies which have been discussed in this research. In most American Indian tourism projects, the cultural aspect is the main focus of their efforts. The tourism on the Havasupai reservation probably offered the least amount of cultural information. The educational component is essential to tourism operations. It can be an effective management tool for reducing visitor impact as well as a catalyst for tribal cultural knowledge and interest in the reservations (Hoare 1993).

Table 7.2: Case studies used in the analysis of sustainability.

| Name | Location Context | Tourism Type | Control |
|---|---|---|---|
| Mashantucket — Pequot | Connecticut — close to metropolitan markets | Gaming | Tribal Council/Foreign Investor |
| The Eastern Band of Cherokees | North Carolina — Gateway to Smoky Mountain National Park | Arts and Crafts Cooperative | Tribal Members of the Cooperative |
| Pueblo Indians | New Mexico — surrounding growing cities and federal lands | Cultural Education | Tribal Communities |
| Havasupai | Arizona — bordering Grand Canyon National Park | Recreational | Tribal Council and National Park Service |
| Navajo Nation | Arizona, New Mexico, Utah — containing or adjacent to several federal lands | Recreational, Cultural, Educational | Individual members, tribal council and federal agencies |
| Hopi | Arizona — adjacent to Navajo Nation and federal lands | Educational | Tribal council, local colleges and Elderhostel Coordinator |
| Flathead/Blackfeet Reservations | Montana — bordering Glacier National Park | Recreational, Educational | Individuals, tribal council and local colleges |
| Sinkyone | Northern California — within confines of state park | Conservation | The wilderness council and state agency officials |

## Environmental Factors

When the development follows the community's beliefs, including environmental considerations, a project is much more likely to succeed. Many American Indians who still practice their traditions believe that nature is not to be manipulated as a land management practice (Hoffman 1997). The American Indian land ethic does not imply that American Indians have no sense of reality and the resources are merely there to be worshiped and honored, but rather that they should be respected and not exploited to the point of destruction (Jostad 1996). The use of the resources is part of the survival of all people, yet abuse is part of the demise of the nation, including American Indian people.

Many of the cases may not have focused specifically on the environment, but they did support the sustainability of the resources through the need for the continued use of the lands. Also, without the area's scenic beauty and recreational opportunities, the tourism businesses could not thrive. Therefore, the cases do support the need for environmental protection and the argument that tourism offers an alternative to resource extraction for income.

## Socio-Economic Factors

In order to sustain the communities, a level of support by the community must be retained and the benefits must be felt by all members. Therefore, in order to develop social systems, improvements must be made for the entire tribal community. Many of the reservations were able to provide better health care, childcare, housing facilities and substance abuse programs. The cases illustrated how small improvements in development activities can create significant benefits for the entire system. It is essential that community improvements be made, and not allow just one individual to benefit from the development.

## Political Factors

A manifest imperative in Indian Country is maintaining the cultures and strengthening sovereign powers. Only when individual tribes both control their own resources and sustain their identities as distinct civilizations does economic development make sense (Smith 1994a, b). The need for sovereignty and tribal ownership was the most pivotal element in the development of tourism projects. In order to avoid conflicts and problems during development, all members must be aware and support the actions that are occurring on the reservation.

Tourism has been supported through the community colleges and businesses. This is true for the communities of the Hopi, Navajo and Flathead and Blackfeet Tribes, who have full participation in the programs and have advocated the programs to other reservations looking for development ideas. The combination of education and community participation can help achieve community empowerment (Hoare 1993: 45). Thus, in respecting cultural traditions, the community and environment are also respected and maintained.

## Discussion

Tourism has been gaining greater acceptance and recognition as a sustainable tool for economic development. However, in order to continue on the path of success, all tourism must be carefully implemented through policies that assure minimal negative impacts on the cultural, environmental, socio-economic and political components of the region. Alternative tourism developments must be careful to respect local people and resources, avoiding the invasive philosophy of mass tourism. A new intellectual and environmental component has been added to the complex mix of tourism. People have begun to realize that wildlife, biodiversity, ethnic diversity, the land and its human, animal and natural resources are all important.

Environmentalism and concern about sustainable development have dramatically increased globally, including American Indian communities. Grassroots organizations such as Native Americans for a Clean Environment in Oklahoma, the Kaibab Earthkeepers of Arizona, The Navajo Dine CARE, and the Native American Rights Foundation based in Colorado have all successfully opposed environmentally damaging developments. Most of these developments have been nuclear and hazardous waste sites, or multinational mining and timber operations. The grassroots efforts have made undeniable progress in the struggle for clean and healthy environments, despite the advantage that the corporations have had regarding technical expertise and financial capital.

Environmental organizations are important, but their efforts are futile if reservation economies remain stagnant. Denying certain development activities, such as hazardous waste facilities and resource extraction, does not help tribal communities unless alternative developments can be accepted that will help improve communities. While tourism should not replace all other economic activities and become the single industry on which an entire tribe depends upon, it can be successfully integrated into tribal economic development plans, providing balance and equity while sustaining and enhancing environmental and cultural security. American Indian tribal communities must protect themselves from all unsustainable development, including inappropriate tourism.

The Alliance of Tribal Tourism Advocates is an organization that seeks to secure the future of tribal tourism. This organization comprises tribal members, individuals, governmental agencies and environmental organizations. It was established to ensure the development of responsible tourism on American Indian reservations. The following identifies the Alliance's beliefs and priorities:

> support cultural integrity and traditional values
> acknowledge sovereignty of tribes
> preserve sanctity of sites, artifacts, rituals and ceremonies
> protect the natural environment of tribal homelands
> assist in tourism codes of conduct and policy development
> publish and distribute intertribal tourism materials
> host tribal tourism workshops and training
> provide assistance to members in developing promotional materials
> (Alliance of Tribal Tourism 1997).

While this organization is important to the development and initiation of tourism on reservations, the long term impacts of tourism development are still unclear. Therefore, it is just as important for similar organizations to monitor and assess all developments for extended time periods. Simply because a project incorporated all of the sustainability factors when it began, that in itself does not ensure that they will be upheld throughout the project's duration. Placing the accountability for reservation development on tribal councils forces the communities to be responsible for their actions. Therefore American Indians must continue to be involved and stay informed about development proposals and the impacts of the activities. According to the Sage Group, a travel research center, most public parks are not equipped to take advantage of the increased demand for educational travel (The Ecotourism Society 1997). Expanding upon this gap in services offered at public parks represents an excellent opportunity for American Indian nations to take advantage of this demand for educational tourism, teaching visitors about their culture and environment. While, the future of tourism and its sustainability relies on several factors, this research has provided examples of some acceptable tribal developments and the methods used to implement the sustainable factors. Tribal associations must continue to strengthen tribal control and power, continue to insist on equal access to and control of resources and develop projects that are not influenced by outside interests.

## Conclusion

The purpose of this chapter was to use examples of sustainable tourism being promoted on American Indian reservations to describe which factors determine sustainability. Through the examination of the case studies, it was determined that most of the tourism activities did implement all of the sustainability factors into their tourism developments. Indeed, some contain concrete examples of sustainability, but the recognition of cultural, environmental, socio-economic and political sustainable factors exist, thereby possibly creating tourism developments that mitigate negative impacts as much as possible. Since American Indians are increasingly able to control how progress is to occur, such developments follow traditional beliefs of the tribal communities. Thus, in most cases they insisted that the development occurred with minimal impacts, so that their lands were not further harmed by economic developments.

While tourism will not remedy all of the problems that reservations face, it will offer some stability on which to grow. Even though American Indian cultural integrity and self-esteem was once destroyed by past federal policies, there have been some speculations that increased economic self-sufficiency will only further destroy a tribe's cultural integrity. However, attaining economic independence on tribal terms can only raise tribal dignity. Without strong cultural identity, economic development can lead to simple consumerism, and without economic development, cultural identity is not self-sufficient (Smith 1994a, b). Therefore, it is essential that cultural integrity is maintained throughout the development process.

Economic development is a process which occurs over many years. While reservations may not instantly rid themselves of the social and environmental deterioration that has been occurring, tourism certainly has the potential to aid tribal communities in their struggle for economic independence. The future of reservation life looks brighter as communities gain greater control of their futures. The knowledge that has been gained from previous experiences will only provide the tribal communities with greater strength on which to build their cultural, environmental and political systems, resulting in successful and sustainable community development. Tourism has proven to be a powerful form of cultural rejuvenation. Economic development is a means toward the end of sustaining tribal character (Smith 1994a: 178). Once the tribal organizations have gained greater strength and ownership of their resources, they will have the power to develop stronger economies and choose the type of activities desired. Tourism has proved to be an appropriate form of development and the future of tribal tourism offers many promising benefits. However, before reservations develop much more, there are a few items which need consideration regarding this growth of tourism.

## Implications

Research has not yet indicated what long-term impacts successful economic development will have on reservations. Therefore, the perception and definition of sustainability needs to be clearly stated and understood at the beginning of each individual tribal development. What does each tribe really want to gain or achieve from the tourism? A program that may be considered appropriate on one reservation can be considered disrespectful and unsustainable on another. Future studies should examine what barriers might exist in the implementation of certain types of tourism developments.

More research is also needed regarding the impacts that federal lands and nationally protected sites may have on reservations. The viability of tribally controlled tourism on reservations which are close to nationally protected locations needs special attention since so many reservations either border or are within a short distance of federal lands. Are the markets for tourism in certain locations already saturated due to the establishment of national parks, monuments and forests? This research has indicated that in some cases national parks can have both a positive and negative effect on the reservations. Research into whether or not federally protected lands predominantly hurt or help the tribal tourism could help to determine future federal agency actions. Moreover, as national parks experience greater crowding and degradation, demands for reservation tourism may increase. Many tourists may turn to American Indian tourism destinations since they would be able to offer more remote and "authentic" experiences. Therefore, conservation strategies and controls must be in place to ensure that problems similar to the ones that the national parks are beginning to encounter are not repeated on reservations.

Furthermore, state and federal agencies may be able to gain insightful knowledge from American Indians by adopting similar land management strategies. The land ethic of American Indians is similar to and may be compatible with the concept of ecosystem management which has emerged recently within the field of natural resource management. Ecosystem management is a multidimensional system which focuses on all values equally, thereby seeking a system that is more sustainable for both natural resources and the communities that live in those landscapes.

Chapter 8

# Community-Based Tourism and the Marginalized Communities in Botswana: The Case of the Basarwa in the Okavango Delta

Joseph E. Mbaiwa

## Introduction

This chapter reports research that assesses the contribution of community-based tourism to the improvement of rural livelihoods among Basarwa communities in the Okavango Delta, Botswana. The Basarwa are a minority and marginalized ethnic group in Botswana. They were the first people to live in Botswana and the Okavango Delta before the arrival of Bantu-speaking groups in the eighteenth century. The Basarwa subsequently lost their rights over land and its resources, first, because of the arrival and conquest of the Okavango Delta by Bantu-speaking groups (particularly the Batawana), and second, because of the establishment of Moremi Game Reserve in 1965. The latter resulted in the relocation of some Basarwa groups from areas which were formally their hunting and gathering lands and also led to laws prohibiting hunting and gathering in the game reserve. The centralization of land and its resources in the Okavango Delta, a system maintained even after Botswana's independence in 1966, led to antagonisms, resentment and negative attitudes by Basarwa towards resource conservation and poverty leading to resource conflicts between the government and the Basarwa groups. To address these problems the Botswana Government adopted a community-based tourism programme in the 1990s. The programme aims at the promotion of rural development and natural resource management. The Basarwa who have become participants of the programme are now beginning to derive socio-economic benefits such as employment and income generation. They are also beginning to develop positive attitudes towards natural resource conservation particularly wildlife. However, community-based tourism projects have problems of poor performance, partly because tourism is a new, foreign idea among the Basarwa and thus not fully understood. Second, few possess the necessary experience, entrepreneurship and managerial skills. The problems of poor performance of community-based tourism threaten the sustainability of the programme and the use of natural resources. Therefore, a sustainable community-based tourism sector

Indigenous Tourism: The Commodification and Management of Culture
Copyright © 2005 by Elsevier Ltd.
All rights of reproduction in any form reserved
ISBN: 0-08-044620-5

in the Okavango Delta requires the empowerment of Basarwa communities, particularly with reference to resource ownership, marketing, entrepreneurship and managerial skills in the tourism business. This empowerment will not only promote the sustainability of the programme and livelihood of the Basarwa but also encourage the sustainable use of natural resources in the Okavango Delta.

## The Context of the Study

The indigenous people of Southern Africa are the Basarwa (a collective name for several groups of Khoisan speaking people). Europeans also refer to the Basarwa as the Bushmen or San. The Basarwa are the second largest population of former foragers in Africa (Hitchcock 1996). They are aboriginal groups who resided in an area stretching from the Congo-Zambezi watershed in Central Africa south to the Cape in South Africa. The Basarwa once existed in relatively large numbers, with as many as 150,000–300,000 people dispersed widely in the region (Lee 1976). Hitchcock (1996) notes that even after centuries of conflict, genocide, incorporation and exploitation, the Basarwa can still be found in large numbers in six of the Southern African countries. There are over 104,000 Basarwa in Southern Africa with 9,750 in Angola, 49,475 in Botswana, 38,275 in Namibia, 4,700 in South Africa, 1,600 in Zambia and 1,275 in Zimbabwe (Hitchcock 1996). This shows that half of the aboriginal Basarwa population in Southern Africa live in Botswana while a third of the population are believed to be living in Namibia (Mphinyane 2002). Although Hitchcock estimated that there are 49,475 Basarwa in Botswana, Cassidy *et al.* (2001) and Masilo-Rakgoasi's (2002) estimation is 47,675 people. This means that approximately 2.8% of Botswana's total population of 1.7 million people are Basarwa.

The Basarwa in Southern Africa speak as many as 80 different dialects and exist in a wide variety of socio-economic situations (Hitchcock 1996). For example, in South Africa they reside in refugee camps that were constructed for former soldiers and their dependents (Uys 1994) while others live in freehold farms where tourists visit them as is the case at Kagga Kamma (White 1993). In Namibia, the Basarwa live in urban areas, on freehold farms, in government-sponsored settlements and in small rural communities on communal land where they make their living through a mixture of foraging, pastoralism and rural industries. In Angola, Zambia and Zimbabwe, the Basarwa live in small scattered communities throughout the Kalahari and adjacent areas, growing their own food, and working for other people (Hitchcock 1996). In Botswana, some of the Basarwa reside in government-sponsored settlements which contain water sources and social services (Hitchcock & Holm 1993). A considerable number of Basarwa also live in small villages in wildlife areas such as in the Central Kalahari Game Reserve and adjacent area, the Okavango, Kgatleng, Ghanzi, Kweneng and Chobe regions of Botswana.

Although the Basarwa are found in the different parts of Botswana, the focus of this chapter is on those living in the Okavango Delta. Cassidy *et al.* (2001) and Masilo-Rakgoasi (2002) estimates that roughly 10,850 of the Basarwa live in the Okavango Delta region (Table 8.1). This is about 8.3% of the 122,000 people found in the entire Ngamiland District where the Okavango Delta is located. The Basarwa are the oldest inhabitants of the Okavango. Archaeological evidence based on Early and Middle Age implements found

Table 8.1: The number of Basarwa in different districts of Botswana.

| Name of District | Number of Basarwa |
|---|---|
| Chobe | 1,500 |
| Ngamiland District (Okavango Delta) | 10,850 |
| Ghanzi (including Central Kalahari Game Reserve) | 14,150 |
| Kgalagadi | 2,900 |
| Kweneng | 2,500 |
| Southern | 2,175 |
| Central | 11,470 |
| Kgatleng | 680 |
| Urban Areas (Gaborone, Mochudi, Molepolole, Serowe, Francistown, and Maun) | 1,450 |
| Total | 47,675 |

*Source:* Cassidy *et al.* (2001) and Masilo-Rakgoasi (2002).

at sites on or near the margins of the Okavango Delta seem to indicate that the Basarwa inhabited the southern periphery of the Delta for about 10,000 years or more (Tlou 1985). Other ethnic and Bantu-speaking groups arrived in the Okavango Delta not more than 500 years ago (Mbaiwa 2001). Since the Basarwa were the first people to occupy and live in the Okavango Delta and in Botswana as a whole, they are sometimes referred to as the "first people" or "indigenous people" of Botswana. They are also referred to as the "marginalized people" because they were dispossessed and displaced from their historical land by other ethnic groups such as the Bantu-speaking peoples.

The Okavango Delta is a wilderness and unique wetland located in northwestern Botswana. It is a vast swamp and flood plain area measuring about 16,000 square kilometres (about 3% of the total area of Botswana), of which half is permanently flooded (Tlou 1985). The Okavango River Delta is the most striking geographical feature of Ngamiland, and indeed of the whole of Botswana. The Delta became a wetland of international importance and a Ramsar site in 1997. It is home to 5,000 different types of insects, 3,000 species of plants, 540 birds, 164 mammals, 157 reptiles, 80 fish and countless micro-organisms (Rothert 1997). It is also home to over 122,000 people who live within and around it (Central Statistics Office, CSO 2002). The wide variety of wildlife species and a relatively pristine wilderness habitat attracts tourists from around the world, making the Okavango Delta one of the largest tourist destinations in Botswana (NWDC 2003). Although tourism has rapidly grown in the Okavango in the last 10–15 years, it is enclave in nature and, as such, provides little direct benefit for the local people, particularly the Basarwa. The insignificant benefits result in little mitigation of poverty in the Okavango (Mbaiwa 2003e), which is described by the NWDC (2003) as widespread.

In Southern African countries, particularly in Botswana, the period after the 1990s has become an era of community development fused with natural resource management. This has been implemented through the Community-Based Natural Resource Management programme. In the Okavango Delta, the programme is largely dominated by tourism projects. This chapter seeks to assess the contribution of community-based tourism to the improvement of livelihoods of Basarwa communities in the Okavango Delta, Botswana. The chapter uses the concept of sustainable tourism development and it is guided by the following questions: (a) What factors led to the adoption and implementation of community-based tourism among the Basarwa communities in the Okavango Delta? (b) What is the contribution of community-based tourism to the improvement of livelihoods of the Basarwa? (c) Which are the problems and challenges of community-based tourism in the Okavango Delta? and (d) Which strategies can be adopted to promote a sustainable community-based tourism industry among the Basarwa communities in the Okavango Delta?

This study mainly utilised secondary data sources, notably the data and reports written by this author between 1998 and 2003. The chapter supplemented secondary information with primary sources which were in the form of informal interviews, conducted with government wildlife officers in Maun, Basarwa traditional and CBNRM project leaders in the Okavango Delta, and members of community trusts. Secondary data collection also centered on the use of the available literature such as government policy documents, reports and published and unpublished documents. The remaining sections of the chapter are divided as follows: the next and first section discusses the concept of sustainable tourism development and community-based tourism, the second section and the main body deals with the socio-economic benefits, problems and challenges of community-based tourism as practiced by Basarwa in the Okavango Delta, the third and last section, a discussion, concludes the chapter.

## Sustainable Tourism Development and Community-Based Tourism

Since the adoption of the World Report on Environment and Development, otherwise known as the Brundtland Commission Report or World Commission on Environment and Development (WCED) of 1987, the term sustainable development has become a central theme in much of the tourism literature. This is because tourism as an economic activity has cultural, economic and environmental impacts in destination areas. Sustainable development is anchored on three main concerns, namely: economic efficiency, social equity and environmental sustainability (Angelson *et al.* 1994; Munasinghe & McNeely 1995). Tourism is considered sustainable if it adheres to these three concerns, that is, it should be economically viable; ecologically bearable; and ethnically and socially equitable for local communities (Wall 1997). Sustainable development advocates an intergenerational equity, which says that development is sustainable only to the extent that we can meet our needs today without prejudice to those of the future generations. Therefore, the present generation should leave for the next generation a stock of quality-of-life assets no less than those we have inherited (Pearce *et al.* 1989). Sustainable development promotes the utilisation and management of renewable resources for the benefit of today's generations at the same time making the same resources available for future generations (WCED 1987). Therefore, in relation to tourism development in the Okavango Delta, the concept of sustainable development should address the problems of poverty, unemployment and unequal distribution of tourism particularly for minority groups such as the Basarwa.

Sustainable tourism development in the Okavango Delta is carried out through the adoption of the Community-Based Natural Resource Management (CBNRM) programme in which the Basarwa are participants. The CBNRM approach combines rural development and natural resource conservation (Rozemeijer & van der Jagt 2000). The CBNRM approach also aims at reforming conventional protectionist conservation philosophy and top down approaches because it is based on common property theory which discourages open access resource management and promotes resource use rights of the local communities (Kgathi *et al.* 2002; Rihoy 1995). As an attempt to find alternatives to the failure of top-down approaches to development and conservation, CBNRM is based on the premise that local people must have decision making power over their natural resources in order to encourage sustainable development (Rozemeijer & van der Jagt 2000). It is assumed that CBNRM will alleviate rural poverty and advance conservation by strengthening rural economies and empowering communities to manage resources for their long-term social, economic and ecological benefits (Rozemeijer & van der Jagt 2000; Twyman 2000). CBNRM further assumes that once rural communities participate in natural resource utilisation and derive economic benefits; this will cultivate the spirit of ownership and ultimately lead to the use of natural resources found around them in ways consistent with long-term sustainability (Mbaiwa 1999; Tsing *et al.* 1999). Through CBNRM, the Basarwa in the Okavango Delta have, since the 1990s, become involved in community-based tourism. Despite this positive strategy on rural development, not much is known about the sustainability of the programme or the extent to which sustainable livelihoods among the Basarwa communities are being met through community-based tourism, an omission that this study seeks to correct, at least partially.

## *Factors Leading to the Participation of Basarwa in Community-Based Tourism*

**The loss of land and its natural resource by Basarwa communities**   Land, its resources, and how they are used, by whom and who owns them, is one of the greatest concerns in Southern Africa (Rihoy *et al.* 1999). Since the Basarwa were the first people to live in the Okavango Delta, they are supposed to possess traditional rights over the area and all the natural resources found in it. The Basarwa are famous for their heritage of hunting and gathering. They used wildlife and other natural resources in the Okavango for centuries to sustain their livelihoods. However, they lost their traditional rights over the land and resources of the Okavango Delta in the nineteenth century. Two main factors account for this. First, was the arrival of Bantu-speaking groups from Central Africa in the eighteenth century, and, second, the establishment of protected areas such as the Moremi Game Reserve by the government.

The Bantu-speaking groups such as the Bayei, Bambukushu, Bakgalagadi, Batawana and Baherero arrived in the Okavango Delta after the Basarwa were already fully established in the area. Taylor (2000) states that the entry of different waves of Bantu-speaking immigrants into Ngamiland and the Okavango marked the beginning of the end of the control over land by the Basarwa communities. Of particular interest was the arrival of the Batawana in the last quarter of the eighteenth century. The Batawana, an off-shoot of the Bangwato of the Central District, seceded in the nineteenth century and migrated to the Okavango region.

The Batawana fought and conquered all the different ethnic groups in the Okavango. The Batawana state was thus superimposed on the hitherto stateless societies of the area including the Basarwa. Tlou (1985) notes that the period before the arrival of the Batawana in the Okavango was characterized by the absence of a unitary state and the prevalence of small-scale communities with diversified social and political structures. None of these entities were powerful enough to impose its rule on others. They co-existed in a fairly peaceful and balanced manner and were relatively autonomous until their incorporation into the Batawana State in the early nineteenth century. The conquest of the Okavango Delta by the Batawana meant that all the small ethnic groups as well as land and resources found in it were now under their control (Mbaiwa 1999, 2002b). Although the Basarwa communities lost their rights over the use of land and its resources in the Okavango, they were granted a semi-autonomous status by which they used resources in consultation with their Batawana kings. They were to show their loyalty to the Batawana through payment of annual tribute paid with elephant tusks, leopard skins and hippo teeth (Mbaiwa 1999).

The establishment of Moremi Game Reserve by the government in 1963 affected the semi-autonomous status of the Basarwa. It resulted in the displacement of Basarwa communities, particularly the people of Khwai village. Informal interviews with elderly people in Khwai indicate that the area around Xakanaxa and Chief's Island within Moremi Game Reserve used to be the hunting and gathering grounds of the Basarwa of Khwai (Mbaiwa 1999). The immediate effects of the loss of control over land and its natural resources by Basarwa groups were resentment, antagonism toward the new wildlife authorities and the development of negative attitudes towards wildlife conservation (Mbaiwa 1999).

The location of Moremi Game Reserve in the heart of the Okavango Delta has resulted in tourism becoming an important land use activity in the area. For example, there are three tourism lodges (Camp Okuti, Camp Moremi and Moremi Safaris), four public campsites operated by the Department of Wildlife and National Parks (DWNP), ten campsites operated by the Hospitality and Tourism Association of Botswana (HATAB), a boat safari camp and an airstrip.

Access into Moremi Game Reserve is permitted to individuals for touristic purposes for which gate entry fees are required. The Basarwa communities living around Moremi Game Reserve are generally unable to pay park entry fees, besides, they do not see the need to pay the required fees since they regard the area as historically theirs. The Basarwa communities believe that the DWNP has usurped the resources which previously belonged to them (Mbaiwa 1999). DWNP is actually viewed as a government policing body meant to deny them the use of resources that they believe are historically theirs. This conflict situation over access to Moremi Game Reserve and the use of resources between government and Basarwa communities can be illustrated by the lack of social services at Khwai village. The government has proposed the relocation of Khwai from its present site along Khwai River (which also forms Moremi Game Reserve's northern border with the village) to areas with less wildlife numbers such as the southeastern parts of the reserve. This suggestion was rejected by the people of Khwai, and Mbaiwa (1999) reports that over 97% of the respondents in Khwai were against relocation in 1999.

The refusal by the Basarwa of Khwai to relocate resulted in the government implementing draconian measures designed to indirectly force or intimidate the people of Khwai to consider re-location. These measures included the government suspension of the provision of all social services such as water supply, clinics, shops, schools and communications. Consequently Khwai remained virtually undeveloped when compared to most settlements in the Okavango. However, due to international and donor pressure, the government, in 2002, gave up the idea of relocating the people of Khwai and granted them a permanent status by which they should be provided with all necessary social services (NWDC 2003). The fact that the relocation of Khwai was only likely to result in increased hostility with wildlife management in the Okavango Delta has forced the government to accept the principle of community-based tourism by and for the people of Khwai.

**The need for poverty alleviation and natural resource conservation**   The loss of land, rights over hunting and gathering, and the lack of benefits from enclave tourism sustained and exacerbated poverty among the Basarwa communities in the Okavango Delta. The NWDC (2003) notes that the majority of the people in the Okavango can be classified as rural and living in poverty. The Basarwa community in the Okavango Delta and other parts of Botswana are provided with monthly food rations from the government and donor agencies. Basarwa children travel to developed centers such as Maun, where they attend boarding schools, and where their basic requirements such as school uniform, toiletry, food, transportation and accommodation expenses are paid for by the government. Some of the Basarwa communities living outside what is known as a livestock free zone (for example, the people of Gudigwa) are provided with crop seeds for arable farming and with livestock, particularly cattle, goats and donkeys as a way of introducing them to agriculture and to alleviate their poverty. However, agricultural production among the Basarwa has so far had little success mainly because of drought, wildlife damage to crops and livestock and livestock diseases such as the Cattle lung Disease that resulted in the eradication of over 300,000 cattle in the Okavango in 1995 (Fidzani *et al.* 1999).

Apart from agriculture that has so far failed to eradicate poverty among the Basarwa, the booming tourism industry in the Okavango Delta has equally failed (Mbaiwa 2003e). Tourism development in the Okavango Delta in the last 10–15 years is enclave in nature, and as such fails to meet the needs of the local people but meets instead the requirements of foreign investors and companies. ACORD (2002: 2) notes that in Gunotsoga and Eretsha, unemployment and lack of employment opportunities, low income levels, lack of food, few food sources, crop failure and crop damage by elephants, lack of capacity to advocate for their rights in the use of natural resources, vulnerability to diseases among women, lack of institutional capacity, and lack of opportunities and limited options resulting from various factors like limited education attained are some of the factors that aggravates poverty in the Okavango. Increased poverty levels among the Basarwa in the Okavango Delta contributed to the adoption of community-based tourism in the area.

In addition to poverty problems, the need to deal with negative perceptions by the Basarwa towards natural resource conservation and land use conflicts also prompted the Botswana Government to include the Basarwa in the community-based tourism programme commenced since the 1990s. Steiner & Rihoy (1995) note that the driving force behind the introduction of Community-Based Natural Resource Management (CBNRM) in Eastern and Southern Africa from the 1980s was a result of factors such as: the threat of species extinction due to over utilisation of resources especially wildlife through poaching, the inability of the state to protect its declining wildlife resources, land use conflicts between rural communities living in resource areas and resource managers (especially wildlife managers) and the need to link conservation and development. The antagonisms and resource conflicts between the Basarwa and the central government in the Okavango Delta presented a threat to natural resource conservation. Darkoh & Mbaiwa (2001) note that security and control over natural resources, or the lack of these, may prevent appropriate management of natural resources, exacerbate dissatisfaction, competition, and worsen conflict and unsustainability of resource utilisation. Even though the adoption of CBNRM was also meant to alleviate poverty in rural areas, it was also designed to achieve the conservation of natural resources particularly wildlife. Economic benefits were perceived as a means of achieving conservation (Gudjuhur 2001; Mbaiwa 2002a).

### Wildlife Management Areas (WMAs) and Controlled Hunting Areas (CHAs)

Access to land and its resources by the Basarwa and other ethnic groups in the Okavango Delta for community-based tourism has been made possible through the adoption and implementation of several government policies and strategies, notably, the Wildlife Conservation Policy of 1986, Tourism Policy of 1990, National Conservation Strategy of 1990, Tourism Act of 1992 and the Wildlife Conservation and National Parks Act of 1992. These strategies laid the foundation for CBNRM in Botswana (Rozemeijer & van der Jagt 2000). According to Rozemeijer and van der Jagt, each of these documents call for increased opportunities for local communities to benefit from wildlife and natural resources through tourism development. Community-based tourism in the Okavango Delta among the Basarwa and other communities is largely based on wildlife utilization. Wildlife utilization can broadly be divided into two categories, namely, consumptive and non-consumptive. Consumptive (e.g. hunting) includes subsistence hunting, spot hunting (recreational hunting) and commercial safari hunting or trophy hunting. Non-consumptive wildlife uses largely constitutes photographic tourism activities.

Both consumptive and non-consumptive wildlife uses are carried out in sub-divided areas known as Wildlife Management Areas (WMAs) and Controlled Hunting Areas (CHAs). The concept of WMAs in Botswana arose from the need for conservation and controlled utilisation of wildlife outside national parks and game reserves, along with the desirability of creating buffer zones between protected areas and human settlements. WMAs are therefore zones between protected areas and surrounding areas, especially human settlements. The primary land use option in WMAs is wildlife utilisation and management, other types of land use are permitted provided they do not prejudice the wildlife population and their utilisation (Mbaiwa 1999; Thakadu 1997). WMAs are further sub-divided into Controlled Hunting Areas (CHAs) which become the "unit of production" (Rozemeijer & van der Jagt 2000). CHAs are administrative blocks used by DWNP to allocate wildlife quotas (Rozemeijer & van der Jagt 2000). The Okavango area is divided into 28 WMAs and 49 CHAs. CHAs are allocated to various communities geographically located in different parts of the Okavango Delta where community-based tourism projects are carried out. The off-take wildlife quotas are set each year on the basis of wildlife census data and population trends for each CHA. In each of the CHAs, two types of tenure are established, that is, commercial CHAs which are leased by tourism or safari hunting operators, and community CHAs which are managed by the rural communities who live in or adjacent to them. In each of the CHAs, the type of wildlife use is designated as either multipurpose or photographic. Multipurpose CHAs permit hunting or photographic use, or both, whereas only non-consumptive use is permitted in photographic areas. After allocation of a CHA, a community decides on the type of land use for that particular area, that is, either for hunting or photographic purposes.

## The Socio-Economic Benefits of Community-Based Tourism

### *Access to Land and Resource Use*

Access to land and resource use is one of the socio-economic benefits that the Basarwa have achieved through community-based tourism organizations in the Okavango Delta. Access to, and management of, natural resources and participation in tourism by the Basarwa is carried out through local institutions known as Community-Based Organisations (CBOs) or trusts. Communities should have legally registered trusts before they are allocated a Controlled Hunting Area by the Tawana Land Board (government land authority in the Okavango) and a wildlife quota by the Department of Wildlife and National Parks (Mbaiwa 2002a, 2003b). Trusts provide leadership in the use of land and wildlife resources for tourism purposes. In 2001, there were 12 trusts in the Okavango Delta, that is, about 27% of all trusts in Botswana (National CBNRM Forum 2001). Of the 12, eight of them have been allocated CHAs for tourism purposes as shown in Table 8.2. The table also shows names of Community-Based Organization (trusts), CHAs allocated to them (coded NGs), the villages that compose each trust (CBO), population and ethnic composition and the type of tourism activity in each CHA. A trust can comprise one or more villages and this depends on geographical location and availability of land with wildlife resources.

Although Khwai was one of the first villages to be encouraged to participate in community-based tourism, it was amongst the last villages in the Okavango to implement it (Mbaiwa 2002b; Taylor 2001). This is mainly because they wanted a concession for Basarwa only, an idea which the Government did not accept because it would exclude other ethnic groups within the village and this delayed the registration of the trust (Mbaiwa 2002b; Taylor 2000). Apart from the Khwai Development Trust, all the CBOs in the Okavango Delta have followed the Department of Wildlife and National Parks (DWNP) model of implementing CBNRM projects. This includes the promotion of a joint venture partnership with safari operators (DWNP 1999). However, the KDT decided on a different model where they do not form a joint venture partnership with safari operators but prefer selling their wildlife quota at an auction sale and do not sub-lease their land (Mbaiwa 1999, 2002b). Guided by their constitutions and management plans, CBOs have become de facto owners of the wildlife resources in their respective community areas (Rozeimejer & van der Jagt 2000). The CBOs are engaged in consumptive and non-consumptive tourism activities. However, due to the lack of entrepreneurship and managerial skills in the tourism business, except for Khwai, Basarwa communities in the Okavango sub-lease their CHAs and sell

Table 8.2:  Selected community-based organisations, CHAs and type of land use.

| Name of Community Based organization | Villages and Population size | Name CHAs and its Size | Type of Land Use | Ethnic Composition of CBO Villages |
|---|---|---|---|---|
| Sankuyo Tshwaragano Management Trust | Sankoyo (345 people) | NG 33 and NG 34 (870 km$^2$) | Community multipurpose CHA (Hunting & photographic) | Bayei and Bambukushu are dominant groups, Basarwa numbers are small |
| Okavango Community Trust | Seronga, Eretsha, Gunotsoga, Beetsha, Gudingwa (2,200 people in all villages) | NG 22 and NG 23(1,220 km$^2$) | Community multipurpose CHA (Hunting* & photographic) | Gudigwa is 100% Basarwa. Basrwa comprise almost half the population in other villages |
| Cgaecgae Tlhabololo Trust | Cgaecgae (360 people) | NG 4 and NG 5(2,640 km$^2$) | Community multipurpose CHA (Hunting & photographic) | Half the population is Basarwa while the other half is Herero |
| Okavango Kopano Mokoro Community Trust | Ditshiping, Boro Xaxaba, Daunara, Xharaxao, Xuxao (2,400 people) | NG 32 (1,223 km$^2$) | Community multipurpose CHA (Hunting & photographic) | Xaxaba is 100% Basarwa while they compose half the population in other villages |
| Mababe Zokotsama Development Trust | Mababe (400 people) | NG 41 (2,181 km$^2$) | Hunting and photographic | Mababe is 100% Basarwa |

| Khwai Development Trust | Khwai (360 people) | NG 18 and 19 (1,995 km²) | Community multipurpose CHA (Hunting & photographic) | Khwai is 100% Basarwa |
|---|---|---|---|---|
| Okavango Jakotsha Community Trust | Jao, Etsha 1–13, Ikoga, Thaoge (10,000 people) | NG 24 (589 km²) | Community Photographic CHA | Bambukushu and Basarwa |
| Phuduhudu Trust | Phuduhudu | NG 49 (1,180 km²) | Community multipurpose CHA (Hunting & photographic) | Phuduhudu is 100% Basarwa |

*Source:* (Mbaiwa 2002).

*Hunting suspended in 2003 in favour of photographic tourism.

their wildlife quotas to safari companies to generate employment and income for their respective communities.

Although the Basarwa are given partial rights to manage land and wildlife resources in the Okavango, much of it remains centralised as land is only leased to them for a 15 year period and wildlife resources wholly remain the property of government except the quota allocated to the community. Cassidy (2001) states that there is very little monitoring of the natural resource and management decisions made by the rural communities. Key decisions over key resources remain the responsibility of government; for example, the hunting quotas are determined by the Department of Wildlife and National Parks without the involvement of the rural communities. Despite these limitations, it is important to note that government policies and the zoning of the Okavango into WMAs and CHAs for community-based tourism purposes indicates the success and achievements of the project in an attempt to promote rural livelihoods.

### Financial Benefits

The Basarwa communities in the Okavango Delta have successfully generated considerable income through their participation in community-based tourism projects (Table 8.3). Financial benefits have accrued to Basarwa communities through joint venture partnerships with safari companies that sub-lease their CHAs. Safari companies pay land rentals and buy annual wildlife quotas allocated to CBOs by the Department of Wildlife and National Parks. Safari operators also pay some funds known as community development funds to the CBOs. Community development funds are those which a safari operator provides to a community-based organization for small projects such as providing sponsorship to a local soccer team, construction of community halls used for social activities (mainly entertainment based) or any other small project assumed important and necessary by community members.

Income generation in the Okavango Delta can be one way in which the Basarwa and other communities in the region can sustain their livelihoods. The funds are used for various devolvement projects such as the establishment of kiosks which sell food products to the communities. Funds have also been used to buy vehicles which have become an important source of transport to better service areas such as Maun. The Okavango generally has poor roads and because of the dispersed and small populations, investors have not been keen to invest in transport or shopping businesses in these areas. Through their participation in community-based tourism, the Basarwa have as a result had better access to socio-economic services which are generally difficult to provide in these remote areas. Revenue generated by CBOs has also been used to provide loans to community members, particularly in times of deaths when financial costs become a burden to individuals, family and tribal groups. In terms of increasing monetary income, CBNRM among the Basarwa and other ethnic groups in the Okavango Delta has been widely successful. In 2001, CBNRM generated an estimated 4.8 million pula (about US$ 800,000) into the Okavango community-based organisations through contracts and joint venture partnerships with safari operators, sale of hunting quotas, crafts and veld products, and small-scale tourism ventures (North West CBNRM Forum 2001).

Table 8.3.    Revenue generated by selected CBO in the Okavango Delta (in Botswana Pula*).

| Name of Community Based Organization | Year | Land Rental | Quota (Pula) | Others** (Pula) | Total Revenue (Pula) |
|---|---|---|---|---|---|
| Sankuyo | 1997 | 285,000 | | | 285,000 |
| Tshwaragano | 1998 | 345,000 | | | 345,000 |
| Management Trust | 1999 | 140,000 | 202,850 | 120,000 | 462,850 |
| | 2000 | 154,000 | 223,135 | 148,940 | 526,075 |
| | 2001 | 169,400 | 245,450 | 180,610 | 595,460 |
| Okavango | 1997 | 264,000 | 204,050 | | 468,050 |
| Community Trust | 1998 | 290,400 | 335,250 | | 625,650 |
| | 1999 | 319,440 | 332,900 | | 652,340 |
| | 2000 | 350,240 | 336,000 | | 686,240 |
| | 2001 | 600,000 | 400,000 | 500,000 | 1,500,000 |
| Cgaegae Tlhabololo | 1997 | 45,000 | | | |
| Trust | 1998 | 40,750 | | 30,000 | 70,750 |
| | 1999 | 70,000 | | 35,000 | 105,000 |
| | 2000 | 25,000 | 290,167 | 27,095 | 342,262 |
| | 2001 | 265,000 | 265,000 | | |
| | 2002 | | 150,000 | | |
| Okavango Kopano | 1999 | 110,000 | 320,000 | 250,000 | 680,000 |
| Mokoro | 2000 | 200,000 | 700,000 | 200,000 | 110,000 |
| Community Trust | 2001 | 220,000 | 735,000 | 200,000 | 1,155,000 |
| Mababe Zokotsama | 2000 | 60,000 | 550,000 | 65,000 | 675,000 |
| Development Trust | 2001 | 69,000 | 632,000 | 63,250 | 764,250 |
| Khwai Development | 2000 | 1,100,000 | | | 1,100,000 |
| Trust | 2001 | 550,000 | | | 550,000 |

*Source:* (Mbaiwa 2002a; NWDC 2003).
* 1.00 USD = 6.00 BWP (November 2002).
** Community development and craft production funds.


## Employment Creation

The Basarwa communities also derive employment opportunities from their community-based tourism projects. Table 8.4 shows employment figures in selected CBOs in the Okavango Delta. For example, Khwai Development Trust had 78 people employed in various activities of the trust in 2001 (Mbaiwa 2002a). The Okavango Community Trust which includes the Basarwa village of Gudigwa, had 95 people employed in its three photographic

Table 8.4.  Employment figures in selected CBOs in the Okavango Delta.

| Name of Community Based Organization | Positions and Number Employed | Total No of Employed |
|---|---|---|
| Sankuyo Tshwaragano Management Trust | 3 Assistant Camp Managers, 1 Community Liaison Officer, 1 Bookkeeper, 1 Driver, 8 Escort Guides & others | 15 in each of two hunting camp (30 in total) and 19 in a photographic camp Total = 49 people |
| Okavango Community Trust | 1 Manager, 3 Assistant Managers in photographic camps, 3 Staff managers in photographic camps, 1 Apprentice Manager, 1 Bookkeeper (Treasurer), 2 Motor boat drivers & several Community Escort Guides and drivers | 95 people in 3 photographic camps 50 people in 2 in hunting camps Total = 145 people employed |
| Cgaegae Tlhabololo Trust | 1 Crafts Manager, 1 Buildings Manager, 1 Tourism Manager, 3 Community Escort Guides & 3 Shop attendants | (a) 22 in hunting season & 10 part time in 1998, (b) 27 in hunting season 10 part time in 1999, (c) in 2000 an increase of 10% expected |
| Okavango Kopano Mokoro Community Trust | | 100 people in 2000, data for other years not available |
| Mababe Zokotsama Development Trust | | 49 jobs during the hunting season as per 2000 contract |
| Khwai Development Trust | | 78 people in 2001 |

*Source:* (Mbaiwa 2002a; NWDC 2003).

camps and 50 people in employed the two hunting camps. Additionally, Xaixai, which is part of the CCT, had 69 people employed specifically for hunting activities, Mababe had 49 jobs and Sankuyo had 49 workers (NWDC 2003).

The creation of employment opportunities in community-based tourism projects is one way in which rural livelihoods among the Basarwa communities can be sustained. Mention has been made that subsistence hunting that used to dominate economic activities has since been prohibited, and thus new livelihood strategies like the CBNRM process are essential. The Okavango, as a rural and remote area, is characterized by an absence of industrial development. This therefore reduces employment opportunities for local residents. Community-based tourism therefore serves as an alternative form of employment in the region. In addition, employment in tourism is relatively more sustainable when compared to that provided by government through the Drought Relief Projects which usually take 18 months to complete. Drought Relief Projects are mainly manual and involve small projects such as gravel road construction between settlements and brick moulding that generally have a finite life as a source of employment; although possessing value as a means of improving the local infrastructure, which in turn also aids tourism enterprises.

### Cultural Tourism

In Botswana, and in the Okavango Delta in particular, resources such as museums, national monuments, historical sites and ruins, rock paintings, cultural events, sports and recreational activities remain relatively untapped in terms of their potential contribution to the tourism sector (Government of Botswana 1997). However, the Okavango Delta has a rich cultural diversity that can aid the promotion of cultural tourism. This includes cultural sites such as the Basarwa rock painting Tshodilo Hills, the Gbhwihaba Caves which Basarwa used as refuge areas when attacked by Bantu-speaking groups, Basarwa craft products such as bows and arrows, beads, skin clothing as well as the diversity of Basarwa life.

Although the Okavango Delta has a rich cultural diversity, enclave tourism mentioned earlier in this chapter partly contributes to the poorly developed cultural tourism in the area. In such tourism, there is little interaction between tourists' enclaves and the local communities (BoB 1999) or between the operators and the host communities (Mbaiwa 2002a). However, if tourists are able to access and appreciate the cultural heritage of a destination, that appreciation can stimulate the host's pride in their heritage and foster local crafts, traditions and customs. Despite the limited interaction between the tourism sector and tourists on the one hand and the local communities on the other, and the consequently weak development of cultural tourism, attempts are being made to promote cultural tourism through the CBNRM programme. Some of the Community-Based Organisations (CBO) such as the Khwai Development Trust, Bukakwe Cultural Conservation Trust and Sankuyo Tshwaragano Management Trust are developing traditional villages. The traditional villages are meant to provide tourism services such as accommodation (in huts), music and dance, and dishes for the tourism market (Mbaiwa 2002a). The Bukakwe Cultural Conservation Trust (BCCT) of the Basarwa of Gudigwa established tourist camp (Gudigwa Camp) in March 2003. According to Mbaiwa (2003d), the Gudigwa camp has six grass-thatched chalets designed in the style of traditional Bukakwe huts. The huts can accommodate up to 15 guests and rely on solar energy and borehole water. In addition to accommodation services, Gudigwa Camp provides Basarwa music and dance performances, traditional Basarwa dishes, bush walks, Basarwa methods of tracking wild animals during hunting and story telling. Although it is too early for Gudigwa Camp to generate profits, it can be credited for providing employment to 15 Basarwa workers, of which 2 are respectively managers and assistant managers (Mbaiwa 2003d). The camp can also be noted for its role in promoting the preservation of the Basarwa culture through tourism.

The participation of the Basarwa in cultural tourism has both positive and negative effects. Positively, it has the potential to diversify tourism development in the Okavango Delta from a concentration on wildlife and wilderness nature to include culture. This results in socio-economic benefits from tourism accruing directly to Basarwa and local people. It can also promote the preservation of culture which is otherwise slowly dying as new forms of living are adopted. For example, traditional dishes served at Gudigwa Camp and Basarwa music and dance that are performed for guests help revive traditions. The new generation that goes to formal boarding schools away from their communities now possess an opportunity to learn their culture that might not otherwise exist.

The commercialisation of culture in tourism also has negative effects in that it can lead to over-utilisation of natural resources particularly where the production of craft products for the tourism market is concerned. For example, Mbaiwa (2003a) notes the scarcity of *Hyphaene petersian* (mokola), *Euclea divinorum* (motlhalkola), and *Berchemia discolor* (montsentsila) which are raw materials used for the production baskets by the Basarwa at Xhaoga, a small settlement in the western side of the Okavango River Delta. This community walks roughly 20 kilometers to collect raw material used for basket making instead of the 2–3 kilometres that they used to walk about 10–15 years ago; partly due to over-harvesting to meet the demand of tourists. Consequently a need arises for new plantings; which also helped sustain insect and other life that are dependent on such vegetation.

## Problems and Challenges of Community-Based Tourism

There exist, however, a number of problems in community-based tourism projects organised by Basarwa communities in the Okavango Delta. These problems threaten the sustainability of community-based tourism, they include the following:

### *Lack of Entrepreneurship and Managerial Skills*

The Basarwa and other communities involved in community-based tourism in the Okavango Delta lack business management skills as well as the necessary experience in developing viable tourism projects (Mbaiwa 2002a, 2003b). This deficiency in entrepreneurship and managerial skills has resulted in these communities forming joint partnerships with safari companies. Most joint ventures are in the form of contract agreements rather than community-private sector partnerships; hence the sub-leasing of community areas to safari companies that originate mainly from Europe and North America. In the longer term it is thought that joint venture partnerships will be very important for the success of CBNRM projects (DWNP 1999; Gujadjhur 2001). As Basarwa lack knowledge about how to commercially utilise their natural resources, and lack the capital to do so, the joint venture partnership is expected to fill the gaps and in the process transfer entrepreneurship and management skills to the local people (DWNP 1999). This goal has not been successfully implemented in CBNRM projects in the Okavango Delta. Rather, the joint venture partnership system in the Delta is very weak and it directly hinders the successful performance of community-based projects (Mbaiwa 2002a). As a result,

Gujadjhur (2001) and Rozemeijer & van der Jagt (2000) state that there is no transfer of skills between communities and safari operators in the development of community-based tourism. Gujadjhur (2001) further notes that there is no example of real collaboration and learning between safari companies and communities. Therefore, what was intended as a true joint venture partnership through community-based tourism projects has resulted in a management contract where Basarwa communities have little to do with the management, monitoring or practicalities of running a tourism business. Instead of being managers or being in the forefront in the development of community-based tourism, the Basarwa communities have become labourers and land lords who are aware that money will come regardless of participation or performance (Boggs 2002; Gujadjhur 2001). CBNRM has created a system of passive participation, raised expectations and provided disincentives to work (Boggs 2002).

The lack of entrepreneurship skills by Basarwa communities has also resulted in funds obtained from the sale of wildlife quotas and land rentals being kept in the bank without being re-invested or alternatively they are misused or misappropriated (Ngamiland CBNRM Forum 2001). For example, DWNP (2000: 4) notes that with the Okavango Kopano Mokoro Community Trust (OKMCT), there is an "apparent misappropriation of funds (P12, 500 or US$ 2,083). The Village Technical Committee was requested (on a majority vote by the community present at the 2000 Annual General Meeting) to ask the Department of Economic Crime and Corruption to investigate the allegations." Another example is that of the Khwai Development Trust which was refused a wildlife quota for 2003 by the Department of Wildlife and National Parks mainly because it failed to provide audited financial accounts to the government in the last two years as required by their contract agreement. It is alleged that the trust has embezzled about P 500,000 (US$ 83, 333) in the two years (National CBNRM Meeting, May 2003). Government has also raised the same issue of poor handling and mis-use of funds earned from community-based tourism projects, failure to have audited reports on financial management and the misappropriation of funds by some community trusts (Molale 2001). Because of these reasons, government has since instructed that all funds earned from community-based projects should be placed in trust by the District Councils instead of having safari operators dealing directly with participating communities. However, this has not yet (by 2003) been implemented due to opposition by community trusts and UASID which spearheaded the formation of trusts in the country (Kgathi *et al.* 2002).

### *Lack of Understanding of the CBNRM Concepts*

The CBNRM concept in Botswana and the Okavango in particular is relatively new and generally the Basarwa and other local communities have failed to fully understand its implications (Mbaiwa 2002a). This is shown by the failure of communities to create tourist projects that match their skills and knowledge. For example, in an attempt to re-invest funds generated from land rentals or sale of wildlife quotas, some Basarwa communities are either proposing or are engaged on tourism projects that are too elaborate and complicated for them to understand and manage such as kiosks, bottle stores and guesthouses. Some projects have closed down due to the lack of management and investment skills (Mbaiwa 1999, 2002a). Tsaro Game Lodge (which was given to Khwai Development Trust as part of the agreement between government and Chobe Holdings) has been closed since 2001. The Khwai Development Trust lacks the necessary capital, marketing, entrepreneurship and managerial skills to run the lodge. The irony is that the Tsaro Game Lodge should succeed because it is located in a rich wildlife area that links Moremi game Reserve and Chobe National Park. Additionally these communities have also bought Land Cruiser vehicles which are used as free public transport instead of being used for community tourism projects as initially planned. DWNP (2000) also notes that villages in the OKMCT have no development plans on how they are to use funds derived from CBNRM. This too indicates a lack of understanding by the rural communities on CBNRM issues.

### Reliance on Outside Assistance

Related to the failure by Basarwa to fully understand the CBNRM concept, is the reliance on outside assistance, particularly from government and donor agencies. The Department of Wildlife and National Parks (DWNP) mobilises communities to form CBOs and provides communities with most of the technical advice in joint venture partnership with safari operators. Rozemeijer & van der Jagt (2000: 10) state that "DWNP does not have the resources for long-term facilitation and at times endorses the establishment of a trust with a quota knowing that it will not be able to provide the necessary follow-up, leaving behind a resource rich but institutionally puzzled community."

In addition to support from DWNP, CBOs heavily rely on donor support mainly from Europe and North America. NGOs such as the Agency for Cooperation and Research in Development (ACORD), Conservation International, People and Nature Trust, German Development Services (GES), Kuru Development Trust and TOCADI, work with Community Based Organizations as advisors. ACORD is working with the Okavango Community Trust. It is helping the trust to undertake a Participatory Rural Appraisal in all their five villages located in the eastern side of the Okavango Delta. In addition, ACORD has helped the trust to secure funding for the preparation of the management plan for NG 22 and 23. TOCADI, (formerly the Kuru Development Trust) works with the Okavango Jakotsha Community Trust. The People and Nature Trust helped the Sankoyo Tshwaragano Management Trust in establishing traditional tourism enterprises of Shandereka and Kazikini (these two offer traditional accommodation, dishes, music and dance). The GES provided an advisor to Mababe Zokatsama Development Trust. The NGOs provides specialized training to the Basarwa communities in the tourism business.

Donor Agencies have also been supportive in providing funds for training, production of management plans and for establishing tourism infrastructure. The European Development Fund (EDF) funded the construction of both the Aha Hills and Ghwihaba caves campsites in collaboration with CgaeCgae Tlhobololo Trust. PACT/IRCE provided funds and consultants that produced the strategic plan for NG3 (Okavango Kopano Mokoro Community Trust). The BCCT project is a result of several donations, Conservation International-Botswana facilitated the project as well as raising funds for it in 1997. Financial donations for the BCCT were provided by organizations such as the European Union Micro Project Fund, United States Ambassador's Fund, the Swift Foundation, the Swiss Development Corporation, the National Conservation Strategy Co-ordination Agency and the Business Link Strategy. The Okavango Wilderness Safaris provides training for lodge workers and marketing of the lodge at a cost of P 200,000 (US$ 33,333) per annum. Marketing is carried out both locally and internationally. Donations by these different donor agencies were made on an understanding that the project should promote eco-tourism among the people of Gudigwa who happen to be one of the minority and disadvantaged groups in Botswana.

This dependence on outside assistance in providing the direction in which community-based tourism should take may subsequently lead to setbacks, even perhaps the collapse of projects once the outside assistance is withdrawn. This therefore provides a challenge to community-based tourism to come up with ways by which Basarwa trusts become self-supporting and independent. Only in this way will tourism be culturally, environmentally and financially sustainable in the longer run while achieving greater economic well-being for the Delta communities.

### Poor Distribution of CBNRM Financial and Employment Benefits

The uneven distribution of financial and employment benefits derived from CBNRM also threatens the sustainability of the programme in the Okavango Delta. For example, Taylor (2000, 2001) states that the Gudigwa community alleged that they were not receiving a fair share of the benefits accrued to the OCT from leasing out their land, such as jobs, meat, cash and the use of OCT vehicles. Taylor attributes the problem of a lack of benefits by the Basarwa of Gudigwa from their CBO to ethnic differences with five other villages that form the trusts. These villages have substantial numbers of Bambukushu and Bayei who generally look down upon the Basarwa community (Taylor 2001). Despite the existence of laws in Botswana that discourages discrimination of an individual based on ethnicity and colour, the Basarwa are generally discriminated against by other ethnic groups in the country (Bantu-speaking groups). In the past, the Basarwa were perceived to be good as servants and livestock herdsmen by other ethnic groups but were not regarded as part of an elite. As a result, the issue of the Basarwa of Gudigwa not deriving benefits from the Okavango Community Trust demonstrates the problem of power relations between different ethnic groups that form a single trust wherein the Basarwa have been the casualties. Because of their alleged unfair treatment by other ethnic groups, the people of Gudigwa are noted by Taylor (2000, 2001) as being interested in forming an independent trust from the rest of the Okavango Community Trust.

In addition to ethnic differences between members of a trust, the poor distribution of benefits from community-based tourism projects is a result of a number of other factors including poor co-ordination between those in trust leadership (i.e. Village Technical Committees/Board of Trustees members) and the rest of the general membership (Mbaiwa 2002a). DWNP (2000) notes that in the OCT, there is poor communication between trusts board members and the wider community members. The Board of Trustees is accused by general members of running the trusts without much participation by other community members; hence disparities in benefit sharing particularly with the Basarwa of Gudigwa

(Rozemeijer & van der Jagt 2000). The rural elite and influential people in Village Technical Committees and Board of Trusts, were alleged to be paid high setting allowances (e.g. P500.00 or US$ 83 at OCT in 2000) while the general members obtain little or nothing (Rozemeijer & van der Jagt 2000). The OCT has also developed into a powerful village institution, and because of its power, Rozemeijer & van der Jagt (2000: 10) state that "the Board of Trustees live a life of its own in very close harmony with the safari operator and, in the process, loses contact with its constituents." DWNP (2000) also notes that there is an apparent strong private sector and political influence over OCT board activities and decisions. This has excluded other members from meaningfully participating in the development of their trusts, particularly the Basarwa of Gudigwa. This implies that only the emerging elite who are at the helm of trusts management benefit from CBNRM while the majority of the community members derive little or no benefit. Government also notes that only a few people benefit from funds derived from community-based tourism projects but they are meant to benefit larger sections of the community (Molale 2001). While this is the case, the distribution of benefits is probably the most crucial component of the CBNRM programme, and if not worked out in a sufficient detail, becomes a potential stumbling block for the success of community-based tourism.

### Contradictory Goals of Government Towards Community-Based Tourism

Although the government has policies that support community-based tourism, notably the Wildlife Conservation Policy of 1986 and the Tourism Policy of 1990, it has also come up with contradictory statements directed against the programme. These statements have the potential to hamper the programme. For example, a government savingram of January 2001 from the Permanent Secretary in the Ministry of Local Governments raised the following concerns that: (a) there is a strong feeling that there should not be a departure from the policy of natural resources benefiting the whole nation, as is done with diamonds and other revenue earning natural resources; (b) only participating communities in CBNRM benefit from national resources; and (c) CBNRM projects tend to be discriminatory in that if, for instance, there are job opportunities, they are reserved for participating localities to the exclusion of other citizens from outside (Molale 2001).

The contradictory goals on natural resources being a national resource to be used for the benefit of the entire nation, as compared to a particular community and employment opportunities being restricted to participating communities, are likely to affect the success of CBNRM in the Okavango Delta. The exclusive access to wildlife by Basarwa communities is necessary mainly because they are an ethnic group which until recently entirely depended on the natural resource to sustain their livelihoods. Such natural resources have been centralized; hence the Basarwa have limited livelihood alternatives. The Basarwa as a disadvantage society that lost its land and resources to both the central government and other powerful Bantu-speaking groups such as the Batawana should have more access to wildlife resource use than other groups as a positive discrimination measure to have them sustain their livelihoods. This should be the basis upon which community-based tourism should incorporate issues of empowerment among the disadvantages societies such as the Basarwa in Botswana in natural resource utilisation.

## *Enclave Tourism*

One of the main challenges facing CBNRM in the Okavango Delta is a predominately foreign owned tourism industry otherwise described as enclave tourism (Mbaiwa 2003c). Enclave tourism in the Okavango Delta is characterised by predominately foreign ownership of tourism facilities, top management positions are in foreign hands, repatriation of revenue from Botswana and the failure to effectively contribute to poverty alleviation in the district (Mbaiwa 2002c). The fact that expatriates dominate the tourism business in the Okavango Delta creates resentment, antagonisms, and resource conflicts between the local people and foreign investors. Many local people assume the Delta, which has sustained their livelihoods for centuries, has been usurped from them and has been transferred, at least temporarily to foreign tourism operators (Mbaiwa 1999, 2002a). As a result, citizens view enclave tourism negatively because they perceive the domination by non-citizens as "selling out" their resources (Mbaiwa 1999). The dominance of the tourism industry by foreign investors can reduce control over local resources and that this loss of local autonomy is the most negative long-term effect of tourism (Glasson *et al.* 1995). Glasson *et al.* note that a local resident may also suffer a loss of sense of place, as his/her surroundings are transformed to accommodate the requirements of a foreign-dominated tourism industry.

The lack of equal access to tourism resources, decision making as well as limited economic benefits to local people when compared to foreign investors is contrary to the ideals of sustainable development. Sustainable development emphasises equal access and participation in decision-making on natural resources management by all user groups and stakeholders (WCED 1987). A sustainable tourism industry should be sensitive to the needs and aspirations of the host population and provide them the opportunity to participate in the decision-making process (Ceballos-Lascurain 1996; Glasson *et al.* 1995). Enclave tourism is not sustainable, the challenge for community-based tourism, therefore, is to address the issues of sustainability in tourism development in the Okavango Delta. Community-based tourism has to prove the fact that it has the potential to make tourism in the Okavango Delta economically viable; ecologically bearable; and ethnically and socially equitable for local communities.

# Conclusion

In conclusion, this chapter has shown that even though the Basarwa in the Okavango Delta were dispossessed of land and its resources, there are attempts to return custodian of such resources to them through community-based tourism. The Basarwa communities are allocated land and an annual wildlife by government for tourism purposes. Apart from the Khwai Development Trust, all the community-based organization in the Okavango Delta sub-lease their community wildlife areas to safari operators and sell their wildlife quota to these safari investors. This arrangement has benefited Basarwa communities in terms of financial benefits, employment, meat and other intangible benefits. This has as a result influenced the development of positive attitudes by Basarwa groups towards natural resource conservation particularly wildlife. Although the introduction of community-based tourism was primarily designed to promote natural resource conservation, it also contributes to rural poverty alleviation. It has also provided information on the economic value of natural resources in the Okavango Delta.

Even though community-based tourism is beginning to positively contribute to rural livelihoods among the Basarwa communities in the Okavango Delta, the programme is also performing poorly. This is mainly because of the lack of empowerment particularly on marketing, entrepreneurship and managerial skills in the tourism business by Basarwa communities. Therefore, if community-based tourism is to succeed, priority should be given to the empowerment of the Basarwa. This can be achieved through both formal and informal training of Basarwa communities with those intending to start tourism projects. Tourism business skills can also be passed to Basarwa communities through joint venture partnership system with safari operators as currently done in the Okavango Delta subject to caveats. While the joint venture partnership is in place, it is not yet effective. There is no effective transfer of skills between safari operators and the local Basarwa communities involved in tourism. As a result, for the transfer of skills to be effective, all parties in the joint venture partnership (government, safari operators and local people) will need to be committed to agreed and expected results to be derived from the community-based tourism programme. Government will need to enhance its role of facilitation of the programme, and safari operators will need to come up with clearly designed and objective training programmes for Basarwa tourism organizations. The Basarwa tourism organizations on the other hand will need to remain committed to learning modern ways of natural resource conservation particularly wildlife utilization through tourism development. The transfer of skills between operators and local communities are needed from participatory planning and natural resource management to operation of a tourism commercial enterprise and marketing. The provision of entrepreneurship and managerial skills to Basarwa should led to a sustainable tourism industry in the Okavango Delta where all parties are equal partners in benefit sharing as compared to the current situation where tourism is predominately foreign owned and largely benefits foreign companies and individuals.

Since the key objective of community-based tourism is local community participation in natural resource management and tourism, issues of resource ownership need to be given much attention. The current situation is that full ownership of land and its resources is not given to Basarwa communities. Land ownership for example is limited to lease parts of sub-divided sections to Basarwa groups for a period of 15 years and an annual wildlife quota. The Basarwa are not involved in the decision-making process that decides on wildlife quotas. Land and its resources in the Okavango Delta remain wholly centralized and controlled by the central government. Therefore, if natural resource conservation is to be achieved in the Okavango Delta, the ownership and control of land and its resource will need to give more priority to the Basarwa and other communities in the Okavango Delta.

Previous studies such as that by Mwenya *et al.* (1991) in Zimbabwe portray the idea that people's attitudes are largely based on the personal or community ownership they attach to wildlife resources. Mwenya *et al.* assessed people's attitudes and perceptions about wildlife conservation on the issue of "who owns wildlife" and "who should manage it." Their findings indicate that people view wildlife resources as "theirs" because they realise the benefits of "owning" wildlife resources, and they understand wildlife management as a partnership between them and the government. This suggest that if the Basarwa of the Okavango Delta are to appreciate wildlife and land as theirs, they will need to be involved in deciding annual wildlife quotas as well as deciding the allocation of wildlife and tourism areas. This will turn Basarwa from being passive recipients of wildlife quotas and wildlife areas to be major players in deciding the use and management of land and its resources in the Okavango Delta. The local involvement and ability to derive economic benefits from resources as well as full ownership of resources will make Basarwa have positive attitudes towards natural resource hence ensure the sustainability of natural resources and the community-based tourism programme.

Finally, the introduction of community-based tourism in the Okavango Delta provides an alternative sustainable model of tourism development that is likely to be appropriate for the wetland. Appropriate in the sense that it yield economic benefits to the local people as compared to enclave tourism which has insignificant benefits to locals and is controlled from outside. It is also appropriate in that it promotes rural community development, community participation in tourism development and the sustainable use of natural resources.

Chapter 9

# Limits to Indigenous Ecotourism: An Exploratory Analysis from the Tl'azt'en Territories, Northern British Columbia

Sanjay K. Nepal

## Introduction

This chapter explores the potential for building capacity to plan and develop ecotourism in a traditionally forest-dependent indigenous community. The Tl'azt'en Nations in the Omineca Peace Region of Northern British Columbia (BC) represent communities seeking to revitalize their economic base, due to a significant decline in forestry. This study is based on fieldwork conducted in 2001 and 2002, which involved two workshops, informal and formal interviews with members of the Tl'azt'en Nations, semi-structured interviews with selected guide and outfitters, and an exploratory survey of key tourism sites. Results show that there is significant potential for ecotourism development in the Tl'azt'en territory. The Tl'azt'en First Nations have a strong desire to be involved in ecotourism, however, they seem to be incognizant of the challenges and opportunities that come with its development. There is a general lack of commitment to a shared responsibility in the planning and management of ecotourism. Four potential obstacles to fully realize the development of ecotourism include: (a) the speculation that most commercial "niches" are already filled; (b) lack of clearly identified target markets; (c) competing interests from other northern BC communities that have similar resources; and (d) stereotypical images of First Nations in Canada. The chapter suggests several strategies, including the capitalization of Tl'azt'enne knowledge of resources, measures preventing the negative effects of ecotourism, building networks with other Aboriginal and non-Aboriginal agencies and individuals, persuading the provincial government to fund projects and provide technical support, and exploring opportunities for educating and training the Tl'azt'en youth in tourism and small enterprise development.

## The Context

Ecotourism is often regarded as one of the fastest growing sectors of global tourism. Ever since the term was coined in the mid-1980s, "ecotourism" has been of special interest to policy and decision-makers, academics and business communities including aboriginal people (Ceballos-Lascurain 1996). The International Ecotourism Society considers ecotourism as "responsible travel to natural areas, which conserves the environment and improves well-being of local people" (TES 1991). Ecotourism has been heralded as an alternative, sustainable development initiative particularly in remote communities located in northern British Columbia (BC). Areas such as northern BC possess significant potential for ecotourism development but owing to the domination of forestry as the key employer in the region ecotourism has been slow to develop. However in the early years of the twenty-first century an air of uncertainty emerged in the forestry sector, and favorable attitudes developed toward tourism that made northern communities more cognizant of their unique location and resources. Many First Nations' communities in BC commenced the necessary steps to develop ecotourism. As the Vancouver Sun (2001) noted, the Ksan Historical Village in Hazelton, Doig River Rodeo in Rose Prarie, Wilp Syoon Wilderness Lodge in Chatham Sound, Qat'llnagaay Lodge and Heritage Centre and the Gwaii Haanas Park in Haida Gwaii emerged as successful examples of First Nations owned and operated tourism businesses.

Indigenous tourism is characterized as any tourism product or service that is owned or operated by native peoples (Zeppel 2002). Fennell (2000: 43) considers ecotourism as a sustainable activity that is primarily focused on "experiencing and learning about nature . . . ethically managed to be low-impact, non-consumptive, and locally-oriented." However, ecotourism as a concept is ambiguous, and has been interpreted to mean different things to different people (Wall 1997). For the purpose of the discussion here, indigenous ecotourism is defined as an activity and enterprise focused on maintaining the natural and cultural integrity of the land and people where it is developed. Due to effective marketing strategies, modern communication media, access to information and technology, and the awareness of environmentally friendly tourism practices, remote communities have also become aware of ecotourism development as a viable economic activity (Howe *et al.* 1997).

There are conflicting reports about whether the development of indigenous tourism is an essential element of self-determination, or a process to assimilate indigenous societies into mainstream culture. Those in favor of indigenous involvement in tourism argue that through the provision of economic stability and the reinstatement of traditional cultural practices, indigenous people can achieve self-determination and self-reliance. It is believed that by "showcasing" native culture and values, especially through the art of native storytelling and interpretation, non-indigenous society will gain a fuller understanding and insight of indigenous people's views, whilst providing these peoples opportunities to assert their rights and autonomy through economic empowerment (Pfister 2000; Smith & Ward 2000). Development of indigenous controlled tourism is also expected to bring positive social and economic changes (Beltran 2002; Butler & Hinch 1996; Nepal 2002). Given that indigenous peoples in Canada have lagged behind in economic development and face many social challenges, ecotourism appears to be a viable alternative. Ecotourism development is seen not just as an economic strategy, but also as a means to strengthening First Nations positions in regional and national development policies (Taiga Rescue Network 2003). The development of ecotourism is seen as integral to this process toward indigenous control, self-reliance, and improvement of social and economic conditions.

This chapter explores the potential for building capacity to plan and develop ecotourism in a traditionally forest-dependent indigenous community. The community in question is the Tl'azt'en First Nations, comprising four native bands located in northern BC. The study is important for two main reasons. First, the alarming scale and speed at which tourism is spreading into remote and peripheral areas, driven by the search for new destinations and marketing of things natural and unspoiled, has become a concern to local communities. Secondly, problems of indigenous peoples have been recognized at several international forums. While there is no doubt that ecotourism can play an important role in the revival of stagnant economies in many parts of northern BC, it must be ensured that ecotourism plans adequately consider the needs, aspirations and values of indigenous communities, and protection of natural resources.

With the exception of the works cited by Butler & Hinch (1996), Robinson & Boniface (2000) and occasional papers in refereed journals, empirical research on whether ecotourism leads to heritage conservation and ultimately toward self-determination of indigenous societies is lacking. This research aims to fill that gap by examining these issues in the Tl'azt'en Nations Territories in northern British Columbia. An analysis of Tl'azt'en Nations' perspectives of ecotourism development provides specific insights into economic development opportunities among many indigenous and remote communities in northern BC and acts as a case study contributing to a wider debate about these issues. The study also provides knowledge with regard to BC's First Nations' willingness to embrace change and adapt to changing socio-economic circumstances and thus illustrates problems associated with managing change in a cultural and community setting.

## Methods

It should be noted that this research is ongoing, and the analysis conducted thus far is mainly qualitative. Various qualitative research methods were applied in this study. First a comprehensive literature search on indigenous tourism was conducted (Bass & Nepal 2002). A rapid appraisal of ecotourism opportunities in the Tl'azt'en Territory was conducted during April–May 2001. This appraisal was based on existing literature, particularly the Fort St. James LRMP Forest Recreation and Tourism Opportunities Study (Meredith & Associates 2000), Internet sources and informal interviews with key informants (Oussoren *et al.* 2002). Secondly, two half-day workshops were held at the Band office in Tachie, the administrative center of the Tl'azt'en Nation, in May and July 2001. The workshop discussions focused on local visions for community development and understanding of ecotourism issues. Two follow-up interviews, one with Tl'azt'en elders and the other with Band members working in the Reserve administration, were conducted (Joseph *et al.* 2002). At the workshop, community members were also asked to identify potential ecotourism sites and recreation opportunities at these sites. Based on the initial feedback, and existing literature on recreation opportunity analysis, selected sites were surveyed during July and

August, with help from native research assistants (John *et al.* 2002). Several guide and outfitters active in the Tl'azt'en territory were interviewed between January and February 2002, to gain their perspectives on ecotourism opportunities and constraints in the region (Sears *et al.* 2002). Finally, a household survey in Tachie was conducted during January and February 2002. A total of 135 individuals were interviewed, of which 128 survey forms were used for analysis, and is the focus of this chapter.

### Household Survey Questionnaire

The survey questionnaire was six pages long, and contained 21 questions on various aspects of ecotourism (Nepal & Zeiger 2002). The questionnaire was initially designed as a mail-survey; however, it was assumed that the return rates would be low, and that a face to face interview could result in better responses, and would also give researchers the opportunity to establish rapport with the First Nations community. A Tl'azt'en Nation woman was employed to conduct the interviews. The first version of the questionnaire, designed by this author, was discussed with the enumerator and changed as necessary. A pre-test survey in the field revealed that some questions required clarification and were subsequently amended. For example, the original question: Where do you think are the potential ecotourism sites? was changed to If you have a tourist coming to visit for 5–6 days, where would you take them? What would you do with them? After necessary revisions were made, house-to-house interviews, which were typically between 45 and 60 minutes per interview, were completed. The household head was the target respondent. In the absence of the household head, other adult members were interviewed.

Following the introductory letter, the first part of the questionnaire solicited respondents' background information. The second part contained 20 questions: questions 1–3 were related to respondents' knowledge of potential ecotourism sites; questions 4–6 solicited respondents' interpretation of ecotourism and attitude towards tourism; questions 7–9 were related to respondents' perceived opportunities and constraints of ecotourism; questions 10–11 were about control measures; questions 12–14 asked if ecotourism would improve First Nations' social, economic and environmental conditions; questions 15–16 solicited respondents' opinions about community-managed or independent ecotourism operations; questions 17–19 were related to their opinions regarding any potential contributions they could make, and if any outside support was needed; Q. 21 solicited additional comments.

Questions were both closed- and open-ended. A closed question often included "Others (please specify)" as a category, to generate ideas from the respondents. Survey data were coded, and Microsoft Excel was used to develop the database. Analysis is mainly descriptive.

## Study Area

The Tl'azt'en Nation, a sub-tribe of the Carrier linguistic group of the Dene (Athabascan) family, inhabit 47 registered Indian Reserve Lands, spread over approximately 6,560 square kilometers in a relatively pristine natural environment in central British Columbia (Morris & Fondahl 2002). The Tl'azt'en Nation territory is situated on the Interior Plateau, approximately 250 km northwest of Prince George and 60 km northwest of Fort St. James on the north side of Nak'al Bun (Stuart Lake). The majority of Tl'azt'enne reside in four reserve lands, namely Tachie, Binchie (Pinchi), K'uzche (Grand Rapids), and Dzitl'ainli (Middle River), of which Tachie is the largest community with 501 residents. Tl'azt'en refers to "people by the edge of the bay."

Eighty-two percent of the total native population of 1,281 is under the age of forty years. Approximately 641 members live on reserve lands, while the rest is scattered throughout northern BC, with a large cluster in and around Fort St. James. Oral history suggests that for thousands of years prior to the 18th century arrival of Europeans, the Tl'azt'en existed as a hunter-gatherer society (Morris 1999). Woodland caribou, deer, elk and black bear were hunted extensively throughout the territory for their meat and hides and salmon were fished in the Skeena and Fraser rivers. The Tl'azt'en demonstrated an ability to sustain themselves as a people through traditional forest management practices for centuries prior to the arrival of Europeans. However, the Tl'azt'en economy underwent several changes after the 1880s. After the arrival of Europeans, the Tl'azt'en incorporated the fur trade into their existing fishing and hunting economy. Some researchers have argued that the native land and space in the Tl'azt'en territories have been influenced not just by the early European settlers expansionist policies, but also due to the Tl'azt'en Nations' often successful negotiations with the white settlers to control and manage vast tracts of land under their jurisdiction (Morris & Fondahl 2002). They also added to this gardening and animal husbandry to produce products that could be sold and traded to non-natives to supplement their own consumption of wild food. Hunting, fishing and trapping continued to be viable and socially important activities for the Tl'azt'en. In the 1940s the Tl'azt'en economy began to include more seasonal wage labour in mining, forestry and guiding (Morris 1999). Today, Tl'azt'en families hold keyohs or traplines that have been passed from one generation to the next. There are 30 keyohs within the Tl'azt'en Nations territories. While traditional economic activities such as trapping hunting and fishing continue to be carried out by a number of band members, by the 1990s the Tl'azt'en's predominant industry was forestry.

In 1982, the Tl'azt'en Nation was granted the first, and up to that point the only, Tree Farm License (TFL) in British Columbia operated by a First Nation. In addition to Tree Farm License # 42, the community established Tanizul Timber Ltd., a Tl'azt'en owned and operated logging company. However, the TFL did not provide many jobs, and those that were available required experience and heavy equipment. In a quest to create more employment and more revenue, the Tl'azt'en opened Teeslee Forest Products, a sister company to Tanizul Timber Ltd. in 1990. In 1998 the Tl'azt'en moved into the value-added sector of the forestry industry with the opening of the Tl'azt'en Cabinet Shop in Tache. These three enterprises, which were owned and run entirely by the Band, provided the majority of the employment on the reserve. Poor markets in the mid-1990s along with outdated technologies and a lack of management expertise caused the shut down of Teeslee in 1998. High overhead costs, especially in the area of employee skills and knowledge development, and inexperienced management appear to have contributed significantly to its current status (Baruah 1998; Booth 2000; Morris 1999). Tl'azt'en active in the labour force are primarily seasonally employed in the forest industry with a much smaller portion employed across the government, public and private services sectors. The unemployment rate for Tl'azt'en is 60%, which is significantly higher than the provincial average. The relative absence of

Tl'azt'enne with the experience, training and education needed to establish and operate local enterprises that, to some degree, must interact and compete with external enterprises has led to the erosion of confidence among several community members.

Given their history of adaptation to changing economic circumstances, the Tl'azt'enne recognized the need to diversify their economic base, and have naturally turned their eyes to ecotourism. With spectacular landscapes dotted with hiking mountains and navigable lakes and rivers, rich wildlife population, and cultural heritage, outdoor recreation and ecotourism opportunities abound in the territory. Angling is a particularly popular recreational activity as the lakes in the area support healthy populations of rainbow trout, char, whitefish and kokanee. Currently, 45 lakeshore lots have been leased out to mostly non-native guide and outfitters (Sears *et al.* 2002). There are also historic native pictographs that are a testimony to the rich history of the area, a great opportunity for cultural heritage interpretation and photography.

# Results

## *Tl'azt'en Perspectives of Ecotourism Development*

In order to examine whether ecotourism attributes and their meanings are understood by the Tl'azt'en Nations, questions were asked about First Nations' interpretations of ecotourism. Their responses indicate that the majority of respondents view it as a form of sustainable tourism that involves wildlife and nature, respects local culture and traditions, and creates job opportunities for local communities (Table 9.1). Interestingly, 74% of the respondents also indicated that ecotourism may also involve traditional wildlife hunting, as it was argued that wildlife hunting and living off wildlife (food, medicine, construction materials, etc.) could not be separated from First Nations' livelihood strategies. Under these circumstances, ecotourism should allow sustainable extraction of wildlife resources. This latter interpretation is sharply in contrast to existing norms of ecotourism, as discussed in current literature (Fennell 2000; Weaver 2002). Responses relating to the negative environmental and social impacts associated with tourism were muted and the impression was gained that these were perceived as inevitable but acceptable. To this author, this is a realistic perspective. Ecotourism was also seen as a community initiative in which community members are consulted and involved.

A highly significant proportion of respondents were in favor of ecotourism development, as they held the opinion that there are significant natural and cultural resources appropriate for ecotourism development (Table 9.2). The overwhelming majority answered positively to all nine questions about ecotourism. Ecotourism, they believed, could positively influence public appreciation of First Nations' culture and traditions. When asked if ecotourism development will have negative impacts (for example, increased drug and alcohol consumption), 60 out of 125 respondents or 48% indicated that it is inevitable. Overall, 95% of the respondents indicated that ecotourism is good for the community. Such a high proportion of positive attitude toward ecotourism is unusual, as research on indigenous involvement in tourism has indicated that local attitudes vary highly (Butler & Hinch 1996; Grekin & Milne 1996). One likely explanation is the declining state of the

Table 9.1: Tl'azt'en Nations' interpretation of ecotourism ($n = 128$).

| Interpretation of Ecotourism | $f$ | % |
|---|---|---|
| Includes wildlife viewing and enjoying natural scenery | 117 | 91.4 |
| Includes wildlife hunting using traditional methods | 95 | 74.2 |
| Respects local culture and traditions | 113 | 88.3 |
| Creates awareness among First Nations on visitors perspectives toward nature, wildlife, and society in general | 106 | 82.8 |
| Provides economic benefits such as jobs and cash income to local communities | 104 | 81.3 |
| Facilitates dialogue between First Nations and other people | 96 | 75.0 |
| Has minimum negative environmental impacts | 74 | 57.8 |
| Has minimum social impacts | 51 | 39.8 |
| Includes community members in its planning processes | 95 | 74.2 |
| Has a community-based management structure | 80 | 62.5 |

*Notes:* $f =$ Frequency of responses; percentages are calculated from total number of responses.
*Source:* Field Survey (2002).

Table 9.2: Tl'azt'en Nations attitude toward ecotourism/tourism development.

| Question | Yes | No | Don't Know |
|---|---|---|---|
| Is it good to develop ecotourism in your area? | 119 | 4 | 3 |
| Does your area have good potential for ecotourism? | 115 | 9 | 1 |
| Do you think tourism will generate revenue for the region? | 110 | 6 | 8 |
| Do you think tourism will enhance understanding between native and non-native cultures? | 116 | 6 | 3 |
| Do you think tourism will improve economic conditions in your area? | 109 | 10 | 6 |
| Do you think tourism will improve social conditions in your area? | 100 | 17 | 6 |
| Do you think tourism will result in greater appreciation of First Nations' cultures? | 112 | 8 | 5 |
| Do you think First Nations will value their culture more if visitors show appreciation of First Nations' cultures? | 122 | 3 | 2 |
| Do you think tourism will have negative effects on First Nations (e.g. drugs, alcohol)? | 60 | 53 | 12 |

*Source:* Field Survey (2002); Figures indicate frequency of responses.

forest industry, which could be the main reason why the Tl'azt'enne see ecotourism as a potential economic alternative.

### Potential Sites for Ecotourism Activities

Discussion during the two workshops, and follow-up interviews with the Tl'azt'en elders and employees of the Reserve administration, focused on identifying potential ecotourism sites and activities. Based on this information, selected sites were evaluated for their suitability and inclusion in a tour itinerary. It was deemed necessary to examine whether these areas would be the preferred choice of the respondents too. The question was open-ended, so as to compile a reasonable list of potential sites. Discussion during the workshops had indicated that areas around Pinchi and Stuart lakes, Middle River and Shass Mountain were the preferred locations. An earlier study had identified areas northeast of Tezerron Lake, lakeside area around Stuart, river corridors between Stuart, Trembleur and Takla lakes, Middle River, north of Trembleur Lake (Mt. Sidney Williams and areas), upper reaches of Stuart Lake (areas around Tachie) and North Arm Lake as areas of high recreation potential (Meredith & Associates 2000). These were the areas most frequently mentioned by the respondents also. References were frequently made to Stuart, Pinchie and Tezerron lakes, Middle River, Grand Rapids (along the Middle River), Pinchie Point, Pinchie Falls, Mt. Sidney Williams, North Arm Lake, Jenny Chow Island on Stuart Lake, Cunnigham and Whitefish lakes, Stones Bay, Mud Bay, and Tanijul Tree Farm License Area (Cinnabar Resort).

With respect to questions regarding recreation activities, almost all respondents referred to a combination of water-based and land-based recreation activities. Canoeing, hiking, camping, fishing, spelunking, guided hunting, wildlife viewing, bird watching and boating were mentioned most often. Many respondents also indicated the possibility of developing a tour centered around First Nations cultural activities such as a tour of native traplines and smokehouse, storytelling, dance and festivals, and traveling to sites of native petroglyphs. Also mentioned were demonstrations of native craft works such as bead making, skinning moose and beaver hides, and other traditional ways of life. Specific references were made to activities including fishing in Rosetie Creek, hunting in Steamboat Bay area, Leo Creek and Tanijul Forest, hiking on historic trails along the Middle River, horseback riding in areas around Pinchie Point, beach camping at Pinchie Lake, and canoe trips through Lake and Middle River. Several respondents also indicated that it would be possible to organize trips that would take advantage of immensely popular recreation areas such as canoeing through Babine Lake (Babine Provincial Park), Nation Lake chain, and Takla River. Overall, the Tl'azt'enne were highly enthusiastic when talking about local attractions and activities, as summarized by a young high school student from Tachie:

> ... I would bring them [visitors] on a tour of the [Stuart] lake and show them where we get our food from .... if successful, show them a lot of our wildlife ... which ones we live off and which we leave alone ... I would show them which wild berries we eat, and the plants from which we make our medicine .... where the trap lines are, and what trap lines mean to us and our way of life.

## Perceived Opportunities and Constraints

Many northern communities in BC view ecotourism development as a direct response to the need for generating more tax revenues, and providing local income and employment opportunities. The Tl'azt'en Nations were asked what their perceived social, cultural, economic, and environmental opportunities are (Table 9.3). Jobs and skill development, building partnership, enhanced appreciation of Tl'azt'en Nations culture, outlets to showcase art and crafts, and cultural promotion were the most cited opportunities. Strong attachments to wildlife, stewardship of natural heritage, youth leadership, cultural exchange,

Table 9.3: Perceived opportunities from ecotourism.

| Opportunity | *f* | % |
|---|---|---|
| Economic | | |
| Jobs | 125 | 97.7 |
| Business opportunities | 110 | 85.9 |
| Infrastructure development | 111 | 86.7 |
| Skill development and training | 118 | 92.2 |
| Others | 13 | 10.2 |
| Social | | |
| Shared understanding of outside culture | 108 | 84.4 |
| Enhanced appreciation of Tl'azt'en Nations' culture | 117 | 91.4 |
| Partnership among Tl'azt'en Nations | 120 | 93.8 |
| Improved relations with communities from outside | 106 | 82.8 |
| Outlets for dialogue and communications | 99 | 77.3 |
| Others | 6 | 4.7 |
| Cultural | | |
| Enhanced cultural awareness among Tl'azt'en Nations | 112 | 87.5 |
| Opportunities to showcase local arts and crafts | 114 | 89.1 |
| Traditional values are made known to outsiders | 112 | 87.5 |
| Opportunities for cultural promotion | 113 | 88.3 |
| Others | 5 | 3.9 |
| Environmental | | |
| Wildlife conservation | 114 | 89.1 |
| Natural heritage protection | 117 | 91.4 |
| Awareness of values of wildlife | 114 | 89.1 |
| Demonstration of importance of wildlife to society | 113 | 88.3 |
| Strengthening of the value that we are part of nature | 110 | 85.9 |
| Others | 5 | 3.9 |

*Notes: f =* Frequency of responses; percentages are calculated from total number of responses.
*Source:* Field Survey (2002).

self-respect, craft promotion, and alternative economic opportunities were also frequently mentioned.

Considering the sensitivity and remoteness of the Tl'azt'en communities, careful local planning and development of ecotourism resources are vital to ensure longevity of ecotourism projects. Communities should be capable of controlling undesirable and harmful effects of ecotourism. Communities that are not sensitive and proactive enough to minimize harmful effects of ecotourism will fail to sustain positive benefits, and in the long run, may very well erode the resources that brought ecotourists in the first place. Thus, it was essential to examine the Tl'azt'en Nations' perceptions of potential constraints for ecotourism development. The results were somewhat unexpected: the total number of responses to questions related to ecotourism constraints was much lower compared to the earlier questions about opportunities (Table 9.4). It was a clear indication that the respondents were

Table 9.4: Perceived constraints from ecotourism.

| Constraint | # | % |
|---|---|---|
| Economic | | |
| Few jobs | 55 | 43.0 |
| Seasonal, low paying jobs only | 68 | 53.1 |
| Jobs mainly for outsiders | 54 | 42.2 |
| Income mainly for outsiders | 73 | 57.0 |
| Rich and influential people benefit most | 61 | 47.7 |
| Others | 4 | 3.1 |
| Social | | |
| Erosion of Tl'azt'en Nations' values | 41 | 32.0 |
| Conflict between community members | 78 | 60.9 |
| Others | 9 | 7.0 |
| Cultural | | |
| Cultural erosion | 36 | 28.1 |
| ~ Youngsters imitating tourists' lifestyles | 69 | 53.9 |
| Youngsters not showing respect to elders | 56 | 43.8 |
| Youngsters developing bad habits | 60 | 46.9 |
| Others | 5 | 3.9 |
| Environmental | | |
| Wildlife disturbance | 36 | 28.1 |
| Lakes and river pollution | 69 | 53.9 |
| Wildlife exploitation | 56 | 43.8 |
| Wildlife habitat threatened | 60 | 46.9 |
| Others | 5 | 3.9 |

*Notes:* $f$ = Frequency of responses; percentage calculated from total number of responses.
*Source:* Field Survey (2002).

very positive about ecotourism opportunities, and did not consider the constraints to be very important. In terms of economic constraints, the highest frequency of references (57%) was made to the speculation that most income from ecotourism might go to outsiders. This is a valid concern, as research in other indigenous communities have shown that low level of tourism infrastructure and the lack of a strong production base means goods and products needed to provide for visitor services and facilities will have to be imported, resulting in significant economic leakages (Nepal 1997, 2000). Similar concerns were expressed in regard to seasonal and low paying jobs. The potential for conflict among community members was seen as a social constraint, while erosion of First Nations values was cited by only 32% of the respondents. This may imply that the Tl'azt'en Nations, by and large, believe that ecotourism will not erode traditional values. There were some concerns about potential impacts of ecotourism on the Tl'azt'en youth, for example, imitation of tourists' lifestyles and anti-social behaviors. Of the total, 54% of the respondents cited lake and river pollution as a potential constraint while only 28% made references to wildlife disturbance.

When asked what the net effect of tourism would be, almost 45% indicated that it would be positive, and only 4% said it would be negative. Over half of the total respondents believed that both positive and negative effects would occur. Respondents were also asked to indicate whether or not they would be capable of controlling undesirable impacts of ecotourism. The majority (78.9%) indicated that the Tl'azt'en Nations are capable, while 16% indicated they do not have the capability, and 5% were not sure what capability the Tl'azt'enne possessed.

Respondents were also asked their opinion with respect to impact mitigation measures (Table 9.5). It became apparent during the workshop deliberations that not all sites would be open to visitors. Specific concerns were expressed regarding tourist visits to sacred grounds and burial sites, and during traditional rituals and events. Community reaction is manifested in the responses recorded here, for example, 76% of the respondents made it clear that certain areas had to be closed off, and that restrictions would be placed on certain

Table 9.5: Potential measures to control impacts ($n = 128$).

| Measures | $f$ | % |
|---|---|---|
| Control number of visitors | 92 | 71.9 |
| Control timing of visit | 88 | 68.8 |
| Control on sites to be visited | 97 | 75.8 |
| Control on type of activities permitted | 94 | 73.4 |
| Others | 10 | 7.8 |
| Control number of visitors | 92 | 71.9 |
| Control timing of visit | 88 | 68.8 |
| Control on sites to be visited | 97 | 75.8 |
| Control on type of activities permitted | 94 | 73.4 |
| Others | 10 | 7.8 |

*Notes:* $f$ = Frequency of responses; percentages calculated from total number of responses.
*Source:* Field Survey (2002).

types of activities. It was indicated by some community members that offensive behaviors or activities that are not suited to their lifestyles would not be welcome. There were no specific mention of what these offensive behaviors would be; however, some community members referred to hiking etiquette and respect of local customs.

### Preferred Ecotourism Projects

Respondents were asked to indicate their preference for potential ecotourism projects that could be launched in the immediate future. Access improvements, and facility development were accorded high priority. Large sections of the Tl'azt'en Nations territory do not have an adequate network of trail systems, and with the exception of the main road from Fort St. James to Tachie, others are gravelled and used mainly as logging roads. While this may add to the adventure of ecotourism, many residents expressed the view that paved roads are essential for reducing travel time and distance, especially for supplies. Some community members referred to the presence of historic trails that could be of interest to many visitors, however, these trails have become overgrown and require maintenance. One such trail connects Tachie to Grand Rapids via the river corridor. Facility-related projects included portage or marina development, bed and breakfast, visitor information center, native heritage interpretive center, and boats and canoe rentals. Site development referred to campsites and shelters, rest stops, viewpoints, signage and maps, and development of special interest points, for example, limestone cliffs suitable for rock climbing. Information brochures and pamphlets were cited by relatively few, as these could be considered at a later stage of ecotourism planning. The most important consideration was to have some basic infrastructure in place before the area could be opened to visitors, as one of the elders stated:

> ... ecotourism cannot happen overnight ... we need to have the basics put in place first, and start marketing ... with the right kind of strategy ... it will work!

The overwhelmingly positive reactions to ecotourism development from the Tl'azt'enne indicated that irrespective of age differences and access to income and employment opportunities, community members had common perspectives about ecotourism. Respondents were asked whether they would prefer a community-managed ecotourism development, or one based on *laissez faire*. The majority was in favor of the former type, due to their concern that this would prevent individuals from taking undue advantage. Management based on shared responsibilities would inspire a sense of ownership as opposed to independent initiatives. Suggestions were made to have equal representation from the elders, youth, and adult Tl'azt'en members, and ensuring a gender balance. Consultations with the Keyoh holders, when planning access improvements and development of sites and facilities, were strongly suggested, as was the suggestion that a strong involvement of the Tl'azt'en elders is crucial in ecotourism planning and management processes.

   With reference to questions about individual contributions, in the event that ecotourism projects are realized, almost 80% of the respondents indicated that labor is their only contribution, while 40% offered their business advice and training skills. The need for governmental support was mentioned unequivocally; however, respondents also realized that given the current level of cutbacks and reductions in social assistance programs at the provincial level, government help is appreciated but unexpected. Funding and technical support were the two key items most referred to, while some references were made also to leadership and guidance.

## Limits to Indigenous Ecotourism

As stated earlier, ecotourism could revive stagnant economies in rural areas of northern BC; however, the process of visioning, planning, developing and managing must be community-driven. Tourism in many remote communities is often dominated by outside interests, as some examples suggest. The beach hotels have displaced traditional fishing communities that once lined the coasts of Penang in Malaysia and Phuket in Thailand. A Mohawk uprising in Canada in 1990 was triggered by plans to extend a golf course onto Mohawk burial grounds. In the Black Hills, the native Sioux work as low-wage laborers in a white-owned tourism industry that promotes their culture and lands (McLauren 1999). In the Navaho Reserve, authentic ecotourism experience has been compromised in favor of commodified products, packaged and placed front-stage without tourist penetration into personal lives (Smith 1996). While this may be a deliberate attempt to protect indigenous cultures, many critics point out that it defeats the purpose of educating or sensitizing visitors about indigenous cultures, and thus undermines any attempts towards greater cross-cultural understanding. There are also dangers that indigenous populations may increasingly become dependent on the global tourism market. Thus, careful planning is necessary if the Tl'azt'en Nations are to benefit from ecotourism ventures in their territory.

Indeed, there are several good examples of indigenous involvement in ecotourism in northern BC: the "Ksan Historical Village" in Hazelton, Doig River Rodeo in Rose Prarie, Wilp Syoon Wilderness Lodge in Chatham Sound, Qat'llnagaay Lodge and Heritage Centre and the Gwaii Haanas Park in Haida Gwaii (The Vancouver Sun 2001). Gwaii Hanaas is considered one of the bright spots in the spectrum of relationships between Canada and First Nations (Taiga Rescue Network 2003). While treaty talks have been officially underway in British Columbia since 1993, and by 2002, talks of referendum had started to take a definite direction, it should be recognized that resolution of these complex issues takes time. Many First Nations in BC are beginning to take their place as part of the economic mainstream, and in doing so are contributing more than ever to the economic health and well being of BC.

Remoteness, and lack of information and economic development strategies place First Nations communities at a competitive disadvantage with other destinations. Communities such as Tl'azt'en Nations are in serious need of gaining the ability to make themselves known to a wider market and to establish local networks to actively apply local points of view on development issues. The support and cooperation from existing guide and outfitters active in and around the Tl'azt'en territory is crucial, as these are people with business acumen and marketing connections. The 45 active guide and outfitters offer a range of services including bed and breakfast accommodations, campgrounds, helicopter, fixed-wing and float planes, rafting, horseback riding, skiing, and golf (Meredith & Associates 2000; Sears *et al.* 2002). Interviews with these guide and outfitters indicated their positive views of ecotourism development potential in the Tl'azt'en territory. They believed that with a right attitude, marketing strategy, financial help, and development of key sites and facilities, the Tl'azt'en Nations should be able to successfully establish the area as an important ecotourism destination in northern BC. The recreation resource survey showed that the Tl'azt'en territory could attract visitors interested in wildlife viewing, canoeing and rafting, hiking and camping, native cultural events and storytelling, guided hunting, and demonstration of drying and hiding techniques. Some individuals were identified as having previous experience in the tourism industry as guides and outfitters, and given some support they could provide leadership in planning, developing, marketing and management of ecotourism. The Tl'azt'en Nations also need to familiarize themselves and establish connections with several information technology providers, and approach the provincial and federal aboriginal business development assistance agencies. Indeed, information technology works in favor of remote communities and the ecotourism industry.

There are some limits to the development of indigenous ecotourism. First, it could be argued that the existence of 45 tour operators active at different locations in the Tl'azt'en territory may indicate that most ecotourism "niches" are already filled. Although this was not mentioned by any of the existing operators, it nevertheless requires a careful assessment of what is feasible, where, and how priorities are to be accorded. Secondly, many rural areas in northern BC are experiencing economic uncertainties, and may possibly look toward tourism. Given that rural areas in northern BC have similar natural and cultural attributes, unless "niche" products are developed and target markets identified, the risk of too many ecotourism ventures sprouting everywhere may eventually be disadvantageous in terms of prices and markets. It can be argued that communities that are progressive in their thinking, and proactive in the development of new products and experience will edge out the others. This raises the question whether indigenous communities such as the Tl'azt'en Nations can sustain a product against competing interests from other areas of equal potential. What if 25 other rural communities start to compete with each other for potential ecotourists? Will this lead to stiff competition, price undercutting and lowering of standards? An equally valid concern is the size of the indigenous tourism market, both in Canada and overseas (Williams & Richter 2002). Is the market for indigenous tourism economically viable? What indigenous ecotourism products will be marketed, what are appropriate marketing channels, and how will these be tapped, and by whom? How do isolated communities access a global market, and how do potential tourists physically access the attractions? These are questions among others that require further considerations.

One major obstacle in promoting indigenous ecotourism in Tl'azt'en territory is overcoming the stereotypical images of native people and their lifestyle, which are very different from current realities. Tourism brochures in Canada typically depict First Nations wearing feather headdresses, painted faces and outfits made of animal hide. Historical images of native Americans with bows and arrows, riding horses, living in tepees, or depicted as fearsome warriors, have nothing to do with modern day realities of drug and alcohol addictions, domestic violence and suicidal tendencies, some of which can be traced back to the abuse many native children received at residential schools (Reed 1999). The economic reality in many First Nations communities in BC is that the majority is unemployed, lack education and trade skills, have low self-esteem and limited knowledge of the outside world, thus making them vulnerable when choosing to leave the life of a reserve. It has been observed that First Nations youth might do very poorly in European-oriented school curricula, but would make significant impressions if they are asked to perform activities suited to their ways of life such as hunting, fishing, tracking wildlife and plants, and other bush skills. Therefore, it is argued that these youth would easily adapt to ecotourism that is focused on nature and cultural heritage of First Nations, and that they could become excellent guides, interpreters and storytellers, just as they did during colonial periods (Rideout 2000). In essence, ecotourism would provide them a lifestyle that is not too different from their traditional ways of life and values.

Recognition of indigenous conservation systems as well as recovery of indigenous rights has been the global movement in recent years. International conventions including the United Nations Convention on Biological Diversity recognize the need to protect and promote indigenous knowledge systems (Johnston 2001). In the spirit of the Convention, indigenous people in Canada believe that they have legitimate rights to stop, or at the very least minimize, damaging forms of tourism — or initiate positive tourism alternatives — on their ancestral lands. Co-management, and partnership approaches have been initiated in several business and resource management practices. One such example is the Clayoquot Sound Agreement 1994, and Clayoquot Sound Interim Measures Extension Agreement 1996, which was established between the Nuu-chah-nulth First Nations and the Canadian government (Harris 2002). There are several examples, such as in the Gwaii Hanaas National Park, where the Haida Gwaii First Nations have managed to set and enforce terms of visitation, agreements for access and benefit sharing, codes of conduct, and other management tools. The Tl'azt'en Nations can draw lessons from these examples. There is a strong need for skill development, which is crucial for their effective participation in planning management, and ownership issues. Recognizing that the Tl'azt'en Nations lack the resources to fully realize the potential of ecotourism, governmental support in providing tourism education and training are essential.

## Conclusion

The fascination of Canada's First Nations people predates the 1860s (Nicholson 1997). Nineteenth century travelers and pioneers depended upon indigenous knowledge and guidance when exploring Canada's vast areas. With this fascination came a fictitious indigenous identity that had to be nationally overcome in the 20th century, but the identity persists even today, particularly in Western Europe, where native mythology, imagery and stereotypes have created a typecasting of Canada's First Nations people among the general public. Through their direct involvement in ecotourism, First Nations in Canada have the opportunity to assert their historic rights and ways of life, and demonstrate these to Canadians and international visitors. Tourism's role as an educational tool and vehicle for cultural exchange can help to create a better understanding of the reality and culture of First Nations people in Canada.

The Tl'azt'en Nations have struggled to achieve control over its economic, political, social and environmental circumstances through the negotiation of land claims, the development of economic enterprises, and the implementation of community initiatives. The renaissance of language and culture in the community, and awareness and recognition among its members to preserve and perpetuate key elements of traditional culture may steer the community toward a sustainable future. The greatest challenge lies in bringing together sound practices of the past with the constraints and realities of the present in a manner that allows the community to prosper in the most desirable manner (Baruah 1998). The idea of ecotourism development on traditional territories is a possibility for First Nations communities to gain economic self-sufficiency, empowerment and the perpetuation of their customary practices and ways of life.

In the Tl'azt'en Nations territory, and particularly at the John Prince Research Forest (JPRF), which is a co-management initiative between the Tl'azt'en Nations and the University of Northern British Columbia (UNBC), prospects exist for funding opportunities for a pilot project. In 2003 one development in the JPRF was the purchase of the Cinnabar Resort located at the Tanijul Forest, which action provides an opportunity for a pilot project that can involve renovating the resort and transforming it into a multi-functional facility. Such a facility could house an eco-lodge, a native interpretive centre, and a research and education centre. This would be beneficial to both the Tl'azt'en Nation and the University. It would not only speed up the process of ecotourism development in the Territory but also be useful in evaluating the sustainability of future ecotourism projects in the Tl'azt'en Territory.

While the interests of the Tl'azt'enne, from a social standpoint, are paramount in the development of ecotourism, all parties within the community need to cooperate effectively in ensuring that a high quality product is delivered without diminishing the natural and cultural integrity of the Tl'azt'en Nations. This will also ensure the long-term sustainability of the Tl'azt'en economy. Barriers such as lack of training, education, operating funds and control can hinder the potential for successful tourism ventures by First Nations. Addressing these issues along with controlling growth, maximizing benefits while minimizing impacts, and ensuring community acceptance, can help the Tl'azt'en Nations and other First Nations in British Columbia and Canada to start planning for ecotourism in the right direction. In the words of a Tl'azt'en elder, it is time to start a new era of opportunities:

> ... this [ecotourism] is an excellent idea .... it is about time the outsiders come in ... Tl'azt'en Nations get a bad reputation from people who have never been here ... we get so many visitors but all activities are concentrated around the lakes ... there is much more ... so much potential here ... so much to offer ... given the opportunity, the Tl'azt'enne can excel ..."

## Acknowledgments

The Forest Renewal British Columbia, a public agency now defunct, provided funding for this research. Support from the Tl'azt'en Nations community members is greatly appreciated. Field assistance from Damian John, John Bass, Josh Sears, Kylie Oussoren, Kulraj Bhandary, and Vanessa Joseph is greatly appreciated and acknowledged.

Chapter 10

# Public Sector Initiatives for Aboriginal Small Business Development in Tourism

Jeremy Buultjens, Iain Waller, Sasha Graham and Dean Carson

## Introduction

The National Aboriginal and Torres Strait Islander Tourism Industry Strategy (ATSIC 1997) recognised the potential for tourism to generate economic benefits for Indigenous people and help overcome their disadvantaged position in Australia. This view is supported by federal and state governments and various Indigenous communities and individuals throughout Australia. However, for indigenous people to become successfully engaged with the tourism industry there needs to be development of entrepreneurship and capacity building amongst Indigenous communities and individuals. In addition, aspiring and existing tourism businesses need to access start up and developmental capital. The public sector can and should play an important role in helping communities build capacity as well as providing venture capital. This chapter examines the funding and assistance packages provided by federal and state governments to Indigenous communities and individuals interested in establishing or expanding a tourism enterprise. The findings indicate that there is generally poor coordination between programs within and across jurisdictions; the focus of many programs is on promoting the idea of Indigenous participation in tourism rather than providing resources to realise this participation; many programs may be difficult to access for Indigenous enterprises in regional areas due to poor support services and lack of access to technology; programs provide little assistance in "visioning" and applying techniques of market research to feasibility assessment; and programs provide little ongoing support for businesses beyond the business planning phase, despite the heightened pressures on Indigenous enterprises to succeed over the long term.

### The Context of the Study

Indigenous Australians are, in general, more likely than non-Indigenous Australians to be unemployed, to be living below the poverty line, to experience lower levels of education and to suffer health greater problems (for example, see Norris 2001). This situation has not improved despite many years of specific programs designed to address this issue (Norris 2001; Taylor & Altman 1997). In recent years the tourism industry has been identified by Governments, at State and Federal level, and various other interested parties, as providing a potential panacea for overcoming the disadvantages suffered by many Indigenous communities, especially in regions, but also in urban areas (see Department of Industry, Tourism & Resources 2003).

Despite this enthusiasm for tourism there has been a less than desirable success rate in Indigenous tourism enterprises, although this rate may not necessarily be lower than for non-Indigenous tourism enterprises (ATSIC 1994: 5). There are a number of factors likely to impinge on the ability of Indigenous people to effectively participate in tourism. Aboriginal Tourism Australia (ATA) has identified the development of entrepreneurship and capacity building amongst Indigenous tourism businesses and the Indigenous workforce in the tourism industry as a major concern. In addition, access to start up and developmental capital is also a key to the sustainability of Indigenous tourism ventures (Finlayson & Madden 1995; Fiszbein 1997).

The National Aboriginal and Torres Strait Islander Tourism Industry Strategy (NATSITIS) recognised the importance of government agencies at all levels in effectively providing the delivery of resources to Indigenous people in order to better enable them realise tourism employment and business opportunities (ATSIC 1997). Unless this occurs it is likely that many Indigenous people will be excluded from participation in tourism. In recognition of this need for government support, a number of public sector initiatives have been developed. These initiatives are intended to stimulate Indigenous participation in the tourism industry, not only through funding for product development, but through promotion initiatives, infrastructure development, training and skills development and coordination of public sector resources. However, Boyle (2001) notes little is known either about the structure or intentions of these initiatives, and the utility of these initiatives from the perspective of both suppliers and consumers (i.e. Indigenous operators).

This chapter examines the range of public sector initiatives for assisting in the development of Indigenous tourism products as they existed as of March 2002. The objective is to determine if there are gaps in the provision of services. It is possible some initiatives were not identified and it is important to note that there may have been some significant changes since that date because of the dynamic nature of policy development in Australia with reference to this subject. It should be noted that the study identified several private organisations involved in promoting Indigenous tourism, but this research focussed only on public sector programs.

### Method

Information on Indigenous tourism initiatives were identified through a web search and personal contact with important stakeholders including ATSIC and the various state, territory and federal departments. Once a public sector initiative was identified, the organisation responsible for its administration was contacted for information regarding how a prospective Indigenous tourism enterprise could access the programs. Based on the information received

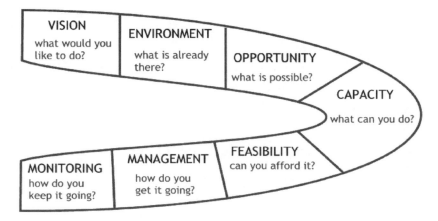

Figure 10.1: The Aboriginal tourism enterprise management potential tasklist (ATEMPT) framework. *Note:* Created by Dean Carson & Iain Waller (Centre for Regional Tourism Research) in conjunction with Lois Peeler and Leanne Miller (Aboriginal Tourism Australia).

via online sources, the phone, and/or from pamphlet literature, the initiative was assessed in terms of its ability to deliver outcomes within the Aboriginal Tourism Enterprise Management Potential Tasklist (ATEMPT) framework.

The ATEMPT framework was developed after discussions with ATA revealed that several cultural factors made the implementation of standard approaches to business development problematic when involving Indigenous participants. The ATEMPT approach acknowledges the cultural, experiential and goal differentiation between Indigenous and non-Indigenous participants in business development (Figure 10.1).

This framework was used as the basis for assessing the initiatives available for Indigenous tourism development. It is recognised that ATEMPT is only one of a number of possible evaluation frameworks. The initiatives will all be addressed on the items shown in Table 10.1 that were generated from the ATEMPT framework:

### The Assessment and Scoring Process

Individual initiatives were described and scored against each of the assessment questions in each aspect of ATEMPT. Table 10.2 describes the scoring system.

## Results

### Federal Initiatives

At the federal level there are 10 initiatives available to Indigenous people. There is also one initiative being developed by Centrelink but the details of this program were still unclear

Table 10.1:  Assessment questions for each component of the ATEMPT framework.

| Assessment Question | Vision | Environment | Opportunity | Capacity | Feasibility | Management | Monitoring |
|---|---|---|---|---|---|---|---|
| | …To develop ideas. | …To determine competition. | …To test market potential. | …To conduct skills/resource audit. | …To develop business plans. | …To bring concept to market readiness. | …To ensure sustainability. |
| 1. Is funding available … | ✓ | ✓ | ✓ | ✓ | ✓ | ✓ | |
| 2. Is the funding a grant or loan? | ✓ | ✓ | ✓ | ✓ | ✓ | ✓ | ✓ |
| 3. Does the funding require matching or in-kind contributions? | ✓ | ✓ | ✓ | ✓ | ✓ | ✓ | ✓ |
| 4. Is the funding paid to the enterprise or a third-party service provider? | ✓ | ✓ | ✓ | ✓ | ✓ | ✓ | ✓ |
| 5. Who decides how the funds are used? | ✓ | ✓ | ✓ | ✓ | ✓ | ✓ | ✓ |
| 6. Is there direct (face to face) consultation? | ✓ | ✓ | ✓ | ✓ | ✓ | ✓ | ✓ |
| 7. Are projects funded on completion or at specific milestones? | ✓ | ✓ | ✓ | ✓ | ✓ | ✓ | ✓ |
| 8. Is there access to successful examples? | ✓ | ✓ | ✓ | ✓ | ✓ | ✓ | ✓ |
| 9. Is there access to unsuccessful examples? | ✓ | ✓ | ✓ | ✓ | ✓ | ✓ | ✓ |
| 10. Are cultural differences specifically accounted for? | ✓ | ✓ | ✓ | ✓ | ✓ | ✓ | ✓ |

Table 10.2: Scoring for indigenous initiatives.

| Assessment Question | 0 Points | 0.5 Points | 1 Point |
|---|---|---|---|
| 1. Is funding available . . . | No | Possible | Yes |
| 2. Is the funding a grant or loan? | No funding available | Loan only | Grants |
| 3. Does the funding require matching or in-kind contributions? | Matching cash only | Cash and in-kind | Flexible |
| 4. Is the funding paid to the enterprise or a third-party service provider? | No funding | Service provider only | Flexible |
| 5. Who decides how the funds are used? | Funding body only | Joint decision | Community/ enterprise |
| 6. Is there direct (face to face) consultation? | Not possible | Possible | Yes |
| 7. Are projects funded on completion or at specific milestones? | No funding | Completion | Milestones |
| 8. Is there access to successful examples? | No | Possible | Yes |
| 9. Is there access to unsuccessful examples? | No | Possible | Yes |
| 10. Are cultural differences specifically accounted for? | Not indicated | Implied | Clearly stated |

in March 2002 and it was not included in the analysis. ATSIC provide seven programs, one of which is in partnership with the Department of Employment Workplace Relations and Small Business (DEWRSB). The Commonwealth Department of Tourism and Tourism Training Australia provide the remaining programs. Consequently the programmes being considered in the chapter are:

| | |
|---|---|
| F1 | Indigenous Small Business Fund. |
| F2 | Business Development Programme (BDP). |
| F3 | Tourism Our Way Brochure. |
| F4 | Business Self Assessment and Information Kit. |
| F5 | The Business of Indigenous Tourism Booklet. |
| F6 | On Our Own Terms. |
| F7 | Community Development Employment Projects (CDEP). |
| F8 | New Enterprise Incentive Scheme (NEIS). |
| F9 | Nature Based and Indigenous Tourism Promotional Brochure. |
| F10 | Pathways. |

and these are each briefly described as follows.

**F1: Indigenous small business fund (ISBF)**   The *Indigenous Small Business Fund (ISBF)* was developed by ATSIC in partnership with DEWRSB. The fund was announced in the 1999–2000 Budget as part of the *Indigenous Employment Programme* and was expected to complement the *Indigenous Business Development Program*. The *ISBF* objectives are to foster the development of businesses owned and operated by Indigenous people and to promote Indigenous employment opportunities.

The *ISBF* will fund Indigenous organisations that provide services to other Indigenous people or groups in order to foster Indigenous businesses through the development of business skills. Funding is available to:

- Identify and facilitate business opportunities.
- Help Indigenous people start businesses.
- Provide advice or support services to small business owner/operators in developing skills, markets and networks.

Indigenous organisations may receive funding to:

- Provide entrepreneurship and business facilitation training.
- Identify possible business opportunities, including undertaking feasibility studies at the local level or more broadly.
- Clarify business opportunities and developing business plans and proposals.
- Provide advice or support services to small business owner/operators in developing their skills, markets and networks.

Funding for Indigenous organisations is available in the range of AUS$5,000 to AUS$100,000 for business development projects. Funding is generally available for up to 12 months and a contribution to the cost of the project is expected from the applicant, in particular where requested funding exceeds AUS$30,000. Advice on eligibility is available at the State offices of DEWRSB and Regional and State offices of ATSIC or via the local Area Consultative Committee (ACC).[1] The endorsement of the ACC is not required in making an application.

The *ISBF* also provides assistance to individual Indigenous people seeking to establish or expand their own small business (funding handled by ATSIC). Individual Indigenous Australians can apply for assistance to develop their ideas, where these are assessed as having good business potential. The *ISBF* will help applicants develop business plans and access business capital and support services through ATSIC.

The *ISBF* does not provide direct finance to individuals, but will commit finance for a service provider to help the applicant with an idea by providing business training for up to one year. A business plan is written for the applicant by the provider once the initial application form (attainable from the information brochure or downloadable from the site) has been approved by ATSIC head office in Canberra. The business plan can then be used in applying for further funding for other sources such as from ATSIC under the *Indigenous*

---

[1] ACCs are a regional network working in partnership with government, business and the community.

*Business Development Program.* Organisations and individuals needing business finance and venture capital will need to approach commercial lending agencies or ATSIC for possible assistance. For example, financial assistance for organisations can be obtained from DEWSRB. Despite this program being promoted regionally in workshops with Indigenous networks and contractors around Australia, ATSIC has received very few applications. The *Indigenous Business Development Program*, which is provided for organisations and individuals, is more popular.

**F2: Business development program (BDP)**   The *Business Development Program (BDP)*[2] offers an alternative to mainstream financial institutions. The aim of the *BDP* is to promote Indigenous economic development by enabling Indigenous people and communities to acquire or develop commercially viable enterprises. Proposals that do not clearly demonstrate commercial viability will not be considered for assistance from this program. Unlike the *ISBF*, which will only commit funding to a service provider for the provision of business training and writing of business plans, the *BDP* will provide financial assistance to cover the costs of business materials and equipment.

The BDP tailors assistance to the needs of individual businesses, and provides two basic types of services:

- Business finance.
- Business support.

Business finance is available as loans, grants, guarantees or a combination of these. Interest charged on loans is linked to the lowest commercial bank business rate. Interest concessions, interest-free loans and grants are also available where a project needs: (a) assistance to be commercially viable; and (b) will produce sufficient benefits to Indigenous people. Business support may include professional assistance to develop and present a business plan and application, business or management training, or ongoing access to professional assistance.

Average annual funding provided by the *IBDF* is around AUS$36 million. There is a considerable demand for loans and grants that existing funding could not (as at March 2002) satisfy.

**F3: Tourism our way brochure**   ATSIC also provides the *Tourism Our Way Brochure, Business Self Assessment and Information Kit, the Business of Indigenous Tourism Booklet* and *On Our Own Terms Booklet. Tourism Our Way* is a guide/brochure containing free "help yourself" information for autonomous self-referral. The aim is to enable Indigenous managers and employees to develop skills in achieving Best Practice in Tourism. The brochure includes:

- Telephone listings of State and Regional ATSIC offices.
- Tourism Data sources, such as ABS and Industry Groups (the majority of which are located in metropolitan areas).

---

[2] The Business Development Program combines the former Business Funding Scheme (which mostly offered loans) with the Indigenous Business Incentive Program (which offered grants and training).

- State Tourist Commissions (for marketing purposes).
- Training and Employment agencies/organisations.
- Department of Aboriginal Affairs; Industry Policy Departments.
- Commonwealth Finance Banks, state by state, and small business advice (for metropolitan areas in selected States only) to contact for further information.

**F4: Business self assessment and information kit**   The *Business Self Assessment and Information Kit*, with catch phrase "*Good Business? Or Just a Good Idea?*" is offered by ATSIC as a self start-up kit that assists in evaluating the business idea and helps individuals determine if they are prepared to start up a business. The kit provides an insight into the viability of the business concept and also provides further directions and contacts. The kit also enables proponents to determine the funds required up-front to begin the business and how to apply for funding, if required.

**F5: The business of indigenous tourism booklet**   Prepared by ATSIC and the National Centre for Studies in Travel and Tourism, the *Business of Indigenous Tourism Booklet*, is similar to the *Business Self-Assessment and Information Kit*. The *Business of Indigenous Tourism Booklet* includes an audio tape that explains how Aboriginal and Torres Strait Islanders interested in tourism can start a tourism business, or begin a career in the tourism industry. It is part of the implementation of the Recommendations of the Royal Commission into Aboriginal Deaths in Custody, which suggest ways of advancing self-determination for Indigenous peoples in Australia. One of the initiatives is an examination of whether Indigenous peoples can take a more active part in the tourism industry and, if so, how this might be supported by government.

**F6: On our own terms**   *On Our Own Terms* is a booklet and video package that highlights some of the success stories in Indigenous tourism across Australia and explains the reasons behind their success. In addition, problems and important issues that need to be considered by an Indigenous community or individuals thinking of starting a tourism venture are also covered. The issues covered include the need for community consultation, business planning and market research.

**F7: Community development employment projects (CDEP)**   *CDEP*, a community and participant led initiative, is a job creation program that provides opportunities for Indigenous employment and skills development. ATSIC fund Indigenous community organisations to run *CDEPs* in urban, rural, and remote communities via the funding application process. Examples of programs include the provision of housing, municipal services, road maintenance and development, artefact production and enterprise development. Community organisations responsible for managing projects receive funding to pay the wages of participants and also to cover the costs of administration and capital items required for undertaking the project.

**F8: New enterprise incentive scheme (NEIS)**   The *New Enterprise Incentive Scheme (NEIS)* is available to all Australians. The difference between *NEIS* and the *ISBF*, is that applicants of *NEIS* are provided financial assistance by Centrelink during the process of being trained by one of Centrelink's service providers while developing a business plan. Once the plan has been endorsed, NEIS will commit a grant equivalent to one year's unemployment benefits. During this time the recipient will be allowed other earnings. Under *NEIS*, no loans are offered by Centrelink for the provision of business equipment or materials.

**F9: Nature based and indigenous tourism promotional brochure**   The initiative provided by the Commonwealth Department of Tourism is the *Nature Based and Indigenous Tourism Promotional Brochure*. This brochure showcases a range of established, successful Indigenous tourism businesses. The brochure does not provide any advice but offers case studies and criteria that made these businesses successful. Contacts for further details are also provided in the brochure.

**F10: Pathways**   The final national initiative, *Pathways*, is provided by Tourism Training Australia. Pathways is a guide for Aboriginal and Torres Strait Islander peoples seeking training and certified qualifications in the tourism industry. Tourism Training Australia also provides (free of charge) a comprehensive "Guide to the Tourism Training Package." The guide has been developed by Tourism Training Australia with funding provided by the Commonwealth Department of Education, Training and Youth Affairs (DEETYA). The guide provides self-education enabling people to meet industry competency standards. The publication has been written for Aboriginal and Torres Strait Islander peoples in order to "support their achievement of national qualifications in tourism" and covers the following areas: attractions and theme parks; meetings and events; tour operations and guiding; and visitor information services. The Guide also lists training resources, such as video-based resources and teacher's manual available for purchase by anyone. The assessment principles have been endorsed by vocational education and training ministers and should be undertaken by, or auspiced through a registered training organisation or provider.

The training packages provided through *Pathways* allow up-skilling for service providers/NGOs or other networks in remote areas contracted by ATSIC to support applicants of the ATSIC *Indigenous Small Business Fund*. Trainer manuals are available for: food and beverage; room attendants; kitchen attendants; hospitality industry; interpersonal skills; housekeeping; hygiene; customer relations; restaurant operations and so on.

The Training Packages have two parts:

(1) Endorsed Component containing a complete set of National Competency Standards, Assessment Guidelines and a National Qualifications Framework with requirements for achieving a qualification at each level.
(2) Training Package Support Materials that may include trainer guides, trainee workbooks, professional development materials, supervisor and mentor guide and assessment materials.

The Guide contains comprehensive descriptors of competency standards and an outline of topics/units covered in each package support and instructions for use. The Guide also provides an overview. Suggestions, options and strategies for training and assessment are included with regard to considerations for trainee needs, resources, training and assessment venues and other possible strategies.

Various general resources, including video-based resources are also available. The Regional and Rural Tourism Modules include: Australian Indigenous Culture; Cultural Interpretation; Cultural Awareness Training Package; Employers Guide to Recruitment of Aboriginal/Torres Strait Islanders. Other Relevant Material includes:

- Strong Business, Strong Culture, Strong Country — video and workbook.
- Australian Indigenous Culture Trainer Manual.
- Australian Indigenous Culture — Cultural Interpretation Manual.

## Analysis of the Federal Initiatives

Each of the above initiatives were then assessed using the frameworks indicated in Tables 10.1 and 10.2. The authors worked first alone in attributing scores, and then met to discuss their rankings to arrive at the consensus scores shown in Table 10.3. The maximum score possible for any initiative is 70.

The scores for the various federal initiatives suggest that only three could be considered as being relatively effective for Indigenous communities and/or individuals. These are the *Indigenous Small Business Fund*, the *Business Development Program*, and *Community Development Employment Projects. Tourism Our Way* is much less effective. The rest of the initiatives appear to provide few practical outcomes. Only one initiative (the *Indigenous Small Business Fund*) provides support for the visioning stage at the beginning of the product development process. This result was a surprise to the authors given the claims of many of the initiatives and their providers and also given the importance of visioning for creating successful businesses. The lack of support for the visioning stage could partly explain the problem of a lack of longevity and sustainability of many Indigenous tourism products.

Be that as it may, another significant omission is the lack of support for helping to monitor Indigenous tourism enterprise and products. All new businesses have difficulty in sustaining themselves for a myriad of reasons. However, Indigenous businesses will clearly have even greater pressures and barriers, both from external sources and from within, to succeed. Therefore, given the level of investment already in place to develop new products it seems almost wasteful to not continue support beyond the initial stages of development. It is clear that the provision of networking and other associated marketing opportunities at this stage of the development of the business is available, but our research tends to indicate that these are not the only problems, nor the most significant, that Indigenous operators are likely to encounter. The authors therefore turned to the individual States and Territories to assess whether the necessary support programmes existed at that level. It could be argued that more "local, on the ground" provision needs to be made to sustain new indigenous businesses, and that such support would be more forthcoming at this level of government rather than at the Federal level.

Table 10.3: Analysis of federal programs.

| Initiative | Vision | Environment | Opportunity | Capacity | Feasibility | Management | Monitoring | Overall Score[a] |
|---|---|---|---|---|---|---|---|---|
| Indigenous small business fund | 6 | 7 | 5 | 6.5 | 7.5 | 7 | 3.5 | 42.5 |
| Business development program | 0 | 7 | 6.5 | 7 | 7 | 6.5 | 0 | 34 |
| Tourism our way | 2 | 2.5 | 1.5 | 1 | 1.5 | 2 | 1 | 11.5 |
| Business self assessment kit | 0 | 0 | 0 | 0 | 0 | 0 | 0 | 0 |
| Business of indigenous tourism | 0 | 0 | 0 | 0 | 0 | 0 | 0 | 0 |
| On our own terms | 1 | 1 | 1 | 0 | 1 | 1 | 1 | 6 |
| Community development employment projects | 0 | 5.5 | 5.5 | 5.5 | 5.5 | 5.5 | 0 | 27.5 |
| New enterprise initiative scheme | 0 | 0 | 0 | 0 | 0 | 7 | 0 | 7 |
| Nature based and indigenous tourism | 3 | 0 | 0 | 3 | 0 | 3 | 0 | 9 |
| Pathways (tourism training Australia) | 0 | 0 | 0 | 0 | 0 | 3 | 0 | 3 |

[a] Maximum score is 70.

## State Initiatives

### New South Wales

In New South Wales (NSW), in addition to *CDEP* there are six initiatives that are available to Indigenous individuals or groups. However these are offered through TAFE, the universities and private companies, while the tourism industry and state commissions appear to be offering extensive marketing exposure to aid successfully established Aboriginal tourism enterprises. Many case studies have been included that highlight factors for successful Aboriginal tourism businesses. However, tourism bodies appear to offer little in the way of funding, training and business plan development. Our experience in this research suggests that, if an Aboriginal person sought direction for development of a business concept, generally the Tourism Commission would direct the individual to ATSIC. The New South Wales programmes are:

| | |
|---|---|
| N1 | Aboriginal Business Link Programme (ABLP). |
| N2 | Tourism NSW Policy Development. |
| N3 | NSW Indigenous Cultural Experience. |
| N4 | Murray Outback Aboriginal Cultural Trail. |
| N5 | Indigenous Tourism. |
| N6 | Online Home Based Business Kit (HomeBiz Kit). |

Again, each will be briefly considered in turn.

**N1: Aboriginal business link program (ABLP)**   In NSW, the Department of State & Regional Development (DSRD) provides the *Aboriginal Business Link Program* (*ABLP*). The ABLP program provides a subsidy towards the cost of a project that demonstrates a direct benefit to Aboriginal communities. The program aims to increase the number of Aboriginal businesses by supporting business owners and activities that are sustainable and profitable and lead to the development of skills, new markets and growth.

There are two streams of assistance — Link 1 and Link 2.

Link 1 provides networks for Indigenous businesses and enables Aboriginal business people to network by providing funding assistance to participate in mainstream trade shows and access to specific industry marketing and promotional opportunities. Link 2 is designed to help Aboriginal business people build business networks, overcome regional isolation and develop business skills by linking them to DSRD programs and by supporting collective participation in trade shows and industry marketing through subsidised participation. Programs include the Small Business Expansion Program, Women in Business Mentoring and Regional Business Development.

To be provided assistance under the program, businesses should be:

- Individual or groups of three or more Aboriginal businesses which can demonstrate significant sales or employment potential as an outcome of an ABLP project.
- 50% or more Aboriginal owned and operated.
- Have a current sales record and be trading in products or services for profit.

The conditions of the *APBL* are:

- Maximum subsidy payable is 75% of the project cost.
- For Link 1 projects the maximum subsidy rate is AUS$2,500 per participant per project.
- The maximum subsidy per group project is AUS$15,000.
- Businesses can only claim an *ABLP* subsidy once per six month period, with a maximum of four projects over two years.
- Payments are made when milestones are achieved, as agreed with DSRD.
- Participants must agree to complete sales and employment evaluation surveys six months after completion of the project and each 12 months for another three years.

The *ABLP* program is widely accessible via DSRD Regional Advisory Centres throughout NSW: Northern Rivers; Coffs Harbour; Port Macquarie; Central Coast; Illawarra; Murray; New England; North West; Far Western; Orana; Central West; Greater Western Sydney; Hunter; South East; and Riverina.

**N2: Tourism NSW policy development**   Tourism NSW is involved in a number of initiatives including *Policy Development. Policy Development*, which was developed in February 2002 to consist of Tourism NSW Website exposure for Indigenous tourism via case studies and fact sheets.

**N3: NSW indigenous cultural experience**   *NSW Indigenous Cultural Experience* is a promotional brochure produced by Tourism NSW showcasing a range of established, successful Indigenous tourism business in the Sydney, Hunter Valley, Murray/Darling and Wentworth regions. The businesses are engaged in retailing traditional Indigenous arts and crafts and providing cultural and bush tucker experiences.

**N4: Murray outback aboriginal cultural trail**   Another promotional brochure, *Murray Outback Aboriginal Cultural Trail*, is produced by Tourism NSW in partnership with Tourism Victoria and Murray Outback Tourism. The promotional brochure provides visitors with details of a trail of Indigenous cultural businesses, experiences and accommodation throughout the Murray Outback Region along the Murray and Darling Rivers. The brochure also lists affiliated Tourist Information Centres and connects visitors with NSW National Parks and Wildlife Service, the Victorian Department of Natural Resources & Environment, Parks Victoria, State Forests of NSW.

**N5: Indigenous tourism**   Another initiative undertaken by Tourism NSW was a two page commercial special-feature, *Indigenous Tourism located in Sydney — The Official Guide* (*Spring/Summer 2001*). This two page feature included details of Sydney and Blue Mountains museums, art galleries, Indigenous commercial galleries, shops, performance, food, art and rock carving sites, boomerang throwing and three Aboriginal sites' tour operators.

**N6: Online home-based business kit (HomeBiz Kit)**   The *HomeBiz Kit* is provided by the Department of State and Regional Development and is available to Indigenous and non-Indigenous people. The *HomeBiz Kit* is a free online service that incorporates business planning with links to other advice and sources of funding.

## Victoria

In the state of Victoria four programmes were identified, namely the Koori Business Network, the Victorian Small Business Counselling Services, the Enterprise Improvement Programme and the Regional Assistance Programme. Hence these form one Indigenous specific initiative and three general initiatives. In addition, Tourism Victoria publicises successful Indigenous tourism enterprises, however, there appear to be no strategies geared to Indigenous tourism development.

**V1: Koori business network**   The Department of State and Regional Development provides the *Koori Business Network*. The Network provides funding for Indigenous business, but information about this initiative proved difficult to access.

**V2: Victorian small business counselling services**   The Department of State and Regional Development also provides the *Victorian Small Business Counselling Services* initiative. This Service is available to anyone in Victoria aimed at mentoring small businesses by providing counselling via a website and helping develop networks. There is a "minimal fee" required to access counselling services, for example, one basic session with a counsellor costs AUS$80.

**V3: Enterprise Improvement program**   *The Enterprise Improvement Program* provides small business grants to businesses in regional Victoria wanting to improve their productivity through technology and innovation. Grants of up to AUS$10,000 are available to assist businesses in priority areas such as manufacturing, regional industries, food and services. Innovation, Industry and Regional Development (formerly State and Regional Development Victoria) is responsible for this program and they forward all enquires to the regional office in Victoria closest to the inquirer.

**V4: Regional assistance program**   The *Regional Assistance Program*, provided by DEET Victoria, consists of a training website that lists a large number of educational networks and training services. The website demonstrates best practice in training. The site also includes a self-educational guide in developing community links and partnerships.

## Queensland

There is one initiative in Queensland that is available to Indigenous businesses and another initiative available to Indigenous and non-Indigenous businesses.

**Q1: Aboriginal and torres strait islander business development scheme**   The State Development Department manages the *Aboriginal and Torres Strait Islander Business*

*Development Scheme* that provides funding and assistance with business planning. The Department assists clients with mentoring, advice and face-to-face assistance in regional areas. A maximum subsidy of 75% of the project or program costs is available under this initiative.

**Q2: The tourism assistance database**   The database, accessible on the web and provided by Tourism Queensland, is a referral service that directs businesses to possible funding and assistance sources. Prospective applicants are advised to contact the nominated funding or assistance agency direct regrading eligibility.

### South Australia

In South Australia there are two initiatives provided by the South Australian Tourism Commission, one in partnership with ATSIC.

**S1: Industry development team initiative**   The South Australian Tourism Commission's (SATC) *Industry Development Team* offers advice to the tourism industry including individual operators. An officer position, specialising in Indigenous tourism, was created within that team in late 2002. The team provides workshops, phone advice, and an industry advice kit for anyone with a business idea. A strategy brochure was developed in 1995 in conjunction with ATSIC's National Aboriginal and Torres Strait Islander Tourism Industry Strategy applying guidelines for tourism joint ventures between Aboriginal and non-Aboriginal partners. The SATC aims to foster the Aboriginal tourism industry by developing employment programs and negotiating contracts and leases. The SATC will also support development of Aboriginal tourism training by providing eco-awareness seminars, tourism training workshops and membership of the Aboriginal Hospitality Employment Strategy Committee. The SATC is also exploring with DETYA ways in which to present and encourage participation in tourism career workshops. The SATC markets existing Aboriginal tourism businesses extensively.

**S2: Guidelines for tourism joint ventures between aboriginal and non-aboriginal partners**   These guidelines have been produced by the SATC in partnership with ATSIC. The guidelines have been written to help develop successful relationships between potential or existing partners based on genuine commitment, real and accurate cultural perceptions and recognition of all aspects of a tourism joint venture. The guidelines have been developed to provide practical approaches to developing joint ventures and identifying problems that may arise. The guidelines have also been designed to test the commercial viability and potential Aboriginal employment gains in the long term. The document caters for student interest in cultural tourism joint ventures based on a realistic understanding of what they might involve. The booklet contains examples of successful Aboriginal tourist enterprises and provides information regarding the process of planning and establishing a commercially viable joint venture. In addition, descriptions of business structures are provided with an explanation of ways to operate a business and the different types of joint venture available, including Aboriginal inputs, locations, local Indigenous cultures and tourist products. There is a listing of accredited and non-accredited cultural tourism training/university/TAFE courses available in Queensland, Western Australia, South Australia and the Northern Territory.

### Tasmania

No funding initiatives were found in Tasmania but Tourism Tasmania was working with the State Office of Aboriginal Affairs on a development plan.

### Northern Territory

There is one initiative, *A Guide to Tourism Business Brochure* available in the Northern Territory but it is not Indigenous specific. In addition, the NT Tourist Commission, in collaboration with the Office of Aboriginal Development and the Aboriginal Land Council, provides advice and direction for Indigenous people. If Aboriginal persons approach NT Tourism for direction referral would be given to the Office of Aboriginal Development. Initial contact with the Northern Land Council (NLC) is essential in any development proposal in the NT under the *Native Title Act* (1976). The NLC can offer direction and mediation for ceremonial owners and persons seeking to operate on Native-owned land. Cases are treated on an individual basis and therefore no reference material is available.

**T1: A guide to tourism business brochure**    *A Guide to Tourism Business Brochure* does not address Aboriginal tourism specifically and it does not provide strategies for establishment or expansion. The brochure is directed towards newcomers to the tourism industry and existing operators seeking to expand their businesses. The brochure follows a step by step approach, beginning with helping operators to ascertain the appropriateness of establishing a business. In addition, advice is provided on developing financial, marketing and business plans. No funding is offered via this initiative.

### Western Australia

In WA, a range of assistance programs are provided by the Office of Aboriginal Economic Development (OAED). The Western Australian Tourism Commission and the Small Business Development Corporation also provide some initiatives available to Indigenous and non-Indigenous people and groups.

The OAED is a directorate of Western Australia's Department of Industry and Technology. It was established to support and encourage the development of enterprises that are owned by or employ Indigenous people. The OAED also works cooperatively with other State, Commonwealth and non-government agencies and tries to help Aboriginal clients access the full range of available business development and support services. The website includes a useful field "*How to apply for Assistance*" with a contact number as well as a list of the Regional Offices. Some of the other ATSIC publications outlined within this chapter are downloadable from this website.

**W1: The enterprise solutions initiative** *The Enterprise Solutions Initiatives* assists clients to identify, develop and grow enterprises that have substantial outcomes for Indigenous people. There are project officers/mentors located in designated regional areas and funding of up to AUS$10, 000 available via this program. The initiative helps Indigenous people to identify enterprise opportunities and supports enterprise development through the provision of feasibility studies, business planning, marketing plans and the provision of professional expertise. The initiative also supports projects, at the industry sector or regional level, that provides benefits to other enterprises, for example, the development of industry sector websites and support for industry representative bodies.

**W2: Business and management expertise initiative** *The Business and Management Expertise Initiative* attempts to improve the skills that contribute to enterprise sustainability by providing project officers/mentors in designated regional areas and funding up to AUS$10,000. The initiative includes identifying business skills and training needs and providing small business management training and corporate governance training. In addition, the initiative supports business mentoring.

**W3: Strategic financial investment product** *The Strategic Financial Investment* policy was established because of the recognition that investments by Indigenous corporate entities into Indigenous enterprises are critical elements for developing the long-term economic benefits for Indigenous people. Assistance may include identifying and assessing investment opportunities, identifying funding sources for Indigenous enterprises and assisting access to these and identifying and facilitating joint venture partnerships including negotiating on behalf of clients. The OAED works in partnership with other government agencies to assess the potential of an Indigenous enterprise and provide support required by the enterprise. For example, an individual may need to attend a management course in order to develop a business. The OEAD will contact an agency, such as West Australian Department of Training (WADOT), who will assess funding requirements for the individual to attend the course. For study areas such as tourism, mining, and arts, the OAED can work with private and government organisations. The OAED take a "business case approach" to funding as financial needs change according to business strategy. In mid-2002 the OAED were in the process of developing one financial system. No fixed amounts of funding are offered as each case is assessed individually. Financial assistance schemes currently fund up to AUS$10,000. The OAED, in mid-2002, was in the process seeking Ministerial approval to increase this amount up to AUS$50,000.

**W4: Integrated services provision** *Integrated Services Provision* is aimed at developing partnerships with other agencies and private sector entities to deliver services to Indigenous enterprises. This will involve the development of multi-lateral agreements with other relevant Government agencies.

**W5: Western Australian tourism commission tourism industry development division advice**    The WA Tourism Commission's *Tourism Industry Development Division* provides individual advice to tourism operators based on a business idea. This advice consists of telephone discussions about a business concept and the provision of a marketing plan template on which to base or develop a business plan upon. There is no specific Indigenous focus, funding or program offered by this division.

**W6: Small business development corporation website advice**    The Small Business Development Corporation website provides links to other relevant websites and phone numbers, including relevant funding bodies specific to WA. A link is also provided to a website entitled *Small Business Assistance Officers Available for Rural and Regional Areas*. This website provides details about how regional small business operators can benefit from the AUS\$6 million Small Business Officer Pilot Project that commenced in July 2001. This initiative is designed to provide operators with an information and referral service on a full range of government initiatives available to small business. For example, a local Small Business Assistance Officer will be able to help identify what assistance and support is available to help pursue opportunities in the expanding e-commerce field.

## Analysis of State and Territory Initiatives

Subsequent to identifying the State and Territory initiatives, they too were assessed with reference to the framework laid out in Tables 10.1 and 10.2. Table 10.4 provides the raw scores for the state and territory initiatives where the maximum score possible for any initiative is again 70.

These results for the state and territory initiatives generally indicate that, with the exception of some Western Australia initiatives, the availability of services appropriate to the needs of Indigenous tourism operators is not adequate. It would not have been unreasonable to expect that the areas not covered by federal initiatives would have been the basis of the provision of services by the states and territories. Instead it appears duplication exists and discussions with Indigenous groups suggests these results are indicative of the problems they face in attempting to develop Indigenous tourism product.

Clearly though, Western Australia has generally sought an integrated approach to developing Indigenous tourism opportunities. They even have two bodies responsible for ensuring that the different sectors of the public service, both federal and state, work together effectively to provide appropriate services to Indigenous tourism entrepreneurs and operators. Queensland provides some appropriate support services although it appears that they are not focussed on the needs of the Indigenous communities but more with an economics driven approach to development. South Australia offers little support to Indigenous tourism product start-ups. However, some initiatives are focussed on sustaining these businesses past the initial development phase. This approach appears to complement aspects of the federal approach and offers some potential for South Australian Indigenous tourism product success. Unfortunately, there are almost no appropriate initiatives for helping to scope out concepts that would be appropriate for the market. New South Wales and Victoria offer few effective initiatives for Indigenous tourism development.

Table 10.4: Analysis of state and territory initiatives.

| Initiative | Vision | Environment | Opportunity | Capacity | Feasibility | Management | Monitoring | Overall Score |
|---|---|---|---|---|---|---|---|---|
| **New South Wales** | | | | | | | | |
| Aboriginal business link program | 0 | 0 | 0 | 0 | 0 | 0 | 4 | 4 |
| Tourism New South Wales | 0.5 | 0 | 0 | 0 | 0 | 0 | 0 | 0.5 |
| NSW indigenous cultural experience | 0.5 | 0 | 0 | 0 | 0 | 0 | 0 | 0.5 |
| Murray outback aboriginal cultural trail | 0.5 | 0 | 0.5 | 0 | 0 | 0.5 | 0.5 | 2 |
| Indigenous tourism promotion | 0 | 0 | 0 | 0 | 0 | 0 | 0.5 | 0.5 |
| HomeBiz kit | 0.5 | 0 | 0 | 0.5 | 0 | 0 | 0.5 | 1.5 |
| **Victoria** | | | | | | | | |
| Koori business network | 0 | 0 | 0 | 0 | 0 | 0 | 0 | 0 |
| Victorian small business counselling services | 0 | 0 | 0 | 0 | 0 | 0 | 0 | 0 |
| Enterprise improvement program | 0 | 0 | 0 | 0 | 0 | 0 | 6 | 6 |
| Regional assistance program | 0 | 0 | 0 | 0 | 0 | 1 | 0 | 1 |
| **Queensland** | | | | | | | | |
| Aboriginal and torres strait islander business development scheme | 0 | 2.5 | 2.5 | 2.5 | 3 | 3.5 | 2.5 | 16.5 |
| Tourism assistance database | 0 | 0 | 0.5 | 0.5 | 0 | 0.5 | 0.5 | 2 |
| **South Australia** | | | | | | | | |
| Industry development team initiative | 0 | 0 | 0 | 0 | 0 | 0 | 4 | 4 |
| Guidelines for tourism joint ventures | 0.5 | 0 | 0 | 0 | 0 | 0 | 0 | 0.5 |
| **Western Australia** | | | | | | | | |
| The enterprise solutions initiative | 7.5 | 7.5 | 7.5 | 7.5 | 7.5 | 7.5 | 7.5 | 52.5 |
| Business and management expertise initiative | 0.5 | 0 | 0 | 0 | 0 | 7.5 | 7.5 | 15.5 |
| Strategic financial investment product | 7.5 | 7.5 | 7.5 | 7.5 | 7.5 | 7.5 | 7.5 | 52.5 |
| Integrated services provision | 0 | 0 | 0 | 0 | 0 | 0 | 0 | 0 |
| Watc tourism industry development division | 0.5 | 0 | 0.5 | 0 | 0 | 0 | 0 | 1 |
| Small business development corporation | 0 | 0 | 0 | 0 | 0 | 0 | 0 | 0 |

## Conclusions

There are five key findings of this research which warrant attention as programs and initiatives are developed and implemented. The findings are:

(1) There is generally poor coordination between programs within and across jurisdictions.
(2) The focus of many programs is on promoting the idea of Indigenous participation in tourism rather than providing resources to realise this participation.
(3) Many programs may be difficult to access for Indigenous enterprises in regional areas due to poor support services and lack of access to technology.
(4) Programs provide little assistance in "visioning" and applying techniques of market research to feasibility assessment.
(5) Programs provide little ongoing support for businesses beyond the business planning phase, despite the heightened pressures on Indigenous enterprises to succeed over the long term.

While it can be argued that it is not for the public sector to duplicate the range of private sector consultancy services that exist and which can be used by Aboriginal enterprises, nonetheless given the base from which many such businesses commence, it can be argued that the Federal, State and Territory governments do have a role in opening access to such services and in ensuring that public monies are well spent by offering access to post start-up monitoring/advisory services. Addressing these fundamental issues requires commitment from public and private sector stakeholders to increasing coordination. It also requires a program of research to establish market perceptions of Indigenous product, market readiness requirements for such product, and "best practice" models of enterprise management which are sensitive to the cultural, historical, and political environments in which many of these enterprises operate.

The results suggest that the centralisation of initiatives that appears to be occurring in the federal sphere is an appropriate response to the need for increased coordination between initiatives. It also suggests that the entire range of initiatives require examination to ensure that they offer what is appropriate to helping develop Indigenous tourism product. There appears to be some replication between sectors at the federal level and between some federal and state initiatives. Clearly, the federal approach is orientated to the development of products and the provision of training for operators. Where the states could improve and complement these initiatives would be in the conduct of market research to discover what tourists to particular areas might wish to utilise or engage with; and an assessment of how businesses could manage and develop themselves further in a sustainable fashion.

The large range of Indigenous promotional material, while outlining the success of Indigenous tourism, seems to have relatively little value in providing useful information and support for new and existing businesses. One possible reason is a cultural difference in communication and education approaches. Indigenous people seem more comfortable with small face-to-face interactions for learning and culturally self-help approaches based on written material in particular seem less productive.

There are many and various opportunities to access program information via the Internet, but this kind of assistance may be of limited value to a person in remote locations or without access to computer facilities. Some websites were useful but many programmes included within this chapter were not posted on the net. The greatest difficulty in obtaining information about the initiatives occurred in Queensland, Tasmania, and to a lesser degree, the Northern Territory and Victoria.

Our experience in researching this chapter indicates that the process of making contact with relevant organisations is often convoluted and this may deter people or groups. We made many telephone calls whilst collecting data and in a number of cases were transferred to the wrong people. Some calls never were returned despite numerous attempts being made, and in some cases the process of obtaining basic information or waiting for a return call could take as long as a week. The situation in some states was worse than in others.

However, the most important conclusion that we have reached concerns what products are being developed, for whom, and on what basis has this been determined. Over 60% of all international visitors to Australia expressed an interest to experience Indigenous heritage (Zeppel 1998). And general interest in Indigenous culture from non-Indigenous Australians appears to be increasing according to various media and reports, including the Report of the Royal Commission into Aboriginal Deaths in Custody (1991). Although there is little or no primary research available to support these positions (and indeed Ryan & Huyton 2000; and Pitterlee 1999 of the Northern Territory Tourist Commission have questioned the level of interest by visitors), tourism has been promoted as an economic development mechanism for Indigenous communities. While recognising that Indigenous cultural heritage is a significant potential resource for the tourism industries in Australia our review of literature could not find any specific evidence of:

(1) Research that addressed the potential size and location of a market for Indigenous product.
(2) Research that identified what Indigenous product(s) are sought by tourists (regardless of market).

It would seem essential that this research be given a priority status as the answers go to the fundamental issues associated with successful tourism product development (Leiper 1995). It is difficult to envisage how any enterprise support program could succeed in the face of a lack of such fundamental information.

# Section C

**Events and Artifacts**

Chapter 11

# Events and Artifacts

## Chris Ryan

The values and norms of a culture are signed and symbolized through its artistic expression. Performances, paintings, ceramics, sculptures — all express the degree to which a culture is dynamic and capable of change. Such works also permit distinctions within a culture, the difference between "high" and "low," between the "elite" and the "popular," or alternatively express the degree to which a society imposes conformity upon its members or adherence to traditional modes of expressing thoughts and creating things. Possession of the artifacts of a civilization confirm a sense of self, and sign that self to others, thereby possibly bestowing prestige and status. Consequently it is of little wonder that societies attribute importance to artistic endeavour. In short, the artistic makes tangible, the intangible.

However, that very tangibility means that it is open to influence, replication, modification and seizure. Such concerns have been well expressed in the tourism, heritage and cultural literature. It is not the purpose of this introductory chapter to fully review the research into these issues, but it is nonetheless possible to identify some not uncommon themes. One issue has been what Hughes (1995: 781) termed an "obligato" in the literature, namely the issue of "authenticity." Hughes points out that within western societies the reproduction of reality has been challenged, deconstructed and re-contextualised as "theatre has been taken out of dedicated buildings onto the streets, painting taken off canvass, out of the frame and out of the gallery ... In post-modern constructions the equivocal relation between reality and its representation has been extended" (Hughes 1995: 782). One of the issues pertaining to much of the art of Indigenous peoples is that it has rarely attached as much importance to representation of reality as has been the case of western art in the past. The scientific rationalism of western culture influenced western art in many ways; not only in terms of its content but also in the manner of its execution, where the skill of the artist has been one of the important criteria of determining "quality" of art. Western art has traditionally balanced execution, creativity and aesthetics. Such approaches are not unknown in the traditions of Indigenous peoples inasmuch as, within the modern era, schools of traditional art have been established to retain long-established practices. Even formerly, artists would study and work under the tutelage of a "master craftsman" — but important differences would exist. First, access to the creative arts might be based upon initiation — and in some societies birth would be a determinant of that initiation. Gender too had a role to play. For

**Indigenous Tourism: The Commodification and Management of Culture**
Copyright © 2005 by Elsevier Ltd.
**All rights of reproduction in any form reserved**
**ISBN: 0-08-044620-5**

example, in many Maori tribes, or *iwi*, not only is a female not permitted to carve, but indeed is not even allowed to see the male at work on a carving. Second, often art was concerned not with the representation of nature *per se*, but with personal and communal relationships with the natural. In pre-modern societies strong ties exist between people and land, with developed sensitivities to seasonal change and the realization that well-being depended upon the vagaries of weather. Not being able to control the weather, peoples sought to both sustain themselves through good agricultural practice, and by articulating fears, aspirations and relationships with nature through abstractions. Indeed, abstraction may have been thought necessary so as to avoid the direct challenge to the "gods" by seeking to directly reproduce their likeness.

A third difference between western artistic tradition and that of many indigenous peoples lay in an understanding of the purpose of the art. If art was about nature-human relationships and an understanding of a cosmology perceived important, then issues of personal appreciation of art become secondary to the sacredness of the representation. This is not unknown in western tradition, where for example, the statute of the Virgin Mary in a Catholic Church is not assessed in terms of aesthetic qualities, but as a symbol and representation of a divine intercession by a mother on behalf of the person who offers prayers. So too, as discussed by Ryan & Crotts (1997) in the instance of Maori art, carvings may possess *tapu*, a sense of that which is sacred about life, for it is a representation by an artist even while the materials themselves are part *mauri* or life. "All things, both animate and inanimate, are imbued with *mauri*, an inter-connectedness of all being" (Ryan & Crotts 1997: 903).

However, as has been noted, the tangible expressions of these types of relationships are easily reproduced once made physical. Blundell (1993) provides evidence of this in the instance of Inuit and Indian arts in Canada. The extent of the practice is indicated by her references to trade shows, trade catalogues and the two-dozen exhibitors offering "mass produced 'native-type' souvenirs . . . produced by non-native companies" (Blundell 1993: 68). Consequently, as illustrated by the work of Blundell, and by the following chapters, there remains a continuing concern about how non-native people capitalize upon a growing tourist interest in Indigenous art, and how both they and the tourist commodify and make subject to the price mechanism items that previously existed separately from market exchange in other forms of exchange of reciprocal and mutual obligation. The criticism of the commodification of Indigenous art is that it replaces these former enduring commitments with a situational commitment that is bound simply by the passing of money. Indeed, the preference by the western consumer for an established market even sets aside the transactional process of barter, which was and is itself a form of mutual relationship as psychologically and culturally buyer and seller explore each other's willingness to establish a contract.

Hence there is expressed a concern about the appropriation of Indigenous design and its separation from its context by non-native people, and indeed even where the sale is by an Aboriginal person, it is thought by some commentators that the very submitting of the item to a market transaction is somehow a betrayal of past tradition. Implicit in such a view is the moral ascendancy of the traditional over the contemporary. However, the traditional was once itself a response to both cultural practice and often pragmatic need. For example, Cohen (1993: 140) notes how, in a pottery workshop in Dan Kwien in Thailand, "an oil painting picturing buffalo-drawn wooden carts" lends "a patina of tradition" by including replicas of pots currently on sale. Yet, he argues, the painting is anachronistic, for nothing of that style of pot was sold to the external public, even when Dan Kwien was a viable cart station. So, one concludes, these pots were once used, but were simple and utilitarian, but are now decontextualised from a humble use, blessed with the nomenclature of being "traditional" in order to obtain income from visitors. And as Aramberri (2001) has observed, why not? Artistic creativity now has an outlet in creating "artistic" pots, the tourist has a souvenir of places that interested and fascinated him or her — and what is more a souvenir that fits in their airline baggage, while the retailer and potter now has a more assured and more easily obtained income to remove them and their families from possibly a subsistence existence to one where, if not for themselves, parents might dream of what their children will be able to achieve. And in many ways there is little that is "wrong" with this — it is simply systematic of a changing world, often characterized as a place of globalization where, perhaps, many things are reduced to a commodity, if only because the market mechanism is effective and efficient for those with limited time to conduct transactions.

However, the underlying process is one of a change in sign value. The reason why it is thought that the changing use of artifacts is thought important is that they acquire new values, and each new generation arguably only has direct experience of the new signs and re-interprets the signage value of past artifacts in the light of their own current understanding. In consequence, while there may be a developmental line of meanings from one generation to another, there may not be a replicable understanding. For Watson & Kopachevsky (1994: 650) the process of commodification also means that human relationships themselves become "objectified as relations between *things*, and money is hoisted as the universal 'doubly abstract' medium of exchange, the primary measure of value, if not the symbol of general alienation."

These arguments are replicable across a number of cultural activities, including events, fairs, festivals and performance arts. Each location or happening is a nexus of meanings, some serious, others less so, and each is signing values that are not necessarily consistent, but are situational. Hence, as the situations change, the signs change, and the signs become the new meanings and not simply symbols of meaning. In the post-modernistic world, it can be argued that all is reduced to the image, ephemeral, reinvented and perhaps eventually unfulfilling.

The following chapters provide case studies of these processes, even if the authors might differ in their interpretations. Maribeth Erb provides evidence from Flores in Indonesia on two levels. First she offers an interpretation of processes of changing gaze, drawing upon John Urry's (1990) seminal work, *The Tourist Gaze*. She thus analyses material in terms of a normalisation of the new through a specific lens or way of seeing the world. Her case study relates to the nature of events planned by local people, and the tensions that exist within communities that, on the one hand seek to sustain the traditional as a distinguishing feature of their difference (a difference which by the mere existence of being a difference is potentially attractive to tourists) and, on the other, entrepreneurial members of the community who wish to modify and make more easily accessible to larger numbers of people, a product for personal and communal gain.

Takayoshi Yamamura discusses the ways in which the art of the Dongba people in China has been "discovered" as a tourist object, to be sold to visitors not simply by local people but also by outsiders who have readier access to the channels of distribution and capital. A description is offered of how a folk art, held by some in little regard, now becomes valuable to the extent that the authorities begin to see a need to protect it, thereby gaining for it a further legitimacy. Yet this too is a story of tensions and differences of the nature discussed above.

Finally, in this section of the book, there is the chapter by Dieter Müller and Robert Pettersson. This reports findings from a study of the fair at Jokkmokk in Sweden where the Sami people sell their artwork, much of which is derived from their traditional economic dependency upon the reindeer.

While these case studies and research reports come from very different parts of the world, each plays out a series of tensions and dialectical processes. There is the attempt to sustain the traditional in the face of forces of change. Nor should it be concluded that it is solely the outsider that dictates the change. Host communities are not wholly homogenous, and tensions might exist between the creative challenger and the conservative emulator of past tradition, between the young and the old, and between the entrepreneurial and those seeing little need for change or profit. Additionally there is the issue of to what degree communities wish to embrace change, and the degree to which they can retain control over the speed and process of that change. Third there is the issue of cultural tradition acquiring value for previously marginalized peoples, and how their distinctive differences now acquire value in the global process of tourism. Consequently, the sign value of tourist souvenir purchasing is not simply a commercial transaction, but an act of political significance as peoples acquire and rediscover skills, a sense of identity as a community and personal worth as individuals. They are then, no longer a people to be ignored by existing power structures.

However, one common feature in all of these change processes exists — and that is the presence of the tourist. Whatever their motives, tourists by perhaps their very existence are catalysts of change. Their existence and presence as outsiders makes possible the comparison of difference, coming as they often do from different societies and existing within the sub-culture of tourism as spenders of leisure time. They are the gazers and interpreters of what they see. But as interpreters, there is the implication that they too might be subject to change. The native peoples engage with the visitors and the distribution channels they use in processes of dialogue, and while conventionally the academic tourism literature has considered the impact of the tourist on culture, there remains yet the notion that the tourist is also changed by the experiences.

Chapter 12

# Limiting Tourism and the Limits of Tourism: The Production and Consumption of Tourist Attractions in Western Flores ☆

Maribeth Erb

## The Limits of Tourism: An Empty Meeting Ground?

> Are we being encouraged to preserve our culture just so we can be an exotic object for tourists? (question at a seminar given by the author, Ruteng, June 14, 2002).

> Tourism is not just an aggregate of merely commercial activities; it is also an ideological framing of history, nature and tradition; a framing that has the power to reshape culture and nature to its own needs (Dean MacCannell, The Empty Meeting Grounds, 1992, p. 1).

In a paper musing on the "identities" of various people associated with tourism, Edward Bruner (1995) suggests that there is a fundamental, ironic discord between the expectations of tourists and the expectations of local people in regards to cultural tourism in the Third World. "Tourists come from the outside to see the exotic; from the inside tourism is viewed as modernization" (1995: 224). "Native peoples" are caught in a "paradoxical predicament" since tourism is encouraged "as a route to economic development . . . at the same time tourists want to see undeveloped primitive peoples" (*ibid*). This fundamental contradiction and misfit in ideas about what tourism can and should be, is, I suggest, one of the fundamental reasons behind the imagery of the "empty meeting ground," so poignantly used as a title

☆ Research in Flores was conducted under the auspices of the Indonesian Council of Sciences, with the sponsorship of the University Nusa Cendana in Kupang. Some of it was funded by National University of Singapore grant # R111-000-022-112/007. I thank all the above institutions for their support and assistance. Many thanks also to my research assistants, Joseph Jelahut, Ardie Agus, and Marsel Djeer, and special thanks to my good friends in Labuan Bajo, Agus and Jul Jehadut, whose companionship and discussions were most useful in the formulation of this chapter. All conclusions and statements in this chapter, however, are my own.

by Dean MacCannell in his book that reviews some of the contradictions and dissonances of tourism developments around the world (1992). One of the most graphic images of this "empty meeting ground" is to be found in the film "Cannibal Tours," discussed by both MacCannell (1990, 1992: 17–73) and Bruner (1988, 1991). This film is fundamentally about a missed conversation, two parts of a dialogue that never meet in the middle, between the tourists and the "toured" in Sepik villages in Papua New Guinea. What the tourists obtain from the encounter with locals, is fundamentally different from what the locals want, and indeed what the tourists imagine that the locals want. Even more radically, as Bruner argues, tourists are pursuing an image of "the other" that never existed (1996: 157–158), which means that what they are searching for, among living peoples, is a fantasy (*ibid*: 160). They move into what he calls a "borderzone," where they consume images of what they expect to find, that has been constructed for them (Bruner 1991). The locals, on the other hand enter this "borderzone" on cue, to perform for tourists, to do what is expected of them. Bruner again underscores the fact that the perceptions of the two groups are not the same, since one goes to this "borderzone" (or "empty meeting ground"), for leisure and exoticism, while the other goes for work and cash. My suggestion here is that these fundamentally different perceptions, this "missed conversation," between those involved in tourism from different sides of the "border," poses fundamental limits to tourism and what tourism can be in terms of a means for development (as hoped by local peoples and governments in the third world), and as a means for gaining knowledge and sensitivity to other cultures (as hoped by tourists from the first world).

That these ideal goals of a benevolent, sensitive tourism that promises prosperity, are stymied from the start, is due to the fact that tourism is part of a system where, MacCannell (1992: 5) suggests, the "ultimate goal of travel is to set up sedentary housekeeping in the entire world, to displace the local peoples, . . . to subordinate them . . . [and] make them the 'household' staff of global capitalists." Thus in a MacCannellian view, tourism is not about "freedom," that is opening up "limits," or making movement "limitless," but instead about "world-wide containment and control," about boundaries and restrictions, or as Alneng (2002: 484) also states, "the freedom of one [is] the confinement of an Other," making "[b]ecoming a tourist, . . . inevitably a political act." Part of the paradox of the global system, and what MacCannell calls the "double displacement of culture," is that "subjects are manipulated into acting against their own self-interest" (*ibid*: 8); this "volunteering to be exploited," MacCannell argues, "appears to be replacing visibly vicious forms" of exploitation (*ibid*: 8–9). Mowforth & Munt (1998) also analyze tourism, especially the "new tourism" (supposedly more sensitive and "sustainable") to the Third World, as reflective of power and wealth inequalities that make up the global political and economic system. The push for supposedly more "flexible" production and consumption in the post-modern economy has been due to the drive to accumulate capital, and has led to a spread of capital for investment into production and leisure travel for varied consumption into the Third World. Quoting Harvey, Mowforth & Munt (1998: 32) state that a push towards service oriented products, that are ephemeral, makes it possible to increase the amount of consumption that is needed to keep the capitalist system going. Hence it is clear that an emphasis on "consumption," as a very powerful hegemonic discourse, has shaped the development of tourism in the capitalist system. This has implications for the way that people consume "culture." Sites get shaped increasingly like shopping centres, and culture is displayed in snippets, decontextualized scraps that slowly affect the way people envision their own "culture."

The boundaries are felt very differently by the two global classes that are created in this system, the "local" and the "multinational," as MacCannell (1992) calls them, or as Bauman (2000) calls them, the "vagabonds" and the "tourists." Tourists become "contained and controlled" by a system of consumption and status that propels them to consume ever more without necessarily understanding or realizing what they are seeing or doing, while locals are constrained to be what the tourists expect them to be. Locals, if they stay "local" have the option of cashing in, to some extent, on their "locality," that is their exoticism or their servility, but once they are displaced from these localities, they are "vagabonded," and "criminalized." Bruner suggests that in the Third World tourism border zones there is an excess of "visuality," an overabundance of seeing (1996: 160), while "at home" in the First World, there is a conscious attempt "not to see" the migrants from the Third World, to keep them "distant or hidden" (*ibid*). In reality though, in both places there is an absence of sight, and an absence of a holistic image and understanding of the peoples who are encountered: "Western peoples fail to see the joy and beauty of the Other in First World space, just as they fail to see the poverty and suffering of the Other in Third World space" (1996: 161). This reminds us that sight is always selective and what is seen is always interpreted.

An additional reason for "miscommunication" that resides within tourism, I argue, has to do with the mixing of different audiences. Some attention has been paid in recent years to the important issue of "domestic tourism," and the differences that exist in a number of ways between "domestic tourists" and foreign tourists. A particularly insightful look at this is given by Bruner (2001), where he compares a number of different locations where Maasai culture is presented for tourist consumption. Where foreign tourists might be looking for the "exotic" and the "primitive," domestic tourists, as at the government museum of performing arts in Kenya, consume cultural attractions as part of the "heritage" and "tradition" of the "nation" (Bruner 2001). Displays like this, and at other miniature parks around the world (Adams 1997a; 1998; Hitchcock 1998; Oakes 1997; Pemberton 1994) are designed to build a sense of national identity, a feeling of history, heritage and pride. What I am proposing here is that if displays meant for one audience are consumed by a different type of audience, there could be room for "dissatisfaction" on the part of the consumer, who does not feel that the image s/he had of the place has been fulfilled. This might particularly be the case where foreign tourists, who are expecting something more "exotic," and perhaps a little like a "show," attend cultural displays that are in essence designed for a domestic audience.

The suggestion, therefore, is that certain forms of tourism, most especially to the "Third World," are a paradoxical meeting of different subject groups who are not only separated by class, wealth, culture and language, but very different expectations and hopes about what the relationship of tourism should be and can be to them. These paradoxical "empty meeting grounds" or spaces of the tourist "borderzones," are, MacCannell (1992: 2) suggests "not really empty" therefore, but "vibrant with people and potential and tense with repression," or as Bruner (1996: 159) argues "a creative space, a site for the invention of culture on a massive scale, a festive liberated zone," but also "sites of struggle." My intention in this chapter is to examine one of these tourist border zones or "empty meeting grounds"— the small town of Labuan Bajo in Western Flores, Eastern Indonesia. I suggest that this is a creative site of repression and struggle, which is a useful locale in which to analyze the local production of a "tourist system" over the past decade, and how this system is produced despite the "missed conversation" that is taking place between the "locals" and the "tourists." In Labuan Bajo not only do the tourists' ideals and the ideals of the locals "miss" or bypass one another within the context of producing and consuming tourist "attractions," but this "missed conversation" is also taking place among "locals" themselves, as they are represented by different groups with different interests. Part of this has to do with different ideas about what should be done, how "culture" should be displayed for tourists. The government tourism board, I will suggest here, has a particular category of tourists in mind that they wish to attract. On the one hand in their minds, the kind of displays that this category of tourists desires to see are displayed in a particular, quantifiable, packagable way. On the other hand, the only way that the Tourism Board, and other actors in official capacities in the regency, know how to "display" "culture" is to a "domestic" audience. Hence what they are creating and offering for foreign tourist consumption is subject to a "double displacement," and destined from the outset to be misinterpreted and mis-consumed, leading to a certain dissatisfaction and disorientation on the part of the tourists who do go to these "tourist" events. In addition this style of production leads to conflict with some local entrepreneurs and others tangentially involved in tourism in Labuan Bajo, who perceive tourism and their own culture in different ways.

Contestations between various groups at the local level, particularly vis-à-vis the government, have become particularly intense in Indonesia, since the opening of an era of "reformasi" with the fall of the long serving President-dictator, Suharto, in 1998. There has been a move towards a process of democratization, politically installed through regional autonomy laws in 2001, and many different undercurrents have been developing with radically different voices being raised about how things should be done. The space to demonstrate against and criticize the government with impunity has been opened in Indonesia, and people have been using this space, with differing success, to make their voices and opinions heard. Of course at times the anger of the reactions have ended up being a threat to tourism, where outbreaks of violence and at times purposeful acts of "terrorism" against tourists have resulted in loss of life and waves of fear that inhibit most travellers. It is in the face of these various threats to tourism such as the riots in Jakarta in 1998 with attacks against Chinese in particular, and the massive evacuation of foreigners from Indonesia; the massive violence in the Moluccas in 1999 and 2000; the referendum in East Timor in 1999, and the violent response of the Indonesian military and militias to the vote to secede from Indonesia; the attacks in Lombok against churches, Chinese hotels and shops in 2000, when tourists were evacuated to Bali; the "sweeping" of foreign tourists from hotels in East Java in 2001–2002 in response to the U.S. plans for retaliation and invasion of Afghanistan; the bomb in Bali in 2002 that killed over 200 people, many of them foreign tourists, the bombing of the Marriot hotel in Jakarta in 2003, and the bombing of the Australian Embassy in Jakarta in 2004, has meant that every year over the past six years there have been events that have adversely affected the idea of Indonesia as a "safe" tourism destination. In response to this there have been many attempts to do something to recharge Indonesia's highly traumatized tourism sectors. Again the "misfit" between Indonesia's boiling political environment, and the image that the government wants to present to tourists, about the existence of a cultural and natural paradise despite these problems, is a very strong comment about the kinds of paradoxes that tourism represents, which the authors' work discussed above have been highlighting.

These various misfits and contestations as they emerge within tourism will be explored in this chapter through the issue of producing and consuming culture and other "tourism products" in the town of Labuan Bajo. The two ways in which I will explore these various issues is through an exploration of various "discourses" about Bali in Labuan Bajo (as the "model" for tourism development), and the varying ideas about "sustainability" within tourism. Both issues raise the question of "limits"; how far should tourism developments be limited, controlled by the community and determined by community concerns? How far does tourism limit people's freedom? And finally, what should be the limits of tourism?

## The Gaze and Govern-mentality

> Power is no longer repressive but productive; does not say no but yes; does not prevent but invent; does not prohibit but promote; does not negate but affirm; does not annihilate but create (Caputo & Yount 1993: 6).

A particular government stand on tourism, which developed during the "New Order" (the 32 years of President Suharto's rule), is at the moment being affected by changes due to regional autonomy and democratization. At the same time there are continuities, because of the renewed emphasis on "promotion," which the various crises mentioned above have necessitated. Some of the more dramatic changes have had to do with the rising voice of the "community" to safeguard their own best interests vis-à-vis capitalist interests that were given free reign through Suharto family investment and control during the New Order. Simultaneously there has been a heightened emphasis on "locality" itself, which regional autonomy brings, and its attendant concern with particular "cultures." This has, in some instances, meant a rethinking of ideas of "culture" and "community" which were shaped and invented during the New Order; however where tourism is concerned, the past ten years, despite, and maybe to an extent because of the crises, has seen an increased emphasis on culture as an "object" to be displayed, on a national, or international stage, while simultaneously emphasising a recovered idealized past.

The processes through which people imagine themselves and reshape their lives because of tourism and government policy about tourism are discussed in John Urry's *"The Tourist Gaze."* Urry shows how the "tourist gaze" is an instrument of *control* both towards tourists and the places they visit because tourists are directed to "gaze" on particular sites, and this "gaze" has consequences for the peoples and places that are gazed upon. It could be argued that "the gaze" is a particularly apt metaphor for tourism *interaction*, or the lack of it. This is so because, despite some words spoken, often, as suggested above, the interactions tend to be "missed" and more monologic than dialogic. This means that the protagonists to the tourism encounter rely much more on their view, their sight, of each other, and what this view tells them, than on the spoken interaction. This emphasis on "gazing," as Foucault argues in his discussion of the Panoptican, becomes internalized, "the state of conscious and permanent visibility that assures the automatic functioning of power" (1979: 201), and becomes itself a very important consequence of the encounter. It is through this gaze, it could be argued, that a "gentle way" is used of "training the body . . . by the traces it leaves in the form of habits, in behaviour" (Foucault 1979: 131) as a "technique in the coercion of individuals" (*ibid*), so that they offer themselves up willingly for exploitation (see above and MacCannell 1992: 8–9). As Caputo and Yount so eloquently say about Foucault's ideas about power, "Power is no longer repressive but productive; does not say no but yes; does not prevent but invent; does not prohibit but promote; does not negate but affirm; does not annihilate but create" (1993: 6). This so aptly sums up the way that power works through the institutions of tourism, which by no means seem institutions of oppression, but instead those of "invention," "promotion" and "creativity"; institutions that say "yes."

Once this "tourist gaze" gets internalized by people, it becomes the way they see themselves and their culture. But, as many have said about tourism and the shaping of culture, it is not just about "tourism" per se, but a particular stance on "culture" that gets shaped in a national interest, to build national integration, and to create an international image. And indeed tourism development, promotion and cultural management, have been powerful tools of what Foucault calls "normalization," during the New Order era. As Picard relates (1997: 196), once the "unity" of the post-independence Indonesian nation was secure, via policies of a standard language and educational structure, standard political, administrative structures, and the acceptance of a hegemonic ideological structure (*Pancasila*),[1] which guaranteed religious belief, but also adherence to a set number of "universal" religions, then the state could comfortably acknowledge and promote "unity in diversity." But as Picard, and many other writers, have said about "culture" in Indonesia, it had to remain at the level of "display," what he calls a "showcase vision" (*ibid*: 197), and what Acciaioli (1985) calls "culture as art." This way of conceiving culture includes all the decorative and visual things that can neatly be co-opted into a touristic display of the nation: music and dance, handicrafts, costumes, architecture, as indeed they were in the pet project of Ibu Tien, President Suharto's wife, in a Miniature Indonesian Park, her answer to Disneyland, opened in the late 1970s, that has since become one of the most popular domestic tourism attractions in Indonesia (Hitchcock 1998; Pemberton 1994). However as Picard points out, this vision of culture does not include the things such as "language, religion, legal systems, economic practices, social organization, and so on — and that which sustains the sense of identity of the participants in this culture" (*ibid*: 197). In fact these things were purposefully and somewhat forcefully reshaped during the New Order, so as to be part of the standard "Indonesian culture." Thus showing how "culture" had been reduced to a touristic recipe of culture, making Indonesia ripe in the 1980s for the increased promotion of tourism.

Tourism was part of the national planning as early as 1969, where Adams states that Indonesian leaders had envisioned it as contributing to nation building through: "first as a source of foreign revenue; second, as a way of enhancing Indonesian's celebrity on the international state; and third, as a strategy for fostering domestic brotherhood" (1997: 156). As Picard (1997) relates, on the advice of the World Bank, foreign experts were commissioned to create a master plan of tourism development in Bali, which had already

---

[1] Pancasila — "five principles," is the Indonesian state ideology of: (1) Belief in God; (2) nationalism; (3) humanitarianism; (4) social justice; and (5) democracy. During the New Order there were regular "retreats" to indoctrinate these principles. This was particularly important as a buffer against proponents of radical Islam, who wanted an Islamic state, and communism, which was perceived as a major threat and led to massive killings in 1965 after a reputedly aborted communist coup.

been a favourite haunt of Dutch and American artists and intellectuals before World War II and the Indonesian fight for independence. However, it was not until the slump in oil prices in 1986 that tourism development entered centre stage in Indonesian development policy. Repelita V and VI (*Rencana Pembangunan Lima Tahun* — Five Year Development Plans numbers 5 and 6) focused extensively on tourism as a means of increasing foreign exchange earnings (Booth 1990; Sofield 1995). Major changes in the organization of investment, both foreign and domestic, occurred when the central government "de-regulated" the banking system in 1988, which led to a manifold increase of foreign and domestic investment in Bali for purposes of developing the tourism sector (Picard 1997: 203; Warren 1998a: 230). With the "euphoria" that was generated by the idea of tourism development in Bali, the restrictions that were initially imposed on tourism developments in areas outside the "tourism zones" pinpointed in the master plan, were essentially ignored, once investment was deregulated (Picard 1997: 203). As Warren says, "Despite a continuous flow of rhetoric espousing earlier commitments to 'Cultural Tourism' and 'Tourism for Bali, not Bali for Tourism,' development policy had become almost entirely geared towards gross maximisation of the number of tourists visiting the island and the income they might generate" (Warren 1998a: 231). Aditjondro (1995) details the extensive networks focusing on the first family and their cronies that controlled Balinese tourism developments in the late 1980s and in the early 1990s, while Warren (1998a), Suasta & Connor (1999), Ostrom (2000) and Picard (1997) among others, tell of some of the mostly fruitless struggles of the Balinese against these tourism developments that disenfranchised them.

These authors show how the government manipulated policies, which were always "pro-development" to the advantage of outside investors, "with little regard for local interests" (Suasta & Connor 1999: 111). For example farmers and fishing folk were, in a number of instances, strong-armed into giving up their land for luxury resort developments, that defied not only local economic interests, but local cultural and religious sensibilities.[2] Cocteau, perhaps the most critical of the writers, says that there was a "thirty year conspiracy of silence on the expropriation the island has been subject to" (2003: 42), in the name of tourism, basically due to fear on the part of some, and "euphoria" on the part of others. Cocteau tellingly shows that development through tourism became such a "hegemonic discourse," that "few . . . [were] . . . aware or even able to warn the local population about the wide-scale appropriation that was taking place" (2003: 51). "Cultural tourism" became so much the "mantra" of both central government policy towards Bali and Balinese elite hopes for the "development" of Bali, that Cocteau points out "both the proponents of the New Order's policy for Bali and its opponents used the same vocabulary of reference to push contradictory arguments" (2003: 53). As he shows ". . . it was in the name of 'cultural tourism' that the Balinese resisted 'outside'— mainly Jakartanese investments, but in its name also that investors stealthily appropriated much of the island's economy" (*ibid*). Not being able to escape the language and ideology which ensnared them, the Balinese therefore ended up being "manipulated into acting against their own self-interest" (MacCannell 1992: 8) and thus "volunteering to be exploited" (*ibid*). In the case of Bali in particular, but also true

---

[2] The most controversial project being the construction of a luxury resort villa and golf course right next to the Tanah Lot temple. See Warren (1998a, b) and Suasta & Connor (1999) for accounts.

for other places in Indonesia, this had to do with the "normalization" of "culture" as an "asset," and as an attribute of a particular group. "Culture" became the lens through which to perceive oneself politically, as a "citizen" (though "national," "regional" and "ethnic" cultures, as forms of displays at theme parks, festivals, and other events, see Acciaioli 1985; Adams 1997a; Hitchcock 1998; Pemberton 1994; Picard 1997) and economically as a "producer" (Picard 1995), to raise the "growth" of the nation's economy (Booth 1990).

This culture, though, as stated above, was a "culture" that was tamed and neutered, so as to be appropriate for the "tourist gaze." Adams (1997a) discusses the "Tourism Consciousness Campaign" of 1991 and 1992 (in conjunction with the Visit Indonesia Year 1991 and Visit ASEAN year 1992), wherein Indonesians were informed, via the media, handbooks and plaques posted in various places, of the "seven charms" (security, orderliness, friendliness, beauty, comfort, cleanliness, memories) to which they should aspire, that would be pleasing to tourists (1997a: 157). People were encouraged to think of their culture as an object for display, not only for foreign tourists, who increasingly visited and consumed Indonesia during the New Order period, but also for domestic tourists, who also increasingly consumed their own country and the myriad cultures (Adams 1998). Adams rather cynically points out that "national integration" was best promoted by the emphasis on "ethnicity" and "culture" as tourism assets, which sparked some inter- and intra-regional rivalries over who had the most "charms," and could be counted as a "*primadonna*"[3] tourist attraction, while distracting attention and resentment away from the power and wealth that was increasingly held in the centre, that is Jakarta (1997a: 175).

The push towards shaping "charms" that would please and serve tourists, was accompanied by a push to find something to show them, to think of one's culture in terms of quantifiable objects which could be displayed and admired. As mentioned earlier, the prototype for this was the Beautiful Indonesia in Miniature Park in Jakarta, which had on display all that people should think about and delineate as presentable for tourist consumption, both domestic, as those who were admiring the diversity of their nation, and foreigners, who had come to see the variety and uniqueness that was Indonesia. This rather "museum" like display, however, is not as popular with certain categories of foreign tourists as it is with domestic tourists. Western foreign tourists, "back-packers" and perhaps the "new breed" (Mowforth & Munt 1998), who claim to be "alternative," or "eco-tourists" would prefer to see the "exotic" *in situ*, in what they would prefer to think of as the "authentic" setting, and hence many places in Indonesia over the past several decades have been penetrated by adventurer tourists, and subsequently more cautious travellers who wanted to experience the "primitive" or "exotic" Indonesia. The fact that "official" Indonesian culture is not particularly of interest to tourists, can be seen in what Picard has to say about the Balinese Festival of the Arts, held every year since 1979 for one month in the Balinese provincial capital Den Pasar. The festival includes performances, seminars, parades and exhibitions. As Picard relates: ". . . even though the Bali Arts Festival was

---

[3] Adams tells how the visit of the then Minister of Tourism Joop Ave to Sulawesi particularly fueled this rivalry, since he called the Tana Toraja area the "primadonna" of South Sulawesi, while the capital city, Ujung Pandang was merely a "gateway" to Tana Toraja. Although many people did not have a clue as to the meaning of "primadonna," it spread rapidly as a term of competition between areas and businesses in South Sulawesi, and later became a term widely used within tourism throughout Indonesia (Adams 1997a).

initially presented by the governor as the perfect exponent of cultural tourism, it was never convincingly promoted on the tourist market and soon became a thoroughly Balinese affair" (1997: 202).

I suggest that the reason that tourists were not "convinced" about this festival as a highlight of Balinese culture, is because there is a fundamental misfit between the way that urban Balinese present their culture to themselves, as a consumption item, to display their nostalgia for their "culture" and their pride in their own achievements on a "national stage" (but that had already been fundamentally shaped by a "global-national" cultural style, by a shopping centre way of display), and the way that foreign tourists wanted to "consume" Bali, as a paradise of the "exotic." The Balinese have accepted the "official" version of their culture, which has evolved over the decades under Indonesian nationalism, but foreign tourists prefer a different form of display. My suggestion is that foreigners may have been happy to have consumed their own culture in this way, domestic tourists imbibing an illustration of their achievements and their place within the nation, but in a Third World destination, many of them are looking for something different. This was too similar to what they had come to expect in their own backyard. An important point to remember, however, is that it depends on the kinds of tourists (Cohen 1972), and what they are looking for (Cohen 1979b), as to whether they will be satisfied with these more "official," showcase-types of displays, or even satisfied with more "exotic," "real-life" village ritual. As a number of commentators have shown, the exotic too, can be "too" exotic (Gewertz & Errington 1989) or too long (Bruner 1995). This very much depends on who these tourists are and what they want from their trips to "exotic" places.

## Tourists and Tourism in Labuan Bajo

I was told by the government Tourism Board (Dinas Pariwisata) in Labuan Bajo when I first talked to them in 1996, that, according to them, the first tourists to visit the Manggaraian regency (*kabupaten*), were a German couple by the name of Kuhn, who arrived by sailboat in 1967, stayed with the district head for a number of days, and then traveled on to the capital of the regency, Ruteng, by horseback (Erb 2000). They were clearly "adventurous" tourists, maybe even what Cohen had referred to at around that time as "drifters" (1972), since at that time Flores was an unknown destination; there was no tourist infrastructure at all on the island, not even very many roads (still true to a considerable extent for a large part of the island in the present day), and there was nothing yet designated as "worth seeing" on Flores. However in the late 1960s there was already research being undertaken by foreign researchers on the unique *Varanus komodensis*, a large monitor lizard, nicknamed the "Komodo Dragon," located on Komodo and neighbouring islands, as well as the western shoreline of Flores. The government was becoming aware of the unique attraction that this endangered species could provide, and in the 1970s conservation efforts were started with technical aid from the FAO, to develop a National Park (Wickaksono 1996). The Komodo National Park was opened in 1980 and in 1982–1983 construction started for the government run holiday bungalows located on Komodo Island. Since 1986 Komodo Island has been a World Heritage Site, and since 1995 The Nature Conservancy (TNC) has been present in the Komodo National Park, and has been ostensibly pushing ecotourism work as an alternative livelihood for the fishing folk, who they deem as threatening the conservation of the marine and land resources within the Park.

There have been other developments in terms of the defining of "tourist attractions" over the decades on Flores, which have brought Flores to the fore as a still difficult to reach, but worthwhile destination. In 1983 the Indonesian government declared the tri-coloured lakes of Kelimutu in central/eastern Flores a national park (Schalcher 2001: 7). These volcanic lakes, which periodically change colour, have been featured a number of times in National Geographic magazine, and have become a "world-class" destination, along with the Komodo Dragons. In the late 1980s an "adventure" travel agency started bringing visitors to some of the traditional villages in Ngada, villages that seemed to be "out of the stone age," because of their traditional houses and "megalithic culture" (Cole 2003). Hence with a number of *"primadonna"* natural attractions on Flores, and some supporting cultural sites, Flores went from a peripheral unknown area, to a fairly well known, though still off the beaten track, tourist destination in less than two decades. In fact in 2002 when the Minister of Tourism, I. Gede Ardika visited Flores, he proclaimed that he wanted Flores to be part of the "golden triangle" of tourist attractions in Indonesia: Bali, Sulawesi (Tana Toraja) and Flores.[4]

With the gradual growth of Flores as an island of interest to tourists, many changes have occurred in infrastructure over the past three decades. The sector of the main Flores road between Labuan Bajo and Ruteng, went from a path, to a dirt track, to eventually paved roads in the 1990s, where dozens of buses every day now ply the route between Labuan Bajo and the capital of the Manggarai regency, Ruteng. The improvement can be best gauged in the amount of distance that one can cover in one day. In the 1980s, one was lucky to get from Labuan Bajo to Ruteng, about 120 km away, in one day, whereas now it is possible to by pass Ruteng altogether and go straight onto the capital of the next regency, Bajawa (which many tourists now do).[5] With these improvements in transportation infrastructure, it became possible also for "tour buses" to ply the roads of Flores, though they do so still with great caution and uncertainty (Figure 12.1).

Air travel also has changed quite dramatically. A small airport opened in Ruteng in the 1970s and was expanded in the late 1980s and 1990s. However, with the subsequent growth of Labuan Bajo this airport has shrunk almost into oblivion; with no more flights to Den Pasar, this airport serves only the provincial capital, Kupang. A small airstrip in Labuan Bajo opened in 1983 and is now one of the major airports on the island, with turbo propellered Fokker 27s making the trip to Den Pasar in less than two hours. However air travel into Manggarai regency has always been erratic, with flights in the 1990s very frequently being cancelled, and almost always overbooked (since fish until recently had first priority).[6] With

---

[4] Friends, who personally spoke with him about this plan, said that he had picked these three sides of a triangle specifically to promote because they were non-Muslim, and thus represented less of a threat to foreign tourists, and less of a likelihood of erupting into anti-tourist, anti-Chinese violence, such as that which had occurred in Lombok in 2000.

[5] This somewhat "dramatic" improvement in the roads meant that Ruteng, which had been the major "gateway" to western Flores in the 1980s, has been increasingly bypassed by tourists, and because of the way the "guiding" and selling of attractions works in Labuan Bajo, no one is interested in promoting Ruteng, because it is not to their advantage.

[6] People who trade in live fish, sending them by air to Den Pasar and then on to Singapore or Hong Kong, pay good money for their fishes' place on the plane. However in August 2003 I was surprised to find that things were

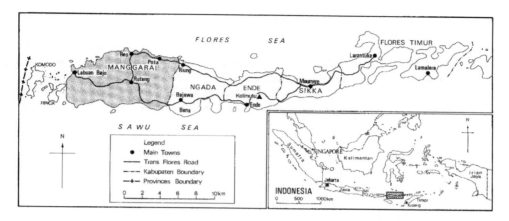

Figure 12.1: The island of flores.

the economic crisis of 1997 and 1998, the numbers of flights dropped drastically, to, at one point, only once a week. Efforts have been made to improve this situation, and a few new airlines opened, but they have closed again, and at the moment one airline services Labuan Bajo three times a week. An alternative flight route that many of the small "package groups" (of usually between 10–20 people), have used over the years, are flights into the larger town of Maumere, in eastern Flores. There continue to be flights every day, or almost every day, in and out of Maumere, though the town is a good 3–4 days trip from Labuan Bajo, over rough roads.

The more common means of tourists arriving in Labuan Bajo, from the beginning and to the present day, is by boat. PELNI, the large ships that travel around Indonesia, stop at Labuan Bajo once every two weeks, and some tourists have used this option. Much smaller, fishing style boats have brought many intrepid travellers to Flores over the years, to land in Labuan Bajo, travelling from Bali and Lombok. It was a man who originated from Lombok who had the innovative idea to start the three to four day trip from Lombok to Labuan Bajo, back in the 1990s. Tourists had the opportunity to snorkel and dive at various places along the route, enjoying the sun, sand and sea. Some of these boats are owned by local fishing folk, while others belong to people in Lombok.

Places of accommodation have also grown up over the years to support the tourist visits. The first "hotel" was opened in 1971 by a Chinese man from the town of Ende in middle Flores, who used to bring the mail by boat from Bima, on the island of Sumbawa (the next island to the west) to Flores in the 1960s and 1970s. He insists that he brought the first tourists to Labuan Bajo in 1970 (in a contradiction with the Tourism Board's story) when they asked him to take them to Labuan Bajo so they could find a means of getting

---

changing. On one occasion I witnessed the fish being bumped off the flight instead. Styrofoam containers of fish, that always in my experience had been readily loaded onto the flights in the past, were actually wheeled out, and then wheeled back again, because of the fact that the flight was full, and there was no extra weight allowance for them.

to Komodo Island. He started ferrying passengers in the 1970s on his mail run, and saw the opportunities that tourism would provide. The next private hotel to be opened was by another Chinese man, a resident of Labuan Bajo, who had been involved in the building of the government bungalows on Komodo. He was privy to the governments' plans, and realizing that tourism was a major goal, he opened a small hotel in the early 1980s. In the late 1980s, when the numbers of tourists all of a sudden exploded, many others started to enter the business. A few who opened some of the early small homestays to accommodate the increasing tourist numbers were civil servants, who had originated from the central regions of the Manggaraian regency. They had been allocated land in the 1960s or 1970s, and later used this land to accommodate tourists. Increasingly during the mid-1990s, residents who had access to land on the islands surrounding the national park, or within it, attempted to open small bungalows so that tourists could stay on these islands. However, most of these places no longer operate, since the various crises that adversely affected tourist arrivals in the later 1990s and early 21st century, have diminished the demand. At the peak of tourism arrivals, in around 1996–1997, the number of guest houses/hotels/homestays in Labuan Bajo was about 20. In 2003 the latest figure was around 15, some of which cater almost solely to locals who are travelling by ferry or ship to neighbouring islands.

A few places have been opened in an attempt to accommodate a more "elite" group of tourist. Along the beach to the south of town, a number of people have opened small hotels. One doctor from Kupang opened a hotel, which no longer operates, and never, I understand, made any money; the brother of the owner of the second hotel in Labuan Bajo opened a slightly more expensive establishment on this beach, which was until recently often the preferred place of accommodation for the regent and other more important people in the government. The prices by local standards are considered high, but by international standards very low (maybe at present around US$12–US$15). In 1997 a Chinese Jakartan, who had once been married to a Manggaraian man, opened a "starred" hotel on a peninsula to the north of Labuan Bajo, initially asking US$100 a night. They, however, subsequently dropped their rates to about US$40. In around 2001, a new hotel, now considered the classiest in Labuan Bajo, was opened on the southern beach by an Australian couple who own a hotel in Bali. They charge around US$50 for a room. Most of these "premiere" establishments are very small, having only about 6–8 rooms, while a few places in Labuan Bajo have between 20–25 rooms. The most popular tourist "hotels," located on the main street of town, charge the equivalent of about US$4–US$5 a night. There was at one time a very fierce price war in Labuan Bajo, and with the devaluation of the rupiah, after the 1997–1998 economic crisis, the prices of hotels dropped dramatically to around US$2, and have only started to slowly move up.

A few travel companies started taking an interest in arranging package tours through Flores in the late 1980s, but given the limited accommodation facilities, and the poor transportation infrastructure in Flores, the size of the groups could never be very large (between 10 and 20). In the busiest years, 1995–1997 (when according to the Tourism Board the figures for visits to the Komodo National Park were 28,275; 30,830; and 32,318 respectively, see Table 12.1) the number of travel agents that handled package tours across Flores were 15; the majority from Holland, with two from Italy, one from Austria, one from Switzerland, one from Australia. I was told at the time that the number of groups had to be carefully orchestrated, so that some travelled west, some east, and never met in

Table 12.1: Data on tourist visits to Komodo National Park.

| Year | Int'l | Domestic | Total |
|------|-------|----------|-------|
| 1989 | 7,870 | 991 | 8861 |
| 1990 | 11,840 | 1,080 | 12,920 |
| 1991 | 15,071 | 969 | 16,040 |
| 1992 | 16,553 | 678 | 17,231 |
| 1993 | 15,338 | 1,090 | 16,428 |
| 1994 | 20,421 | 2,000 | 22,421 |
| 1995 | 26,034 | 2,241 | 28,275 |
| 1996 | 29,040 | 1,790 | 30,830 |
| 1997 | 29,841 | 2,477 | 32,318 |
| 1998 | 21,547 | 2,977 | 24,524 |
| 1999 | 15,806 | 2,049 | 17,855 |
| 2000 | 11,137 | 1,313 | 12,450 |
| 2001 | 12,342 | 1,272 | 13,614 |

*Note:* Data compiled by the Tourist Board of Manggarai, Labuan Bajo, based on information gathered from the National Park Service.

one place, so that the fairly limited accommodation could provide for them. As the various crises started to hit Indonesia, starting with the riots of 1998, the package trips to Flores were dramatically affected, and in the subsequent years they dwindled to practically zero. According to the surveys done and statistics compiled by the Tourism Board of Labuan Bajo, tourists who travelled on package tours only ever accounted for about 15% of the total of foreign tourists who visited the province of Nusa Tenggara Timur (Dinas Pariwisata 1999; VI: 9), the majority of travellers to Flores being of the "individual type." That percentage, by 2003, was probably much lower. My observations support the claim that package trips have not been the most significant suppliers of tourists to Flores, although they represent a noteworthy minority in terms of the influence that they have had. This is because these tour agencies employ "professional" guides, who set a particular standard for what a guide should be, and utilize facilities of a certain quality, that places a certain expectation on accommodation facilities in Flores. They also consume culture in a particular way that, again, sets a particular standard for what a cultural "show" should look like.

In fact, in the imagination of the Tourist Board in Labuan Bajo, and indeed perhaps all government agencies associated with tourism throughout Indonesia, tourists of the package variety represent a certain goal for them.[7] These are the people that they want to attract, people that they see as having money to pay for everything to be arranged in advance for them; people who they consider to be "elites." In fact, when in 1996 I first queried the staff at the Government Tourism Board about their impressions of tourism developments in Labuan Bajo, they regretted the relative absence of "elite" tourists, who would bring more money,

---

[7] Regina Scheyvens (2002) suggests that Third World governments in general tend to assume that "luxury" tourism developments bring the greatest benefits, despite evidence that this is not the case.

Table 12.2: Data on tourist visits to Kelimutu National Park, Ende Regency.

| Year | Int'l | Domestic | Total |
|------|-------|----------|-------|
| 1988 | 2,964 | 9,909 | 12,873 |
| 1989 | 4,772 | 6,881 | 11,653 |
| 1990 | 8,524 | 7,210 | 15,743 |
| 1991 | 8,869 | 7,861 | 16,730 |
| 1992 | 10,627 | 10,641 | 21,268 |
| 1993 | 7,429 | 3,491 | 10,920 |
| 1994 | 12,231 | 7,100 | 19,331 |
| 1995 | 12,249 | 6,458 | 18,707 |
| 1996 | 12,101 | 5,959 | 18,060 |
| 1997 | 10,379 | 4,762 | 15,141 |
| 1998 | 7,272 | 4,746 | 12,018 |
| 1999 | 4,019 | 4,582 | 8,601 |
| 2000 | 2,854 | 3,313 | 6,167 |

*Note:* Based on information gathered from the National Park Service), taken from Schalcher 2001.

they perceived, into the local economy. They recognized that there were few facilities to cater to this type of tourist, but hoped in the future that Labuan Bajo would have something to offer to them. On a number of occasions members of the Tourism Board travelled to Bali and Sulawesi to do "comparative studies" of the kinds of facilities available and the types of tourists who visited. Their stated goal is to create a Labuan Bajo better designed to cater to a different category of tourist than that which has primarily been visiting it over the years. Indeed, perhaps the most "elite" variety of tourists have not really yet set foot on Flores, since the kinds of facilities they normally would expect — swimming pools, golf courses, and shopping malls — do not exist there. There are as yet no fast food outlets (as for example were opened in Lombok in the late 1990s [Bras 2000]). At the moment, as far as I know there are no concrete plans for any of these kinds of developments. However, I understand that one tourism expert from Bali, who purchased a lot of land in Labuan Bajo in the mid-1990s, has plans to someday initiate these kinds of tourism developments. The closest "elite" tourists have gotten to Flores is the cruise ships that visited the Komodo National Park in the busiest years of the 1990s. These passengers inflated the numbers of visitors to the National Park on Komodo Island, but many of them probably did not visit Flores. Comparing data collected by Stephanie Schalcher (2001) on visits to the Kelimutu National Park in eastern Flores (Table 12.2), (which is inland and cannot be visited by cruise ship), with data visits to the Komodo National Park (Table 12.1), suggests a more accurate picture of the numbers of tourists who probably visited the island of Flores itself, in the 1990s (more likely to be closer to her figures).

The primary type of tourist, therefore who has visited Labuan Bajo and other areas in Flores, and utilized the various services that are available (accommodation, transportation, small shops, the vegetable and fruit markets and the like), are "independent," back-packers, "adventurous" kinds of tourist, who are willing to put up with the limitations of facilities in

Labuan Bajo and the rest of Flores, to see something new and interesting, and, of course, because they are cheap. However, one man I spoke to working in the Tourism Board in the earlier years had in fact commented that he felt that it was a mistaken idea that "back-packers" didn't have money. Many of them had enough money to hire automobiles to traverse the island of Flores, which was not a cheap trip (between US$35 and US$45 a day to hire a car and driver),[8] and hence, he argued, it should be more widely recognized that they did have money, and could make substantial contributions to the economy. According to the Tourism Board's survey of 150 visitors to Labuan Bajo in August 1996, the majority (78%) were between 21–40 years old; most were university students, teachers, engineers or other professions. About 49% were men and 51% women. The nationalities of respondents to their survey were: English-32, German-29, French-28, Dutch-14, Italian-9, Swiss-6, Danish-6, American-5, Australian-4, Canadian-4, and a sprinkling of other European nationalities (Dinas Pariwisata 1999: VI: 14–16). The majority stayed in Labuan Bajo for between 2 and 5 days (*ibid*: VI: 18). I found that the profiles of people that I have spoken to over the years since 1996, have been consistent with this. Many of them are on "around-the-world" trips of six months to a year, and have taken off time from work, because of flexible work options in some European countries, or have quit their jobs, expecting that they would be able to find another when they returned. They are certainly not "drifters," in my assessment, but have set plans and goals, with a constant concern to schedule their time and money in the most efficient way possible.

There are basically two "types" of tourists, then, who come to Flores and have an influence on the development of various facilities these. First there are the "around-the-world," often professional or student travellers, who want to arrange their trip to and around Flores independent of a fixed schedule set by a travel agent, though they may purchase set "trips" for a number of days, like overland trips by car to Kelimutu, or a boat trip to the islands of Komodo and Rinca. Second there are the tourists who travel in small package groups of about 10–20 people, who often go for about a month to Indonesia, and travel across Flores for 5–7 days, visiting all the highlights, and being taken care of by both a tour leader (often from their own country) and a local guide. There are different types of "guides" who cater to these two types of tourist. The tour groups have someone who is a "professional" guide, who has a license, and training in a tourism academy. These people, in my knowledge are all men and although they are not exactly "pathfinders" (see Cohen 1985) they have the express task of making the island of Flores as interesting as possible for these tourists. One of my friends, who is this kind of guide, prides himself on having made his tour agency, based in Holland, extend the Flores part of their trip for an extra day, because of all the interesting things that he was adding to the trip. Their counterparts, the tour leaders (often taking on the role of "animators," see Cohen 1985), have often been women as well as men, and have the power to decide whether or not they are satisfied with the local guide. The independent tourists will not usually have the option of getting a "professional" type guide, though some of them have been freelance at various times. Often the "guides" who facilitate the journeys of the independent tourists are "wild guides" (see Adams 1997b;

---

[8] It is impossible to hire a car without a driver on Flores; since the roads are very dangerous, no owner would dream of renting their car to someone who had not had experience driving on Flores.

Bras 2000) without a license, and often without much education. Depending on them and the people who are using their services, they may actually not "guide" the tourists at all, but only "facilitate" their access to others who can transport them to where they want to go.

These two "types" of tourist perceive and consume Flores very differently. The "package group" tourists know they are being taken care of at every move, and so do not have the anxieties about arrangements and prices that independent tourists often have. Independent tourists, on the other hand, sometimes arrive in Flores rather traumatized by the aggressive selling that they experience in places further west in Indonesia, and I have noticed they react to this in a number of ways. Either they are reluctant to buy anything, and follow closely their guide books, to tell them what to do, or they retaliate with aggressive bargaining themselves towards the local vendors, sometimes trying to haggle over items that are actually not negotiable (like cigarettes), because they feel as if all the prices have been marked up in their honour. This haggling is often done to the point that it exasperates, irritates and confuses local people who are trying to sell them something. The package tourists who are on a set schedule know that things will be arranged for them, and that if they witness a "cultural show" it is something that is specially arranged for them. Some of the independent tourists will want to see these cultural displays as well, but often they will be turned off by the price, and think the display is not worth the cost. They often like to wander off on their own, walking or hiking to beaches or scenic sights without a guide, or even as one couple I met, renting a motorbike and daring to ride off into the interior to experience some kind of adventure and see the country side on their own. This couple also met one lad, a "guide" of sorts, who took them to his own village and were thrilled to have witnessed the sacrifice of a chicken. These kinds of tourists often look for spontaneous adventures such as this, and are not as interested in the set schedules or the fixed shows. However even many of the independent travellers, as I have suggested above, are pressed for time, and they will rent available transportation, for as cheaply as they can, to take them overland to see Kelimutu, villages in Ngada and other sites in the east. They may return to Labuan Bajo and go back to Bali/Lombok by boat, fly out of Maumere or go to some other island by boat or plane.

Despite the reality in terms of numbers, and facilities, as I have suggested above, the kind of tourist that is most uppermost in the minds of the government Tourism Board in Labuan Bajo is an "elite," luxury tourist, who demands the most extravagant of facilities, as are found on Bali, and because of whom the Balinese landscape and society were rearranged in the 1990s (see above). These kinds of tourists have not yet even materialized on Flores. The closest to this "elite tourist" that visits Flores is the small package tourist, who it is presumed by most people, has more money than the independent travellers. Although they do not actually spend very much money themselves on Flores, the money that they pay for their trip is used to pay for the better hotels available, and the cultural displays given by various cultural groups found in the Labuan Bajo vicinity (Erb 2000, 2001b). The least desired, but in fact the most numerous type of tourist are the independent travellers, who it is assumed have the least amount of money, and will give the least benefit to the economy of Flores, but who often end up contributing far more to its development at the local level then other types of tourists, because of their direct interactions with locals (Oppermann 1993). Another category of tourist that I have not yet discussed is the "domestic tourist," who, it can be seen by comparing Tables 12.1 and 12.2, visit the Komodo National Park in far smaller proportions, in comparison to the Kelimutu National Park. In many respects domestic tourists are not even recognized as a particular factor within tourism developments in Labuan Bajo, although they figure in the statistics and a small part of the report of the Tourism Board (Dinas Pariwisata 1999). However, as I have discussed elsewhere (Erb 2000), the archetype for a "tourist," particularly in Labuan Bajo, is the foreign, "white" tourist, and this is the prototype that fires the imagination of people in the tourism sector and Government Tourism Board in Labuan Bajo. And yet, at the same time, the way that the Tourism Board and other government agencies go about trying to cater to and attract tourists, shows that in many ways their ideas of what tourists want is geared towards a "domestic audience." It must be understood here that "domestic tourists" also figure into an "elite" category, those from the major cities, those with money to travel and indulge. Often the most widely travelled Indonesians are those in business, or in the government and they will demand the best types of facilities, if they can get them (see also Booth 1990).

The fundamental misfit, between the kinds of tourists that actually come to Labuan Bajo, and the kinds of tourists that the Tourism Board wishes would come to Labuan Bajo, can best be seen in the totally different "discourses" that revolve around the idea of "Bali." In the Tourism Board's imagination, and in their plans, Bali figures prominently as to what they would like Flores to be, what they would like to have Labuan Bajo achieve. This is partially to do with the amounts of money that they see revolving around Bali, but also partially illustrates, what one friend called a "photocopy" tendency in Indonesia. One can see this in the way that people are reluctant to serve local food in Flores, for example, but instead serve Javanese, Chinese or Western Food, that which has been proven to work elsewhere. People are afraid to try out something new to offer to tourists, not recognizing that the large majority of the kind of tourists that come to Flores in fact want to try something new.

While Bali represents everything the Tourism Board wants Flores to be, Bali represents to a large majority of the tourists who come to Flores, what they want to get away from. When asked what they like about Flores, or why they came to Flores, many people told me they wanted to escape Bali, which is too overcrowded with aggressive vendors and aggressive tourists. Bali represents "tourism" in Indonesia to the tourists who want to distinguish themselves as "travellers" (Gewertz & Errington 1989; Mowforth & Munt 1998). Thus, one can see the irony here of a "missed conversation" between the actual tourists who come to Flores, and the people who are partially responsible for shaping the way Flores is to be developed for tourists.

## Planning for Tourism: Elite Tourists or Backpackers?

Apart from the Tourist Board's idea about tourists being fundamentally at odds with the majority of tourists that actually appear in Labuan Bajo, there have been fundamental disagreements over the years between people associated with tourism business, between them and the Tourism Board, and among themselves. This, to simplify the matter, has to do with the vision of tourism developments that they felt would be most appropriate for Labuan Bajo, centring on the different kinds of tourists that they hope will visit.

In one of my earlier trips to Labuan Bajo, inquiring about tourism, I had the opportunity to speak with Haji Abdul,[9] someone who had a different idea about tourists and tourism developments than the Tourism Board. Originating from a different island, he had lived in Labuan Bajo since the early 1970s, taking a wife there. When tourism started to gain the attention of the government and local entrepreneurs, he bought some beautiful beach-front property about 15 minutes by boat from Labuan Bajo and built some simple bungalows. He told me of his encounter with another man, Haji Mohamed, also originating out of the area, who bought up a lot of land in Labuan Bajo in hopes of the future tourism boom. Mohamed had hotels in Bali and was waiting for the time when Labuan Bajo would fulfil its potential. The two, though both outsiders, and both hoping to get profit from Labuan Bajo's tourism potential, had very different ways of thinking about tourism. Abdul, at first close to Mohamed, later became alarmed at his plans, and reported him to the regent (of the 1988–1998 period),[10] warning him not to let Mohamed get permission to use the land he had bought in Labuan Bajo. Abdul frustrated another land deal of Mohamed's, when he told the people who were ready to sell their land that they would end up as "sweepers in their own land in the future," and that he did not want to see these people "go crazy with regret." Mohamed wanted luxury hotels and elite tourists, Abdul knew the danger to the local people of this kind of tourism development.

Abdul was aiming for a different type of tourist and a different type of tourism development. He was the one, he informed me, who introduced the small boat trips from Lombok to Labuan Bajo in 1991, that subsequently became a popular way to travel to and fro, for the "back-packer" type of tourist. At the time he spoke to me, two operators ran boats from Lombok to Flores and back, using boats owned by a number of owners. Abdul himself retreated from the business, because, he regretted his idea, once he saw how these trips contributed to a problematic development of tourism in subsequent years. The guiding of tourists in Labuan Bajo became just the sale of "trips" to and through the town — east to Kelimutu, and west back to Lombok — instead of giving the tourists an opportunity to see anything of interest in the area. The reason, he said, was because of the system of "commission" on which the guides worked. The long trip, from Labuan Bajo to Moni (at the foot of Kelimutu), by automobile, and the long trip from Labuan Bajo to Lombok by boat, were substantial outlays of money on the part of the tourist (hundreds of thousands of rupiah). The guide who brought the tourist to the automobile or boat owner stood to gain 10% commission on the price that the tourist paid. It was therefore worth their while to sell this kind of "product" to the tourist. Trips around Labuan Bajo, to villages in the neighbouring hills or down the nearby river, was not worth promoting for the freelance guides, since these were inexpensive trips and would yield small commissions.

[9] This is a pseudonym. All names have been changed, except where they are a matter of public record. It also needs to be understood that what I say about "Haji Abdul" in this chapter is only in the context of his opinions on tourist developments that I personally heard from him. He is a very controversial figure in Labuan Bajo, and what is said here does not accurately reflect him as a person, or how he is viewed by others.

[10] This regent was very against the purchase of land by this man, and tried to stop him. The next regent however ended up being, apparently, sponsored by him during the election, and has therefore been facilitating his re-entrance into Labuan Bajo.

Abdul, on the other hand, wanted to see tourism develop in a different way. He wanted to see real benefit for the local people in the visits of foreign tourists. He himself, was trying to open a trip to a local village located on a beautiful river (where, incidentally one of his wives lived). Local guides would not sell it, because he only was charging 15,000 rp and the 10% commission wouldn't give them very much. The trip, however, he was certain would be pleasing to the tourist. The tourist would be brought up the river by canoe, to visit the village. The river trip itself was a beautiful experience, he said, with lots of wildlife. At the village, as lunch was being prepared, the traveller could wander around and see how people lived, and play with the children. After lunch a trekking trip would be planned to visit a nearby lake, where many animals came to drink, wild buffalo, deer, lots of birds and even the chance Komodo dragon. It was a trip that would be a very satisfying experience for the nature lover, and Haji Abdul was convinced of its worth.

Not only had Haji Abdul had disagreements with other tourism entrepreneurs, and with local guides, but he also had had a run-in with the Head of the government Tourism Board. He had criticized the staff at the Tourism Board for not providing adequate information for tourists, and not trying to promote the numerous "attractions" to be seen locally, such as the river village, or the local lake. He had been told by the Head that the locals were "not ready" for this kind of thing; that they were not ready for the visits of tourists. Abdul was incensed at this kind of reply. What was needed? What could be readied? It was not as if they had to build any specific recreational sites or anything, he said to me. It was clear to my mind that there was again a different impression of what kinds of tourists would and should be coming to Labuan Bajo, and what they wanted to see. The Tourism Board staff had an image in their mind of "elite" tourists, and the attractions of a place like Bali, or even Europe and America, where there were many sophisticated and varied things to see, both cultural and natural. In comparison to a place like Bali, Flores would always come up short in their mind. They did not see the "back-packer" tourist as a desirable kind of tourist to attract to Labuan Bajo, so what was of interest to backpackers, was not the kind of thing that the Tourist Board at the time wanted to promote.

## Tourist Attractions of Manggarai

The tourism board is always going about counting the various different attractions that there are to be seen in Manggarai, but actually everything is a possible attraction (one tourist guide, Ruteng, 2000).

I would much prefer to have the group come to Flores first, then I have lots of things to show them, coffee, bananas, rice, how these things grow, how people live here. If they have been to other islands already, and seen the way Indonesians live, Flores will not be so readily saleable, so interesting to them, and we can't keep them here so long (one tourist guide, Ruteng, 2000).

The Komodo National Park is our primadonna — (representative from the Kupang Provincial Tourism Office, at a meeting December 18, 2001).

When I first went to the Tourism Board Office in Labuan Bajo in 1996, to ask about tourism in Manggarai, I was told that there were 128 tourist attractions in Manggarai regency, the vast majority of them being "natural" attractions. The staff there were proud of the number of natural attractions, the *primadonna* of which was, of course, the Komodo Dragon, while they were a bit embarrassed about the paucity of attractions of a cultural nature. The staff were critical of the people of Manggarai who had "lost their culture," and therefore had lost their attractiveness for tourists, while they praised the people of Ngada, who still had their traditional houses, a number of villages in Ngada being the major cultural attractions on Flores (see Cole 2003). In reality people of Manggarai had not "given up" their culture, of course, but they weren't as aesthetically displayable as Ngada folk. There is among the civil servants working in the Tourism Board, as well as quite a number of other "middle class" Manggaraians, a very strong "discourse of the vanishing" (Ivy 1995). Things hadn't vanished as much as they were just not always readily displayable for tourists, and therefore could not be counted as an "asset."

This became particularly clear at one meeting that I attended in December 2001, when a representative from the Provincial Tourism Board in Kupang had come to Labuan Bajo to discuss with the Tourism Board staff, and the local branch of the Indonesian Guide's Association, on how to coordinate the provincial and regional goals in tourism planning. The main concern of the Provincial Tourism Board was to set up a "calendar of events," which could be publicized widely so that internationally every tourist agent would know when certain events were going to take place in various places in the Nusa Tenggara Timur Province. He was especially keen for inputs from the local tourism entrepreneurs and the Tourism Board, so as to construct this calendar, which could be replicated year in and year out. Teams were being sent to all of the regency capitals within the province to gather data about annual attractions that could be added to this calendar of events. Clearly the Provincial Tourism team was hoping to be able to imitate the kind of "calendar of events" which exist in all first world countries, compiled by tourism boards, and which also is done in Bali. The attendees to this meeting, in particular the guides, who had "practical" experience on the ground, were very concerned about this kind of plan however. There were a number of issues that they brought up to query it, and it was clear that the main problem was a fundamental misfit between "life" in Manggarai, and "display" for tourists. "Life" goes on in a manner which is hard to pin down. For example, if a date was set for a particular ritual, some worried, it would be very hard to stick to it. Decisions about timing were not made by one person, or from the top down, in a Manggaraian village, but by everyone. If a big ritual was to be held that would have something interesting for tourists to see, such as the famous Manggaraian whip games called *caci*, it would be impossible to force villagers to put this on every year. *Caci* is only done for weddings, and the New Years' ritual if the harvest is good. Also major Church events, such as an ordination, or the opening of a new Church, would normally have *caci* games sponsored by the community. Additionally major government events, such as receiving important guests, and of course the National Day celebrations, would always have *caci*. But outside of National Day, it was impossible to pin down a date for a *caci* game. That is why various different cultural groups had started to traffic in displays of *caci* for tourists, which could be ordered in advance, or even put together on the spot if there were enough participants available. But these displays of *caci* were not "ritual," they were just that, "displays," shadows of the real game, and critically viewed by many. In addition, of course, it is quite expensive for tourists to "order" these special displays, and many tourists, especially the individual ones, as mentioned above, will not do it.

The concern with setting up a "calendar of events," is clearly geared towards a "standardization" process, "normalizing" the times and ways that particular rituals and other events could be presented. It also had to do with pinpointing "assets" in a quantifiable and orderly manner, that could be displayed, in a more festival-like style. There have been a number of attempts to organize festivals in Manggarai over the past several years, in an attempt to cater to this particular image of tourism displays. Except for the festival of 2000 (see below), which was organized by Haji Abdul, these recent festivals have always been an attempt to mix local ritual events with tourism displays. A look at these "festivals" underscores the issues raised above, that if an event is a ritual of the village, trying to sell it to tourists is going to cause major contestations at the local level. It is also going to cause problems of consumption. How are these events to be consumed, and do the kinds of tourists that come to Manggarai want to witness or partake in these kinds of events?

By the year 2000, with a number of crises already wreaking havoc on Labuan Bajo tourism, the regent of Manggarai approached a number of government civil servants associated with tourism and handicrafts to try and make some plans to attract the tourists back. One of these civil servants suggested approaching Haji Abdul, well known for his good ideas, to help organize some kind of event that would attract tourists. Abdul responded that since tourist arrivals were at a very low point, they would have to do something that would be really surprising to attract attention and get people to come to Flores. So Haji Abdul took advantage of this opportunity to promote his trip to his wife's village and the nearby lake, by suggesting a cross-country race, where the participants would go around the lake. The prize, he said, would be the pulling attraction; they should set it at 100 million rupiah (at the time around US$10,000). The staff from the Regent's office were rightly shocked, since with the economic crisis still affecting the country, the government did not have that kind of money for a prize. However Abdul was clever and devised a scheme whereby no one could actually win the prize.[11] So the idea of a tourist promotion festival, "Komodo Flores Big Promo Year 2000," with a number of different competitions, a canoe race, a cross-country race, and cultural displays of various kinds, was born.

Despite advertisements in Lombok and Bali, the cross-country race with its grand prize did not attract very many tourists. A few signed up (and paid their 10,000 rupiah registration fee), but dropped out when they saw the meager numbers. In the end only two tourists took part. The majority of participants were local guides, about 30 in all, who were pressured into participating by the organizing committee so they would gain the experience and know the local landscape, that is the river village and nearby lake, a hike of about 5 hours round trip. Abdul saw this as an opportunity for local guides to be introduced to the beauty of the place, even if there were practically no tourists.

---

[11] The prize was not given to the person who finished first, but would only be given to the person who finished the race in the exact time, to the second, which was determined before hand. They sealed up the time in a coconut and opened it on the last night of the festival, after the race. Not surprisingly no one had finished the race to the exact second which they had pre-determined. Second prize, 2 million rupiah, would go to the person who finished the race within 10 minutes of the time determined. Third was within 20 minutes. Some one won third prize, which was one million rupiah (a far cry from 100 million), about US$100.

The low level of tourist attendance for the whole three-day event, since there were very few tourists in Labuan Bajo at the time, meant that the government itself did not take the affair entirely seriously. Everything started late, not according to the program that was distributed, so that the few tourists who did show up left a number of events in disgust and disappointment. The location of events was also regularly changed, and in general the whole three day event had the air of disorganization. What struck me as being particularly amusing was that even though the three day program of activities was organized specifically for tourists, no one involved in most of the organization or the announcing of various activities spoke in English. When the rules were read for the race, or the prizes distributed finally at the last days' "rama-tama" dinner, no one was designated to tell the two tourists involved what was going on. Speeches that were made, etc., were all in Indonesian, and it was clearly more a government affair than a tourist affair. The sense of misfit was strong and the cultural miscommunication was palpable. I got the sense that though the government really wanted to do something about tourism, they really did not know how to go about it.

Indeed on many occasions since then numerous people have criticized the government Tourism Board in Labuan Bajo on exactly these issues. Few who work there were ever specially trained in the field of tourism. Though some acknowledge that the current Head is far superior to the last Head (whom I met in 1996), it is still pointed out that he is not a "professional" in terms of tourism, because he has not had the training or any experience. Some people have commented that the only thing the staff does is count the hotels and restaurants in Manggarai, (with all the chairs, beds, etc.), in addition to all of the tourist "objects," and then catalogue them and submit the information to their superiors. To be fair, there has been considerable effort in the past years to do various things; they have opened information kiosks, there are plans to open a small museum, construction is underway for a government run hotel and restaurant, and meetings and seminars have been held for people involved in the tourism sector. There is criticism, however, as to how appropriate or useful these activities are for actually promoting tourism in Manggarai.

If the "Big Promo Year 2000" was a tourism event designed for local sensibilities, the same can be said of "Penti Manggarai 2001," which was held a year later. I have already written on this event, and analyzed it as basically a "domestic tourism" festival (Erb 2003). What I want to mention here is that as a local event it was the source of a considerable amount of contestation, precisely because it was presented only incompletely as a "ritual," (Penti is the ritual of the "New Year"), but more as a tourism display. But this tourism display was not meant for international tourists, even though there were some in attendance, precisely again because it was organized as a government style event, with speeches and special welcoming of particular VIPs, and of course everything was in Indonesian. It was sponsored by a Manggaraian organization interested in culture that is based in Jakarta, and the people who designed the event, were mostly expatriate Manggaraians, who had a different understanding of their culture than those still living in Manggarai. It was a massive event attended by people from all over the regency. As a tourism event, it attracted considerable numbers of guides and international tourists from Labuan Bajo, into the capital of Ruteng where it was held. It was not designed as an international tourism festival, however, even though the "opening" of the event took place in the Miniature Indonesia Park in Jakarta, and then was "brought" to Manggarai in later months. Apart from the main ritual event, there were "shows" every night of different types of Manggaraian dances and songs, and even a theatrical show, which was a true "showcasing" of Manggaraian cultural offerings as "assets."

Partially in response to this event, the following year, a man from a rival village, planned another great ritual event in an attempt to outshine the "Penti of 2001" However cognizant of the criticism towards Penti 2001, he had every intention of doing this ritual in an entirely "traditional" manner, that is, it was not to be full of showcased cultural displays. Another issue that he and some of his associates and advisors were critical of in the Penti ritual was the "protocol" of the Penti events. At every stage, the ritual of Penti in Ruteng was carefully introduced and explained to the attendees, even though the majority of the people who attended were Manggaraians. The implication was that people did not know or understand their own culture (in fact one of the stated aims of the Penti 2001 event was to suspend cultural loss). The organizer of the ritual of 2002, entitled *"Wajo Mora Empo Pahu"* ("to fulfil the promise of Grandfather Pahu"),[12] wanted his ritual to proceed as it normally would in a village context, without anyone explaining it to the audience. More forthrightly than the Penti ritual of 2001, however, the organizer of *Wajo Mora* had every intention of promoting his ritual as a tourism event. He hired a Balinese consultant, who was famous for promoting Balinese rituals to tourists, and approached the Minister of Culture and Tourism for his "seal of approval." What this included was asking for the designation of his village as a *"desa wisata"* (tourist village) and also the explicit invitation of the Minister himself to bestow this honor to the village.

This ritual, which took place on June 15, 2002, had its own controversy. There were those who thought it was totally inappropriate for a private citizen to invite a Minister to visit his village. The necessary facilities and preparations to accommodate a visitor of this calibre set the sub-district head (*camat*) and the people of the village into a whirlwind of activity, especially since the head was only informed one week before the visit. This, it appears, was primarily because of various conflicts within the wider community. Many did not believe that the Minister would come, and others, though perhaps believing it, wanted to see the event fail, because of their rivalry with the organizer. Hence, though the invitation was accepted formally in April, the news did not officially get relayed to the *camat* until June. The sub-district head was obviously very displeased, and the village leader (*kepala desa*) and staff, unsupportive of their fellow villager, were also not at all happy with the arrangements, which they were forced to be involved in.

Others, however, felt that in the present era of democratization and regional autonomy in Indonesia, this was a very positive step to make, that is inviting an important person to visit a village. Although they may not have agreed with other things about the ritual, they were very pleased that it had taken place. "History has been made," one informant commented, although he had his own reservations about the event, and refused to attend. Some criticism, of this individual and others, was levied at its cultural inauthenticity, even though the stated aim was to be as culturally authentic as possible. One reason for this was the nature of the ritual itself. The event, clearly designed initially as a tourism promotion event, had the requisite *caci*, whip games, which they knew tourists would like. This was not a "display," however, as it had been in Jakarta at the opening of Penti there, or at the "Big Promo Year 2000" event, but was the "real" thing. A guest team arrived two days

---

[12] Wajo means "to make," mora means "to disappear." The ritual was intended to "make disappear" all of the difficulties that had occurred to the descendents of Empo (grandfather) Pahu because the promise he had made over a century ago had not been fulfilled.

before the peak of the ritual, (which was the sacrifice of a "red" buffalo, to fulfil the vow made 150 years ago by Grandfather Pahu), and "fought" with the host team in the village for two full days. However, the play of *caci* did not belong to a ritual such as this, these critics claimed, since the ritual was actually an admission of wrong-doing (since the vow should have been fulfilled many years earlier). *Caci*, on the other hand, is appropriately played only at "happy events."

As a tourism event, the ritual was quite successful, but its organization, with which I was peripherally involved, shows again many misconceptions about various kinds of tourists and what they want. Since the man who was leading the ritual asked for a Balinese consultant to advise him, the kind of things that were originally planned, and the kinds of prices that he was asking for were those that one would find in more luxurious tourism in Bali. The price that the consultant had suggested that the organizer ask for the five day event, was US$1500 per participant, and this did not include airfares. They were hoping that about 100 people would attend. When I asked a tour leader friend of mine who had brought tours to Flores to comment on the plans, she was shocked at the price, but also critical of the plans. For the five day event, there was not enough variety to please the kind of tourists who would pay that kind of price. When eventually the plans were amended in accordance with her and my suggestions, she ended up bringing a group of about eight to the village. My friend, the tour leader, told the organizer that her group would not pay the kind of fee they were looking for, but that they would make a contribution to the ritual. This inspired the organizer to include them, just as would be the case with any attendees who would come with their obligatory contributions. They were incorporated as "*panga Europa*," (the European lineage), as if they were actually part of the village family. This was also in line, he argued, with the politics of his ancestors, who became powerful kings because of their diplomatic ties with many other clans, and their ways of absorbing foreigners into their village network through kinship and marriage ties. In this way his interpretation of the history of his clan (also a contested matter, see Erb 1997) could be justified by the way he handled the tourists who came to attend the event, and the past, as it were, was repeated and integrated into the present.

## The Future and Limits of Tourism in Labuan Bajo

Despite setbacks in the numbers of tourists that have visited Indonesia, and specifically Flores, over the past five years, people in the government have total confidence that tourism arrivals will recover, because of the *primadonna* nature of Komodo Island as a tourism attraction. However there has been a recent move to "improve" the management of the Komodo National Park, in order to better serve the kinds of tourists that the Tourism Board is hoping to attract, and this has been rather enthusiastically embraced by a number of people within several government sectors. The proposal is one put forth by the TNC (The Nature Conservancy), who as mentioned in the beginning of this chapter, have been active in conservation efforts in the National Park since 1995. The TNC's *modus operandi* is actually to buy the "Earth's Last Great Places," but since Indonesian law would not allow them to do that (Dhume 2002), they have come up with an alternative plan to co-manage the park, with the National Parks, and a Malaysian born tourism expert-businessman, who had already made himself a rather controversial figure about 10 years earlier, by purchasing from local poor fishing folk, a lot of land around Labuan Bajo. The company that TNC and this businessman have formed, called P. T. Putri Naga Komodo (The Dragon Princess of Komodo Pte Ltd), have a plan to manage the Komodo National Park more like the Galapagos Islands, which has an entrance fee of US$100. Government officials, and a number of others involved in tourism in Labuan Bajo were treated to a "comparative study" trip to the Galapagos, in order to convince them of the benefit of modelling the Park after that famous place. In September 2003, the entrance fee to the Park was raised from about US$2 to US$30 as a way of putting into place an incremental rise in the entrance fee. Local people within the tourism sector find this move very disturbing, since, the majority of tourists who go to Labuan Bajo, the independent traveller types, are bound to find these higher entrance fees inhibiting, and may in fact, decide to give Komodo, and hence Labuan Bajo, a miss in the future. In addition there has been massive protest about the heavy handed approach the TNC has taken towards local fishermen, to stop them using what they consider destructive fishing methods within the Park. About a dozen people have been killed or wounded by the TNC and National Park patrols since 1995, when the TNC started to patrol the park.

This inevitably brings to my mind the question of "sustainability" within tourism developments, a highly slippery concept (Mowforth & Munt 1998). The TNC claim to be concerned with conservation and sustainability, and say they encourage local community participation. But as Mowforth and Munt show, "participation" takes place at many levels, and many local people in Labuan Bajo and the surrounding islands, feel as if they have been sidelined by the TNC and the National Park.[13] It is possible to see that there is a particularly sharp division in the way that people think about "sustainability"; sustaining what and for whom, is indeed the question that arises in my mind in the context of the contestation over tourism developments in the Komodo National Park and elsewhere in Manggarai. Luxury tourism developments, of the kind which the TNC and their joint business venture with the tourism expert are planning, would disenfranchise not only the local fishing folk, but local guides working in tourism, who cater to independent/backpacker tourists. This would certainly limit the participation of local people in tourism and also limit the kinds of tourists who would have access to the Komodo National Park.

If the Tourism Board continues to imagine a tourism that is different from the tourism that actually exists in Labuan Bajo and elsewhere in Manggarai and the wider province, this will continue to create misfits in the kinds of attractions that are created and promoted in the regency. It may also very well end up shaping a very different kind of tourism in the future from what currently exists, allowing outside, luxury investments to control and change Komodo and Flores, as they have done to Bali. I hope that I have illustrated in this chapter that different understandings of tourism can end up being a mismatch and can result in limiting the benefits of any type that tourism is supposed to have for the local people who are encouraged to live off of it, or the tourists who are encouraged to seek and enjoy.

---

[13] This is particularly so on the islands within the Park, as had been shown already by the research of Walpoole and Goodwin (2000) in a study done in 1996, which indicated that leakage of tourism benefits was very high overall, and that the islanders in the Park were particularly marginalized in tourism developments. This study was done before the TNC influence in the Park had grown strong.

Chapter 13

# Dongba Art in Lijiang, China: Indigenous Culture, Local Community and Tourism

Takayoshi Yamamura

## Introduction

This examines the current status of the preservation of intangible resources in World Heritage cities and the use thereof in tourism with specific reference to culture of the *Naxi* people in Lijiang, China. The study will also consider the role played by local communities as the successors to, and perpetuators of, such intangible cultural resources. As a specific case in point, the study examines the old town of Lijiang, China. In particular, traditional handicraft techniques are looked at and on-site interviews with local manufacturers of handicraft items are reported, in order to illustrate the processes involved in the creation of new tourism-related merchandise in accordance with traditional handicraft techniques. In light of these findings, some proposals concerning the roles of local government and regional communities in perpetuating their intangible cultural assets will be presented.

Through focusing on the production of "tourist art" and this specific case study, the aim of this chapter is to discuss the situation, (as it existed in 2003), regarding the protection and tourist use of intangible resources in world heritage cities and communities, and to illustrate the issues which face local communities in coping simultaneously with both sustaining and exploiting tourist use of these resources. Culture that is adapted for tourist use, or existing culture that is stimulated by tourism to be renewed for tourist use, is known as "touristic culture" (Picard 1990). Within this touristic culture, "tourist art" refers to folk art (works of art and craft which have been developed within and have real relevance for the way of life of a specific cultural or ethnic group) that is produced for and marketed to tourists (Graburn 1976). Consequently, both culture and art are commodified to fit into the perceived needs of their own the visiting tourists, who are often time constrained and not immersed in the culture of those they visit. Therefore, almost by definition, compromises emerge in the presentation of culture and art, and arguably new meanings may emerge.

## The Research Context

As UNESCO and other international organizations have pointed out, the number of tourists visiting world heritage cities and communities has increased in recent years following their listing as world heritage sites, and the question of how local communities and administrations can control the impact of this phenomenon is becoming a major issue. In other words, the issue is how to manage the conservation and succession of traditional culture, while at the same time promoting sustainable tourism use (Office of the UNESCO Regional Advisor for Culture in Asia Pacific 2000). However, discussion of such issues thus far has been almost entirely confined to tangible property listed as world heritage such as buildings, monuments and sites (physical cultural properties, real estate and so on). On the other hand, there has been insufficient discussion about the issue of intangible cultural heritage, which is passed down from earlier generations for each specific region. Indeed, at the present time the body of research available on this aspect is notable for its comparative absence.

Recognizing this situation, Yamamura (2002) and Drdácký (2002) reported the case of old towns in Asia and Europe listed as world heritage sites, where the outward appearance and scenery of designated buildings is carefully planned and conserved by the nation, but where the population structure and people's lifestyle patterns have been drastically transformed by the rise in tourism. Consequently significant and far reaching changes in traditional culture have taken place to the point where its very existence has been threatened. As a result, they express concern about heritage preservation policies that are skewed towards physical structures. Taking this situation into account, it could be claimed that there is an urgent necessity to examine and advance methods of "holistic heritage preservation" that attribute

■ : Lijiang Naxi Autonomous County

Figure 13.1: Location of Lijiang. *Source:* Map courtesy of the author.

a higher importance to intangible heritage as one element of the structure of the heritage environment of such preservation sites. As mentioned before, there is a significant lack of basic research on this matter, and so the first task would be to better understand the situation of intangible heritage in various world heritage cities and communities, then use this as a basis to deepen discussion on ways of protecting, maintaining and enhancing a culture while promoting means of sustainable tourism use.

Using the context of the Old Town of Lijiang, which is situated in the Lijiang Naxi Autonomous County in Yunnan Province, China (hereafter referred to as Lijiang, Figure 13.1), this chapter will deal with art and craft works utilizing religious images. Specifically, attention will be paid to tourist art based on the motifs and production techniques of *Dongba* painting, which is the religious painting characteristic of members of the *Naxis* of Lijiang. To the knowledge of the author, no prior study has been undertaken on the actual situation of tourist art relating to *Dongba* painting, and it is thought that this is the first such study.

## The Native *Naxi* People of Lijiang and *Dongba* Painting

The *Naxi* Tribe is a minority group of people who have their own language, writing system and religion (Photo 13.1). The total population of the group is estimated at 278,000, and

Photo 13.1: The *Naxi* living in the Old Town of Lijiang. *Source:* Photograph courtesy of the author, September 2001.

Photo 13.2: A townscape view of the central area of the Old Town. *Source:* Photograph courtesy of the author, September 2001.

66.5% of the population, or 198,000 *Naxis*, live in Lijiang, where they are the native people (population figures from 1996). Situated in the center of the city, the Old Town of Lijiang, Dayan town, is designated as a world cultural heritage site (Photo 13.2). *Dongba* culture is a culture specific to the *Naxis*, based on "*Dongba* religion," a religion that is centered on animism. The term "*Dongba*" signifies a male shaman, and the priesthood is passed down specific families in a hereditary fashion (He ed. 2000). On December 26th 2002, the Chinese State Council decided to re-establish Lijiang Prefecture as Lijiang City, and at the same time revise the administration by abolishing Lijiang Naxi Autonomous County. Since April 1st 2003, the local administration has been carried out under a new structure and from that date "Lijiang Prefecture, Lijiang Naxi Autonomous County, Dayan Town" became "Lijiang City Old Town District, Dayan Town." However, as all accounts in this chapter are based on the results of surveys carried out before April 2003, the text refers to the old titles and nomenclature as was used by respondents.

Originally, *Dongba* art were paintings created for religious purposes, and they depict myths and scriptures, using motifs such as spirits, people, plants, animals, monsters and *Dongba* pictographs (over 1,400 pictographs specific to the *Naxis*' writing system) to illustrate sutras and festival scrolls (Guo ed. 1999, see Photo 13.3–13.5). However, from

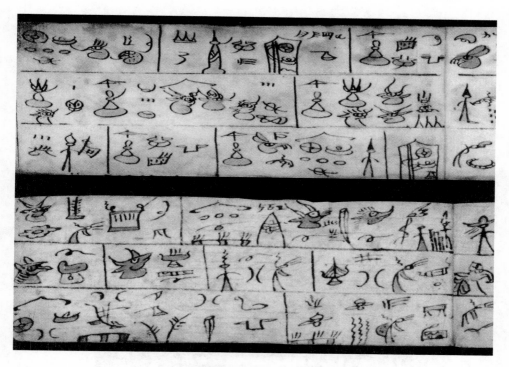

Photo 13.3: *Dongba* pictographs illustrated sutra in a festival scroll. *Source:* Photograph courtesy of Yang (2000: 76).

the establishment of the People's Republic of China in 1949 until the adoption of open policies at the end of the 1970s, the *Dongba* religion, like other religions during that period, had its beliefs restricted by the government, and in particular it was banned during the period of the Cultural Revolution (1966–1976). During this time, not only did *Dongba* festivals practically disappear from the Lijiang area, but the succession of *Dongba* culture from generation to generation was also severely threatened (Gao ed. 2001). As a result, *Dongba* paintings, as a traditional religious art, virtually ceased to be produced. On the other hand, since 1949, *Dongba* art had started to be produced, not as religious art, but as an aesthetic work of art complete in itself without reference to religious symbolism. Artists from Lijiang, who have acquired the traditional methods of *Dongba* art, have also absorbed new techniques and, using traditional designs and motifs and *Dongba* pictographs, have started to produce pictorial works using new means of expression. In the region, this new form of *Dongba* painting is known as "Contemporary *Dongba* art" (Guo ed. 1999, for an example see Photo 13.6). Since the designation of the Old Town of Lijiang as a world cultural heritage site in 1997, and the consequent sudden rise in tourism, contemporary *Dongba* art has started to be produced as tourist souvenirs, that is, adapted as "tourist art" to use the terminology previously defined (Yamamura *et al.* 2001). These tourist souvenirs are mainly produced using wooden blocks, on the front of which are carvings of *Dongba*

Photo 13.4:  An example of *Dongba* painting: a part of *"Shen-Lu Tu"* (the road to heaven).
*Source:* Photograph courtesy of Li *et al.* (1998: 42).

art. However, there are a wide variety of styles depending on the craftsperson, and there is no standard umbrella term for existing products. Therefore, for the sake of convenience, the phrase "contemporary *Dongba* crafts" will be used in this chapter as a general term for the craft products which are produced for tourists, using *Dongba* art (Photo 13.7).

## The General Situation of Contemporary *Dongba* Craft Workshops

In June 2000, in the main tourist area of the Old Town of Lijiang (Figure 13.2) there were 27 shops producing and selling contemporary *Dongba* crafts (Yamamura *et al.* 2001, see Photo 13.8). All of these 27 are workshop-type, individually managed shops that produce and sell crafts on-site (hereafter referred to as contemporary *Dongba* craft workshops). Table 13.1 shows the types of proprietors and the length of time for which the present workshops have been operating. Based on the family registration system currently used in China, the proprietors have been divided, according to their registration types, into "permanent inhabitants," who reside permanently in Lijiang, and "temporary residents (immigrants)," that is, permanent inhabitants of areas outside Lijiang who only

Photo 13.5: An example of *Dongba* painting: *"Ba-Ge Tu." Source:* Photograph courtesy of Li *et al.* (1998: 59).

have a "provisional residence permit" (Table 13.1). The result is that just over half of the proprietors (14 people) are permanent residents, mostly the *Naxi*s, while almost half (13 people) are immigrants, 12 of whom belong to the *Han*s, the major ethnic group of China. In other words, approximately half of the contemporary *Dongba* craft workshops are managed by immigrant *Han* people who have no previous contact with *Naxi* culture.

## Research Methods

Taking the above situation into account and in order to clarify the actual conditions of the creation and production of contemporary *Dongba* crafts, empirical research was carried out in September 2001 in the following manner:

Photo 13.6:  An example of contemporary *Dongba* art. *Source:* Photograph courtesy of the author with permission of the artist at Guang-Yi Street.

Photo 13.7:  An example of contemporary *Dongba* art crafts as tourist souvenirs. *Source:* Photograph courtesy of the author with permission of the artist at Xin-Hua Street.

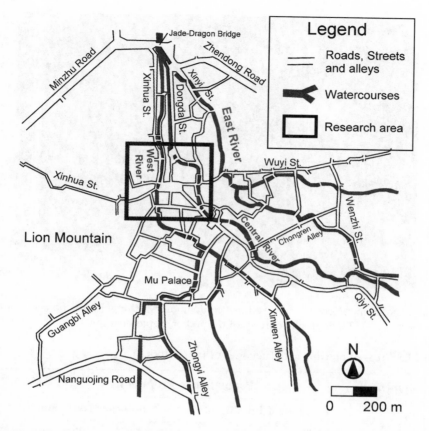

Figure 13.2: Research area: The main tourist area of the Old Town. *Source:* Map courtesy of the author on the basis of a map by Xu (2000).

(1) Participants were selected from among the proprietors of contemporary *Dongba* craft workshops (hereafter, workshop proprietors) to provide a balance of representation including workshops that: (a) have been in operation for a long period; (b) those that have recently opened; (c) workshops run by local *Naxi* proprietors; and (d) those run by immigrants. Of the selected representatives, five proprietors agreed to take part in the study.

(2) The author visited the workshops in person and carried out one-to-one interviews in Mandarin Chinese directly, gathering and confirming basic information about the proprietors themselves and the conditions of operation of the workshop.

(3) In addition to the above, supplementary data were also collected as necessary from other workshop proprietors, ordinary inhabitants and local public institutions (albeit at times on a less formal basis).

Photo 13.8: A handicraft shop selling contemporary *Dongba* art objects. *Source:* Photograph courtesy of the author, September 2001.

Table 13.1: Year of opening and categories of proprietors.

| Year of Opening | Population of Proprietors | | | | Total |
|---|---|---|---|---|---|
| | Permanent Inhabitants | | Temporary Residents | | |
| | The *Naxis* | The *Hans* | The *Naxis* | The *Hans* | |
| 1996 | 1 | 0 | 0 | 1 | 2 |
| 1997 | 2 | 0 | 0 | 1 | 3 |
| 1998 | 0 | 0 | 0 | 1 | 1 |
| 1999 | 9 | 0 | 0 | 4 | 13 |
| 2000 | 0 | 2 | 1 | 4 | 7 |
| N.A. | 0 | 0 | 0 | 1 | 1 |
| Total | 12 | 2 | 1 | 12 | 27 |

*Source:* Based on survey results conducted by the author in June 2000 from interviews of 27 proprietors. For detailed information on survey methods, see Yamamura *et al.* (2001).

## Results

Based on data obtained from interviews with workshop proprietors, Table 13.2 shows the fundamental demographics and circumstances of the proprietors, while Table 13.3

Table 13.2: Basic data on interview respondents.

| Proprietor (Age/Sex/Ethnic Group) | Address of Workshop | Category of Family Registration (Place of Origin) | Last Educational Institute | Previous Employment (Employer) | Details of Workshop | |
|---|---|---|---|---|---|---|
| | | | | | Year of Opening | Ownership of the Shop Building (Monthly rent) |
| A (33/male/the Naxi) | Guangyi St. Xinyuan Alley | Permanent inhabitant (Lijiang) | High school | Researcher (Lijiang County Museum) | 1996 | Private owner rented house (1,100 CNY) |
| B (27/male/the Naxi) | Guangyi St. Xianwen Alley | Permanent inhabitant (Lijiang) | Junior high school | Package designer (Lijiang Beer Factory) | 1997 | Public owner rented house (700 CNY) |
| C (20/male/the Naxi) | Guangyi St. Xianwen Alley | Permanent inhabitant (Lijiang) | Primary school | Part-time craftsman (Woodcarving workshop) | 2000 | Private owner rented house (200 CNY) |
| D (33/male/the Han) | Market Square | Temporary resident (Sichuan) | College | Teacher (Vocational junior high school) | 2000 | Private owner rented house (1,150 CNY) |
| E (29/male/the Han) | Xinhua St. Lower Huangshan Alley | Temporary resident (Guangxi) | Primary school | Jade seller (Self-employment) | 2000 | Private owner rented house (300 CNY) |

*Note:* 1 CNY (China Yuan Renminbi) = 0.12 USD.
*Source:* Compiled by author on the basis of information gained in interviews with proprietors, September 2001.

Table 13.3:  Motivation for opening workshop and acquisition of craft techniques.

| Proprietor (Ethnic group) | Motivation for Opening Workshop | Acquisition Process of *Dongba* art Knowledge and Techniques/Product Design Method | Acquisition Process of Woodcarving Techniques |
|---|---|---|---|
| A (the *Naxi*) | "The wages of my previous job were no good and I thought I would use my skills and start my own business." | "I originally had some basic knowledge of *Dongba* art. I studied *Dongba* art and drawing techniques in my previous job. I arrange and design my own products freely based on the design of original *Dongba* art." | "I learnt woodcarving techniques through my daily life and now they are part of my nature." |
| B (the *Naxi*) | "I wanted to make a living from what was originally a hobby — woodcarving and engraving" | "I knew to some extent the meaning in *Dongba* art. I use my own style for drawing. The majority of my products are creations based on *Dongba* design. I often refer to books on *Dongba* art for inspiration." | "Through my daily life, woodcarving techniques became part of my nature." |
| C (the *Naxi*) | "In Lijiang, the income for woodcarving is good." | "I knew to some extent the meaning in *Dongba* art. I use my own style for drawing. The majority of my products are creations based on *Dongba* design. I often refer to books on *Dongba* art for inspiration." | "Woodwork is a skill passed down from our ancestors. My parents taught me the skill. Later, my skill was improved through my part-time job." |
| D (the *Han*) | "I had no interest in my previous job." | "Mr. A taught me the meanings and drawing techniques. I have two types of designs. One is fully creative, another is using traditional designs as they are." | "After I moved to Lijiang, I learnt the basics of woodcarving techniques from Mr. A." |

| E (the *Han*) | "The local government banned selling jade and income was no good. In Lijiang, woodcarvings are a popular souvenir recently and the income is good. Although I have no experiences I thought I would try it." | "I learnt the basic knowledge of *Dongba* art from the *Naxis* and some books in my daily life in Lijiang. I use my own style for drawing. The Design of my products is fully creative. Although I don't follow any examples to create them, I often refer to my own handicraft experiences and other craftsmen's *Dongba* art for inspiration." | "I have experience making and selling woodcarvings in business before. I learnt the techniques then." |

*Note:* (1) A–E corresponds to the people in Table 13.2. (2) See Yamamura *et al.* (2001) for details regarding the prohibition of sales of jade in the Lijiang Old Town.
*Source:* Created by the author based on interview survey results of proprietors, September 2001 (author's translation).

summarizes the motivation for starting the shops and the acquisition of production techniques.

According to the interview, Proprietor A, who was originally employed at Lijiang County Museum to research the disappearing *Dongba* pictographs and art, decided to set up his own enterprise, using the skills he had researched, in order to increase his income. He resigned from the museum in 1993 and took up the production of original paintings and engravings in paper and wood using *Dongba* art as his subject matter. This is said to be the beginning of the production of contemporary *Dongba* crafts as tourist souvenirs in the Old Town district (according to interviews with Proprietor A himself and other workshop proprietors). Later, Proprietor A opened a shop directly marketed at tourists in the Old Town of Lijiang in 1996, and this was the first such shop to open in the Old Town district. Following this, Proprietor B, who at the time was in charge of package design at "Lijiang beer factory" and is a *Naxi* and friend of Proprietor A, was influenced by Proprietor A, and decided to resign from the factory in 1997 to set up his own workshop, saying that he "wanted to make a living from what was originally a hobby — woodcarving and engraving." As is apparent from Proprietor C's comment that "woodwork is a skill passed down from our ancestors" (Table 13.3), *Naxi* men have a long tradition of using tree roots from the mountains around Lijiang, which are rich in timber resources, to make furniture and ornaments in the shape of animals. This is generally known as "*Gen-diao*" (woodcarving) and is popular even now as a hobby, with *Naxi* men often learning the skills from their families (Guo ed. 1999). It appears that the trigger for organizing the production of contemporary *Dongba* crafts, mixing traditional woodwork skills with techniques of *Dongba* art, was the original idea of young *Naxi* locals, but once Proprietor A opened the first workshop in 1996, *Han* immigrants soon started to arrive (Table 13.1), and the number has increased to the point where, in 2000, almost half the workshops are managed and owned by the *Hans*.

## The Acquisition of Knowledge and Techniques of *Dongba* Art

When Proprietor A and Proprietor B opened their workshops in 1996–1997, preceding the designation of Lijiang as a world heritage site, there was a trend of re-assessing the value of native culture in Lijiang. Concerning *Dongba* pictographs and art, Lijiang County Museum set up a short course for local residents in February 1995 entitled "*Dongba* Culture School," where reading and writing were taught. At the time, Proprietor A was actually one of the teachers on this course. This course was continued until 1998, and produced a total of 135 graduates. Most of the course participants were local residents in their teens and twenties, and some went on to open the early workshops (according to interviews with Proprietor A. and Interviewee M, a researcher at Lijiang County Museum). Considering that there was no place for the production of *Dongba* art as religious art, and that the religious significance of *Dongba* art was being lost among ordinary people, the creation of this kind of opportunity for citizens to gain a common knowledge of original *Dongba* art, and the resulting spread of the knowledge and skills of production of contemporary *Dongba* crafts can be seen as serving an important role. Also of importance was the fact that the period when this course was held coincided with that when Lijiang was experiencing a sudden rise in tourism, and gradually the number of course participants who purely wanted to learn about the values of *Dongba* culture was exceeded by those who wanted to learn the techniques in order to produce tourist souvenirs. As a result, there was a strengthening of the opinion among members of the administration and in the museum that "although the aim of the course is the protection and succession of cultural heritage, the existence of the course was actually encouraging the commercialization and misuse of cultural heritage, and thus could not be acknowledged as an educational activity of the museum" (Interviewee M). Furthermore, the museum itself suffered from a lack of funds for running the project, and so the course was discontinued in 1998. Since then, the museum has consistently taken the standpoint of opposing tourism use of *Dongba* art, and there are no prospects for restarting the course (according to an interview with the aforementioned Interviewee M).

At present, systematic research into, and conservation activities for, *Dongba* art in Lijiang are mainly carried out by two institutions, namely, the County Museum, which is a public institution of Lijiang County, and the *Dongba* Culture Research Institute. In particular, the *Dongba* Culture Research Institute has gathered 8 young people in their teens from various parts of Lijiang who already have some familiarity with *Dongba* culture, and is taking charge of training them as the next *Dongba* generation. Through these kinds of activities, the revival and succession of painting production techniques is gradually being advanced. However, both the Research Institute and the Museum are taking a standpoint of consistent opposition to the commercial use of *Dongba* art for tourist purposes, claiming that "clear abuse of the meanings of pictographs and paintings is striking, leading to disorder in ethnic culture," and they will have nothing to do with the production of contemporary *Dongba* crafts (according to an interview with *Dongba* Culture Research Institute Assistant Researcher Shi-Ying Wang).

## Product Pricing and Average Monthly Sales

Table 13.4 summarizes the product sales and business situation of the 5 workshops where interviews were conducted. As can be seen, in those workshops managed by the *Naxis*, product prices are at a relatively high level but average monthly sales are low. On the other hand, in workshops managed by immigrant *Han* people, product prices are at lower levels yet overall sales figures are higher. In terms of capital for setting up business, the immigrants possess an advantage. It can be contended that the role of immigrant *Han* people is significant in the commercialization of contemporary *Dongba* crafts as a trade. It is probably valid to say that this shows a discrepancy between different ethnic groups, with the *Naxis* lacking the funds, know-how, skills and linkages in the distribution chain that reaches outside the region in order to produce commercial products for profit in Lijiang, which still has a very short history as a tourist region. Regarding the price difference, Proprietors A, B and C all answered that "*Naxi* proprietors spend a lot of time making highly elaborate products, so they can't reduce the prices" (according to interviews with the three). On the other hand, the level of knowledge of *Dongba* art and woodcarving techniques of the immigrant *Han* people is comparatively low. However, their ability to produce commercially viable trade products is superior, as are their capital reserves and business know-how, and they have started to make products that are cheap and at the same time interesting as souvenirs (according to interviews with Proprietors A, B and C, and with *Dongba* Culture Research

Table 13.4.  Product prices and business situation of workshops.

| Proprietor (Ethnic Group) | Approximate Capital Amount for Starting the Shop (Means of Preparing Capital) | Average Price | | Average Sales Volume (Monthly Total) |
| --- | --- | --- | --- | --- |
| | | Wooden Engraved Picture (Large) | Wooden Engraved Picture (Small) | |
| A (the *Naxi*) | 12,000 CNY (From personal savings) | 500 CNY | 100 CNY | A little more than 1,000 CNY |
| B (the *Naxi*) | 1,000 CNY (From personal savings) | 4,000 CNY | 1,000 CNY | A little more than 1,000 CNY |
| C (the *Naxi*) | 2,000 CNY (From personal savings) | 500 CNY | 200 CNY | Nearly 700 CNY |
| D (the *Han*) | 12,000 CNY (From personal savings) | 300 CNY | 40 CNY | Nearly 3,000 CNY |
| E (the *Han*) | 15,000 CNY (From personal savings) | 280 CNY | 40 CNY | Nearly 3,000 CNY |

*Note:*  (1) A–E corresponds to the people in Table 13.2. (2) 1 CNY (China Yuan Renminbi) = 0.12 USD. (3) Wooden engraved picture (large): Circular wooden block of approximately 30–40 cm diameter carved and colored in *Dongba* art. Wooden engraved picture (small): Circular wooden block of approximately 15 cm diameter carved and colored in *Dongba* art. In all cases, the same raw materials obtained by the same sales route are used, with the wood of an equal standard, so prices are comparable.

*Source:*  Created by the author based on an interview survey of proprietors and on-site verification of the workshops, September 2001.

Institute Assistant Researcher Shi-Ying Wang). This explains why, in spite of the fact that the product prices of immigrant *Han* proprietors are much lower than those of *Naxi* proprietors, the overall sales of the *Hans* are about three times higher than the sales of the *Naxis* (see Table 13.4).

Obviously, the trend of prices and sales outlined above comes from only the five workshops represented in this study, and does not constitute statistical proof since the prices of all shops in the Old Town were not surveyed. However, *Naxi* proprietors of other workshops have also remarked that: "the immigrants have too strong a business sense. We local *Naxis* are creating culture, but they're just making crafts for money." This indicates the existence of a price difference between ethnic groups (according to an interview with *Naxi* workshop proprietor F). From these findings, it appears that *Naxi* proprietors tend towards producing contemporary *Dongba* crafts with the aim of making high-quality products related to their own culture. For example, the previously mentioned comment by a *Naxi* proprietor that he was "creating culture" demonstrates the consciousness that contemporary *Dongba* crafts, based on *Dongba* art and woodcarving, are still an aspect of ethnic cultural heritage which should be protected by the *Naxis*.

## Discussion

### *Issues Concerning the Preservation and Succession of Intangible Heritage*

First, attention should be drawn to the fact that the production of *Dongba* art as religious art and as it has traditionally been passed down for generations, is now hardly practiced in the local community. This means that the original intangible heritage that should guarantee the quality of contemporary *Dongba* crafts has been virtually lost from general social life. However, such a loss is not due to tourism, but to the past social upheavals in this part of China. This does mean however, that an intrinsic quality which along with being informative to tourists in the products they buy is, if not lost, then no longer a part of contemporary everyday life for the majority of the population. Basically, this kind of intangible heritage was handed down from generation to generation because it constituted the wisdom and values of an ethnic lifestyle, and once the social significance of the heritage was lost, as is arguably the case with *Dongba* religion, it becomes impossible to continue the heritage within the regional society. The task of protecting and continuing intangible heritage is both unprofitable and impossible given the loss of the sustaining social fabric. While, though for the time being, it is realistic for the *Dongba* Culture Research Institute and other existing public sector institutions to sustain the form of the cultural expression, it requires a great deal of expense for which specific public aid from the government and other bodies is indispensable. It is also questionable whether form without substance should be perpetuated. Additionally, in general, when it comes to the protection of cultural heritage, the restoration and repair of historical buildings and suchlike tends to take priority, and the protection of intangible heritage, being difficult to grasp, tends to be pushed into second place. This is exactly what happened in Lijiang, where specific protection plans exist and are implemented only for the buildings of the Old Town designated as a world cultural heritage site, and there are no current plans or public aid for intangible heritage protection (Yamamura *et al.* 2001).

Indeed, at the time data was collected (2001), at the *Dongba* Culture Research Institute, the public institute where efforts are being made to assure the succession of *Dongba* art, the situation is such that almost all the funds for activities come from international financial aid (according to an interview with *Dongba* Culture Research Institute Assistant Researcher Shi-Ying Wang). Furthermore, there is no system for using financial aid and profits from the tourist trade for these kinds of protection activities that might sustain and permit the continuance of old traditions. If therefore such activities are to be promoted, there exists a need for a financial aid structure for which administrative policies and support are urgently required.

Second, attention should be drawn to the way in which information regarding the significance of *Dongba* art is provided to producers of tourist art. Current research indicates that, in present Lijiang, there are hardly any *Dongba* people presiding over the *Dongba* religion, and that associated religious events and events are also in decline. This means that it is almost impossible to obtain information about past religious daily practice. As noted, the past suppression of *Donga* and *Naxis* life has been largely effective. Also, as mentioned above, the County Museum and the *Dongba* Culture Research Institute, which are carrying out activities to protect and continue *Dongba* art, both refuse to have anything to do with contemporary *Dongba* crafts. In other words, there is no system or network for ensuring that the results of protection and succession activities are reflected in the quality of actual tourist art. In these circumstances, the producers of tourist art are making and selling products according to their own individual and arbitrary interpretations of the meaning and skills of *Dongba* art. It appears that even if workshop proprietors are motivated to study *Dongba* pictographs and *Dongba* art, their only options are to study under former researchers like Proprietor A, or to gain fragmented knowledge from books, existing *Dongba* art or local residents. In other words, the quality of contemporary *Dongba* crafts is entirely entrusted to individual proprietors, and it is difficult to assert that the producers have a correct understanding of what information is available. Therefore, it has to be said that it will be very difficult to improve the overall quality of contemporary *Dongba* crafts and to ensure their continued development with reference to traditional criteria, although of course, new criteria and realities may emerge.

Taking into account these circumstances, it seems that in order for producers to obtain accurate information about heritage, it is necessary for some kind of link or network to be established between producers and institutions in charge of protection and succession, and for access to information about heritage to be established. On this point, the necessity can be understood as the right stressed by ICOMOS in the International Cultural Tourism Charter as the "physical, intellectual and/or emotive access to heritage and cultural development" (Brooks 1999). In this way, if access to heritage information could be assured, and accurate information could be transmitted to producers, and if the quality of contemporary *Dongba* crafts could be improved, then tourists' interest and knowledge could be heightened through the marketing of what would be perceived as more "authentic" traditional-tourist art, and subsequently people might become more interested in the original heritage and the art forms to which it gave rise. In the author's view it is necessary that institutions responsible for the protection of heritage understand this point and thus provide access to information to those in the tourist trade in a more pro-active way.

It has been noted that, when focusing on the business conditions of contemporary *Dongba* craft workshops, *Naxi* residents, who should arguably be the beneficiaries of a culture that is their own, are relatively weak in a competitive market, and that there is a possibility that they are not able to exert sufficient independence and influence in the commercialization and industrialization of their own heritage. The lack of appropriate policies in this area does little to help them. As part of its policy for the promotion of tourism the Lijiang County administration gives priority to businesses which make and sell contemporary *Dongba* crafts in granting permission to open souvenir shops in the central district of the Old Town. However, its responsibility is restricted solely to the granting of licenses to trade and there is no policy of business aid in terms of the provision of capital and skills needed for starting up businesses (Yamamura *et al.* 2001). As a result, the local *Naxis*, even if they want to enter the tourist trade, tend to miss opportunities. In other words, it can be seen that it is relatively difficult for the local *Naxis* to compete with immigrant *Han* people in terms of capital and know-how and thereby effectively sustain the existing business ventures much less start new ones.

In these circumstances, there arises a need for the administration to support residents who need such capital and know-how. For example, if the *Naxis* are able to become more actively involved in regional industry through the support of local administrative industrial promotion policies, one can conclude that not only would there be an increased production of art works that are closer to the spirit of the original, but the *Naxis* would themselves be able to more effectively promote the area's cultural attractions of the area and the importance of its heritage to tourists through their better understanding of its historic customs. Simultaneously it may be argued that the *Naxis* would be less marginalized, be better able to enter the mainstream of economic and social life in contemporary China and deal more effectively and harmoniously with *Han* immigration. In other words, the wider issue is not only the production of tourist art, but one of how the immigrant population can integrate into the society as a whole as new residents, and how both new and original residents together can work to construct a new community.

## Conclusion

Because this chapter is restricted to an analysis of contemporary *Dongba* crafts as tourist art, the knowledge that can be gained from it is bound to be limited. However, what can be strongly asserted is that, in order to balance the succession of intangible heritage with tourism use in a sustainable fashion, a reciprocal relationship on both the information and financial fronts need to be properly constructed between the tourist art market and the protection and sustenance of its cultural parent body. The role of the government and other public sector bodies is important in this process. That is, in terms of information, knowledge regarding the value and importance of heritage needs to be taken to the tourist art market and used to raise the quality of tourist art. In financial terms, if public aid and profits from the tourist art market could be used as capital for the protection of heritage, it would become possible to promote the protection and maintenance cultural standards. By creating a virtuous instead of the current vicious cycle it will become possible to widen tourist interest in and opportunities for studying intangible heritage. This could lead to repeat visits to the area by tourists who have become interested in the original heritage, and increased co-operation in conservation activities, thereby generating yet further educational and financial gains.

Chapter 14

# What and Where is the Indigenous at an Indigenous Festival? — Observations from the Winter Festival in Jokkmokk, Sweden

Dieter K. Müller and Robert Pettersson

## Introduction

Indigenous experiences are coveted, but often hard to catch. Thanks to a growing industry of indigenous tourism the accessibility increases. According to Smith (1996) there are four different elements which are influential in the development of indigenous tourism, and can be a part of the tourist experience: *habitat, history, handicrafts* and *heritage*. Particularly, access to non-commercialised heritage is difficult to find due to its allocation in space and time (Müller & Pettersson 2001). Smith (1996: 290) writes that the heritage "*comprises that body of knowledge and skills which ensure human survival together with the beliefs and values that give meaning to life....*" Hence, heritage, i.e. the ethnographic tradition, is mainly presented in institutionalized forms for example in museums and exhibitions, or at other manifestations, more or less arranged to suit the tourists. Otherwise indigenous culture often remains invisible or inaccessible for the tourist gaze. This, is particularly the case if the indigenous population is an invisible minority, well integrated into the surrounding society, as is the case for the Sami population in Sweden.

The recent decline in reindeer husbandry, the traditional economy of the Sami, has meant that tourism is identified as an alternative source of income. Even the Swedish *Sametinget*, the parliament of the Swedish Sami, has consequently pointed to tourism as a new Sami industry with heritage as main asset. However, it is claimed by the Sami that the Sami themselves should control tourism development to guarantee an authentic tourist experience and survival of Sami culture.

The annual winter festival in Jokkmokk is one of a few occasions where the general public has the opportunity to meet Sami and Sami heritage. This makes the festival a good occasion to increase the visitors' knowledge about Sami issues. There is a history of antagonism between Sami and non-Sami in Sweden. The antagonism often springs from poor knowledge about each other, and the indistinct rules about the right to land, including hunting and fishing.

Indigenous events form exceptional occasions where the otherwise invisible heritage is brought into the focus of tourists. Here heritage can be displayed and put up for sale in cultural shows presenting e.g. music, dance and traditional clothing. It can be traded in form of handicrafts, art and food. It also can be presented and discussed in exhibitions and seminars. However, what is it that the tourists are observing and purchasing? Is it the authentic expression of a living culture or is it, as MacCannell (1976) asserts, a staged authenticity only and thus a variation of the institutionalized displays of museums and exhibitions?

Despite the rather high number of indigenous events, academic attention for this expression of indigenous tourism has been limited. The research that nevertheless has been published predominantly focuses on economic concerns, and less attention is paid to the social context of the festivals (Hinch 2003; Hinch & Delamere 1993). This seems to be remarkable last, but not least, with regards to the symbolic, meaning and touristic importance of events (Hall 1992).

The purpose of this chapter is therefore to analyze how heritage is displayed at an indigenous festival: the winter festival in Jokkmokk, which is an annual gathering of Sami and tourists in northern Sweden. This is based on two dimensions. First, the spatial distribution of Sami heritage at the festival site is mapped, and then the content of the displayed heritage is analyzed, according both to the festival site and to media presentations.

## Indigenous Heritage and Authenticity

Carrying out a cultural festival like the winter festival in Jokkmokk is an act of balance between opportunities and risks. In this context the discussion of genuine cultural representations and authenticity is central. In his initial work on tourism MacCannell (1976) argued that striving for authentic experiences is crucial. However, tourists are usually exposed to staged authenticity only and are seldom able to reach backstage. This notion has often been contested in the tourism literature and hence, it is reasonable to ask what authenticity in tourism actually is all about (Wang 1999). Current knowledge of the past is incomplete and selective, and consequently questions regarding the authenticity of heritage are always objected to societal negotiations (Timothy & Boyd 2003).

According to Hall & McArthur (1998) heritage is what society wants to keep from the past, or as Ashworth & Turnbridge (1999: 105) put it, it is the "*contemporary use of the past.*" Hence, tourists always experience a distorted past only influenced by their demand, economic and business processes, and political pressures (Timothy & Boyd 2003). Consequently, indigenous heritage is socially constructed and thus a dynamic representation of current values and beliefs (Timothy & Boyd 2003). In other words, it is dependent on what tourists would like to see and what indigenous people would like to display. These attempts to define heritage differ from Smith's definitions (1996) who presents a more normative statement, not acknowledging the dynamic conditions surrounding heritage.

If heritage is dynamic, even authenticity becomes a relative concept dependent on various stakeholders' expectations (Chhabra *et al.* 2003; Fawcett & Cormack 2001). Lowenthal

(1985) goes even further stating that a comprehensive authentic heritage never can be achieved or experienced owing to a lack of knowledge about the past. Hence heritage places and attractions are often sanitised and idealized (Timothy & Boyd 2003). Therefore, heritage tourism is always staged. Still, tourists do not necessarily experience apparently staged experiences as inauthentic. McIntosh & Prentice (1999) therefore ask to allow people to create their own subjective experiences of "authenticity." Departing from Bruner (1994) Ryan & Huyton (2000b) suggest that the term *authorisation* may be a better term than *authenticity* as it redirects the questions to who authorizes and what is authorized instead of trying to define something permanently changing.

Indigenous heritage is thus not a comprehensive collection of past practices and commodities. It is a selection only, that is constantly objected to negotiations, both within the indigenous group, and in wider society. Use of fur or indigenous hunt, for example, is contested by environmental organisations (Smith 1996), and has sometimes disappeared from the heritage on display or for sale. However, there are also commodities and events which have been added to the heritage supply. Indigenous handicraft is produced for sale and display mainly and not for use by the indigenous community itself. Although the items are "authentic" in that sense that they follow traditional patterns and can be used in a traditional way, their meaning as well as the scale of production has changed and has been adapted to a touristic demand. This occurs partly owing to economic pressure and interests within the indigenous groups, partly owing to outside political pressure on the indigenous groups to widen their economic activities including an increase of commodified heritage supply.

Indigenous heritage thus exists in a societal context implying a constant contesting of its content and meaning. It is strongly influenced by the ongoing ethnopolitical discourses on the role of indigenous peoples in contemporary societies. These discourses can be divided into two interlinked parts. One comprises the internal debate on ways of development for the indigenous group; the other is conducted by tourists, politicians, media and other outside stakeholders. Their perceptions of the indigenous group influences demand, but also political and economic pressure on the supply and display of indigenous heritage.

Consequently, indigenous heritage tourism is always embedded in an ethnopolitical context influencing its content and scope. Studying this kind of tourism thus requires an acknowledgement of these discourses. First, however, a closer look is taken on the setting of the heritage display.

## Events and Indigenous Heritage

Festivals and events attract visitors and can thus be called tourism attractions. However, the key difference, between festivals/events and tourism attractions, is the period of time over which they make impacts on the host community. Festivals attract visitors during a limited period, while attractions tend to draw visitors for a more continual period of time (Getz 1991). Festivals offer the host area something else other than the everyday life, and several studies show that tourism festivals not only serve to attract visitors but may also assist in the development of community identity (Hall 1992). The annual, three days long, winter festival in Jokkmokk can be said to be an indigenous event, including cultural performances, exhibitions, seminars and a large trade fair.

Events, including festivals and fairs, exhibit a broad range of economic, social and physical impacts at various scales (Getz 1997; Hall 1992; Janiskee & Drews 1998). These impacts are of both positive and negative kind. Positive impacts can be increased incomes, creation of employment, strengthening of regional traditions and an increased awareness of the region as a tourism destination. On the other hand there is a risk of negative impacts such as price increases during the event, ecological damage, overcrowding, noise and a commercialisation of activities.

Due to Wilson & Udall (1982), cultural festivals are characterised by the movement of culture away from the hosting area to people of a larger society. At the winter festival in Jokkmokk there are forces striving for a commercialised and more externally oriented festival, and in addition there are people with indigenous and local ambitions. Hence, the festival is a place where traditional heritage display is contested and negotiated. This is mirrored in various ways at the festival. The indigenous heritage at display as well as their location in the festival area indicates the position of indigenous heritage in relation to outside influences. The items at display and for sale as well as cultural shows allow assessing the content of the heritage that indigenous groups as well as non-indigenous group choose to exhibit.

Peripheral locations may indicate marginal influence and a suppressed existence, meanwhile central locations indicate a core role also for the festival itself. Hence, in relation to ethnopolitical discourses on tourism and indigenous heritage, the festival area can be interpreted as a representation of power relations between indigenous peoples and outside stakeholders.

## Method

Over the last decades there have been few attempts to make theoretically refined or methodologically systematic approaches of touristic images and indigenous representation (Cohen 1993a). Nevertheless, according to Cohen a typology of touristic images can be constructed (Figure 14.1).

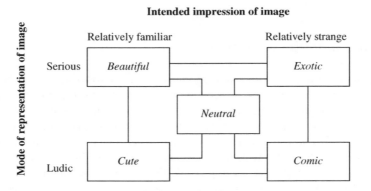

Figure 14.1:  A typology of touristic images (redrawn after Cohen 1993a: 43).

In the typology images are classified vertically due to the *mode of representation of image* (serious to ludic), and horizontally due to the *intended impression of image* (familiar to strange). The boxes in the figure distinguish five images; *neutral* images in the middle and more metaphoric images in the corners. The latter are divided into four types: (i) *beautiful* images, which elicit a serious appreciation familiar to the viewer; (ii) *exotic* images with a serious sense of astonishment beyond the purely aesthetic; (iii) *cute* images, that elicit a ludic sense of enjoyment by familiar traits of sweetness; and finally (iv) *comic* images, that is structured to bring forth a sense of merriness by relatively unfamiliar traits of incongruity. The lines connecting the boxes in the figure indicate that there are no distinct borderlines between the different categories, why some images may fall between neighbouring categories.

Data for this chapter were collected during the winter festival in 2003, and particularly on Saturday (8th February 2003) which is the main festival day. The data collection covered several aspects of Sami presence at the festival. First, the Sami exhibitors were mapped and categorized according to their location at the festival site and according to their supplies. Second, scheduled activities related to the Sami were registered. Third, other appearances of Sami or expressions of Sami heritage were observed and noted. To ensure a validation of the collected information, the authors decided to collect the data parallel, but independently of each other. Altogether three independent data collections were conducted. After the festival the data were compared, assembled and analyzed.

Mapping the indigenous is of course a highly individual process. Certain cultural expressions may be interpreted differently within the indigenous community (i.e. among the *insiders*), and be considered either indigenous or not. Even tourists and other people not living in the area (i.e. *outsiders*) will have different opinions of what is indigenous or not. This study is conducted from the perspective of non-indigenous tourists. Hence, it could be accused of being interested in superficial interpretation and stereotypes only. However, this view is the dominant; indigenous heritage is often defined from the point of the tourist, but also indirectly from the point of the providers who deliberately choose to use markers to identify their products as indigenous. Tourists are seldom able to reach beyond this staging, and hence the question what they identify as indigenous is relevant. Nevertheless, it can be assumed that a Sami researcher would have had other possibilities to illuminate the complexities of Sami heritage at display.

The markers representing Sami heritage were chosen with regard to earlier studies (Müller & Pettersson 2001, Viken 1997). These indicate that representations of the Sami are often connected to a promotion of Northern Scandinavia as *"The last wilderness with exotic indigenous peoples."* Despite their rather rare engagement in tourism, pictures of Sami and Sami heritage are used in most tourism brochures in the area. The most frequent pictures in these brochures show reindeers and reindeer herding, traditional dresses, handicrafts and Sami tents, i.e. historical Sami markers. Also, Sami themselves identify these markers as central for their heritage (Viken 2002).

Mapping the Sami and the Sami heritage at the winter festival in Jokkmokk is not necessarily an easy thing to do. Although the festival activities are bound in time and space, the Sami appears unannounced and in various forms. Thousands of mingling visitors also obstruct an organized charting of the Sami dimensions. Hence, the presented data do not provide a comprehensive picture, but hopefully a valuable snapshot of representations of Sami and Sami heritage at the festival.

Additionally, to get a picture of which images that are spread to the public, i.e. not only the tourists visiting the festival, a mapping has been done of articles and advertisements connected to the festival and published in Swedish media. This mapping has been done through a media watch conducted by a company specialized in scanning the daily and specialist press in Sweden. The number of papers scanned each day is approximately 1,400. With regard to a similar scan made during 2002 the scan of 2003 started 1st of January and lasted for eleven weeks, with the winter festival in Jokkmokk held in the middle of this period. All together 97 cuttings were collected and analysed.

Finally, focus group interviews were undertaken with Sami in Jokkmokk, who all had visited the winter festival. The 14 respondents were divided into three groups with four or five persons in each group, representing *young Sami, Sami politicians/bureaucrats* and *Sami tourism entrepreneurs*. They were all asked questions about Sami tourism and their experiences of the winter festival in Jokkmokk. Qualitative interviews here, and elsewhere (e.g. Eyles & Smith 1988), proved to be a good complement to the geographically based observations.

## Ethnopolitical Discourses and Sami Tourism

Besides reindeer herding, Sami economic life consists of a variety of activities. The activities are often characterised by small scale, local anchoring and there is generally a tight connection between industry, environment and Sami culture. Living close to the reindeer grazing area in the sparse populated northern Sweden, by Sami called *Sápmi*, often implies a combination of several occupations. The Parliament of the Swedish Sami tries to support the establishment of occupations within Sápmi. Tourism has lately been pointed out as important to make it easier for Sami to stay and work in the traditional Sami areas and to be able to maintain the reindeer herding, at least as a part time occupation.

The Parliament of the Swedish Sami states (Sametinget 2003) a number of things that would improve by a developed Sami tourism:

- increased employment;
- increased income;
- broader economic base;
- decreased antagonism (by increased transfer of knowledge);
- improved infrastructure;
- increased possibilities for Sami to stay in Sápmi;
- increased tourism control (reduce disturbance of grazing reindeers).

Also the Swedish Government proposes a differentiated Sami economic life. Recently, a commission of inquiry set up by the Swedish Government proposed that the legislation connected to the Swedish Sami cooperatives (*Samebyar*) should change (SOU 2001: 101). One of the proposals is that the cooperatives shall receive the legal rights to run businesses other than reindeer herding within the limits of the Sami cooperatives. One aim of this proposal is to make it easier to have spare-time occupations, like for instance tourism, besides reindeer herding. Another proposal is that all Sami, not as before only the reindeer herding Sami, shall be allowed to be members of the Sami cooperatives. In an effort to work against antagonism the Swedish Government has started an information project focusing Sami. The aim of the project is to increase the Swedes' knowledge about Sami. One part of the project focuses arenas where Sami and non-Sami can meet, like at the winter festival in Jokkmokk. In this context it is important to remember that it is foremost the reindeer herding Sami, which is only a minority of the about 20,000 Sami living in Sweden, that is focused in governmental policies. This dividing of the Sami peoples into two different groups has characterised the Sami peoples' political strivings for a long time (Lantto 2000).

Besides the Sami and Swedish authorities, the Sami tourism entrepreneurs themselves try to strengthen Sami tourism. In an effort to control the development of Sami tourism a Sami tourism entrepreneur network was established in the early 1990s. The members established a Sami tourism act of ethics which among other things stated that Sami tourism:

- shall be run in small-scale;
- shall be run with regard to nature and the culture;
- shall be built on the traditional Sami heritage, including reindeer herding;
- shall be authentic and genuine;
- shall be run by professional staff, initiated in Sami culture;
- incomes shall stay in the local area.

Today the network that worked out this act of ethics has closed down, but the act lives on through a new Sami tourism entrepreneur network based in Lapland in northern Sweden. Both authorities and Sami tourism entrepreneurs are of the opinion that Sami tourism will increase and that many possibilities will follow in the Sami tourism footprints. However, a Sami tourism development would lead to a situation where many Sami are exposed to tourists whether they like it or not. This risk is obvious at commercial tourism attractions, like for instance the winter festival in Jokkmokk. For the Sami the festival is a very important meeting place, and many Sami think of the festival as a Sami- rather than a tourism-festival.

Focus group interviews made in Sápmi show that the ethnopolitical discourses influence the development of Sami tourism to a large extent. Interviews made in Norway (Viken 2002) show that most of the Sami think that Sami tourism contribute to the maintenance of Sami tradition and identity. On the other hand, Norwegian Sami highlight risks in the ongoing development of a non-Sami controlled Sami tourism. For instance Sami tourism facilities as hotels and restaurants owned by non-Sami may lead to incorrectness in the presentation of Sami heritage.

The focus group interviews made in Jokkmokk call attention to the fact that politics and regulations may constitute a bottleneck in the development of Sami tourism. For instance, regulations governing the use of motor vehicles in the Swedish national parks are pointed out as negative both to reindeer — and the tourism industry. When it comes to land use questions the Sami regard the Swedish government with suspicion and distrust. A late example of this is the court proceedings concerning reindeer herders and private land owners in northern Sweden.

Furthermore, the Sami respondents in Jokkmokk, and especially the group of young Sami, state that the governmental attempts to adopt the Sami into the non-Sami society is a large threat to the Sami culture, and to the possibilities to developing Sami culture. According to the respondents there are many factors and symbols contributing to a maintained Sami culture but that are hard to hang on to in modern Swedish society. Many of these things like reindeer, Sami dress, Sami food and last but not least Sami handicraft may be strengthened by a developed Sami tourism. Other factors stated as important to Sami culture are for instance reindeer herding, Sami language and the Sami basis of valuation, but these factors are not necessarily strengthened by a Sami tourism development.

## The Winter Festival in Jokkmokk

The winter festival in Jokkmokk has been held every year since 1605 and is therefore one of the oldest indigenous festivals in the world still in existence. It was initiated by the Swedish State to regulate and to assess the trade between the Sami and the Swedish tradesmen, but functioned also as court and assembly for the Swedish Sami.

The former marketplace has developed into a main Sami center in Sweden and today, Jokkmokk hosts several important Sami cultural institutions. *Ájtte, the Swedish Mountain and Sami Museum*, contains important collections representing Sami handicraft, history and heritage. The museum's responsibility for the mountains implies that also the habitat of the Sami is represented in the museum. Close to the museum, at the Sami Educational Institution, courses are given on Sami language, handicraft and design.

Nevertheless, like elsewhere in northern Sweden the Sami population in Jokkmokk is a minority in its own land. Sápmi, the Sami homeland, is scattered by international and national borders distributing the Sami over four countries and several municipalities in Sweden, Norway, Finland and Russia (Pettersson 2001). The 20,000 Swedish Sami are distributed over a vast area. However, Stockholm, the capital of Sweden located outside Sápmi, hosts the largest concentration of Sami in entire Sweden. This pattern indicates that the majority of the Sami has assimilated with the Swedish population and hence, the Sami can be characterized as a non-visible and economically not deprived minority. In fact only about 2,500 of the Swedish Sami are still engaged in reindeer husbandry. These reindeer herding Sami are found in the 51 Sami cooperatives in northern Sweden, with grazing land in 41 Swedish municipalities. This situation entails that tourists rarely experience encounters with Sami and hence, intended encounters particularly occur in staged forms.

Jokkmokk is also a symbolic place. It is found only a few kilometers north of the Arctic Circle, and thus, it functions as a gateway to the Arctic and the wilderness of the North Calottes, sometimes considered the home of the Sami. Moreover, since the late 1990s it is also the southern entrance to the UNESCO world heritage area *Laponia* preserving the Sami habitat and heritage in Northern Sweden. Jokkmokk is thus a place of great symbolic power not only to visitors to the North, but also to the Sami themselves.

The original winter meetings in Jokkmokk have changed considerably until today. Nevertheless, it continued to keep a significant presence of Sami, Sami activities and Sami products (Pettersson 2003). The trade fair is traditionally from Thursday to Saturday in the first week of February, which also is one of the coldest during the year, often with temperatures below −30°C. These sometimes harsh conditions contribute to the mystification of the festival as a truly indigenous happening at the border to wilderness.

Particularly since 1955 the festival has developed into a tourism event, nowadays attracting approximately 40,000 visitors during the three festival days in early February (Pettersson 2003). This means that the number of inhabitants in Jokkmokk, during the festival, is redoubled about ten times. The traditional activities are complemented by Sami seminars and exhibitions at the museum Ájtte and the Sami Educational Institution. Also several outdoor activities as *renrajden*, a procession of Sami into the festival area, put additional focus on the Sami. The festival displays are not only Sami, but feature various rather typical festival supplies. Sami products represented cover mainly handicrafts and food. However, being a Sami holiday, Sami in traditional clothes usually not used in everyday life, can be spotted all over the festival area.

The festival thus becomes a place for encounters between the Sami, the local population and the tourists. At this occasion the Sami choose to leave anonymity and appear in public easily identifiable by their clothing. Journalists sometimes criticize this, accusing the Sami of selling out their heritage to tourists.

## The Winter Festival "Saminess"

### Sami Representation at the Festival Area

The festival mapping resulted in a definition of three separate festival areas (Figure 14.2). The *commercial area* is the area where the traditional trade fair is found. About 200 tradesmen are distributed along 1.5 kilometers of sales places. This is an area with trading, bargaining and crowding from opening to closing hours, i.e. 10 a.m. to 6 p.m., during Thursday, Friday and Saturday.

The modern trade fair still shows Sami influences based on the 400 year old tradition of trade between Sami peoples and tradesmen in Jokkmokk. Nowadays, the commercial area offers rather traditional tourism adapted sights, like for instance Sami handicraft including knifes and pewter embroidery besides reindeer products, like meat and hides. About one fifth of the assortment is Sami related (Pettersson 2003). Remarkable is that Sami related assortment like pewter embroidery on handbags and bracelets, as well as Sami influenced knifes, are sold also by non-Sami tradesmen. Reindeer meat is, on the other hand, a product that seems to be sold only by Sami.

Although the fact that the winter festival in Jokkmokk is a traditional Sami event rather few tradesmen of today, Sami or non-Sami, use Sami attributes. The attributes and symbols found in the commercial area, except for the assortment for sale, is the Sami flag, Sami dolls and reindeer accessories like reindeer horn and a reindeer head (trophy). Also non-Sami tradesmen sometimes use these Sami attributes, independent of the assortment for sale.

Only a small number of the Sami visiting the festival wear the complete colorful Sami dress with trousers, coat and headgear. However, a larger number wear attributes like Sami shoes, belts, and rugs. A concentration of Sami dresses is found in the central parts of the commercial area, where some of the Sami tradesmen wear their dresses. Parts of the traditional Sami dress, and the Sami heritage, are also found among the visitors, though limited to the use of certain Sami dress colored ribbons, caps in Sami style, Sami influenced shoes and small Sami flags.

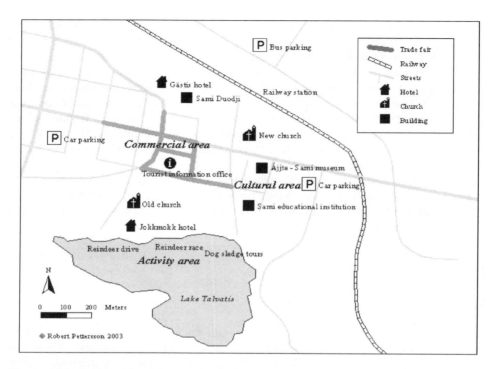

Figure 14.2: Jokkmokk with the three identified festival areas, *the commercial area, the activity area* and *the cultural area*.

Even more adapted to tourism are the activities offered at the Lake Talvatis. The lake has in this study been defined as the *activity area*. At the lake the visitors can try reindeer drive, dog sled tours, snowmobile or compete in the reindeer race. Many of these activities are loosely connected to Sami heritage due to the presence of reindeers and snowmobiles, where the latter is used in modern reindeer herding. Here also another historically strong Sami symbol is to be found: the Sami tent (*kåta*). The Sami tents found at the lake are manufactured in modern design and material, but they are still non-stationary.

One of the Sami tourism entrepreneurs at the lake is not only offering reindeer drive, but is also interested in informing the visitors about Sami. For this purpose he has got a small-sized Sami tent with a coffeepot waiting for the visitors at the fireplace. Inside the tent the visitor can sit down at the soft and warm reindeer hides to listen and ask about Sami culture.

In the eastern part of the festival area the Sami museum Ájtte and the Sami Educational Institution are located. Together they form the area here called the *cultural area*. The museum offers a number of Sami related exhibitions and seminars, all sanctioned and planned by the museum managers. The Sami Educational Institution has its own Sami fashion show and exhibit the handicraft work of the Sami students. Moreover, here are about 30 Sami craftsmen selling their handicraft, of whom more or less all are labeled with the Sami

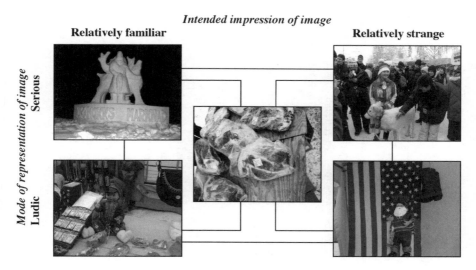

Figure 14.3: Touristic images at the winter festival in Jokkmokk connected to Cohen's typology. Photo: Robert Pettersson.

proof of authenticity (*Sami Duodji*). In common for all products and activities offered in the cultural area is that they are sanctioned by, or at least established firmly in, the Sami community.

Besides the Sami dresses found in the central parts of the commercial area the cultural area is where the largest concentration of dresses can be found. A large part of the Sami craftsmen in the Sami Educational Institution wear Sami dress, and costumes from all over Sápmi are also found in the exhibitions at the Sami museum, Ájtte. Also visitors in this area are more likely to wear Sami clothing. Among the interviewed Sami the Sami museum Ájtte and the Sami Educational Institution seem to be the most attractive places during the festival. On the other hand some Sami in the focus group interviews state that these institutions, and consequently also the Sami, have been pushed to a remote corner of the festival area.

Table 14.1 systematises and quantifies the observations carried out during the winter festival in Jokkmokk (2003). The observations are divided according to the identified festival areas.

As the table shows many of the traditional Sami images are found in the festival area. The Sami representation, that is foremost found in the commercial and cultural area, differ from the one found in the tourism brochures to a certain degree. During the festival no reindeer herding, or Sami every day life, is to be found.

Cohen's earlier presented typology of touristic images (see Figure 14.1) has been used to analyse some of the images experienced at the winter festival in Jokkmokk. Figure 14.3 shows five photos from the festival in Jokkmokk. Central (neutral, metanymic) is a photo showing reindeer meat for sale at the trade fair. Different products from the reindeer, such as meat and hides, have been found at the market area since the establishment 400 years

Table 14.1: Observations during the winter festival 2003, systematised due to the identified festival areas.

| Observations | Commercial Area | Activity Area | Cultural Area |
| --- | --- | --- | --- |
| Area characteristic | The trade fair with about 200 tradesmen in central Jokkmokk. Sami products in about every fourth sale place. Appr. 40,000 visitors during the festival. No entrance fee. | Five entrepreneurs offering activities at Lake Talvatis. Appr. 3,000 visitors. No entrance, but the activities cost. | Sami Educational Institution (SEI): 30 Sami craftsmen. Appr. 20,000 visitors. No entrance. Sami museum, Ájtte: Appr. 10,000 paying visitors (fee: 5 €). |
| Information about Sami | No official Sami information centre. Some information thus available at the tourist information office. | Sami heritage is often a part of the tourism attraction, and more or less all entrepreneurs inform the visitors. | SEI: Information only about Sami handicrafts. Ájtte: Exhibitions, seminars, films etc., foremost from a historical perspective. |
| Sami dress and textile | Four tradesmen with complete dresses. Parts of Sami dress among some visitors. Sami textiles in six sale places. | Used by one of the five entrepreneurs. | SEI: Used by almost every craftsman. Ájtte: dress exhibition. |
| Sami handicraft | In 34 of the sale places, sold by Sami (27) as well as non-Sami (7). Both genuine handicrafts and souvenirs. | No. | SEI: All 30 sale places offer genuine Sami handicraft. Ájtte: new handicraft in the museum shop and old exhibited. |

| | | | |
|---|---|---|---|
| Reindeer | Four reindeers in the renrajd, one used for political propaganda and two stuffed. | Used by two of the entrepreneurs (reindeer drive and reindeer race). | SEI: No. Ájtte: Only on photos and in films. |
| Sami tent | Two among the tradesmen and three big Sami tents used as restaurant/pub. | Used by three of the five entrepreneurs. | SEI: No. Ájtte: One, besides photos and films. |
| Sami food | Found in 17 out of the appr. 200 sales places. | No. | SEI/Ájtte: One cafeteria each offering reindeer based meals. |
| Sami related activities | Reindeer procession (renrajd). | Reindeer drive, dog sled, snowmobile, reindeer race. | SEI: Sami fashion show. Ájtte: Seminars, speeches. |

ago. Upper left (beautiful, metaphoric) is a snow sculpture that in an artistic way shows two of the most common Sami symbols: a traditionally dressed Sami and a reindeer. This sculpture is found in the western roundabout and is the first Sami image to be seen for many of the festival visitors.

Upper right (exotic, metaphoric) is a Sami girl in her richly colored Sami dress and a reindeer. They are both a part of the exotic reindeer drive (*renrajden*), the procession of Sami and reindeers that each festival crosses the festival area. This procession shows how the Sami peoples historically used to travel to the winter meetings in Jokkmokk. Today the procession is an appreciated part of the festival, and one of the most common motifs for photographers. Lower left (cute, metaphoric) is a pretty Sami doll for sale at one of the non-Sami tradesmen. All together Sami dolls were found among four of the sale places. Lower right (comic, metaphoric) is a dancing Sami-Santa doll, aiming to help its owner, a non-Sami, to sell country music.

It is hard to quantify the observations carried out during the festival, but the accent of the Sami images is, according to Cohen's typology, found in the center of the figure, i.e. as neutral images, and to the left, i.e. as relatively familiar images. In other words, there are not so many images exemplifying exotic or comic representations.

## The Winter Festival Displayed in Media

Besides Sami heritage seen in Jokkmokk during the festival Sami heritage and the winter festival is displayed in media. The pictures and texts in media that illustrate the festival may be one of the most efficient ways to spread knowledge about, and market, the festival. Due to distance, time-consumption and so on, a lot of people are not able to go to Jokkmokk during the festival, even though they would like to. Therefore, the main aim for the media scan is to study in what way the festival is displayed outside Jokkmokk, and consequently how it may be experienced by the ones who have not visited the festival themselves. The study also shows which expectations the first time visitors may have, provided that the expectations are based on media presentations.

In total, 97 cuttings were collected during the eleven weeks in 2003. About two thirds (62/97) of these cuttings were published during the festival week, and the remaining cuttings were published during the three weeks before and after the festival week. This indicates that a majority of the festival reports were covered by the media scan, which prolongation was eleven weeks. The two local newspapers (*Norrländska Socialdemokraten* and *Norrbottens-Kuriren*) published about two thirds (69/97) of the cuttings. Many of the newspapers' cuttings were from the annual winter festival supplement that each local newspaper publishes a few days before the festival. Some of the cuttings (8/97) were published in the Sami magazine *Samefolket*, published monthly.

Besides the local newspapers and their supplements the cuttings were published foremost in papers from the northernmost parts of Sweden. The rest of the cuttings were from papers in southern Sweden, who often reach a large number of readers with editions up to 360,000. Hardly any cuttings were published in papers from Mid-Sweden. A large majority of the cuttings (57%) was published in daily press and almost one third (30%) was found in the two supplements of the local newspapers. The rest of the cuttings was distributed between

| | | Intended impression of image | | |
|---|---|---|---|---|
| | | *Familiar* | | *Strange* |
| **Mode of representation of image** | *Serious* | Beautiful 3% | | Exotic 25% |
| | | | Neutral 66% | |
| | *Ludic* | Cute 1% | | Comic 4% |

Figure 14.4: Sami related pictures in media scan classified according to Cohen's typology $(n = 95)$.

specialist (10%) and popular (3%) press. The media scan showed that all together 19 different papers reported from the winter festival.

Four out of five cuttings carried one or more picture in the festival report. These 78 cuttings together used 219 pictures. The most common picture is portraits (26%) of Sami and non-Sami persons, often more thoroughly presented in the text. More or less all other pictures show traditional Sami symbols like Sami dresses (16%), Sami handicrafts (15%), reindeers/herding (8%) and Sami tents (1%). Besides Sami related pictures musicians (13%) and festival crowds (5%) are rather common, and the rest of the pictures (*others* — 15%), show for example activities and goods.

In the media scan Sami heritage was connected to about every second picture (95 out of 219), to be compared with the one third to one fourth of the festival activities that is connected to Sami heritage (Pettersson 2003). Figure 14.4 shows these Sami related pictures, classified according to Cohen's typology.

Most pictures are found in the center (neutral images) and to the upper right (exotic images). These results partly differ from the observations made at the festival area in Jokkmokk, where the main point was in the center and to the left (see Figure 14.3). One has got to bear in mind that, besides the papers, also other media not analysed here, for instance radio and television, report from the festival, and this is why the winter festival in Jokkmokk can be said to be given rather large attention in media.

## Concluding Remarks

One will not find Sami everyday life like for instance reindeer herding at the winter festival in Jokkmokk. The colorful dresses and other Sami attributes are all examples of a Sami representation that is more or less staged. On the other hand it is very much the staging of the culture that makes the attractiveness.

In the three different festival areas the occurrence of Sami heritage differs. It is notable that also the cultural area shows a rather commercialised and historical image of the Sami. The Sami themselves know the differences between everyday life and the life showed at the festival. A tourist, without any previous knowledge, has to talk to the Sami to be conscious about the differences, otherwise the tourist will only see superficial representations at the festival only. There are a lot of Sami showing their Sami origin by wearing the Sami dress but for the tourist the most accessible, and comfortable, source of information may be the

Sami tourism entrepreneurs in the activity area that use the transfer of information and knowledge as an attraction. A lot of information is of course available at the museum, but it is static, impersonal and has often got a historical perspective. It is however not really obvious to what extent the tourists are looking for authentic experiences. There are certainly many other reasons to visit the festival.

The media scan shows that the staged authenticity at the festival area is reproduced in the papers. However, the pictures differ to some extent. The differences between the representations at the festival site and in media may be explained by the fact that exotic motifs are better suited for catching the attention of the paper readers. A large part of the exotic motifs in media are pictures showing the reindeer procession, which has become a trademark strongly associated to the winter festival. Furthermore, the predominance of portrays in the paper medias can be explained by the possibility of presenting single persons in a way that not is possible at the festival site.

In this context it can be stated that analyzing the representations of indigenous heritage according to Cohen's (1993a) model is a viable approach. However, problems classifying the pictures into the outlined categories are unavoidable.

The festival experiences are to the tourists (outsiders) more or less staged. The local inhabitants and the Sami peoples (insiders) are on the other hand having non-staged experiences. The different experiences occur during the same three days in February, but the experiences may differ in time and space. For instance outsiders have not got access to the Sami-dances that are held in the festival evenings. Another difference can be found in the fact that Sami are staying at Sami friends and relatives, while tourists in general are staying at places of tourism accommodation. Thus, the everyday festival experience differs according to who the participant is.

Hence, there is a co-existence of a variety of Sami and non-Sami activities and attractions. In the cultural area the authorized heritage at display for the tourist mainly comprises handicrafts, dresses and historical representations of Sami heritage. In the commercial area even non-Sami stakeholders use Sami symbols like flags and reindeer horns to attract the attention of the visitors. Moreover, Sami food plays an important role. In the activity area finally Sami heritage is used in the context of activities. Thus, the festival offers a broad variety of aspects of Sami heritage appealing to various groups of visitors. It is probably this co-existence of more or less staged, authorized and unauthorized representations of Sami heritage that makes the festival that attractive. In the end the festival is an arena where indigenous heritage is displayed, tested, contested, and re-negotiated by Sami, tourists, tradesmen, planners, and public servants. The festival is thus not only an important indigenous attraction, it is also an annual meeting point and display for the redefinition of indigenous heritage.

## Acknowledgments

The authors would like to acknowledge the support of Stefan Leonsson who participated in the data collection during the festival. Moreover comments from Arvid Viken and Seija Tuulentie on previous versions contributed to the realization of this paper.

# Section D

**Conceptualization and Aspiration**

Chapter 15

# Conceptualization and Aspiration

## Chris Ryan and Birgit Trauer

For those of a certain disposition, and probably age, the familiar refrain derived from the U.K. television series, *Monty Python* series, "And now for something totally different" will have certain connotations and meanings. In this comedy series the line was often used to introduce another sketch that was apparently a *non-sequitor* to that which had preceded it, but nonetheless, paradoxically, often by the end of the show the new sketch had formed part of a whole wherein various links could be observed. This chapter seeks to introduce three remaining contributions to the book, these being the work of Johan Edelheim, Freya Higgins-Desbiolles and Jenny Cave. From one perspective these appear to be three unrelated chapters; and indeed might have been located in one of the previous sections of the book. First, Edelheim offers an analysis of perception of place to argue that images of Australia are dominated by the four "Rs" — namely the Roo, the Roof, the Reef and the Rock. Again, issues of "authenticity" are discussed. Are these authentic images of Australia and would Australians recognize them as being such, and wherein does the "Outback" and the Australian Aboriginal presence lie? The reality of much Australian life is one of surburbia, so how important are these images not only to tourists, but to Australians; and if the images are saying something of importance, what then of the silence about Aboriginal Australia?

For Freya Higgins-Desbiolles, that silence is a gap to be bridged, and one possible bridge is that of tourism. But the metaphor of bridging gaps is a "loaded" one in this instance as she discusses the role of tourism as a means of developing understanding for the Aboriginal peoples involved in the Hindmarsh Bridge Controversy. She offers the concept of "reconciliation tourism" by which cultural understanding might lead to real political re-appraisal.

Finally Jenny Cave offers a chapter derived from her own long involvement over several years with the Pacific Island communities that live in both the Islands of the South Pacific and in Auckland, the world's largest Polynesian city. It can be objected that perhaps strictly this chapter does not fit in this collection of studies, in that it pertains to an emergence of entrepreneurial cultures within a migrant community rather than in an indigenous people as defined in chapter one of this book. However, there are many parallels and lessons to be learnt from Cave's chapter that are applicable to the main concerns of this book. The peoples involved are marginalized, have a history of colonization by the major European and

American countries and have, potentially, as their main tourist product, their own culture. Again, it is "difference" that forms the product, but in this instance the indigeneity of a Polynesian culture comes to the site of tourist generation, rather than being a place separate and to be visited away from home. In a sense it is a displacement of people, cultural offering and touristic experience that is appropriate in a post-modern world where boundaries are shifted physically. Ours is a world of liquid modernity where the spatial certainties of past generations are continually challenged by new and old forms of mobility. Such a shifting of spaces emphasizes a different, but fundamental property of borders. Borders are no longer simply physical locations, but increasingly are places of engagement and discussion between different groupings. Thus the context is one of participation in a process of discussion within a wider community as groups seek to articulate their own presence in mainstream society. It is interleaved with, but remains separate from the host community in different spheres of its own life. It clings to traditional practices as a means of assuring itself of its own identity, and from that reassurance is able to better communicate its own needs to mainstream society. From this experience she has crafted an analysis based upon tensions of European vs. Pacific Island business orientations, and the notion of public vs. private space.

Consequently commonalities exist between these chapters, although the authors allude to it implicitly rather than explicitly. One such issue is the question of identity. Whose identity is to be adopted? What identities might be selected? How might those identities and roles be implemented? That this is the case is not surprising given the argument that cultural performance and artefacts are signs of values and shared norms. Indeed, it might be said that these papers represent a continuing *lei-motif* of all the contributions, namely that Indigenous peoples through tourism, (and through other means), are constantly restating their presence and identity, and seeking to engage with visitors to develop new understandings of what multi-culturalism implies.

Trauer and Ryan, in a paper submitted to the *Journal of Travel Research* suggested an amendment to Leiper's framework of the "tourism system," which is here further amended as a description of the processes being described by the three following chapters. Trauer and Ryan suggest that given spatial liquidity, Leiper's tourism generating and receiving zones are effectively metaphors for tourism demand and product supply; and they further divide tourism demand into two components, intra- and inter-personal motives. Having replaced the two zones they add a third to emphasise the role of the media. It is argued that tourists are increasingly familiar with the places and the roles they enact at those places by seeing those places in the mass media, and equally those supplying the product supply product to fit the images as both tourist and product supplier obtain satisfaction and commercial success by fitting the signage of what is appropriate to the activity. Writing within the framework of adventure tourism, they note the role of signing and symbolizing the activity as conveying meaning and acquiring self-image for the parties involved. The framework of analysis that is used is reproduced in Figure 15.1. However, given the role of media as an expression of culture, and bearing in mind the themes of the following chapters, the framework can be modified to better describe the role of the cultural milieu and the difficulties facing marginal groups as they seek to re-negotiate that milieu into structures that are more beneficial to them.

Implicit in Figure 15.1 is a cultural environment which is common to all parties. In the case of tourism based upon Indigenous People's culture that is not the case. Consequently

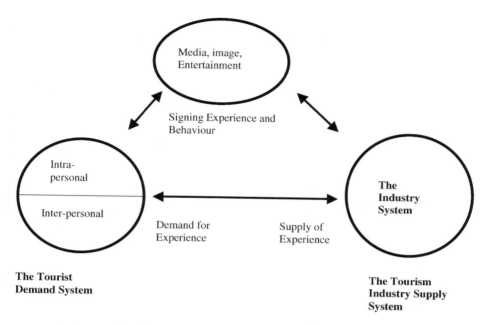

Figure 15.1: The "post-modern" tourist system (after Leiper 1990).

the cultural role of the media as a signage and expression of modes of behaviour and belief needs to be more explicitly stated in the model. The intra- and inter-personal nature of demand for the experience of penetrating and sharing to a degree the culture of a non-minority group is arguably shaped by cultural beliefs and representations of those actions as being personally satisfying, pertinent and appropriate to the potential tourist. Consequently in Figure 15.2 the role of the dominant culture is symbolized by its positioning between the zones of tourist demand for an experience and the zone of product and experience supply. However, surrounding the supply there is the culture of the minority group. That group and its culture is subject to representation by the dominant culture and its media; which media is also to a large degree consumed by the minority group, although in turn their ability to influence that media is limited. Consequently they need to sell the tourism experience through a cultural veil of the assumptions adopted by the potential client, while perhaps indirectly seeking to change the perception of themselves by the dominant group by, where possible, obtaining representation of themselves in the media (shown by the dotted line in Figure 15.2).

Figure 15.2 thus helps to illustrate the themes of the remaining three chapters. Edelheim's chapter highlights the non-appearance of the Aboriginal in the touristic image of Australia, and the role of myth in that cultural imagery. As previously stated he notes the role of myth in that the reality of much of Australia, he argues, is that of a suburban society. Higgins-Desboilles also picks up the cultural and mythic components with reference to the Hindmarsh bridge controversy, and difficulties that the Ngarrindjeri people had, and the need for and the means of negotiating for recognition of their position. Thus Camp Coorong

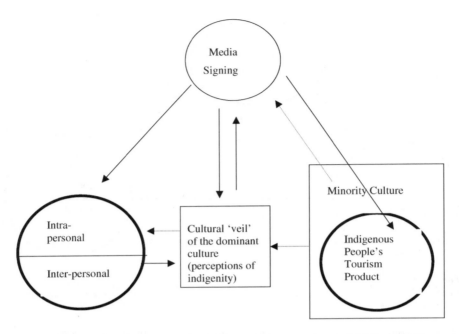

Figure 15.2: The indigenous tourism system [After Leiper (1990) and Trauer & Ryan (2004)].

assumes an importance beyond simply being a location for a touristic experience of inter-cultural difference; it is also a political statement. Cave's paper picks up other means by which minority groups seek to use the interest in cultural difference and "otherness" for social and economic gain, and how individuals are seeking to control the commodification of their culture. In consequence tensions can emerge between the collective sense of decisions making and the capital needs and individual risk taking inherent in the dominant western oriented culture of New Zealand — and these are described in her chapter. Additionally she examines how differences between public and private space are also inherent to the design of given tourism product and the manner in which identities are portrayed to the tourist domain.

Chapter 16

# Reconciliation Tourism: Challenging the Constraints of Economic Rationalism

Freya Higgins-Desbiolles

## Introduction

In this era of economic globalisation, the focus of tourism is upon its profitability as an industry and its context is overwhelmingly shaped by the neo-liberal market paradigm (Higgins-Desbiolles 2003a). Tourism as an industry is subject to the same forces of reduced governmental support, competitive market practice in an increasingly global arena and the tight economic constraints that all industries are currently facing. However, there is another way of viewing tourism than through the economic prism; tourism is also a social force that has profound impacts upon societies and peoples. It is in this vein, that the rhetoric of tourism as a force for peace and understanding is engaged (Higgins-Desbiolles 2003b).

This chapter will examine the context of reconciliation tourism in Australia and present a case study of Camp Coorong Race Relations and Cultural Education Centre of South Australia. While reconciliation is now a marginalised endeavour within Australia following such a promising launch in the new millennium with the Sydney 2000 Olympics and the walk across Sydney Harbour Bridge in 2000, there are still many Aboriginal communities and tourism operations which see tourism as a useful vehicle to secure Reconciliation. Camp Coorong is one such facility. It was started by the Ngarrindjeri community in 1985 and has catered to school groups, community organisations and tourists from all around Australia and the world. It has since won tourism awards and has been cited as a model of Aboriginal tourism in such publications as *A Talent for Tourism* and *Strong Business, Strong Culture, Strong Country*. It has some notable achievements to record as well as some amazing setbacks such as the Hindmarsh Island (Kumarangk) bridge controversy. One battle is still being waged; the Ngarrindjeri are seeking a "Reconciliation" ferry which would enable appropriate access for them to maintain their cultural obligations to Kumarangk.

This case study illustrates how tourism can be an ambivalent force for some Indigenous communities but many resort to it for its capabilities as a social force for breaking down barriers and healing social divisions.

Indigenous Tourism: The Commodification and Management of Culture
Copyright © 2005 by Elsevier Ltd.
All rights of reproduction in any form reserved
ISBN: 0-08-044620-5

## Indigenous Tourism

Indigenous tourism is a significant phenomenon worldwide. Whether the recent upsurge in interest in Indigenous tourism experiences is due to a seeking out of the "exotic Other" due to the homogenising forces of globalisation (MacCannell 1992; Turner & Ash 1975),[1] a "New Age" orientation of a segment of the tourist population (Attix 2002), or to a desire to express solidarity,[2] there is no discounting the drawcard of Indigenous tourism experiences. Butler and Hinch characterise Indigenous tourism as ". . . tourism activity in which indigenous people are directly involved either through control and/or by having their culture serve as the essence of the attraction" (1996: 9). Importantly, Butler and Hinch have formulated a model which distinguishes four categories of Indigenous tourism based upon the factors of Indigenous control and Indigenous theming (1996: 9–10).[3] It is important to distinguish the different demands of the different stakeholders in Indigenous tourism: tourists are seeking some special encounter through the experience; the tourism industry is seeking some marketing advantage through usurping the Indigenous theme; governments are seeking sources of Indigenous community development in order to reduce governmental welfare spending; and Indigenous communities are seeking control in order to secure beneficial outcomes for their communities. As Butler and Hinch emphasise, there is an important power differential as the global tourism industry is dominated by non-Indigenous interests and this limits the ability for Indigenous communities to exert control over tourism to secure such goals as self-determination or mitigate harmful impacts (1996: 11–12).

## The Context of Aboriginal and Torres Strait Islander Tourism in Australia

Aboriginal and Torres Strait Islander (ATSI)[4] involvement in the Australian tourism industry has been of increasing importance in recent decades. Its economic importance to Australia has begun to draw attention and valuation (Zeppel 2000). The highlight to date of the

---

[1] Turner and Ash's work refers to tourism in the Third World and they note the irony that in the tourists' seeking out of difference, they actually serve to spread the uniformity of modernisation to the "exotic" locales they visit.

[2] For example, see http://www.globalexchange.org/tours/faq.html#1. This website from the American organisation, Global Exchange, promotes "reality tours" which have at their heart the concept of solidarity.

[3] In this model, if the tourism has a low degree of Indigenous control but has an Indigenous theme present, it is characterised as "culture dispossessed"; if it has a high degree of Indigenous control and an Indigenous theme present, it is described as "culture controlled"; if the tourism has a low degree of control and it lacks an Indigenous theme it is called "non-Indigenous tourism"; and finally tourism with a high degree of Indigenous control but lacks an Indigenous theme is characterised as "diversified Indigenous" (such as Native American casinos) (Butler & Hinch 1995: 10).

[4] The term "ATSI tourism" (used by Whitford, Bell & Watkins 2001) is a preferable term because it specifies the two Indigenous groups of peoples rather than relying on the more commonly used generic term "Indigenous Australian tourism" which refers to both Aboriginal communities and Torres Strait Islander communities involved with tourism. Some merely speak of "Aboriginal tourism" because it is so overwhelmingly predominant in the market and because Aboriginal imagery is what has been used to distinguish Australia internationally in the competitive tourism market (i.e. the 3 "d's," the dot paintings, the didgeridoo and the desert nomad).

This case study illustrates clearly the politics and power of development playing out in a local and regional context, but it also illustrates more. The catalyst to a marina and residential development on this rather unimposing island is a facet of the insatiable demands for new "playgrounds" for the activities undertaken in the "culture/ideology of consumerism" (Sklair 2002). In particular, Australia is in the midst of a property boom as demand for coastal residences is phenomenal and recreational boating becomes increasingly popular. Since its expansion following completion of the bridge, the Marina Hindmarsh Island has been named one of the top five seaside property "hotspots" in Australia (Dunlevy 2002), was designated in the 2003 Australian Marine Awards "Marina of the Year" by the Australian Marine Industry Federation[17] and featured in Club Marine boating magazine as a "boating playground" (Robinson 2002). It is apparent that the marina developers have been very successful in tapping into the national and global networks to promote their facility in a competitive market. The key feature that they have capitalised upon is the proximity to the Coorong National Park.[18] Neither the environmental nor Aboriginal heritage attributes of the area were allowed to obstruct the plans to build the bridge that was required in order to create "the largest marina complex in the southern hemisphere." Since then, ironically, Ngarrindjeri attachment to the island and the larger region have been utilised as tourism assets.

## Tourism to Ngarrindjeri Country Since the Bridge Conflict

In addition to the Coorong's many resources and attributes that serve as tourism drawcards, Ngarrindjeri culture, and the signs of their archaeological occupation of the area are also important attractors. Besides there being a small but lucrative niche market for Indigenous tourism products, these products also serve to "add value" to the Coorong tourism experience by contributing to the diverse range of tourism opportunities available to potential tourists and thus increasing the region's drawing power.

This is apparent in such brochures as the *Secrets* brochure for the Limestone Coast/South East for 2002.[19] On the pages devoted to the Coorong, the brochure itemises what it designates as "must see and do." This list starts with "search for ancient middens along a series of captivating walking trails"[20] and "learn about Aboriginal heritage at the Coorong Wilderness Lodge or Camp Coorong" which is then followed by the other attractions of nature tours, boating and bird watching among others.

---

[17] See: http://www.marina-hi.com.au/news/Awards.htm.

[18] One of the Marina Hindmarsh Island's ads entitled "Live Next Door to Mother Nature" features the Coorong as its selling point; it calls the Coorong "one of the world's great nature reserves." See: http://www.marina-hi.com.au/news/18586-MH000-1..otherNature1.pdf.

[19] Some Ngarrindjeri have expressed suspicion that the SATC's use of the concept "Discover the Secrets" marketing campaign is an attempt to capitalise on the notoriety of "Secret Women's Business" which became the popular and media cliche to describe the proponents assertion of sacred women's association with Hindmarsh Island which became the much of the focus during the Hindmarsh Island controversy.

[20] This is incongruous with Ngarrindjeri concerns to protect these significant midden and burial sites dotted throughout the Coorong.

connection between ATSI people and the tourism industry has been the Sydney 2000 Olympics in which the Opening ceremony in particular featured a strong ATSI presence and the victory of Aboriginal runner Cathy Freeman became symbolic of Australia's Olympic aspirations and achievement. Since then Freeman has been appointed "ambassador for Indigenous tourism" by the national peak body Aboriginal Tourism Australia (ATA 2003). Hoping to translate the 3.7 billion viewers of the Games into higher visitor numbers to Australia, the Australian Tourist Commission (ATC) has seized the opportunity of the heightened profile of Indigenous Australians through the Games to market Australia by appointing an Indigenous tourism coordinator to implement an Indigenous Tourism Strategy and quench ". . . [the] incredible thirst by the world to understand our indigenous culture," in the words of John Morse, then CEO of the ATC (ATC n.d.).

However, to understand ATSI tourism,[5] it is necessary to examine it from the positions of its various stakeholders. This includes the tourists who assert the demand for ATSI experiences, the tourism industry who obtain advantage from ATSI imagery in marketing Australia, government policymakers who establish the policy context of ATSI tourism and the ATSI communities who utilise tourism for their own needs.

As a counter to those in the tourism industry, government and specialised agencies who envision tremendous demand for ATSI tourism (such as Morse above), tourism research is indicating that the volume and the nature of the demand for ATSI tourism experiences might have been misrepresented previously (Ryan & Huyton 2000a; 2000b; 2000c). In their work on visitors to Central Australia, Ryan and Huyton found that the majority surveyed indicated little interest in Aboriginal culture compared to other experiences offered but of those who indicated a strong interest in it, satisfaction levels with these experiences were strongly linked with the importance attributed to it (2000c: 639). It would also seem that certain nationalities in the international tourism sector (American, German and British) as well as young women have stronger interest than others (Ryan & Huyton 2000c: 643). Research into the appeal of ATSI tourism experiences for domestic tourists would be helpful in light of Ryan's findings on the lack of interest in Maori tourism product by *pakeha*[6] tourists due to the lack of "spatial distance underlying exoticism" (Ryan 2002: 965); such a phenomenon might also be at work in other settler-colonial states such as Australia. It is apparent that while most tourists are not "amateur anthropologists" (Ryan & Huyton 2000a), there is a small niche market that is very keen on ATSI tourism experiences and seek out intensive experiences such as visiting communities[7] and in-depth cultural encounters such as offered by the Bush University in the Kimberley region of Western Australia, Desert Tracks and Camp Coorong. However, as Ryan & Huyton (2002c) show, a larger number of respondents did value Aboriginal culture but only as it fit their image

---

[5] ATSI tourism could be defined as any products or experiences featuring ATSI people, ATSI spirituality, ATSI bushcraft skills, ATSI cultural practices or ATSI artefacts (based on Zeppel 1999: 124). However, the National Aboriginal and Torres Strait Islander Tourism Strategy (NATSITIS) emphasises the involvement of Indigenous peoples as key in the defining of Indigenous tourism: as employers, as employees, as investors, as joint partners, as providers of Indigenous cultural tourism products and as providers of mainstream products (1997).

[6] A Maori word for Europeans which is used here to refer to non-Maori New Zealanders.

[7] However, as noted by Ryan, a Northern Territory survey revealed only 2% of visitors actually visited an Aboriginal community (Pitterlee cited in Ryan 2002: 642).

of the Australian outback. There is undoubtedly more work to be done in order to refine understanding of the nature of tourists' demand for ATSI products and experiences in order to capitalise on the good work of Ryan & Huyton (2000a; 2000b; 2000c), Moscardo & Pearce (1989) and others. There is also a recognised need for further research which analyses tourism satisfaction with ATSI tourism products (Pitcher, van Oosterzee & Palmer 1999: 28) (Figure 16.1).

If demand is small, why does international marketing feature Aboriginal tourism products and imagery, in particular, so prominently? The Australian tourism industry does this because marketing Aboriginal "product," which is frequently characterised as representing the "oldest living culture on Earth," helps create "Brand" Australia[8] and distinguish Australia as a destination in a highly competitive market . For example, this thinking is apparent in the appointment of Olympic athlete Cathy Freeman as Indigenous Tourism ambassador as stated in the press release:

> Cathy is an Australian icon and can do much on both a national and international level to raise the level of awareness of Indigenous art and cultural experiences offered through tourism. Her profile will add value to the Australian tourism industry, particularly at a time when international tourism is suffering because of world events (ATA 2003).

Some attention has been given to critically analysing the representation of Indigenous Australians in Australian advertising (Waitt 1997) but little has been said about the economics of the use of ATSI imagery to sell Australia. Zeppel has noted, the use of ATSI images, music and dance have benefited the mainstream tourism industry, while generating ". . . little benefit for Aboriginal-owned tourism operations" (2000: 114).

Governments, both State and Commonwealth, have been important facilitators of ATSI involvement in tourism. This has been for a number of reasons, but not least important is the goal of moving ATSI people from welfare rosters and gaining marketing advantages from ATSI products. But as Altman has cautioned in his analysis of the national tourism strategy, "tourism will not provide an instant panacea for Aboriginal economic disadvantage" (1993: 12). Concerted analysis by Whitford, Bell and Watkins of tourism policy making by both the Commonwealth and Queensland governments reveals that most of the policy formulation has been in the economic rationalist paradigm whose emphasis upon the economic bottomline ". . . would appear diametrically opposed to stated social and environmental aspirations of ATSI people" (2001: 177). Well-recognised expert on ATSI tourism and ATSI economic development, Jon Altman has advocated recognition of the value of the "indigenous hybrid economy" which serves to deliver economic development but with appropriate cultural and environmental qualities for ATSI communities (2001). More recently, Altman has been scathing of the policy process of governments for ATSI community development:

---

[8] This is the name of the promotional campaign to create an international "brand" image of Australia as a tourism destination launched in 1995 (see: http://www.atc.net.au/brand.asp).

> In truth, during the last 30 years there has been no sensible governance for
> development, at best there have been policy goals of socioeconomic equality
> but these have never been met because the Australian political process will
> not allow the allocation of sufficient financial resources to make up for
> Indigenous socioeconomic shortfalls. Part of the problem is that the policy
> framework has been deficient — there has been a lack of comprehension
> of the fundamental differences of many Indigenous economies from the
> mainstream because neo-liberal ideological blinkers have distorted the lenses
> (2002).

Altman has suggested that an agenda based on "governance for development" could use such policies as implementing land rights and native title, public funding support for sectors where ATSI people have a "commercial comparative advantage" such as in the arts sector, and remunerating ATSI peoples for their customary activity that yields national benefits such as land management practices; however, none of these suggestions are supported by current governments (2002). Altman elsewhere notes that the mining industry's mineral rents for access to Aboriginal lands gets shared with the appropriate community by statutory requirement and suggests that tourism could be obliged to undertake similar arrangements (1989: 474).

Some ATSI communities have taken up tourism for a variety of reasons. Venbrux has characterised the embrace of tourism by the Tiwi people of the Northern Territory as motivated by development imperatives and a desire for self-determination with valuable outcomes for the solidifying of Tiwi identity (2000). In contrast, a study of Seisia community at Cape York in Queensland describes their resort to tourism as "coping with locational advantage" because the community found themselves receiving four-wheel drive adventure enthusiasts and fishing people who are attracted to "one of the great four-wheel driving adventure" locations and thus the community leaders sought to gain economically from this unsought market (Altman 1996). However, not all have benefited as well as hoped. Dyer, Aberdeen and Schuler's research on the Aboriginal people behind the most recognised and commercially successful Aboriginal tourism enterprise, Tjapukai Aboriginal Cultural Park in Queensland, reveals some benefits have been delivered but at some cost and with some disappointments (2003). The Djabugay people have entered into a partnership agreement with non-Indigenous owners of the Park but find the benefits less than expected and their freedom to take up other opportunities restricted as the agreement ". . . prohibits cultural activities that compete with the Park" (2003: 92). They conclude:

> The relatively limited benefits of the Park for the Djabugay people serve as a
> warning for those indigenous communities and tourism enterprise operators
> contemplating new cultural tourism ventures. Because of the range and
> complexities of tourism impacts, the gap between capitalist corporate culture
> and traditional indigenous culture needs to be addressed openly and honestly.
> Reciprocity, timelines and contingencies should be in place so that cultural
> and intellectual property remains in the hands and control of the rightful
> owners (2003: 94).

However, as some have noted, some ATSI communities will have little choice in allowing tourism access to their lands and communities despite the lofty statement of the *National Aboriginal and Torres Strait Islander Tourism Industry Strategy* (NATSITIS) that communities must have choice in their engagement or not with tourism (ATSIC and Office of National Tourism 1997). Other communities have wholeheartedly embraced some kind of engagement with tourism, both directly or indirectly because:

> ... for many Indigenous communities, cultural tourism and art production offer a way to achieve economic empowerment. This is not an arena into which Indigenous peoples have been unwillingly dragged, but rather one to which Indigenous peoples who have been unwillingly colonized have turned as a means of asserting their rights and autonomy (Smith, Burke & Ward 2000: 14–15).

The preceding discussion indicates that the proverbial "win-win" situation of tourism and ATSI community development may be more elusive in reality than is commonly thought. Because of its complexity, tourism brings an attendant variety of benefits and problems which result in tourism being greeted with an uneasy ambivalence among many of the people that it affects, including Indigenous people. The following case study illustrates one such example and the circumstances that gave rise to such ambivalence.

## ATSI Tourism Case Study: the Ngarrindjeri of South Australia

The Ngarrindjeri are the Aboriginal people of the Lower Murray River, the Lower Lakes and the Coorong.[9] The Ngarrindjeri have had a long engagement with the forces of tourism and capitalism. It was particularly their invaluable craft of mat and basket weaving that evolved from a cultural mainstay, to a cottage industry, to a tourist attraction. Jenkin contends:

> The only major aspect of Ngarrindjeri culture which had survived to flourish during these decades [1890s–1911] was mat and basket making. This was due to the fact that the people by this time had been incorporated into the capitalist system; and since the collapse of the fishing industry, mat and basket making was the only traditional occupation that was at all profitable (1979: 227).

He describes how this quickly led to tours to Raukkan Mission (to which some Ngarrindjeri had been removed) by the paddle steamers who took holidaymakers from Goolwa to buy the handicrafts, hear the children sing and to "gaze" at the Aboriginals. Jenkin takes a critical view of it: "... even in the 1940s tourists were treating Raukkan as a human zoo ..."

---

[9] As Bell states, "the extent of Ngarrindjeri lands and the divisions within their territory are not beyond dispute ..." (1998: 29). Their lands and waters stretch from Swanport on the Murray River, to Kingston in the Southeast, to Cape Jervis in the west.

(1979: 228). However, it should be noted that the transition to selling "trinkets" to the tourists was a vital necessity because the pattern of colonization in South Australia meant that the Ngarrindjeri had lost access to their food and resources by being removed from their lands and placed in missions such as Raukkan or fringe camps on the edges of towns such as Meningie and co-opted into the colonial economy through rations and handouts. Thus selling weaving was one of the few options for earning the money to purchase supplements to meagre rations, or desired or required goods (Gollan personal communication 2002).

## Ngarrindjeri and Contemporary Tourism

Seton argues that in the contemporary system, the lands, cultures and peoples of the Indigenous world are now seen "in economic terms" as unutilized natural resources that can be harnessed as a national and global resource (1999). It can be argued that tourism commodifies the people and lands of groups such as the Ngarrindjeri not only as a "commons" but also for private wealth accumulation of tourism entrepreneurs who wish to "cash in" on the market attraction of Indigenous peoples.

The following discussion focuses on one area of Ngarrindjeri lands because of the limited scope of this chapter and because of the intensity of tourism's pressure on this area. The area selected is that of the Coorong or Kurangk[10] and includes the "gateway" holiday town of Goolwa, Hindmarsh Island, the Murray Mouth and the Coorong National Park.[11]

The Coorong and surrounding areas are extremely attractive amongst South Australian tourism offerings and provide South Australia with one of its few icons. Attributes that contribute to its drawing power include: its short distance from the State capital, Adelaide; its location on the important route between Adelaide and Melbourne that includes the famous Great Ocean Road scenic drive; and its iconic status for South Australia as a rugged and wild coastal area that is easily conjured up in the Australian imagination with a reference to it as "Storm Boy country."[12] The Coorong National Park also attracts particular niche markets that the South Australian Tourism Commission (SATC) has designated as lucrative to pursue, including nature-based, ecotourism, bird watching, water sports and adventure tourists.

---

[10] The Ngarrindjeri name for the Coorong is Kurangk and means "narrow neck" which refers to the narrow neck of waters trapped as lagoons between the Younghusband peninsula's dune system on the Southern Ocean and the mainland.

[11] The area selected involves: two tourism regions, the Fleurieu Peninsula and the Limestone Coast; two local government areas, Alexandrina Shire Council and Coorong District Council; one National Park subject to three international agreements, including the Ramsar Convention on Wetlands of International Importance.

[12] For example, see SATC's *Discover the Secrets of South Australia* Media Kit compiled to take advantage of the Sydney Olympic Games. Here in the section entitled "Aboriginal Dreaming in the Coorong," it starts "It's been more than 20 years since Colin Thiele's gripping short story was made into one of Australia's first feature films, *Storm Boy*, but fortunately the setting for this tale about a boy, his pet pelican and hermit father hasn't changed all that much" (SATC 2000: 17).

## Hindmarsh Island Bridge Controversy[13]

The controversy that emerged in the early 1990s resulted from a plan to expand a marina and residential development on Hindmarsh Island. Such a development sought to capitalise on the area's proximity to Adelaide and its tourism and recreational drawing potential particularly strengthened by its proximity to the Coorong National Park (CNP). As part of the development planning approval process for the expansion, a bridge was required to replace the car ferry that served for access between the town of Goolwa and the Island for the Marina development to proceed with expansion. Opposition emerged from environmentalists, community groups and trade unionists, but it was when some of the Ngarrindjeri[14] spoke out with their opposition based on sacred sites and the spiritual significance of the Island (which became labeled as "secret women's business") that the conflict drew national and international attention. A Royal Commission called by the State government in 1995 found that the Ngarrindjeri proponents of "secret women's business"[15] were fabricators. This determination, however, was undermined by a Federal High Court decision by Justice von Doussa in August 2001 in which he concluded: "I am not satisfied that the restricted women's knowledge was fabricated or that it was not part of genuine Aboriginal traditions" (Briton 2001). Unfortunately for the Ngarrindjeri proponents, this finding came too late to stop the bridge which was officially opened on March 4 2001.

The unfolding of this conflict has taken longer than a decade, five government inquiries and more than thirty legal cases. It has had significant impact not only for the Ngarrindjeri and other locals, but also nationally in its effects on Native Title and Reconciliation policies as well as the international arena of Indigenous rights. The diversity and multitude of frequently contradictory conclusions that are drawn from these events are a result of the variety of perspectives and analytical lenses employed to comprehend this torturous and momentous episode. However, one Ngarrindjeri elder, Veronica Brodie,[16] summed up the experience from an Indigenous perspective:

> Aboriginal people were part of a game of political football. We were being played against one another while the developers and politicians were making as many gains as they could. We now have a better understanding of the issues facing us. The land grab and destruction of Aboriginal sacred sites will continue and we must be sure that the Coorong is protected from the expanding development (Brodie 2001: 4).

---

[13] It is not possible to do justice to the full history and contours of this issue within the space of this chapter. Therefore only the relevant and most basic points will be made. For more in-depth insight, refer to Bell (1998); Taubman (2002); Gelder & Jacobs (1997); and Simons (2003). Hindmarsh Island is called *Kumarangk* by the Ngarrindjeri.

[14] The Ngarrindjeri community fragmented during this event, with the people advocating sacred sites and women's connections with the Island being labelled "proponents" and those denying these attributes being labelled "dissidents."

[15] "Secret women's business" was the popular term for the restricted and sacred knowledge that certain Ngarrindjeri women claimed to hold about Hindmarsh Island.

[16] A Ngarrindjeri "proponent."

It is also evident in many of the planning instruments that relate to the area, that the Ngarrindjeri potential to add value to tourism is recognised and designated for exploitation. For example, despite the damaging confrontation over Hindmarsh Island, a management plan released for comment in 1999 freely recognised their association with the Island, claimed "their cultural values need to be recognised and protected" but with a suspected instrumental purpose, in the statement "there is potential for the Ngarrindjeri's association with the Island to attract additional visitation" (Alexandrina Council 1999: 8). Similarly the plans for the Coorong National Park (CNP) also highlight the importance of Ngarrindjeri cultural values and relationships to the land, water, plant and animal life of the Coorong, however, the instrumental motivation is quickly asserted: "the presence of a continuous living indigenous culture provides a unique tourism opportunity within the Coorong National Park" (NPWSA 1999: 11). The fact that influential organisations utilise Indigenous culture as a drawcard for tourism is not at first glance problematic. But as the following section concerning the relationship between the Ngarrindjeri and National Parks and Wildlife shows, deeper reflection reveals that such relationships are uneasy because of discrepancies in power and principles.

## Relations between the Ngarrindjeri and National Parks and Wildlife of South Australia

In analysing the relationships between Indigenous peoples and national parks on their lands, analysts have pointed to the frequent mutuality of interests that can be achieved by shared management schemes (Hall 2000). Although efforts such as the policy of employing Ngarrindjeri rangers in the CNP show a desire on the part of NPWSA to maintain positive relations with the Ngarrindjeri people, there is at the foundation of the relationship a discrepancy in philosophy and power.

> From what I see of the Parks and Wildlife and the Ngarrindjeri people, the Parks and Wildlife have the power. We're out on a limb when it comes to money and power, to do our own thing with the Coorong. If you could imagine years ago when we didn't have to ask permission to go there, that land was all looked after, it was beautiful, the waters were looked after, we didn't do anything that would destroy it — Veronica Brodie, Ngarrindjeri Elder (Thomsen 2001: 73).

The philosophical difference relates to the divergent views concerning the purpose of national parks. In the era of the ascendancy of neoliberal values, parks must be open to recreationists and tourists whose spending will help pay for conservation.[21] For example, the 1990 CNP Management Plan recognises "national parks are important contributions to local, state and national economies and are an integral part of the tourism industry" and

---

[21] There many significant facets to this paradigm that cannot be explored here including: the right to tour, parks as global commons, market principles regulating conservation and the privatisation of assets with social values.

establishes a clear objective of the park to ". . . contribute to regional and state tourism while protecting the natural values of the park" (NPWSA 1990: 5–7). However, the real outcomes from these policies are of grave concern to the Ngarrindjeri custodians, including the fact that tourists and recreational users can utilise four wheel drive vehicles and jet skis;[22] that recreational boaters want infrastructure such as jetties, moorings and boat ramps; today's tourist drawn to nature wants it to be a comfortable experience with toilets, camp sites and facilities; and tours and guidebooks publicise the middens and burial grounds of the CNP. The Ngarrindjeri look to the national park status to help protect their lands and waters (as shown in the speech below) but their relationship is fundamentally different to the non-Indigenous users in signficant ways. As this statement calling for a handback of the CNP to the Ngarrindjeri explains:

> For us to survive we need the national park, it's the last bit of land that we have got to carry on our culture. I suppose why Ngarrindjeri people feel this is very important is because there are a lot of surviving sites and burial sites within it, important areas. They're still there, unlike across the land where they've ploughed and torn it up and done so much damage. At least Coorong National Park still holds a lot of culture for the rest of our people. We're willing to share that with the rest of the people in the world, but we want ownership of it in order to feel good about it. We need a handover of the park to us and we're willing to do joint management because then everybody benefits. We need the system that's in place, but we also need to have some ownership as well. So the white structure would stay there, but it would be a minority in the big picture, instead of a majority. We could employ people and have our kids off the street. Stop them dying and get them back on the land so they can live again. We're losing too many — George Trevorrow, Ngarrindjeri community (Thomsen 2001: 115).

## Relations between the Ngarrindjeri and the South Australian Tourism Commission: The Launch of the International Year of Ecotourism 2002

The United Nations' International Year of Ecotourism 2002 (IYE 2002) was hailed with great fanfare globally by a tourism industry that promotes ecotourism as a path conducive to economic development and the conservation of environments. However, this initiative came in for early criticism from various sources around the world including networks of Indigenous peoples and non-governmental organisations concerned with development (see Higgins-Desbiolles 2003a). Some of these groups view ecotourism suspiciously as

---

[22] Albeit with restrictions on speed and access. However, using the economic paradigm again, violations are subject to fines. The penalties could be judged as less than dissuasive when enforcement officials are few and fines are paltry. These vehicles can disturb the dune systems and the birds which are meant to be protected by the park status.

Photo 16.1: Talkinjeri performing the Welcome to Country at the Australian launch of the International Year of Ecotourism, 5 February 2002 (photo courtesy of Fraser Vickery).

"greenwash" and see it as a thin disguise for further expansion of tourism and "business as usual." An examination of the Australian launch of the IYE 2002 reveals that ecotourism proponents have failed to live up to their lofty rhetoric of respect for Indigenous peoples and local communities residing where ecotourism development occurs.

In Australia, the Ecotourism Association of Australia and the Department of Science, Industry, Resources, Sports and Tourism led the IYE 2002 initiative. Other supporting agencies included the South Australian Tourism Commission, Australian Tourist Commission, Aboriginal Tourism Australia and Tourism Task Force, among others. The South Australian Tourism Commission (SATC) received the right to conduct the Australian launch of the International Year of Ecotourism, one suspects because of their status as major sponsors of the project. The SATC chose the Coorong as the venue in which to showcase the nature-based and ecotourism jewels of South Australia. Their committee[23] chose Godfrey's Landing in the Coorong National Park. Although the Ngarrindjeri are recognized throughout tourism brochures and planning documents as the traditional owners of this land and frequent mention is made to the need to consult and involve their community organisations in management, they were not consulted during the planning stages for this significant event and only invited along to give the traditional "welcome to country" and for one of their dance

---

[23] The organising committee included representatives of SATC, NPWSA, academics from a local university and tour operators.

troupes to perform some traditional dances (Rigney personal communication 2002). This is indicative of the enduring colonial attitudes that linger in the minds of tourism industry players that Indigenous people are participants to add colour and value, not as Indigenous people with rights that must be respected.

Although this insensitive behaviour caused much distress and offence to the leaders of the Ngarrindjeri community, they ultimately decided to participate and voice their desires for ecotourism to their lands (Rigney personal communication 2002). The *Rupelle* of the Ngarrindjeri *Tendi*,[24] George Trevorrow, gave the opening address. He firstly drew attention to the significance of the event for the Ngarrinderi and revealed the serious nature of the occasion to the guests that when he said:

> . . . I would like to propose a moment's silence in respect of the Ngarrindjeri people who have lived and lost their lives for the protection of this land. Close to here at Punmarung is the resting-place of one of our respected and much loved elders Auntie Leila Rankine. She fought for the preservation of the *Kurangk* and the Ngarrindjeri culture and traditions.[25]

He then shared the Ngarrindjeri view of ecotourism:

> . . . we would like to welcome the idea of ecotourism to our area. We the Ngarrindjeri people have been practising eco-sustainability for thousands of years and we have a strong belief that ecotourism will have less impact on the fragile cultural sites and spiritual beliefs in the Kurangk region.

However, he then embarked on some of the concerns in such comments as:

- Every living thing created for us has a right to survive upon the earth and in the waters. Every race of people has the right to survive, practice and protect their culture and heritage within the ecosystem. Our Ngartji (totems)[26] are at risk if it is not done correctly — we need to ensure their survival.

- As the saying goes "lessons are learnt from the past." And it is very clear that the Kurangk could not sustain another Kumarangk (Hindmarsh Island) development.

- Under normal circumstances the Ngarrindjeri people would take several days to properly welcome visitors to our land and visitors would come by formal invitation only and the

---

[24] The *Tendi* is the traditional Governing Council and the *Rupelle* is the head. This system existed at the time of European invasion of South Australia and is a representative governing structure (Bell 1998). However, it is seen as significant by the Ngarrindjeri that George received his invitation to present the welcome to country in his personal name rather than through his official position.

[25] This is a subtle indication that the launch location chosen was inappropriate.

[26] Some of the *Njartjis* include birds, fish, snakes and insects (Bell 1998). The *Njartjis* reveal how Ngarrindjeri culture and ecology are inseparable, and points to an important distinction with non-Indigenous perspectives on managing parks like the CNP.

traditional owners of the land would give this. Given time constraints today however, we now make the most of the time allocated.

He also referred to a discussion that was held with SATC just before the launch to try to repair the damage of the failure to involve the Ngarrindjeri earlier in the planning of the event. In this discussion, it was proposed that the SATC, the NPWSA and the Ngarrindjeri should conclude a tripartite agreement so that such problems could be averted in future. In the welcome speech, the Rupelle stated "The Ngarrindjeri welcome this idea and look forward to furthering the idea into reality."

So while the planners of the event can feel pleased that they pulled off the event to the desired effect,[27] the Ngarrindjeri were able in a diplomatic yet effective way to express their concerns, their hopes and their cultural protocols. The reaction of the guests was very warm and supportive and the communications during the event breached some significant cultural barriers.

For the purposes of the present discussion, this incident illustrates that the criticisms extend to even the new, more responsible tourisms such as ecotourism. The planners of the Australian launch of the IYE 2002 felt free to designate a South Australian region for the launch assured in their actions that key stakeholders would support the plan as "good for business" by showcasing their product. However, as the Rupelle's speech demonstrates, the Ngarrindjeri priorities diverge significantly, encompassing not just economic aims but also respect, relationships, cultural traditions and survival.[28]

Although the previous discussion has highlighted some of the difficulties that tourism has presented to the Ngarrindjeri community, the fact is that they are also well recognised tourism operators in South Australia. Their work has been characterised as fostering reconciliation and has been categorised as reconciliation tourism (Higgins-Desbiolles 2003b). The coming section will provide a context of the reconciliation movement in Australia before detailing Camp Coorong's contribution to reconciliation tourism in Australia.

## Crossing Bridges: Reconciliation in Australia

Reconciliation is a defining issue for the Australian nation. As Geoff Clark, former chair of the Aboriginal and Torres Strait Islander Commission (ATSIC), has stated:

> The future of Australia is meshed with the future for the First Peoples. We look back, to find a better way forward. Reconciliation is people being different but finding solutions together. It is about Healing, Justice and Truth. For the future, Australia's heritage must embrace all its peoples and cultures (CAR 2000).

---

[27] Which seems to have paid off for SATC in the securing of the hosting rights for the annual Australian conference on ecotourism (supported by the Ecotourism Association of Australia) in 2003 (Eco-tourism Coup 2002).

[28] Since January 2002, the tripartite agreement has yet to be discussed further.

Reconciliation between Indigenous and non-Indigenous Australians became an official aim of the Australian nation when the Australian Commonwealth parliament established the Council for Aboriginal Reconciliation (CAR) in 1991. The vision that inspired CAR was "A united Australia which respects this land of ours, values the Aboriginal and Torres Strait Islander heritage, and provides justice and equity for all" (CAR 1999). It was given a nine-year mandate in which chart a path to reconciliation through consultations with communities, education campaigns and projects. However, much of its work has been undermined by the policies that the Howard Liberal government has pursued since taking office in 1996; this government has promoted what it calls "practical reconciliation"[29] in opposition to Indigenous demands for an official apology for past governmental policies and self-determination as seen in the *Treaty* campaign for example. Thus, when the CAR released its *Corroboree 2000 — Towards Reconciliation, Australian Declaration Towards Reconciliation* and *The Roadmap for Reconciliation* documents in 2000, a great rift was evident between the government's vision for reconciliation and that of Indigenous Australians and their supporters.[30] As a result, reconciliation has returned to a people's movement in the absence of federal governmental leadership. This people's movement for reconciliation was potently symbolised by the quarter of a million people who crossed Sydney Harbour Bridge together on 28 May 2000 and who were joined in other bridge walks around the nation by many thousands more Australians. The hard work still continues in communities around the country as they hold reconciliation events, form reconciliation learning circles and undertake projects large and small to build more bridges to understanding.

It is in this vein that reconciliation tourism operates at a low-key level, fostered by the daily efforts of people, eventually chipping away at the barriers between Indigenous and non-Indigenous Australians.[31] The concern with reconciliation through tourism is evident across the spectrum of ATSI tourism, including the vastly successful Tjapukai Aboriginal Cultural Park,[32] the intense experiences offered by the Bush University and Anangu tours, the commemoration through historical markers such as that for the Myall Creek Massacre in Victoria and such hallmark events as the 2002 Adelaide Festival.

Reconciliation tourism is a new concept that requires analysis and definition. In fact, many definitions are provided for reconciliation and important ones such as the vision for reconciliation declared by the CAR provided above are vague and therefore are open to

---

[29] Practical reconciliation entails a commitment to improve the physical manifestations of Indigenous disadvantage such as ill-health, pre-mature death rates, poor education levels, substandard housing and substance abuse. The services to be offered through this initiative are services that the non-Indigenous Australian community take for granted.

[30] See: http://www.antar.org.au/rec_inquiry_subs.html concerning the inquiry into "... progress towards national reconciliation, including the adequacy and effectiveness of the Commonwealth's response..." which provides many details on these issues.

[31] Joe Hockey, Federal Tourism Minister, stated in a speech to the National Press Club in Canberra "... some 90% of metropolitan Australians haven't even met, let alone sat down and had a meaningful conversation with an indigenous person. Without this happening how can we hope to understand and connect with indigenous Australians?" Accessed on 22 May 2003. Accessed at: http://www.aboriginaltouroperators.com.au/news/april2003/april2.html.

[32] See the Tjapukai website at http://www.tjapukai.com.au/guideinfo.html. This section closes with "thank you for supporting the reconciliation of all cultures..."

diverse interpretation.[33] Contrast, for example the following statements on reconciliation from a non-Indigenous and an Indigenous Australian leader:

> Reconciliation between Australia's indigenous people and the migrants and their descendants requires personal commitment and changes to laws and policies which have driven a wedge between us for so long. We need to become more comfortable with the differences which enhance our lives and cultures, while overcoming the differences which separate us and do violence to our lives and cultures. Reconciliation is both a national task and a personal commitment (Father Frank Brennan in CAR 1999: Module 2.10).

And:

> There can be no reconciliation without justice. Both the Torres Strait Islander people and the Aboriginal people will continue to judge the process of reconciliation against the extent to which justice is delivered (George Mye, former Aboriginal and Torres Strait Island Commission Commissioner for the Torres Strait in CAR 1999: Module 2.8).[34]

The Royal Commission into Aboriginal Deaths in Custody gave a clear indication of reconciliation's meaning when it claimed:

> The process of reconciliation will have as a principal focus the education of non-Aboriginal Australians about the cultures of Australia's indigenous peoples and the causes of division, discord and continuing injustice to Aboriginal and Torres Strait Islander peoples (CAR 1993b).

Utilising the CAR's delineation of the eight key issues in reconciliation, reconciliation tourism might address such concerns as "understanding country" (recognising the importance of land and sea to ATSI peoples), "improving relationships," "valuing cultures" and "sharing history" (CAR 1993a). The remaining key issues are arguably less amenable to address through reconciliation tourism.[35]

Perhaps reconciliation tourism can best be envisioned as a continuum from "light" to "deep" reconciliation tourism, much as ecotourism has previously been characterised. Therefore reconciliation tourism might contain some or all of the following attributes:

---

[33] Tackling the meaning of reconciliation is actually very difficult as a firm definition is automatically divisive and alienating. This may be the reason that a section on the website of Reconciliation Australia (the current embodiment of CAR) entitled "What is Reconciliation?" actually provides no definition whatsoever; see http://www.reconciliationaustralia.org/textonly/info/whatis.html.

[34] Reconciliation is not without its opposition from both Indigenous and non-Indigenous leaders as this quote from an Aboriginal lawyer and academic illustrates: "The term reconciliation is meaningless. How can we as nations of people reconcile ourselves, our sovereign position to a relationship with the Australian government that is vague and ambiguous? Are we to reconcile with our own cultural genocide?" (Irene Watson CAR 1999: Module 2.12).

[35] These include: "addressing disadvantage," "addressing custody levels," "controlling destiny" (self-determination) and "agreeing on a document" (document/s of reconciliation).

- contact between Indigenous and non-Indigenous Australians;
- experiences that educate and foster understanding;
- experiences contributing to healing relationships;
- experiences that develop "bridges" between the Indigenous and non-Indigenous communities;
- experiences that foster justice for Indigenous Australians.

The following case study of Camp Coorong contributes to the understanding of this phenomenon by examining the effort of the Ngarrindjeri who use this facility in their efforts to utilise tourism for reconciliation.

## Camp Coorong Race Relations and Cultural Education Centre

Despite Ngarrindjeri ambivalence to tourism and its impacts, the Ngarrindjeri are successful Aboriginal tourism operators. Ngarrindjeri educator, George Trevorrow, founded Camp Coorong Race Relations and Cultural Education Centre in 1985 as a place for South Australia's school children to come and learn about Ngarrindjeri culture and history with the long-term aim that this experience will contribute to reconciliation between black and white Australians. Camp Coorong is now managed by Tom and Ellen Trevorrow on behalf of the Ngarrindjeri Lands and Progress Association (NLPA); it is a community-based enterprise. Its aim is stated by Tom Trevorrow.

> We don't put a value on the dollar — we put education and love and understanding first... We're not doing this to get rich — we're doing it to help solve a problem (Office of National Tourism 1996).

Since becoming involved in tourism in the 1990s, Camp Coorong has been cited as one of five successful Aboriginal tourism ventures (Schmiechen 1993: 3). Its record of achievement is visible through its use as a case study in tourism documents and videos such as: *A Talent for Tourism* (Office of National Tourism 1996), *On Our Own Terms* (ATSIC 1996) and *Strong Business, Strong Culture, Strong Country* (ATSIC and Northern Territory 1996). Camp Coorong has also received a number of state and national tourism awards.

While Camp Coorong provides many of the economic benefits such as jobs, income and skills development that others in the tourism industry seek, its main motivations are the securing of reconciliation, cultural maintenance and revival and positive futures for Ngarrindjeri youth. To do this, Camp Coorong offers a variety of services and experiences. The facility provides: dormitory style accommodation, three family-size cabins with self-catering facilities and ensuite baths; an ablutions block; conference facility; and large kitchen and dining room. The experiences on offer include: a walking trail highlighting bush tucker and bush medicine at a site known as Bonney Reserve, a rare part of the Coorong with remnant vegetation; a basket-weaving workshop; a field trip to the Southern Ocean via Parkna Point where a large midden is viewed; and a tour of the Cultural Museum or Keeping Place located at the facility.

Each of the experiences offered contributes to the effort at fostering reconciliation:

- The walking trail demonstrates Ngarrindjeri bush tucker (foods) and bush medicine and is conducted at Bonney Reserve, a site where a fringe camp[36] existed as late as the 1980s. During the walk, tourists are told of how the Ngarrindjeri ancestors once lived, how European invasion has impacted on this lifestyle, how the natural environment has been severely damaged by non-Indigenous water and land use practices, and how the Ngarrindjeri community lives today, retains traditional knowledge and uses the bush tucker and bush medicine available.

- In the basket-weaving workshops offered at the Camp, basket-weaving is taught in the context of its place in weaving cultural ties among the Ngarrindjeri community and connecting the people to their environment. The story of how the art of basket-weaving was revived and restored to the larger community reveals how the Ngarrindjeri have had to negotiate the demands of contemporary living with maintaining traditions. It also sheds light on how traditions and culture of Aboriginal peoples are held to external yardsticks of authenticity, a situation that played out with tragic consequences in the Hindmarsh Island Bridge controversy (see Higgins-Desbiolles 2002 for further discussion). During this session, the video made by the South Australian Museum entitled *Ngurunderi: A Ngarrendjeri Dreaming* (1987) is shown which tells how Ngurunderi's journeys and actions are recounted and remembered through the Ngarrindjeri landscape.[37]

- The visit to the Southern Ocean via Parkna Point provides an opportunity to visit a very large midden that is one of many located in the dunes of the Coorong National Park. A talk is held here explaining how the Ngarrindjeri moved camps methodically through the seasons, how burial grounds were placed adjacent to the campsites (which the middens are the remains of) and how the science of archaeology has supported the information passed down in Ngarrindjeri oral traditions. This is also the place where issues of contemporary import are raised, including: the fear that tourism and recreational users of the National Park will violate these places; and the problematic relationship with the South Australian Museum and other museums around the world who hold Ngarrindjeri remains or artefacts within their collections which the Ngarrindjeri would like returned for proper burial or keeping.[38]

---

[36] Fringe camps existed on the outskirts of non-Indigenous settlements and were places people gathered due to displacement from traditional lands. The fringe camps are important in the argument on Native Title because they show that the Ngarrindjeri have an unbroken relationship to their lands and waters that can be more difficult for nations who were more comprehensively removed to missions to prove.

[37] Ngurunderi's Dreaming is a significant creation story of the Ngarrindjeri but Bell argues that the Museum's film has served to make viewers come to see it as *"the* creation story" and has thus displaced and overshadowed other creations stories such as the Seven Sisters Dreaming which has important impacts (1998: 98–99). There is a valuable warning in this for tourism that even well-intentioned interpretation can have significant, un-anticipated outcomes.

[38] A significant precedent for the return of these ancestral remains occurred in April 2003 when Edinburgh University, the Australian Museum and the Royal College of Surgeons in London organised for the return of 300 Ngarrindjeri ancestors to the community at a ceremony held at Camp Coorong (Rehn 2003: 8). This positive event also places a heavy emotional and organisational burden upon Ngarrindjeri elders and the community who are committed to re-burying each individual in their original resting place.

- The visit to the Camp Coorong Museum or Keeping Place provides an opportunity to learn about the laws that governed Ngarrindjeri lives in the past including Aboriginal exemption papers which made certain Aboriginal people "honorary members of the White race"; the life on the mission at Raukkan (formerly Point McLeay mission); Ngarrindjeri contributions to Australian society such as serving as soldiers in Australian forces in the Boer War, World Wars I and II; and the injustice that was meted out in return, as happened, for example, when returned Ngarrindjeri servicemen were denied access to services that other war veterans received.

- The four to five-day tour that covers the entirety of Ngarrindjeri lands provides an opportunity to discuss all of the issues above and a good deal more. On this tour, visitors can realize the breadth of Ngarrindjeri lands, the variety of environments, the diverse groups that make up the Ngarrindjeri (*lakalinyeri* or clans), as well as be reminded that Aboriginal Australia is made up of a diversity of peoples, cultures, traditions and societies. It is during this tour that one can learn about the political/social structures that governed the Ngarrindjeri prior to European invasion including the highly democratic, representative governmental structure of the *tendi* that has been revived in recent times to serve contemporary Ngarrindjeri purposes. This tour includes some of the stories from the Dreaming as it stops at sites where the acts of Dreaming ancestors such as Ngurunderi have left their marks upon the land at places like the Bluff at Victor Harbor and the Granites near Kingston. It is also during this tour that the issues concerning the Hindmarsh Island bridge are sometimes raised if someone inquires and the damage that the conflict has wrought on the Ngarrindjeri community are recounted.

## Who Comes to Camp Coorong?

Camp Coorong was originally designed to cater to South Australian school groups of all ages in order to support their curricula in Aboriginal Studies. However, it has expanded to serve a variety of clients including: university students in such specialized programs as medicine, environmental management and cultural studies; environmental groups; reconciliation groups such as Australians for Native Title and Reconciliation; staff and volunteers of non-governmental organizations concerned with social justice; motoring tourists on the Melbourne to Adelaide route; tour groups on privately run tours such as ecotours and four-wheel drive, adventure tours; and Indigenous groups.[39] Of the tourists who come, there are many local, state and national visitors who compose the domestic market, as well as international visitors coming from some 45 nations from around the globe.

Perhaps the most exciting tours for the Ngarrindjeri are the visits by Indigenous groups, which include: members of the Ngarrindjeri community who come to re-connect to culture

---

[39] While SATC publications, some tourism brochures and some management plans will refer to Camp Coorong as a tourist facility, it remains different from other tourism eco-camps in important ways. Community commitments take precedence over tourist bookings, and so it does not meet the reliability of conventional tourism operators. Camp Coorong does not seek "to grow" the business or increase profits in the way that others do. Camp Coorong also "serves clients" that most other tourism ventures ignore, by hosting Ngarrindjeri community events and welcoming groups of Indigenous people from around Australia and the world. It could be said that Camp Coorong refuses to be disciplined to the imperatives of the market by prioritising social rather than economic objectives.

and country; visits by other Aboriginal groups from around South Australia and Australia who come to network and learn from Camp Coorong's experience; and Indigenous people from around the world who came to learn and share their experiences so that global networks are forged. For example, Port Adelaide's Tauondi Aboriginal College's students in the Cultural Tour Guiding program come frequently to learn about culture and dealing with tourists.

## What Visitors Have Said About Their Experiences at Camp Coorong

From a review of the Guest Books placed in the Museum of Camp Coorong between 1990 and 2002, some insight can be gained into how the experiences at Camp Coorong have affected participants. Some of the non-Indigenous visitors have written:

- "Education is the key to reconciliation — may the stories live forever."
- "Reconciliation is a difficult process. Camp Coorong helps to overcome our ignorance."
- "Much to learn, much reconciliation to take place. All the best in getting back your identity and recognition."
- "A wonderful idea that can help make a difference to how we all live together — we hope."
- "It hurts but we need to know the truth."
- "Thank you for teaching me not to feel guilty but to seek awareness instead" — 4/1993.
- "Hope for the Future" — 4/1993.
- "A most gentle and enlightening experience" — 4/1993.
- "May this Camp prosper and teach Australia its forgotten history" — 3/2000.

Some of the Aboriginal and other Indigenous visitors to the Camp have written such comments as:

- "Exactly what's needed for educating foreigners" — 1/1992.
- "Affirms my pride in being a Ngarrindjeri" — 4/1993.
- "I saw photos of my grandfather and father. Made me proud to be a Ngarrindjeri descendant" — 10/1994.
- "Proud to be a Nunga" — 1/1996.
- "Deadly. Long live our struggle for cultural freedom" — 2/1996.
- "Thank you very much, brothers and sisters — Nacho yungondalya yunkandalya — oh how we yearn for the voices of the past" — 2/1997.

- "Great to see our material out of the museums and within our own Keeping Places" — 1/1997.[40]

While most visitors to Camp Coorong seem to have valuable experiences there and this facility is recognised as an important place to conduct training for reconciliation,[41] reconciliation tourism has its challenges.

## Constraints to Reconciliation Tourism: Tourism Industry Policies and Processes

In the current setting, the tourism industry is promoting tourism as a source of economic development but through private entrepreneurial enterprises and for profit motives. This can present significant barriers to the social aims and objectives of facilities such as Camp Coorong that are not capable of generating the profits expected by the mainstream tourism sector.

This uncomfortable disjuncture in aims was apparent at the 1993 *Indigenous Australians in Tourism Conference* held in Darwin, when the Pacific Asia Travel Association delegate, Robertson E. Collins, took the opportunity to counsel attendees:

And now I speak to the Indigenous people in the room: if you go into tourism, you must be professional. There are plenty of examples where Indigenous people have been professional and highly successful. The Tjapukai Dancers are a classic example and there is an interesting theatre in Sydney.

But I remind you of the real world out there: don't expect me to like you because you are black or white or brown or yellow; don't expect me to like you because you are an Aboriginal or an Indian. As a professional, you must meet my expectations of what I think is a professional performance, be it as a guide, dancer or hotel clerk. You have some advantages, but don't expect any special allowances.

Don't mix your tourism goals with your political agenda. There is an old Hollywood cliché that bears repeating: "*if you want to send a message, use Western Union!*" Don't try to mix it into the script (Collins 1993: 35).

---

[40] While this is only a sketch of the many entries in the visitor books that have been collected since 1988, it is representative of some of the responses which indicate the profound impact of this small facility. However, it must be said the majority of entries are from the school children who visit and are more mundane or humorous in their content. It is striking that there is little negative comment in these books which may be due to the fact that many of the groups who visit the facility are already predisposed to appreciate the experience and also the fact that those who harbour negative views may be constrained in writing them in the visitors books because of the intimate nature of the interactions with the Ngarrindjeri. Please note that some entries in these books have entry dates, while others do not.

[41] For instance, the author first became involved with this community by participating in a fieldtrip to Camp Coorong as part of professional development training through the South Australian Department of Education's Aboriginal Education Unit which usually conducts fieldtrips there every year. Similarly, the Medical School of Adelaide University holds compulsory training at Camp Coorong for its students.

This statement reflects his perspective from a mainstream industry view and fails to acknowledge the roots of ATSI tourism in a different political and social context, as clearly delineated in such documents as the *National Aboriginal and Torres Strait Islander Tourism Industry Strategy*. Also, it must be acknowledged that a good deal of Australian tourism marketing internationally relies upon ATSI imagery to create "Brand Australia" in an intensively competitive market without yet providing returns to Indigenous communities for this service. This in effect is a valuable subsidy (or a "special allowance") which remains hidden and needs to be exposed so that both the tourism industry and appropriate governmental bodies provide the legitimate support that ATSI community development requires.[42]

## A Ferry Would Further Reconciliation

Although deeply wounded by the events in the Hindmarsh Island conflict, the Ngarrindjeri have continued to run Camp Coorong and work towards reconciliation. Because they cannot cross the bridge in violation of their spiritual beliefs and therefore find it difficult to carry out their duties as custodians of the Island, they have sought support for the re-establishment of a ferry service to the Island. While the local council of Alexandrina has demonstrated support of Ngarrindjeri efforts to establish a ferry connection,[43] so far no meaningful state or commonwealth government support has been forthcoming. In an article entitled the *Politics of Surviving*, Bell emphasises the importance of the ferry to the larger project of reconciliation in Australia. She concludes:

> The Ngarrindjeri survivors plan the construction of another ferry to service the island [Hindmarsh]. They cannot use the bridge to visit their sacred places on the island. In my view, if we can't get this one right, there is no hope for the Reconciliation Movement in Australia. The Ngarrindjeri stories are a test case and thus far there are no winners (Bell 2001: 6).

In a way, the ferry is also a test case for the tourism industry. All of the players in tourism in this area utilise the Ngarrindjeri people's culture, history or physical presence manifested in the landscape as a drawcard to attract tourism to the area, including the South Australian Tourism Commission, National Parks and Wildlife of South Australia, local tour operators and regional tourism promotional boards. Tourism and recreational demand are implicated

---

[42] Well over a decade ago, Altman suggested tourism should follow the mining industry's lead in paying mineral rents to ATSI communities for access to Aboriginal lands (1989: 474).

[43] This agreement had unusual origins. The unearthing of Ngarrindjeri ancestral remains during redevelopment of Goolwa's wharf (a site adjacent to the foundations of the bridge to Hindmarsh Island) led to a crisis. The resultant consultations between representatives of Alexandrina Council and representatives of the Ngarrindjeri Native Title Committee, the Ngarrindjeri Heritage Committee and the *Tendi* (a traditional Ngarrindjeri political body), led to a historic statement of apology from Alexandrina Council to the Ngarrindjeri community and established a protocol agreement. The protocol agreement can be seen as a rare model of the kind of understandings that will need to be negotiated between ATSI communities and tourism agencies, government agencies and other relevant organisations if tourism is to be an acceptable force for ATSI communities. See Williams 2002.

in the tragic unfolding of the Hindmarsh Island conflict. Information released in the Von Doussa court decision and in Simon's book (2003) indicates that the Ngarrindjeri proponents have been ill-served in the legal and political battles that comprise the conflict. Support for the ferry would go some way in mitigating the damages of this affair and mainstreaming reconciliation rather than marginalising it.

## Conclusion

It is evident to many that the Australian nation will not be comfortable with itself until the "unfinished business" of reconciliation is addressed and reconciliation tourism is one catalyst to its achievement. This analysis of Camp Coorong[44] demonstrates that some ATSI communities seize tourism's opportunities to bridge social divides and indicates that some tourists value these experiences and use them to engage in reconciliation. While reconciliation tourism may remain limited to a specialised niche market of tourists who are interested in social experiences through tourism, it may, like ecotourism is touted to do,[45] be able to exert much larger effects on not only the wider tourism industry but also the larger society.

The arena of Indigenous tourism is a site of contestation in the tense political relationships between Indigenous and non-Indigenous peoples in the competitive economic and political climate of contemporary globalisation. The reasons for which tourism is embraced and/or resisted may point to the very heart of the question of what future is desired by Indigenous peoples and others impacted by tourism. Is tourism to be valued only for its contributions to economic indicators or is tourism to be recognised for its contributions to a society's identity, social relations and future development? In fact, if tourism was liberated from its economic rationalist constraints, could more socially-oriented relations fostered by reconciliation tourism, peace tourism and other alternative forms of tourism help usher in a more humanistic form of globalisation?

## Acknowledgments

The author would like to thank the Ngarrindjeri who founded, manage and maintain Camp Coorong for their cooperation and inspiration. Thanks are also due to Dr. Olga Gostin of the University of South Australia and an anonymous referee who gave valuable comments on an earlier version of this chapter. Any faults, errors and omissions remain the fault of the author.

---

[44] While this chapter has focused upon the Ngarrindjeri motivation for engaging in reconciliation tourism, there is need for further examination of the motivations of the reconciliation tourist, the long-term impacts of reconciliation tourism experiences and the barriers to achieving reconciliation through tourism.

[45] For example, some contend that ecotourism experiences can contribute to the formation of an environmental consciousness among ecotourists, foster conservation and model sustainability.

Chapter 17

# To Experience the "Real" Australia — A Liminal Authentic Cultural Experience

Johan R. Edelheim

## Introduction

This chapter will pose the question: If a nation's icons are not true representations of that society's culture — then what are true descriptors of that culture? Australia as a Tourist Destination Region (TDR) is defined as having 4 R's; the Roo, the Roof, the Reef and the Rock, as its main attractions. The Roo — the marsupial family of kangaroos and wallabies. The Roof — the exterior areas of the Sydney Opera House. The Reef — refers to the Great Barrier Reef. Finally, the Rock — Uluṟu, the world's largest monolith remotely situated in the middle of the continent. All the 4 R's are icons, and recognised worldwide as being images/pictures that describe Australia. Visitors are, to a certain degree, focused on gazing upon these icons, and the inbound tourism industry of Australia is focused on serving tourists at these attractions. An Australian is likely to regard the images as being too simplified descriptors. A normal response includes suggestions of visits to the outback to experience "the real Australia," to sit in pubs talking to "locals" about "real Australian" professions such as mining or farming. The picture is painted as if to say that the tourist could not have experienced more than an overtly staged front-stage unless they have delved into other areas and activities; in short, to have gone "backstage."

This study will consequently argue that neither front-stage nor backstage icons are authentic. However, if no cultural icon is ultimately authentic then can any description of "real Australia" have a final value as representing a "culture?" An alternative definition that everything is authentic, that the tourists are the persons who experience the phenomena and if they would not be where they are, those very experiences would not happen. It is therefore the tourists that make the experience authentic. If the latter definition is accepted then all descriptors found in Australia can be seen as "real" cultural symbols. In Wang's (2000) terminology the authenticity is experiential.

This chapter therefore suggests that phenomenology might be a means for researchers and industry practitioners to take a "step back" from their normal thoughts and reflect upon the phenomena of which they are part, and how their actions involuntarily help form the

Indigenous Tourism: The Commodification and Management of Culture
Copyright © 2005 by Elsevier Ltd.
All rights of reproduction in any form reserved
ISBN: 0-08-044620-5

visitor experience. Consequently the chapter commences with a brief description of tourism in Australia and a media analysis is subsequently conducted to sustain the argument. It is contended that true descriptors of the Australian culture are an amalgam of interconnected symbols, each from different settings, but together constituting Australia. If, therefore, "real Australia" is an amalgam, each component of that whole might be said to be a liminal facet and hence represent a contested authenticity if decontextualised from the whole. This is a preliminary work of a larger thesis investigating special interest tourism as a contributor to the formation of cultural identity.

## Definitions

From this perspective, the front-stage icons at best have a partial claim to be authentic while the backstage icons, as discussed in this chapter, can claim as equal a verification as those in the front stage. In order to answer the question, "What are the descriptors of Australian culture?" certain concepts have to be investigated and defined. The problem in the question and in the on-going debate in tourism literature is the ambiguity prevalent in the use of different terms. In order to clearly define the context in which this essay is based, concepts of culture are mainly derived from cultural studies, and to a lesser degree from sociology and philosophy.

The main concepts of the title are; "culture," "experience" and "authenticity," and in a lesser degree the words "liminal," "real"/"true" and "Australia." In order to illustrate the prevailing different views of what is "Australia," a media analysis was undertaken in which articles in newspapers for the period 2001–2003 were analysed for content. A division between Australian and international sources was made and the contents were then classified to be either *Romantic*; the view of the nature standing for the "real" attribute; *4-R's*; the international view gazing at just some features; *Political*; as the then Prime-Minister, John Howard, used the phrase to prove his nationalism; *Statistical*; using the phrase in a literal meaning by looking at the "average Australian"; or *Other*; in which case the words "real" and "Australia" were not related to the topic of this enquiry.

Jenks (1993) divides the representations of "culture" into four categories (as shown in Figure 17.1). When analysing Jenks' framework one sees that the first box (*A*) in Figure 17.1 represents a somewhat conventional, but one highly relevant to tourism literature, namely culture as a cognitive category; a state of mind. This is the culture that the Romantic authors described, a lost world, a world before the intrusions of technology and urbanism. This definition is relevant to tourism literature because of the on-going debate of "culturally and environmentally sensible tourism." A significant proportion of the current tourism literature uses the words "culturally and environmentally sustainable" in two senses: (a) being a goal to achieve; and (b) that all development is diverting humans from their "true heritage" or selves, thereby again, arguably, representing an appeal to the romantic or a sense of something lost (see for example on this debate Urry 1990).

The second box (*B*) is looking at culture from an empiricist perspective. Starting from Darwin, anthropological authors claimed that the development of the human race had led to the current civilisation: the current culture. As the then current status (of Victorian England) was seen as the highest achievement of human kind, all the "less developed" people of

**(A) Culture** as a cerebral, or certainly cognitive category: culture becomes intelligible as a general state of mind. It carries with it the idea of perfection, a goal or an aspiration of individual human achievement or emancipation. This links into themes…from Marx's false consciousness to the melancholy science of the Frankfurt school. In origin…mostly in the work of the Romantic literary and cultural criticism of Coleridge, Carlyle and Arnold.

**(B) Culture** as a more embodied and collective category: culture invokes a state of intellectual and/or moral development in society. This is a position linking culture with the idea of civilization and one that is informed by the evolutionary theories of Darwin and informative of that group of social theorists now known as 'early evolutionists' who pioneered anthropology… This notion nevertheless takes the idea of culture into the province of the collective life.

**(C) Culture** as a descriptive and concrete category: culture viewed as the collective body of arts and intellectual work within anyone society: this is very much an everyday language usage of the term 'culture' and carries along with it senses of particularity, exclusivity, elitism, specialist knowledge and training and socialization. It includes a firmly established notion of culture as a realm of the produced and sedimented symbolic: albeit the esoteric symbolism of a society.

**(D) Culture** as a social category: culture regarded as the whole way of life of a people: this is the pluralist and potentially democratic sense of the concept that has come to be the zone of concern within sociology and anthropology and latterly, within a more localized sense, cultural studies.

Figure 17.1: A framework of culture.

the world should be "cultivated" i.e. taught the cultural values of the "civilized" world. This definition of culture is still seen in travel brochures where tourists are invited to experience the "authentic" culture of some remote region in the way MacCannell describes the backstage of tourist experiences (1999). This essay claims that this is still a conservative view of culture that places different traditions and different cultures in a perceptual hierarchy. The hierarchy is based on the western sense of achievement that, in a dualistic way, considers other cultures to be less refined as their own. This definition lends itself, in turn, to concepts of high culture, the culture of museums, opera and art exhibitions. Implicit within this lies a dichotomy between high and low culture, and a perception of the respective position of each. A recent example of this definition might be the debate in Finnish newspapers (in 2003) about the Minister of Cultural affairs, Tanja Karpela. Ms. Karpela, an ex-Miss Finland winner, has been known in her country since her days as a performer in various "popular-cultural" events. She has had a singing career, performed on TV-shows and has been, and is currently, a photo-model. The debate that the "cultural-elite" is pushing, wonders how a person who has not had any connections to the "cultural life" of the nation can be appointed Minister in charge of cultural affairs. Defenders on the other hand, argue that a minister does not have to be an expert in the field in which she or he is in charge and that the ask is more one of allocating funds for cultural events, based on expert judgements received from others (Friberg 2003). The example illuminates the clash between "high-culture" and "popular-culture," a clash that has been appearing in history as long as cultural events in one or another mode have been performed. A small elite sees themselves as guardians of a cultural heritage that is worth keeping and is fighting against the culture the populace is consuming (popular-culture). History has shown that this elite often has substantial power and is therefore able to uphold some of the heritage while parts of the popular culture is transformed into that same heritage as new popular trends emerge. The instances where the definition of culture from box (C) is seen in tourism is for example in "Cultural-tourism" that is tourists attending operas, visiting museums, ruins or different festivals of art, music or performance. Urry goes even further by defining all tourism as examples of popular culture, an amalgam of different forms of culture, regardless of the attraction the tourist is experiencing. He partly bases his notion on Feifer's concept of the post-tourists that can see themselves in a playful way, constantly gazing at frames of representations, changing between moods of sacralization, entertainment and information and constantly aware of being tourists (1990).

The final box (D) defines the realm to which this chapter confines itself. It sees culture as a social category, a way of life of a certain group of people. A modern notion about cross-cultural knowledge highlights this definition. People are aware of the way of life they are living themselves, but have to be educated to recognize differences that appear in other societies and cultures. The way people are brought up, the things people value and acknowledge as valuable, are all reflections of the culture of which they are part. When tourists are motivated to travel because of an urge to experience different cultures they do so based on this definition of culture. The manner in which box (D) is dissimilar from boxes (A) and especially (B) is that this last definition is looking at culture as a neutral value concept. People who want to experience different cultures might, of course, have in their minds perceptions of their own culture as something above and better than the cultures that they are visiting; as perhaps is exemplified by the "Lord Byron" type of tourist described by Wickens & Harrison (1996).

When this study refers to a "liminal cultural experience," the author claims that the manner of life most Australians are living and the common values they possess is the pre-dominant culture of the nation. However when Australians are describing what it means to experience the "real" Australia, they are describing a marginal occurrence that has little to do with the life they live themselves. What this text seeks is the degree to which a "real Australian" culture been formed and continues to (in)form the society and culture in which most Australians are living, and what an "actual" cultural holiday in Australia, from a statistical perspective, might include. The chance exists, of course, that a "statistically average Australian's life," and therefore his or her culture, is so boring that no tourists would like to experience it, and this might then be the reason for the different staged cultures that have been presented. Another possibility is that most developed nations are so similar that a true cultural experience is only knowable if focussed on what differentiates one culture from another. If the latter explanation is correct then both the 4R's and the "real" Australian experience are valid descriptors of what defines the Australian way of life from other cultures.

## Experience

Several of the words defined in this paper were originally described in "The Tourist," and the context for how they are understood in today's tourism literature is often grounded on that seminal work. MacCannell classifies all tourist attractions as "cultural experiences" (1999: 23) and further divides these experiences into two interlinking parts, the *model* and the *influence*. MacCannell's *model* stands for an ideal that is sacralized and commodified through mere existence. The *influence* is the feeling of awe the spectator has when being confronted with the *model* (1999: 24). In a tourist context, the Sydney Opera House is the *model* and the experience of walking around and into this structure, maybe to attend a show or simply to purchase a souvenir, is the *influence*. The tourist has confirmed the correctness of the model by visiting it personally. All attractions can in the same manner be seen as cultural experiences, being representations of diverse cultures and allowing the visitor to experience the verification process that all sightseeing is a part of.

An experience is defined in the Oxford Dictionary as "the process of gaining knowledge or skill over a period of time through seeing and doing things rather than studying" or alternatively "to feel something" (1995). The definition describes an experience as temporal involving the human senses in forming a perception of a phenomenon. The philosophical branch that has focussed mostly on a systematic usage of reflection about experiences is phenomenology. Shapiro (1985: 12) builds on Husserl when he distinguishes between the *noematic* features of a phenomenon, the object and its context, and the *noetic* features, the way the subject is experiencing the phenomena. The dialectic of the two entities is the relation between them, "neither is the cause of which the other is a result, rather, there is a circularity of influence." The reflection of the dialectics between the noematic and the noetic features is what distinguishes an experience. The tourist can take a "step back" from the experience and reflect not only on the attraction and its settings, such as in the example of the Sydney Opera House; its location by the harbour of Sydney, its architecture, its symbolism of being an arena for "high culture," but also on the involvement the tourist themself has with the attraction, the personal closeness to an icon, the pictures taken of it, the souvenirs purchased for later re-consumption of the same experience. Shapiro (1985: 13) sums it up by saying "experience is not somehow only a direct presentation of the object, nor is it merely subjective or mental. It is bodily in that the *body-subject* or individual must actively participate or engage himself in the situation of any moment." This last point is important, as an experience cannot ever be the same while the subject is never the same at two different moments.

## Authenticity, Real and True

MacCannell's overarching theory in "The Tourist" is that every tourist wants to have "authentic" experiences in which they can experience the "real" life of the society that they visit and to see the "true" original sights that made that place famous or infamous in the first place. "The Tourist" is a description of how the tourist industry is divided into two super-structures, the front and the back-stage. MacCannell distinguishes six different stages, between being overtly front-stage, a place built for tourists, to being explicitly back-stage, where the locals live their true lives without being seen by the visitors (1999). Urry builds on this notion by quoting Pearce and Moscado (1986) who claim that a distinction has to be made between the authenticity of the setting; which would be a place inhabited by people simply for the reason of living, and the authenticity of the persons gazed upon; which in turn would be people lacking self-consciousness of their being. He then contrasts this with a statement from Crick (1988) claiming that all cultures are "staged" and to some extent "inauthentic" (1990: 9).

This division is very much still the case on an overt level, where travellers agree on front and back-stage discrepancies. What this paper is claiming is, following Crick's notion, that the backstage is as staged as the front-stage or alternatively that both are as authentic as each other when both constitute the explicit experience of the tourist, the subject. For additional discussions on the authenticity of authenticity see, for example, Frow (1997: 67–75). An example of this dualistic mindset can be given from the New South Wales version of Lonely Planet (LPNSW). Lonely Planet is largely seen as a key for adventurous travellers to open the door to the backstage and make it possible for the travellers to find a way off the "beaten track" to the real scenes and adventures that different regions are offering. The LP instructs its readers to use the guidebook in any way they choose, as "the most memorable travel experiences are often those that are unexpected, and the finest discoveries are those that you make yourself" (LPNSW 2000: 14). It describes the sites worth visiting in NSW and concludes the introduction with: "From ancient Aboriginal sites to atmospheric country pubs, practically everything that is considered 'typically Australian' can be found in NSW" (2000: 16). In a later chapter that is called "Facts about NSW" the guidebook partly corrects this original statement by saying:

> Non-Aboriginal Australians have a self-image as a resourceful, self-reliant people at home in the bush, but this has never been strictly correct. That is not to say that the hardy pioneers didn't exist. They did, but they were objects of bemused admiration for the majority, who lived in towns (LPNSW 2000: 35, 36).

The guidebook is then a combination of facts about destinations and attractions in the state, written in a style that is supposed to be without bias and simply describing for the self-sufficient traveller what there is to see. Clear value statements that reveal the authors' own dispositions to be close to the self-image that earlier was corrected appears in places such as:

> The Central Coast is a strange combination of the beautiful and the awful —
> superb surf beaches, lakes and national parks combined with huge swathes

of rampant suburban housing. There are more urban areas around Lake Macquarie, immediately to the north, which blend into the sprawling city of Newcastle. While you're stuck in one of the Central Coast's suburban-style traffic jams, you might ponder the possibility of this situation spreading over the entire coast of Australia. It's a depressingly likely scenario (LPNSW 2000: 194).

This duality that is evident throughout the LP guides illustrate the frontstage/backstage demarcation that tourism in large is a part of. MacCannell notes that this seems to be a perpetual part of the existence of tourists, the constant urge "to go beyond the other 'mere' tourists to a more profound appreciation of society and culture" (1999: 10). Another author that has pointed out this duality in other terms is Dann (1999) who talks about the *tourist angst* from which many travellers and also travel writers suffer. They do not want to be seen as tourists because of the negative associations the model transmits, they carry a dual hatred towards other travellers and themselves.

The difficulty with words like "authentic," "real" and "true" is that all of them are value statements to a certain degree. Authenticity is problematic on several levels; Lewis (2002) takes examples from popular music and shows how the mixture in the Australian Aboriginal rock music exemplified by artists like Yothu Yindi is both authentic and very much inauthentic. The authentic elements are the usage of traditional instruments and specific arrangements, but the music is at the same time an amalgam of world dance music and Afro-American protest music. He concludes by stating that some of the traditional instruments used in Yothu Yindi's music, such as the Didgeridoo, are not authentically Australian as they in themselves are appropriated from the Indonesian Maccassins three to four hundred years ago (Lewis 2002: 353). Eco is another author who raises the awareness of how the oxymoron "authentic replicas" can become hyper-realities. Eco (1987) studies examples of replicas that are so well made that they become better than the original, not just real, but hyper-real. This hyper-reality is increasingly a part of modern tourism; examples in an Australian context can be taken from the Aboriginal "cultural-park" Tjapukai north of Cairns. Tjapukai has received several awards for being an outstanding exhibition of Australian aboriginal culture which otherwise is hard to encapsulate. The closest most international tourists get to the indigenous population on their holidays in Australia is listening to street-musicians dressed in traditional costumes, or the purchase of commodified, reproduced souvenirs like boomerangs or dot-paintings in the major cities. Tjapukai, on the other hand is developed and run by aboriginal organizations and all music, dance and craft performances are guaranteed to be authentic (Welcome to Tjapukai, n.d.). The notion of hyper-reality comes from the fact that the culture has to be presented in a cultural park in order to be "consumed." The "real," "authentic" life-style is not possible for the average tourist, or for a majority of the indigenous population, to be experienced anymore and that is why staged realities become better than the real thing. Lewis (2002: 374) correctly points out that "tourism re-render local artefacts and ceremonies for the palatability of visitor consumers . . . consume and reproduce images that become 'mainstreamed' for tourism." As this whole process is overt and consumers start to be consistently aware of their position as Feifer's "post-tourists" (1985) and understand that they play the role of being tourists, more emphasis in tourism research should possibly be placed upon phenomenological accounts of experience, not futile discussions about authenticity.

## Liminal and Australia

Urry explains the word liminal by placing it as an opposite to normal social experiences. A honeymoon couple are for example in a liminal zone when they travel in relative anonymity away from their normal commitments (1990: 10). The word liminal shares a root with the word limit, which is defined as "a point or line beyond which something does not extend" or alternatively "to set a limit or limits to something" (Oxford Dictionary 1995: 684). Seen in this context, liminal can be seen as a small physical or mental space that is "on the limit" to be outside the norm, or possibly *is* outside the norm. A tourist that travels to a liminal zone is either leaving his normal mental life or alternatively is leaving physical constraints behind and stays "on his limit." This can be by experiencing things that are not part of the tourists' normal life, such as sex-tourism or extreme sport tourism. In the context of this paper a liminal experience is defined as something that only focuses on a limited part of the collective culture that makes up Australia. To claim that something is "real" is to claim that that entity either constitutes the norm or that it constitutes a limit of the norm. In either case it separates one practice from the amalgam of practices that together makes up the nation's culture.

Australia as a cultural entity, or as a destination to visit is defined as the amalgam of people living in the country and their communal beliefs and shared values. The nation is made up of a minority of indigenous people and a majority of immigrants that have arrived during the two centuries since Australia became a part of the British Commonwealth. As all cultures in themselves are constructed by life and society, Australia like every other nation must be seen as a culture in the making. To discuss any specific feature of the nation is necessarily discriminating against any other feature. The modernist view is to favour the colonial culture and marginalise the colonised (Barker 2000), but the view to take based on box D in Figure 17.1 is rather to look at each cultural form as *re*presentation of the nation. To celebrate the Queen's Birthday is as much an Australian feature as the dreamtime stories, Gewürztraminer wines from the Barossa Valley or a weekend family dinner at a Yum Cha restaurant. The opening ceremony of the Olympic Games in Sydney 2000 was an attempt to *re*present the multi-faceted features of the nation with common symbols in an entertaining setting. The viewer was presented with an array of symbols like dreamtime dances, Ned Kelly costumes, corrugated steel water barrels and, as a satirical joke on the current suburbanisation, dances with "Victa," the lawnmower (Follow the Flame 2000).

## Media Analysis of Images of "Real Australia"

Australia is known for having 4 R's; the Roo; the Roof; the Reef and the Rock, as its main attractions (Heimerson 2000: 56). *The Roo* — symbolising the marsupial family of different types of kangaroos and wallabies. A roo is the symbol painted on each Qantas airplane, Australia's international air carrier. The kangaroo is common in rural areas of the country but it is not unusual that an urban Australian only sees live kangaroos on their rare visits to wildlife parks, or on car tours to the countryside. *The Roof* — the exterior areas of the Sydney Opera House are the closest contacts the majority of Australians get to this institution of high culture. Even though the Opera House was built with five different performance stages in order to cater for a variety of different cultural productions, it still remains a symbol for an elite culture, not the popular. *The Reef* — refers to the Great Barrier Reef, popular as a tourist destination but relatively inaccessible for the average Australian, as it is situated off the north coast of Queensland. Finally *the Rock* — Uluru, the world's largest monolith remotely situated in the middle of the great continent, a centre for aboriginal spiritual beliefs, though far away from where the majority of the population lives and rarely visited by the common citizen of Australia. Many tourists travel to Uluru not only to experience the monolith, but also explicitly to experience the aboriginal culture. Bowry (2003) suggested an additional division by which the international tourist market should not be seen as a homogenous group. She divides international travellers between backpackers and "average" tourists, stating that the average travellers might be more inclined to experience regular 4-R holidays. The youth market of backpackers are on the other hand staying in the country for a longer time in order to experience the "real" Australian way of life, which she describes as: "A relaxed atmosphere, filled with friendly people, outback adventures and an escape from realities of their normal lives back home" (Bowry 2003: 2). A reason for this picture to emerge amongst backpackers might be their extended stays where they get to know the romanticised perception Australians have of "real" holidays.

Visitors are through their pre-conceptions, to a certain degree, focused on gazing upon the icons. A reason why the international tourists are gazing at different attractions from those gazed upon by Australians can again be found in Urry's concept of the Gaze. He states that "The tourist gaze is directed to features of landscape and townscape which separate them off from everyday experience" (1990: 3). Seen from this perspective it can be assumed that everyday views such as the constantly reproduced 4-Rs becomes "too" familiar to Australians and they therefore focus on other more romanticised features for their holiday patterns. This could include the outback, the national parks and the beaches — natural attractions. There is though, a drive for Australians on holiday to visit the Great Barrier Reef and Uluru, but other attractions in Queensland, the Northern Territory and Western Australia are as common to be gazed upon as the aforementioned ones. For international travellers again it seems that the 4-Rs would be the reason for their travel and their gaze would not be fulfilled without having the chance to experience them.

Another perspective on the gaze comes from Hollinshead who has tried to translate Foucault's original thoughts in a way different to Urry. Hollinshead's definition of the gaze is more structured and seems to be closer to Gramsci's concept of Hegemony in the way powers operate (Lewis 2002), thus:

> The panoptic gaze of a group/community/institution is the power of surveillance . . . which individuals within that group/community/institution are found to harness in order to inspect the people and things around them. Such a generally unconscious eye-of-power can enable those individuals in that context to see and then understand phenomena from some vantage points, but not so well at all from others (Hollinshead 1999).

By using this latter definition the different views of what the concept of the "Real Australian" means to international and Australian tourists becomes much clearer. It is also possible to illustrate prevailing different views through a media analysis that was undertaken in June

2003. Database searches were conducted focussing on the words *real* and *Australian* in both Australian and international newspapers from the two prior years. The content of the articles was analysed and then classified to be either:

(a) *Romantic*; which is here seen as equivalent to the western, modernist view of the nature standing for the "real" attribute, building on the dualistic division between nature and culture (Frow 1997). Morris (1995: 181) points out that an Australian national identity is mostly built on "shaky compromises and acts of wishful thinking . . . by white men as a history of desire, uncertainty and fear of a lack of difference." Or

(b) *4-Rs*; the previously mentioned four Australian icons that internationally are seen as icons representing the continent (Heimerson 2000).

(c) *Political*; as there has been a tendency amongst politicians, for example the then Prime-Minister John Howard, to use the phrase to somehow prove their nationalism. Real Australia has in these instances often been an indication of the nation's current state, with a fair amount of Caucasian, Anglican undertows.

(d) *Statistical*; in which the words "real" and "Australia" are understood in a literal meaning by looking at what constitutes the average Australian.

(e) *Other*; this final category constitutes articles in which the words "real" and "Australia" just happened to be in the same sentence but were not related to this topic such as "Get real Australia."

## Results

An Australian is likely to laugh at the 4-R image as being a too simplified descriptor of the "real Australia." A normal response is for example Ball's:

> Mixed in with the colours are the characters. You find them in Gulf Country pubs . . . They are stockmen, road workers, truck drivers, southerners and English barmaids getting a taste of "real" Australia, men and women chatting, playing pool, dancing to juke box selections about somebody leaving somebody, and draining stubbies (2003).

The picture is painted to imply that the tourist would not have experienced more than an overtly staged front-stage if they had not seen more than some of the 4-Rs. In database searches of Australian newspapers for the last two years, 137 full articles where "Real Australia" was a feature and thirty-three articles were found where "Real Australia" was either in the heading or in the lead text. A content analysis of the latter group revealed that sixteen (49%) of the articles were based on the Romantic picture of Australia. One excellent example was Maynard's; "This is the beginning of the real Australia, where country meets town. It is not the Outback, but it is still possible to find solitude here in Ku-ring-gai National Park, which is barely 30 km from the city centre" (2003). Two (6%) were statistical articles regarding the 2001 census, two (6%) were political, one was satirical on the romantic picture claiming that "BUMS, boobs and men drooling in their beer is an image that represents present-day Australia much better than such stereotypes as the swagman" (Tucak 2001).

Eleven (33%) had by chance the words in the heading but related to different matters, such as "Security risk remains real" and finally one article pictured "real Australia" from the 4-R perspective in explaining what American tourists are offered when visiting the country. The mention of "real" Australia can be traced back to Urry's definition of "real holidays" that have two parts. Firstly to spend the holiday away from the masses, thus building on the romantic gaze, secondly to "use small specialist agents/operators to get to the destination" (1990: 95). Tour operators in Cairns, the main gate to the Great Barrier Reef, are specifically pitching certain cruises to Australian tourists by pointing out how personal and small the vessels are compared to the large commercial mass-cruises purchased by international visitors (Jack Stellarer, personal communication, 02.01.2003).

When the search was extended to international sources forty-three full articles were found and eight articles where "Real Australia" featured in the heading. A content analysis of the latter category revealed that six (75%) of the articles pictured Australia from the 4-R tourist stereotype perspective with texts like Gonzalez:

> The mere mention of the land down-under conjures certain images: the striking Sydney Opera House, its roof resembling sails gliding across the city's harbor; the azure, tranquil waters surrounding the Great Barrier Reef; Paul Hogan navigating a new Subaru through the Outback (2003).

Or alternatively with a very strong focus on the aboriginal heritage such as; "So many Canadians visit Australia but so few see the Real Australia — a nation defined by the culture of its Aboriginal people" (Russell 2002). Morris (1995: 183) explains this remark by reminding that many international tourists are more interested "in Aboriginal, rather than non-Aboriginal Australian cultures." One of the analysed articles pictured Australia in the Romantic framework, and one had by chance the words real and Australia in the title.

## Discussion

By summing up the media study it can be seen that both categories were dominated by a majority of articles confirming the dualistic gaze of "real" Australia that has been suggested. Further issues that have to be examined are to see how many of these images are planned measures by tourist authorities. The question that might be asked is: Have the different promotions shaped the gaze or has the gaze shaped the promotions? Morris' view of the matter seems to be clear in emphasising that Australians have

> an anxiety that the culture is somehow dull and its attractions too quickly exhausted, along with . . . a nostalgic wish, that authentic Australian life may not be found in the sprawling coastal cities where people actually live, but only in the . . . 'dead heart' — in myth a source of historic white identity (Morris 1995: 185).

This view is supported by looking at Australia from a statistical perspective instead of any tourist gaze, for it is clear that the nation is one of the most urbanised in the world with

81.8% of the population living in urban areas with more than 3000 inhabitants. Of the workforce, 85.2% is employed in other industries than primary production and 42% of the nation's population are either first or second generation Australians and have therefore been brought up in families where cultural values other than the iconised "real" Australian ones have been fostered (Census of Population 2001).

Salt (cited in Cleary & Murphy 2002) states: "There is no such thing as the average Australian. What you have is a weighted average of a series of tribes: social, cultural and demographic, which meld together to give a statistical average." Based on the earlier definition of culture in Figure 17.1, this last perspective is the closest to what can be called the "real' Australia. However to be attracted to something, maybe it has to be hyper-real, as the real "real" is not distinct and therefore has no tourist pull value in itself. A romanticised picture of suburbia is also possible such as in the following extract:

> "Boring" and "dull" seems to be words of choice to describe city suburbs. Why? I often think of the suburbs of Townsville/Thuringowa where I have lived for more than 60 years. The hills, well-tended gardens, colourful tropical trees and plants and creeks seem idyllic to me. When we celebrate being Australian, let's include suburbia among the things in which we rejoice (Hoolihan 2002).

Nevertheless this still probably remains a minority opinion, most travellers are not gazing upon mundane residential areas, they travel away from such home-environments and want to experience different, "authentic" and fulfilling attractions.

## Conclusion and Implications

This chapter raised the question of what are the true descriptors of Australian culture? In the process of defining the terms culture, experience and authenticity, liminal, real/true and Australia several indicators were found that pointed to the fact that no culture might be authentic. If this is correct then there is no description of real or true Australia that would be more accurate than any other. It is alternatively possible to view everything as authentic, based on the fact that tourists are the persons who experience the phenomena. If they would not be where they were, that very experience would not have happened. In this sense it is the tourist that makes the experience authentic. If the latter definition is accepted then all descriptors found in Australia can be seen as "real" cultural symbols. Shapiro's notion on the usage of phenomenology as a tool for researchers and industry practitioners, to reflect on the dialectics between the noematic and the noetic features in an experience should be taken seriously. Ultimately that is what distinguishes the final phenomena, as the stakeholders' own actions form the experiences involuntarily. Urry's and Hollinshead's definitions of the tourist gaze were analysed and a suggestion was made that each tourist group have their own perception of the "real" aspects of the culture, and that these perceptions are hard to change as they are part of a subconscious value system.

A brief description of tourism in Australia was made and a media analysis was conducted in order to prove the validity of the concepts proposed. The analysis showed that a strong connection exists between the way Australian and international tourists gaze in different ways on the nation and especially on its tourist attractions. Caution should though be used in drawing too far reaching conclusions of this division, as it has been earlier claimed that both groups are to an extent aware of the other gaze and might be participating in that as well.

The closest answer to the original question might at this stage still be that true descriptors of the Australian culture are an amalgam of interconnected symbols, each from different settings, but together constituting Australia. Based on that answer it seems correct to classify an experience of the "real" Australia as a fairly liminal one. Every time something is experienced which is determined "real" by some source, another source is questioning that reality.

This chapter is derived from a larger doctoral study examining Special Interest Tourism and its contributor to the formation of cultural identity. That thesis discusses additional matters such as how a gaze might shape tourist practices. The fact that Australians are proud of mentioning their cemeteries as tourist attractions; that old gaols are popular tourist attractions while functioning prisons are placed out of sight. A deeper study of statistics to prove the dual gaze proposed here is necessary. Finally more studies will also be based on a phenomenological approach where the author will try to examine tourist experiences from a noematic/noetic/reflective perspective. From the perspective of indigenous tourism, what is of interest is how, within definitions of what constitutes "Australia," the Aboriginal is either represented in absentia, or alternatively is the romantic presence of something lost, or again, as a liminal figure. Yet again, the marginal defines the mainstream by presenting the "truth" that for the statistically common Australian, the conceptualisation of self as Australian is defined by what he or she is not, namely Aboriginal.

## Acknowledgments

The author wishes to acknowledge the useful suggestions and acts of assistance he has received from several colleagues and students in the process of compiling this study. The valid and constructive criticism from his supervisor and conference referee have additionally aided in making this a more readable and valid study.

Chapter 18

# Conceptualising "Otherness" as a Management Framework for Tourism Enterprise

Jenny Cave

## Introduction

Tourists and hosts both hold pre-conceived notions about those things that are private to social settings, and those that can be made public to be shared with visitors, and may occupy a continuum that comprises friends at one extreme to strangers at another. Tensions may thus arise as each communicates the content of culture to the other in the framework of cultural tourism across a series of interactions between visitor and host.

For the most part these interactions occur within a framework of intermediaries formed by the formal business structure of the tourism industry. However, in contexts such as those illustrated by European–Pacific Island cultural divides in New Zealand, the formal tourism industry sector may arise from an informal social context, whereby the entrepreneurs are located within an informal context of family, friends and culturally determined manner of business conduct that is not wholly congruous with the expectations of those bringing guests to the location, much less those expectations of the guests themselves.

## Context — Tourism in Marginalised Communities

Physical marginalisation of communities can result from distance between population centres, natural landscape isolation or catastrophic events. Economic marginalisation results from changing global demands for natural resources, out-migration from rural to urban areas, as well as political and technological change. A tourism attraction, community or activity can be considered marginalised if located at the limits of tourism flow, whether rural or urban. Cultural and social marginalisation occurs for groups that experience life at the fringes of mainstream society, with limited access to basic services as well as impediments or disadvantage in many forms (Thaman 2002). In some cases they are self-identified communities. However, frequently they are defined by the attitudes and perceptions of mainstream populations. Indigenous cultures for example, have experienced cultural dilution, reduction in population through disease, violence and intermarriage, as well as homogenisation and relegation to marginalised positions in the modern world (Thaman 2002).

Tourism is a favoured means of reclaiming position in society amongst isolated communities. Enterprise outcomes envisioned by these communities include local control of initiatives and retention of economic benefits from out-of-region tourist spending within the local community (Murphy 1985). As an industry, tourism has a low entry threshold for both investment and training. Thus lower income groups often are capable of entering an industry in which they can benefit directly (Ryan 2002a). Enhanced community self-image and cohesive community, as well as the stimulation of artistic or cultural expression and preservation of culture within local communities (Erisman 1983) are further benefits. Collective hegemony can be used as a political resource in claims against both the state and other racial or ethnic groups (Ryan 2002a). However, in many cases indigenous peoples hold implicit power through their proximity to and control of natural and/or cultural resources.

Hegemony is a crucial element of ethnicity and community. Indigenous and migrant ethnic communities are asserting intellectual and cultural property ownership in cultural tourism products that strengthen the cultural gaze, attitudes, perception and behaviour within these initiatives. Gurian maintains that this is one of the most important issues of this century that cultural industries will have to address (Gurian 2002). This chapter is directed to the analysis of communities, groups or individuals who actively organise intellectual and cultural resources to realise tourism initiatives based on proximity and/or access to traditional ethnic culture or heritage.

The conceptualisation developed in this chapter has emerged from the author's work with the Pacific Island community resident in Waitakere City, New Zealand. Although this text is theoretical in nature, the author would wish to acknowledge the contribution of these communities by briefly describing their situation within New Zealand, and thereby bringing attention to their current situation and aspiration. New Zealand has been ethnically and culturally connected to Polynesia for at least 1,000 years. Less than 200 years ago, its population and cultural heritage were wholly Polynesian, but now are dominated by cultural traditions that are mainly European. About four-fifths of New Zealanders are of European origin, from the British Isles and Europe. This proportion is expected to reduce to a minority by mid-century as the proportions of Maori, Pacific Island and Asian New Zealanders increase. By 2051, it is likely that one in five children will be of Pacific Island birth (MPAC 1999a). The Pacific population in New Zealand consists of 50% Samoan, 22.5%, Cook Islands, 15.5% Tongan, 9% Niuean, 2% Fijian and 1% Tokelauan, plus small numbers of other Pacific groups (MPAC 1999b: 10).

The history of migration and travel from the Pacific Islands to New Zealand extends back over more than 100 years due to New Zealand's colonial presence in the Pacific, occupations during war time and the demand for seasonal workers in New Zealand. However, collectively, the culturally diverse Pacific peoples represent a disadvantaged community. The median annual income for the Pacific Island community as a whole was $14,800 per annum, compared to an annual average taxable income of $24,251 in 2001 (Statistics 2002). Disposable incomes are reduced further by the practice of remitting money to families back in the islands (McLeod, Perrott & Thomson 2002). Occupations are most commonly in the manufacturing and service industries. Approximately 14% hold a tertiary qualification compared with 24% for the total New Zealand population. The population resident in New Zealand is comparatively young, with a median age of 21 years, 40% of which are below the age of 15 years (Statistics 2001).

In 2001 the Pacific Island Advisory Board Waitakere Inc., began to explore potential business strategies and cultural tourism with the intention of addressing marginalisation issues on behalf of the communities of West Auckland. The anticipated tourism audience for such enterprise was expected to be the 2.4 million residents of the wider Auckland region and the domestic visiting friends and relatives market.

### *Dimensions of the Framework*

The dimensions for the framework proposed in this chapter comprises, firstly (but without an implied hierarchy), an "Otherness" or cultural experience dimension and secondly, an "Enterprise" or entrepreneurial dimension. The framework describes a dynamic of interaction in cultural tourism settings which has implications for both sets of people who participate, i.e. Visitor and Host. The term "Visitor" is chosen, rather than "Tourist" since, in this age of extensive international travel and post-colonial global migrations, culturally distinct enclaves of community are evident in almost every country of the world. Thus, localised short-distance experience of cross-cultural contact through ethnic community cultural expression (events, etc) is as much a commonplace occurrence as is domestic and international tourism. "Host" in this context refers to the ethnic community, group or individual who conceives, stages and implements cultural tourism initiatives.

## Cultural Experience Dimension

The cultural experience dimension as envisaged for this framework is enacted by both visitor and host in terms of behaviours, values, perceptions and attitudes to the experience of cultures that are identifiably different than their own.

From the Host's perspective, there may be elements of cultural tradition/identity which can be made public and others which must be retained as private (to individuals or communities) for spiritual and ritual reasons (Adams 1997). And, from the Visitor's perspective, similar dynamics are at play that are in large part dependent upon self-efficacy in unfamiliar environments (Bird, Osland, Mendenhall & Schneider 1999), as well as willingness to participate freely in a new experience, their degree of prior experience or attitudes to intercultural experiences and the influence of their social group.

From the Visitor's perspective, touristic experiences outside one's social norms, have been argued to be *heterotopic* occurring spatially, in "places of otherness," wherein new ways of seeing or experimenting are experienced (St. John 2001). These are real sites or events (Hetherington 1997) that are unsettling, mysterious, challenging, dangerous, and hold multiple meanings. Heterogeneous spaces are those that indicate complex juxtaposition and cosmopolitan simultaneity of difference (Soja 1995).

Utopia, somewhat oppositional to heterotopia, as sites or events with no real place, also exist in touristic experience (St. John 2001). Utopia represent ideas about society (Hetherington 1996), presenting society in its perfected form, or else turned upside down (Hetherington 1997). Utopia is, by its very nature, without conflict — a state of stasis, harmony, and balance (Klaic 1991). Utopia displaces reality into an idealized *other place*, outside the actual boundaries of geographic space and historical time (de Bruyn 2003).

*Utopic* experiences are characterised as places of togetherness, idealised private spaces, in which groups of associates, family, friends and "not strangers" are in state of "being alone together." These are places in which norms are confirmed, reinforced, common language developed and common (cultural) meanings constructed. People who seek to transform the world as it is, are utopic in attitude, holding the future-oriented ethic of "not yet" since interactions continue to be on-going and to some extent unresolved. Such interactions also carry traces of the past since the "face" presented to the Other by the Self is affected by broader social processes and other times, rather than simply the present (Ahmed 2002). The encounter is mediated at the level of the encounter (sociality), and by one's own identity (Ahmed 2002: 563).

The utopia/dystopia binary coincides with the Self/Other binary and language is often the defining characteristic of otherness (Sheridan 1999). However, in this chapter, complementary differences rather than oppositional contrasts are described so that the Self/Other binary is correlated not with dystopia, but with heterotopia, and seen as an element of complexity not of idealized clarity.

### Notions of Otherness and Self

Tourism is frequently dubbed the business of "difference" and "the other," *par excellence* (Hollinshead 1998). It is a strategy for framing and interpreting cultural difference, the driving ideology behind which is a form of *extopy* (Baktin 1981) or appropriation of otherness (Harkin 1995). However, conflicting épistèmes are in operation: one of *difference*, which reduces the "Other" to either a simple mirror of one own society or a dangerous threat, as well as the épistème of *curiositas*, which urges the traveller to self-confidently explore the limits between that which is known or familiar to us and to engage willingly with the "Unknown," seeking out challenges that call into question accepted worldviews (Sobecki 2002).

Notions of Otherness and Self outlined in literature are: (a) reflexive, in that they are constructed from the outside to unpack the characteristics of your identity; (b) actively epistemological, in that they return to the core of "ways of knowing, that which you know"; (c) retrospective, in that those perceptions are fore-known; and (d) experiential, in that they are born of either your own experience or of experiences by another (McCormick 2002).

Reflexive and epistemological notions of "Otherness and Self" encompass several objectified variants: Otherness — meaning "Different from me"; Self — meaning the "Same as me (your identity)"; Othered Selves — meaning "Other people, like me"; Othered Others — meaning "Other people, unlike me." The relationship of Otherness to Self can be drawn: as heterotopic, being different (Irigary 1991); utopic, as a sense of oneness (de Beauvoir 1997); and tempered with the concepts of ambiguity and mutuality (Green 2002). Such objectification implies power, the mutual construction of identity, the development of relations between colonizers and colonized, or "cultural representations" of Otherness (Lester 1998). The designation of "racial others, ethnics, outsiders" purges cultural differences and social practices, re-shaped around a racial hierarchy that sub-categorises at the same time as devaluing those people (Bartolome & Macedo 1997). Care must be taken in discussion of this framework not to repeat the practice of categorization, but to try not to exclude or devalue the peoples here represented, "to write in friendship and be accountable" (Calas & Smircich 1999: 650).

### *"Otherness"*

"Otherness" is often associated with marginalised communities — primitive, exotic, post-colonial societies that are distant somehow from mainstream western thought. "To speak of Otherness, is to speak of that other human being whom I have mistakenly assumed to be just like me and who, in fact, is not like me at all. To speak of Other is to be open to otherness within my self, to the possibility of a foreigner within my own conscious self. As well, to acknowledge poverty, justice, sexuality, gender, race and class and that difference is prob-lematic, threatening, alienating and difficult to live with well" (Ackermann 1998: 13–27).

Our understanding of Other or rather, the mutual construction of identity and creation of the conceptual Other, have been influenced by the development of relations between colonizer and colonized, described by cultural representations (Lester 1998). Metropolitan narratives of European travellers and geographers reflect the political influence of humanitarianism, versus the resistance to colonial authority by indigenes and former slaves (e.g. in Jamaica and New Zealand with the Maori Wars), with the consequent adoption of images of the "irreclaimable savage" who resisted the civilising missions in the mid eighteenth century (Lester 1998).

Otherness is not just about the "look" or gaze, but also about touch and communication — translated, authorized and valued, though being commodified at the will of the user (Ahmed 2002). Little (1999) suggests that Otherness is usually applied in a static sense to individuals and group identity. There is a need to focus on the differences within groups as well as between them in an attempt to understand the degrees of separation and movement (Little 1999). Hence notions of role emerge. In fact, it is less important to understand cultural behavioral patterns and differences, than it is to understand the antagonism and tensions engendered by cultural differences that coexist asymmetrically because of the distance and ignorance engendered by creating social and cultural separateness (Bartolome & Macedo 1997).

Otherness also relates to embodied, sensory and affective encounters with Place. Boundaries transmitted through travel writings can both differentiate and connect the Self in relation to other worlds (Fullagar 2001). Intimacy theory explicates the otherness of lovers and family members and implies in this form, a unity that is independent of time and place (Trauer & Ryan 2005).

### *Notions of Third Space*

However, as this framework has progressed, another concept has emerged. It is perhaps inevitable that where interactions take place, hybridized environments may evolve

(Hollinshead 1998). Such zones of interaction have been called: "third space" environments (Hollinshead 1998), "communal realms of possibility" (Turner 1982), or "liminoid embodiments" and "pleasurescapes" (St. John 2001), "cultural spaces" (McKercher & Du Cros 2002) or places of contact between cultures (Macdonald & Alsford 1989).

Cultural identity is inherently hybrid because the category of "us" simultaneously incorporates the concept of "non-us" or "them" in terms of semiotic, racial, ethnic or national boundaries (Moscovi 2001). It shows connections between racial categories of the past and today. Hybridity reiterates and reinforces the dynamics, tensions and divisions it re-enacts by means of the connections (Moscovi 2001). The hybrid of two cultures does not eliminate differences, but simultaneously incorporates and negates certain, select qualities of its component cultures. Thus, simultaneously the hybrid preserves and cancels the difference between them, forming an asymmetrical power relationship between two societies that is integral to the ideological network (Moscovi 2001).

Finally, it can be noted that the creation of third space may be construed as the development of intentionally created communities.

## Notions of Role

Humans communicate to each other assumptions about their own culture(s) that are shared and reinforced within the cultural and community setting, albeit varied by time, place, setting, and subculture. Paradoxically, those things which define a culture are explicated and shown internally to each other most clearly when juxtaposed with cultures that are not their own. The processes of reflection and definition become dynamic as the contexts change and external triggering events occur. Thus definition can become re-definition (Said 1975).

One could think of settings for cultural tourism interactions as being the stage upon which such interactions take place. McKercher & Du Cros (2002) suggest that socio-historical, physical and access themes must be considered with regard to setting for the cultural tourism assets, along with cultural heritage management considerations such as continuity, historical context and tourism considerations such as physical location, compatibility with surrounding facilities and structures, proximity to other cultural/heritage assets, or location vis-à-vis tourism nodes (McKercher & Du Cros 2002). One could consider these settings to be influenced by the:

(1) Values and intent of both actors and audience.
(2) Degree of programming and design.
(3) Amount of management intervention.
(4) Degree of interaction — i.e. passive viewing to interactive immersion.
(5) Language used (i.e.: language of the ethnic culture; constructed hybrid of two languages e.g. "franglais"; temporal hybrid — constructed for the duration of the specific interaction; or mainstream language).
(6) Degree of familiarization of the Other (such that participants act out roles of known fantasy (Trauer & Ryan 2004).
(7) Ability to engage in unfamiliar environments.

Thus, setting also would relate to issues frequently highlighted in cultural tourism literature such as control, authority, authenticity, conservation, commodification, identity, attitudinal change, self-awareness and fore-knowledge of audience, as well as role of Hosts and Visitor, in relation to each other.

Ap suggests that the theory of social exchange may be one way to explore the results interactions between residents and tourists, expressed in terms of power (Ap 1992). Indeed, the degree of proximity to tourism activities on a daily basis appears to affect the degree of negative perception of the impacts of tourism, in those places where tourism is an integral part of everyday life (Perdue, Long & Allen 1992). Tourism has been cited as a way of bringing cultures together to create understanding. However, Costa and Livio contest this, by demonstrating that previous ideas and stereotypes can act as blinkers that prevent tourists from learning (Costa & Livio 1998). For example, visits to South West American Indian museums and Pueblo Indian ceremonials served to reinforce ethnocentrism and primitivism, convincing tourists of the correctness of their own views (Laxson 1991).

Role theory also informs this framework in terms of: perceptions of culture and the choice of roles available to the tourist (Schwaller 1992); the importance of role scripts, expectations, role taking and congruence or conflicts of role (inter and intra-personal) (Solomon, Suprenant, Czepiel & Gutman 1985); as well as the role of the intermediary (guide, travel agent, impresario) (Arnould & Price 1993; Quinn 2003).

Tourism plays a role in influencing the processes and dynamics of festival event settings, in terms of symbolism, local practices, reproducing cultural meanings and sustaining local myths (Quinn 2003). Interactions between Visitor and Host can perhaps be seen in three broad categories: the Role of Host (the home-based cultural community), the Role of Visitor (the outsider, the audience), and the Role of Mediator (the middle person, the interpreter, the go-between). These three categories can be further refined into roles which describe the nature of interactions between Self, Others, othered Others and othered Selves, and imply a progression from lower to higher degrees of interaction. Figure 18.1 lists these possible roles within Visitor-Host interactions.

| (a) Roles of Host | • Guardian<br>• Teacher<br>• Manager |
| --- | --- |
| (b) Roles of Visitor | • Involved acquisitor<br>• Edutainee<br>• Casual observer |
| (c) Roles of Mediator | • Actor<br>• Designer<br>• Facilitator |

Figure 18.1: Notions of role.

**(a) Roles of host** As Steward or "Guardian" the Host protects and preserves spiritual values and knowledge, cultural treasures, oral and perhaps written material evidence of traditions that are central to the ethnic community. These are passed on only to members of the ethnic community within traditional hierarchical structures and rarely if ever, brought into the realm of the "Other." Reflections on the past, and future, cultural unity, preservation, transmission of knowledge from elder to younger generations are imperatives within such as notion of stewardship or *kaitiakitanga* (Cave 2001).

When the Host acts as Guardian the Visitor (the Other) is regarded as an uninitiated person who has no access to cultural knowledge and is deliberately constrained by the Host from interaction with particular members of the host community (Ryan 2002), or in participation in cultural activities, or from access to portions of the physical site. An example of this might be the Kingitanga movement of Tainui where access to the Maori Queen is protected, viewing of culturally significant carvings is restricted until completed, or the Turangawaewae meeting house is for invited guests only.

As "Teacher," the Host understands that that the visitor needs some degree of interpretation of the cultural expressions in which they are engaged, in order to understand the protocols, language, or significance of the proceedings (Balme 1998).

The Host acts as "Manager" when money is charged for access to objects or sites of cultural expression and an expectation exists of an exchange whether of knowledge, of entertainment, of goods or services.

**(b) Roles of visitor** As "Involved Acquisitor" the cultural tourist is actively motivated to seek cultural immersion experiences (Smiles 2002); authenticity (McIntosh & Prentice 1999; Xie & Wall 2002); customized excursions into other cultures and places to learn about their people, lifestyle, heritage and arts in an informed way that genuinely represents those cultures and their historical contexts (Craik 2001; McKercher & Chow 2001). Such travellers "collect" experiences, unconsciously formalising or "curating" their experiences by acquisition of representative symbolic matériel — photographs, t-shirts, iconic souvenirs, art, and ephemera — that record, preserve, understand and disseminate their experiences during and after travel. Souvenirs are surrounded by text and context in terms of authentication, display, sale, and the ideology of the selling agent. They are perceived as authentic reminders of a particular place and are powerful signifiers of ideological meaning (Shenev-Keller 1993).

As "Edutainees," Visitor-Others interact somewhat passively with community cultural expressions that have been commodified for consumption by the Host. The range of edutainment experiences has progressed from observed didactism to highly interactive, hands-on participation in cultural events. Disney experiences and theme parks have played strong roles in innovating and demonstrating the success of these techniques (Wasko & Meehan 2001) which have been proven successful when adopted in Maori tourism (Tahanna & Oppermann 1998) and Australian Aboriginal performances (Zeppel 1998, 2001). As edutainees, visitors participate in spectacle, which associates strongly with "narcissistic" attitudes to Self (Abercrombie & Longhurst 1998).

The role of "Casual Observer" for visitors would be one adopted by tourists who are present at cultural events, but seem unwilling to become closely involved with the cultural context and are content to watch, listen and be part of the social group that they accompany.

Being a member of an audience becomes a "mundane event" and there is no longer a boundary between the Self and the world of people and things and so what stands outside the Self is merely a reflection, as in a mirror, of the Self (Abercrombie & Longhurst 1998).

**(c) Roles of mediator**    "Mediators" are seen within the local community — representing Same or Self, and at time Others from cultural communities that are not of the same ethnicity, act to bridge misunderstandings, facilitate positive outcomes and problem resolution between the community and visitors, and serve to facilitate cross-cultural communications (Brown 1992).

External "Others" can also perform the role of an actor mediator between cultures by taking part in the normal day-to day-life of a community, as well as deliberately participating in the acquisition of cultural knowledge through mastery of indigenous or ethnic arts, language or perhaps religion. Their motivation in such participation is to develop new forms of cultural expression, or to seek inspiration or enlightenment from such immersion in unfamiliar cultural environments. The effect of such interaction can lead to modelling or adoption of elements of the other culture whilst in the cultural community, and can endure for a long time after the experience has taken place.

The role of "Designer" can be played by ethnic community members, by Other, or in bicultural partnerships to conceive, design, construct and programme cultural experiences of differing levels of authenticity or commodification. Dances and rituals are perhaps shortened or embellished, and folk customs or arts altered, faked, and invented (Graburn 1976). However, new art styles can however be stimulated or the survival of otherwise moribund folk art may occur (Cohen 1983). Such encounters with the traditional performance of cultural Others are usually brief, essentially transitory, non-repetitive and asymmetrical (Cohen 1984). There is some evidence that such brevity can reinforce ethnocentrism and convince tourists of the correctness of their own world views (Laxson 1991) rather than promote cultural understanding.

The "Facilitator" role can be sourced from the host community or from outside. For example: the culture broker interprets, translates and makes accessible those things which are unfamiliar, exotic, strange and unusual in another culture. The culture broker acts as the mediator between hosts and guests, with responsibility for ethnic imaging and cultural trait selection (Calmels 1996; Smith 2001). Further examples are "wild guides" in the context of funerary rites in Sulawesi (Adams 1997), tour guides, or beach boys (Calmels 1996).

Initially, tourists are considered as guests within the traditional host-guest relationship, or perhaps adopted as "family" or "friend" (Adams 1997) so that they can participate in community ritual (made honorary, temporarily identified as the "Same"). However, as numbers of tourists increase, the nature of welcome can change (Doxey 1976) and the relationship transforms from one based on customary (but not precise nor obligatory) hospitality into a commercial one based on remuneration. Eventually professionalism arises to preserve culture and to enhance the areas's reputation as well as ensure long-term flow of visitors (Cohen 1984). This is not wholly neutral. Locals "play the native" and the professionals act to personalize the experience for Visitors (Cohen 1984; MacCannell 1976). Asymmetries in these relationships occur: where the host has an advantage of knowledge over the visitors, accounting for "gullibility" of tourists; or perhaps tourism means work for the locals, leisure for the tourists and creates misunderstandings and conflicts of interest

(Cohen 1984). Authors have suggested that the extent, variety and degree of change from normal life that tourists seek or are capable of seeking in their contacts with host communities are dependant upon the degree of "familiarity" or "strangeness" that each person is able to engage in unfamiliar environments (Cohen 1979).

In summary, an envisaged the cultural dimension envisaged could integrate an experience and interaction continuum described as "heteropic" at one end and "utopic" at the other. The characteristics of each are listed below.

### Characteristics of "Heterotopic" Experiences

- "Otherness."
- *Curiositas*.
- Openness.
- Public spaces.
- Place of expatriates, strangers.
- New ways of seeing, experimenting.
- Spatial and real spaces.
- Mystery, challenge, danger.
- Multiple meanings.
- Opportunity.
- Cultural dissonance.
- Unfamiliar, unknown, exotic.
- Experiences that can be shared with strangers.
- Accessed through intermediaries.
- Role of Visitor.
- Understanding is mediated.

### Characteristics of "Utopic" Experiences

- "Sameness", "Self hood", "Self-Sameness."
- Places of togetherness.
- Private to community spaces.
- Being alone together.
- Familiar, Known, Everyday.
- Share with family, "friends" not with strangers.
- Accessed only with prior understanding.
- Cultural harmony.
- Role of Host.
- Understanding is shared.

## Notions of Enterprise Dimension for Cultural Tourism

The enterprise dimension for the framework is conceived of spanning social (community) entrepreneurial values at one end, through a mix of goal/value complexities to commercially oriented goals at another. The enterprise dimension is of importance to Hosts in terms of their intent for enterprise outcomes, and to Visitors in term of their expectations of authenticity or commodification within the experience.

Issues for the Enterprise Dimension apparent in literature include: packaging, active collaboration ownership of resources, economic goals and commodification, etc (Robinson 1999); notions of cultural values in enterprise; community motives and goals (complementary or conflicting); decision-making (traditional structures and process vs entrepreneurial mind); networks of power; differences engendered within communities (income, control, distribution of benefits); values (cultural values and compatibility with touristic values); range of experiences made available and able to be used; leadership and influencers within the community; robust problem identification and decision making process; good-will and community participation as well as time in which to do achieve them.

### Notions of Goal

The respective goals of Visitor and Host are not always compatible — the Visitor is engaged in leisure and has many expectations; the Host is engaged in work and often has no idea what to expect from the Visitor who is sourced from a multitude of international, domestic cultural and educational backgrounds (Robinson 1999).

With respect to the goals of cultural tourism industries incompatibilities also emerge, to some extent due to relationships with and influence of stakeholders and networks of power. Cultural tourism should provide both learning objectives (about conservation of cultural heritage assets) and tourism management objectives (market appeal, commercial viability of products). In practice however, the achievement of these goals has proved elusive, as the pursuit of one objective has often been viewed as being inimical with the attainment of the other (Boniface 1998; Jacobs 1994; Jansen-Verbeke 1998). In many instances, one goal is sacrificed or traded off for the other.

Many cultural tourism activities are known to not perform well. This may be due to a lack of awareness and naiveté about the respective responsibilities of managers and operators (the intermediaries); a struggle with the imposition of promotion and marketing roles for some managers; cultural insensitivity on the part of tour operators and marketers about local cultural assets; tourists acting inappropriately, either not responding to signals given to them about accepted behaviour, or not instructed how to act otherwise (McKercher & Du Cros 2002).

However, this is far from the case in every circumstance. Two examples of best practise in commercial tourism enterprise are the Tjapukai Dance Theatre and the Tamaki Brothers Maori Village at Rotorua (Cave 2002). Both are based on "authentic" recreations of indigenous performance, structures, customs, food and art/crafts that have been packaged to aid cultural understanding and entertainment for Others. Authenticity is the "pull" which attracts Visitors to the sites. Note however, that in the case of Tjapukai, the traditional portion of the site returns lower financial yields to the operation because of the high staff numbers and costs of authentic materials, and is cross subsidised by the higher yields from the retail, restaurant, events, special exhibitions, themed corporate entertainment and performance services. They also operate in circumstances where the industry, the Elders and the wider community have negotiated and validated the nature of the commodified interpretations of traditional customs. The products are meaningful representations of the culture for both the audience (consumer/Other) and the ethnic community (producer/Same) alike. They have been authorised by senior members of the community who have requisite status, cultural and spiritual knowledge. Further, the songs, art, carvings etc that are presented are developed and checked by the Elders throughout their conception and performance, with appropriate sanctions to alter what is or is not performed. Thus, these cultural tourism products are indisputably authentic as contemporary expressions of indigenous culture. Authority is arguably more important than authenticity (Ryan 2002a).

The goals and boundaries are clear in these contexts. Stewardship or guardianship of the sacred (precious) and those things that are most important to the culture are clearly owned and managed by the cultures concerned, and yet valid forms of performance or interpretation that have meaning are openly shared.

However, circumstances are somewhat different for migrant communities who lack direct access to the traditional lands and tribal hierarchies that define identity. The way in which we are socialised, to a very large extent, influences the way we see the world around us. In the context of the Pacific island community in New Zealand, and in Auckland in particular, inherent contradictions operate and the picture of goals for cultural tourism is not so clear. In this migrant community traditional values and the church play a strong role. Community members are socialised in both the minority and mainstream contexts, operating sometimes in one and sometimes in the other. The experience is often painful (Thaman 1993). On the one hand, Pacific Island cultures have been embraced and publicly celebrated everywhere where there are island inhabitants, whether in New York, Sydney or London. But on the other hand, many Islanders lament the negative changes they see in their cultural society which they attribute to a breakdown of their cultural traditions and a steady loss of cultural values (Thaman 2002). A critical issue for second generation New Zealand-born Cook Islanders is how to maintain identity over the generations (Fitzgerald 1998). The Islander populations are experiencing rapid change from the traditional non-monetised economies of the islands to the commercially driven western society of New Zealand.

Younger outwardly looking generations have high expectations of keeping pace with the rest of New Zealand and are less sympathetic to traditional values and institutions. They become discontented, which at times puts them in conflict with society's traditional leadership (Fitzgerald 1998). As the power and authority of traditional chiefs and leaders are eroded (Thistlewait & Davis 1996), new mechanisms are becoming needed for community decision-making and conflict resolution. Churches have filled this gap but it is a fundamentally important issue in societies which had been hitherto accustomed to a decision making process dominated by tribal leadership, where dissent was not normal, and often unacceptable.

Migrant community entrepreneurs are thus located in a context of rapidly changing cultural values, diffusion of identity, breakdown in community structure and lack of ownership or relationship with the homeland. There is a sense of dispossession, separation from historical continuity and awareness that the issues of indigeneity, which might otherwise facilitate access to land, education, government agencies and financial resources by Treaty rights are not theirs. However, a sense of optimism regarding speed, flexibility, and opportunity for achievement of community, social and entrepreneurial goals is revealed in Pacific Island business initiatives. A recently articulated Pacific Island community business strategy in Auckland is to comprise features such as competitive edge, active partnerships, leadership, and business development based on community goals not on economics (Sheehan 2002).

## *Enterprise Values*

For the most part, Host-Visitor interactions occur within a framework of intermediaries formed by the formal business structure of the tourism industry, some seeing it as a double-edged sword. On the one hand, increased demand by tourists provides a powerful political and economic justification to support the values of cultural conservation, but on the other, overuse, inappropriate use of cultural assets, commodification without regard for cultural values poses real threats to the integrity and survival of the assets (McKercher & Du Cros 2002). It is difficult to balance enterprise values (to ensure that the financial integrity of assets is maintained) with cultural values that are not compromised for cultural gain.

At the level of community tourism tends to loosen informal diffuse solidarities and increase individualization and greater formalization of local life (Stott 1978: 81). But there are instances however, where among marginal ecological or ethnic groups, tourism produces a reaction of group solidarity in the face of intruding foreigners (Boissevain 1977: 530–532), thus enhancing community cohesion values. Community hegemony is a growing trend, even in the context of the debate about the effects of globalisation, whether resulting in localized cultural expressions to counteract generic cultural diffusion, or whether globalised cultures such as tourism create expectations of the same levels and tones of service throughout the world.

Enterprise creates tension: between community groups; between motives/goals that can be both complementary and conflicting; between decision-making processes where traditional structures may not work well with the entrepreneurial mind; differences can be engendered within communities in terms of income disparity, control mechanisms and the power of individuals, and the distribution of benefits; tensions can arise between values, especially the degree of compatibility of cultural with touristic values; and lastly the range of experience made available to visitors.

Yet, Pacific entrepreneurship is known to thrive within a framework of existing social relations and cultural *mores* (Hailey 1987; Tanoi 1993). Hence a grid is proposed below that explores possible management and public access relationships for communities such as these. It provides for a possible analysis of managed environments in circumstances where cultural values are balanced against tourism enterprise values at several levels of meaning, being active "self-management" via community/cultural mechanisms, "mediated" access to cultural assets via an agreed intermediary, and "appropriated" wherein cultural assets are utilised by tourism industries with passive participation by cultural agents. This grid, shown in Figure 18.2, suggests that the factors of control, confidence in cultural identity, and whether community and cultural values can/should be managed by Selves versus managed by professional industry Others.

The clear disparity between tourism industry and cultural community values is seen in comparisons of recent research into the enterprise values of Pacific Island community,

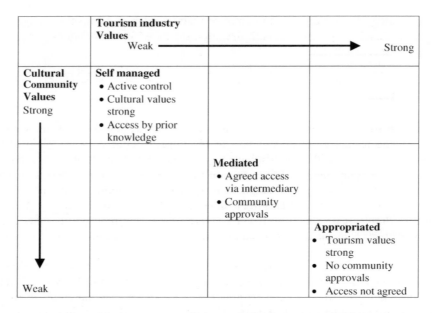

Figure 18.2: Tourism industry values versus cultural community values.

and comparisons with best practise tourism entrepreneurs throughout New Zealand (coincidently mostly European in origin). These are summarised in Figures 18.3 and 18.4, where differences and similarities may be seen.

| Values (Self) | Action |
|---|---|
| Traditions and Capacity Building | • Transmit and preserve cultural traditions<br>• Incubate commercial business capacity<br>• Create a competitive edge<br>• Performance, visual arts and crafts<br>• Link directly to the Island nations |
| Entertainment | • Outdoor shows<br>• Theme park<br>• High quality restaurant |
| Community | • Social and community activities<br>• Family celebrations<br>• Showcase the best of the best |
| Pacific Island Lifestyle | • Experience Pacific Island lifestyle<br>• Supply Pacific Island foods<br>• Meet Pacific Island friends<br>• Chapel for ceremony |
| Retreat | • Create an atmosphere of peace and escape |
| Contemporary | • High energy special events<br>• Touring shows<br>• Interactive displays and high technology |

Figure 18.3: Enterprise values — Pacific Island style.

| Values (Self) | Action |
|---|---|
| **Networks** | Advice, resources, markets |
| **Skills/Background** | Experience, education |
| **Social Values** | People, flexible, lateral, detail, care for environment and culture |
| **Personal development** | Reading, networks, professional training |
| **Staff** | Opinions, team, development, conditions, succession, complementary skills |
| **Systems and Products** | Quality product, online purchase, robust, planned, links and added value, asset plan |
| **Profitability** | Defined niche, strategic game plan, profit and cash flow, know your financial position, diversified, foresight |
| **Relationship with customers** | One-on-one, active participation, authentic |

Figure 18.4: Enterprise values — European style.

### Formal and Informal Notions of Networks of Power

Social networks enable communities to voluntarily provide mutual support and social services, as is seen in the formation of identity of rural communities (Kearns & Joseph 1997). The introduction of information technologies has the potential to make networking in rural communities easier (Barr 2002). People in communities are connected into social networks through their family, working, and social relationships. They are also connected through common tasks, tools and instruments, and ways of doing things (Latour 1987).

Economic development can affect social networks through changes in employment and working hours which have implications for family relationships and social interactions. The design and form of public space in the community affects social networks through the ability of people to spend time together, appreciate the natural environment, and work together to protect it (Statistics New Zealand 2002). Communities are most under threat from pressures upon their social identity, landscape character, and economic interdependence. Communities respond to these pressures by: utilising natural capital, integrating new industries, and strengthening social networks (Parminter *et al.* 2003).

According to Panakera (2003) an appropriate tool to analyse the linkage of economy and culture is offered by the concept of network analysis as developed by the transactionalism school that puts the actor centre stage. It started from the idea that individuals are rational, and whose role is strategising actor instead of being acquiescent in social relations. As such, they seek to attain personal goals and thus proponents of transactionalism focus on contemporary social configurations such as coalitions, cliques, and factions (Boissevain 1977). Through the work of Bourdieu (1997) the relevance of social networks has received a new impetus. Bourdieu's theory focused on the concepts of capital, strategy, and "habitus," or the views and preferences held by individuals, that are themselves in turn moulded within nationality, ethnicity, gender, age, and class (Bourdieu, cited in Gorter 1997).

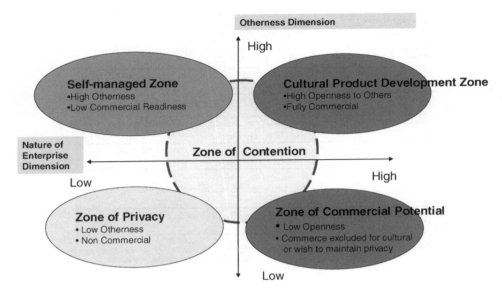

Figure 18.5: Modelling management frameworks.

Consequently in Figure 18.5 it becomes possible to plot both continua to reveal differing cells.

Minority entrepreneurs, such as Pacific Island peoples, operate in both formal and informal economies of minority and majority spheres of influence (Ingram 1990). Economic transactions are also social transactions, since they are usually embedded in social relations and not just determined by market forces (Rutten 1997). Clusters of micro-enterprises intensify the degree of network interaction, can reduce the dependence of small firms on large ones and can increase independent access to markets and supplies. Entrepreneurs socialise in their neighbourhoods and have a voice in local politics, so that social figurations emerge that have similarities in outlook to lifestyle (Gorter 1997). Such networks are a kind of social capital, essential not only for the successful business dealings and enhancement of prestige, but also as insurance against an uncertain future (Rutten 1997).

In summary, therefore, to the continuum of the heteropic-utopic dimension might be added an enterprise dimension of low to high entrepreneurship orientation. The enterprise dimension may comprise the following activities and values:

### Characteristics of the Enterprise Dimension

Community motives/goals (complementary/conflicting).
Decision-making (traditional structures/process vs entrepreneurial mind).
Differences engendered within communities (income, control, distribution of benefits).
Values (cultural values and compatibility with touristic values).
Range of experiences made available/used.
Leadership, influencers.

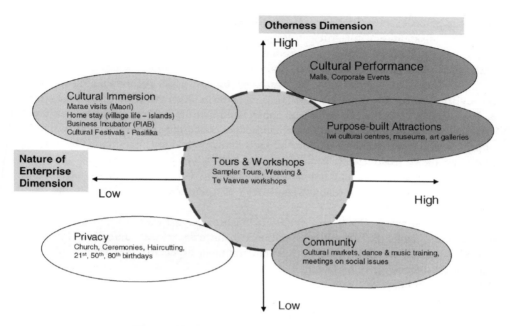

Figure 18.6: Modelling product frameworks.

Robust problem identification and Decision making process.
Good-will and community participation (time to do it).

Figure 18.6 develops the ideas inherent in Figure 18.5 to indicate different types of product that might emanate from the different dimensions of "otherness" and entrepreneurial ethic. Thus where the entrepreneurial ethic is wholly consistent with Indigenous principles of control and management, but where too there is a willingness to engage in and indeed exploit a sense of the "other," the consequence is a product offering genuine opportunities of cultural immersion. Where, however, the enterprise ethic relates more to conventional capitalistic notion, then the tourism product increasingly shares the qualities of commodification, as shown in the top right hand cell of Figure 18.6. The bottom left hand cell represents a zone of privacy which might be intruded upon by the tourist either accidentally or through a close family relationship, while the final cell represents a low level of community engagement with the commercial sector, perhaps on a periodic basis during specific festivals.

## Discussion

A note of caution must be sounded about the dangers of characterisation of cultural behaviour on binary dimensions used as shorthand reference points or categories. While these begin to describe a range of circumstances, many examples can be found which do not fit those reference points exactly (Bird *et al.* 1999). Similarly, such categories might be considered over-generalisations and constructs of European meta-narrative (Lester 1998).

The conceptualisation presented here is researcher-defined, derived from doctoral participant observation in the cultural tourism product development process from 2001 to 2003. Issues of "voice" may be overcome by use of a phenomenographic, post-positivistic approach to generate new items or confirm elements of the framework (Cave & Ryan 2004). Nonetheless it must be appreciated that the ways in which people create imaginative, epistemological and spatial landscapes concerning their own identity and that of people who live beyond the margins of one's known world are underpinned by time and place specificity (Said 1978). Ethnic peoples, responding to representatives of western hegemony might see the interaction between them as being intellectual confrontations — not just of ideas but of strategies, and ways of going about engaging with the world (Wassmann 1998: 2).

Cultural tourism products are sought by visitors as a means of understanding or experiencing "authentic" (traditional) cultures in far away places (Jamal & Hill 2002). Indeed, a lack of familiarity with a new environment, especially in a foreign language may create perceived risk (Mitchell & Greatorex 1990) and can either add to the richness of a holiday, or create negative experience. The intrinsic rewards of participation in an activity, where the level of challenge (physical, intellectual or social) may be placed against levels of competency (language, artistic skill, cultural performance) under circumstances of voluntary participation as described in the theory of flow (Csikszentimihalyi 1975) may have application in understanding in cultural tourism products.

The depth of interaction that takes place in cultural tourism activities should be set against the importance of that experience to that individual (McKercher & Du Cros 2002). One way to minimize such risk is to operate within the boundaries of a social or cultural safety blanket, an "environmental bubble" that surrounds the tourist with the known or familiar, enabling a person to sample the unfamiliar without being overwhelmed by it (McKercher & Du Cros 2002). The extent, variety and degree of change from normal life that tourists seek or are capable of seeking in their contacts with host communities are dependent upon the degree of "familiarity" or "strangeness" that each person is tolerate within unfamiliar environments (Cohen 1979). Communication, involves understanding of the cultures of both speaker and listener and is influenced by at least three cultures: tourist culture, home culture, and local culture (Jafari & Way 1994).

Concepts drawn from sociology, ethnography, epistemology and industry insights permitted the construction of a framework to describe the types of experience in which both hosts and visitors might participate. The significance of this idea is that the relative position of groups and individuals along these continua may influence the types of cultural experience that both are willing to share. The perceptions and experience of Otherness may affect the types of experience being sought or considered for participation. The author's experience of over thirty years in cultural and heritage based products indicates that radical differences in perception of each other's values and norms exist within host groups and potential user communities. Irreconcilable differences in expectation and delivery can result. Underlying tensions arise over time — during development and operation — that affect the viability and therefore sustainability of cultural enterprise. This is important because of the growing number of social enterprise ventures under development and increasing income disparities between cultural communities. It should, however, be noted that analyses such as that advanced in this chapter invariably pose a simplistic view of a hugely variable and complex set of influences at play. For example it assumes that the cultures interacting are distinguishable by language, norms, cultural values and expression, are not just variants of the same culture. For migrant communities, proximity or distance from cultural hierarchies affects the degree of adaptabilty and response to these issues. Finally it should be noted that while parallels based on concepts of liminality and "otherness" exist between the situations of migrants and Indigenous peoples, important distinctions lie in the nature of power sharing and treaty rights for Indigenous peoples with reference to their traditional lands.

Chapter 19

# Concluding Words

## Chris Ryan and Michelle Aicken

While this book has identified several important themes, it is perhaps pertinent to note the absences and silences. First, and perhaps most obvious, for the most part the interpretations offered within the book have been by non-Indigenous people. However, even if the Indigenous voice was more direct, issues would abound as to what degree they might be representative of a wider community. In short, the chapters are texts of interpretation, and well-informed as they are, they themselves remain possible marginal texts. That does not limit their validity as expressions of view given that they are cross referenced and tested by other writings, but the editors are always mindful that Indigenous notions of giving impose reciprocal responsibilities; and as academics perhaps the best gift that we can give in return is to articulate concerns in the fora in which we engage — the classroom, the research environment, as contributors to opinion formation and as advisors to stakeholders derived from governments and communities. Consequently such processes are long in achieving any social change, and that in itself is problematic when the communities themselves arguably require more rapid change to improve their economic and social position. However, such contingencies of time are those of a Eurocentric perspective, and thus the researcher must always bear in mind that cultural differences apply to time and organizational structures as much as to the questions of arts, crafts and performance that are the staple diet of the tourism product.

A second notion that emerges from this text is that the academic researchers themselves are possibly hindered by the mechanisms of research in their own institutions. The authors for the most part have contributed their thoughts to a book, perhaps believing that the totality of the collection is greater than an isolated article. Yet academic institutions in universities value, in research exercises, the book chapter as less than the journal article, no matter how little standing the journal might have. Such a view ignores the role of book as stimulators of concept and debate in a way that many articles, bound by constraints of research empiricism and possibly conservative attitudes of referees, are unable to replicate. Of even greater concern however, is the challenge faced by the tourism academic researcher who adopts the need to immerse themselves slowly, over time, in the communities that they research, to produce traditional research outputs quickly to meet the timetables of external research assessments and internal, generally annual, research evaluations of staff. Thus the academic

Indigenous Tourism: The Commodification and Management of Culture
Copyright © 2005 by Elsevier Ltd.
All rights of reproduction in any form reserved
ISBN: 0-08-044620-5

researcher faces the exigencies of managerialism and power structures within universities that often seem uncaring of the issues of research epistemologies and methodologies, and the fact that some research simply cannot be hurried into publication.

Thirdly, and more pertinent to the main theme, is that issues of gender are also silent in this collection. While liberal minded academics may wish to advance the position of Indigenous cultures, there is yet little recognition in the literature that these cultures may themselves adopt as traditional, practices that would not be acceptable in a western culture. Are these Indigenous cultures truly egalitarian? How, for example, are gender roles allocated? And what role, if any, has the academic researcher to adopt in approaching these issues? Only in some issues such as whale hunting are western academics being faced with a question of choice between wanting, on the one hand, to support and sustain Indigenous practices as maintaining a diversity of human perceptions of the world, and, on the other, wanting to sustain a biological diversity. How does one progress through these moral perplexities?

Fourth, an implicit theme throughout the book has been one of an uneven balance of political power. Some nations have sought to develop answers to these issues by various means of devolution and recognition of customary laws by defining spatial territories within which tribal tradition may hold sway. Thus, in Canada and the United States tribal groups are beginning to exercise increasing levels of executive action in accordance with their own traditions. In Australia, in the Northern Territory, Australian Aboriginal groups are being increasingly involved in management of larger tracts of land including National Parks. However, not every nation has the luxury of permitting spatial allocations of land. For example, New Zealand is a small country and not able to devolve judicial and executive actions in the same way.

This, in turn, raises a further silence. What of the urban Indigenous society? Many of these chapters, with the notable exception of Cave, analyse the position of Indigenous peoples in rural settings where it is thought traditional practice can be adopted unfettered by the constraints of being a minority in a city setting. But in many societies there are as many, if not more, younger Indigenous peoples in the cities as in the rural communities? How then are they to prosper, and can they utilize their culture as a tourist product in a city setting. Evidence from Australia suggests they can, but as yet little of this has appeared in the academic literature.

Consequently, the editors feel that this book represents a stage in thinking and development about the nature of Indigenous people and the commodification and management of their culture as a tourist product. In some ways it summarises past patterns of interest, and illustrates problems as defined by those past patterns. However, as these concluding words are meant to indicate, this is but the start of a long path with many problems of social adjustment yet to be recognized, much less solved. If this book does little more than raise an appreciation of what has been achieved, but what yet remains, then it will have served a purpose.

# References

Abercrombie, N., & Longhurst, B. (1998). *Audiences*. London: Sage.

Aboriginal Tourism Australia (2003). Media Release "Cathy Freeman Appointed as Ambassador", 31 March, from ata@aboriginaltourism.com.au.

Acciaioli, G. (1985). Culture as art: From practice to spectacle in Indonesia. *Canberra Anthropology*, 8(1–2), 148–174.

Ackermann, D. (1998). Becoming fully Huan: An ethic of relationship in difference and otherness. *Journal of Theology for Southern Africa*, 102(November), 13–27.

Adams, K. (1997a). Touting tourist primadonnas. In: M. Picard, & R. Wood (Eds), *Tourism, ethnicity and the state in southeast asia and the pacific* (pp. 155–180). Honolulu: University of Hawaii Press.

Adams, K. (1997b). Ethnic tourism and the regeneration of tradition in Tana Toraja (Sulawesi, Indonesia). *Ethnology*, 36(4), 1–10.

Adams, K. (1998). Domestic tourism and nation building in South Sulawesi. *Indonesia and the Malay World*, 26(75), 77–96.

Adijondro, G. J. (1995). Bali: Jakarta's Colony. Working Paper, Asian Center, Murdoch University.

Agency for Co-operation and Research in Development, ACORD (2002). *Poverty assessment study at gudigwa*. ACORD, Gumare.

Ahmed, S. (2002). This other and other others. *Economy and Society*, 31(1), 558–572.

Alexandrina Council. (1999). *Hindmarsh Island management plan*. Peter R. Day Resource Strategies, South Australia. Available at: http://www.alexandrina.sa.gov.au/publications/management_plan.asp.

Alneng, V. (2002). What the fuck is a Vietnam. *Critique of Anthropology*, 22(4), 461–489.

Altman, J. (1989). Tourism dilemmas for Aboriginal Australians. *Annals of Tourism Research*, 16, 456–476.

Altman, J. (1993). Indigenous Australians in the national tourism strategy: Impact, sustainability and policy issues. Discussion Paper No. 37. Canberra, Centre for Aboriginal Economic Research.

Altman, J. (1996, May). Coping with locational advantage: Tourism and economic deveelopment at Seisia Community, Cape York Peninsula. *The Journal of Tourism Studies*, 7(1), 58–71.

Altman, J. (2001, December). Aboriginal economy and social process. *Arena Magazine*, 56, 38–39.

Altman, J. (2002, 3–5 April). Enhancing economic development: Governance challenges facing indigenous communities within Australia's federal system. Indigenous Governance Conference.

Altman, J. C. (1987a). The economic impact of tourism on the Mutitjulu community, Uluru (Ayers Rock-Mount Olga National Park). Working paper No. 7, Department of Political and Social Change, Research School of Pacific Studies, Australian National university, Canberra.

Altman, J. C. (1987b). The economic impact of tourism on the Warmun (Turkey Creek) community: East Kimberley, East Kimberley Working paper, No. 19, Center for Resource and Environmental Studies, Australian National University, Canberra.

Altman, J. C. (1992). A national survey of indigenous Australians: Options and implications. Center for Aboriginal Economic Policy Research, Australian National University, Canberra.

Altman, J. C., & Finlayson, J. (1992). Aborigines, tourism and sustainable development, CAEPR Discussion Paper, No. 26, Center for Aboriginal Economic Policy Research, Australian National University, Canberra.

Anderson, T. (1997). Conservation Native American style. *Quarterly Review of Economics and Finance, 15*(3), 149–161.

Angelsen, A., Fjeldstad, O., & Rashid-Sumaila, U. (1994). *Project appraisal and sustainability in less developed countries*. Norway: Bergen Print Services.

Ansett Australia (1999). Domestic timetables, Ansett Australia.

Aotearoa Maori Tourism Federation (1995). *Report on the current market position of Maori tourism product*. Rotorua: Aotearoa Maori Tourism Federation.

Aotearoa Maori Tourism Federation (1996). *Report on the current market position of Maori tourism product*. Rotorua: Aotearoa Maori Tourism Federation.

Ap, J. (1992). Residents' perceptions on tourism impacts. *Annals of Tourism Research, 19*(4), 665–690.

Aramberri, J. (2001). The host should get lost: Paradigms in the tourism theory. *Annals of Tourism Research, 28*(3), 738–761.

Arnold, J. (1999). Feminist poetics and cybercolinisation. In: S. Hawthorne, & R. Klein (Eds), *Cyberfeminism – connectivity, critique, creativity* (pp. 250–280). Melbourne: Spinifex Press.

Arnould, E., & Price, L. (1993). River magic: Extraordinary experience and the extended service encounter. *Journal of Consumer Research, 20*, 24.

Ashworth, G. J., & Turnbridge, J. E. (1999). Old Cities, New Pasts: Heritage Planning in Selected Cities of Central Europe. *GeoJournal, 49*, 105–116.

ATSIC (1996). *On our own terms*. ATSIC, Canberra, ACT.

ATSIC (nd). *Good business or just a good idea?* ATSIC, Canberra, ACT.

ATSIC (2000). *National aboriginal and torres strait islander tourism industry strategy*. Proceedings Report. June. ATSIC website: www.atsic.gov.au.

ATSIC, Aboriginal and Torres Strait Islander Commission (1997). *Tourism industry strategy*. Canberra, ACT, Commonwealth of Australia, Aboriginal and Torres Straits Islander Commission and The Office of National Tourism.

ATSIC and Commonwealth Department of Workplace Relations & Small Business (2002). 'Indigenous small business fund'. DEWSRB website: www.workplace.gov.au.

ATSIC and Northern Territory (1996). *Strong business, strong culture, strong country*. Canberra, ACT.

ATSIC and the Office of National Tourism (1997). *The National Aboriginal and Torres Strait Islander Tourism Industry Strategy*. Canberra, ACT.

ATSIC & DEWRSB *Indigenous Business Development Program*. http://www.workplace. gov.au/Workplace/ESDisplay/0,1282,a0%253D0%2526a1%253D537%2526a2%253D627,00. html

Attix, S. A. (2002). New age-oriented special interest travel: An exploratory study. *Tourism Recreation Research, 27*(2), 51–58.

Australian Bureau of Statistics (2002). 2001 Census for population and housing. Australian Bureau of Statistics. Available on-line: http://80-www.abs.gov.au.simsrad.net.ocs.mq.edu.au/websitedbs. Accessed at March 13th 2003.

Australian Tourist Commission (nd). Higher profile for Aboriginal tourism. From: http://atc.world.net/document/200347.htm. Accessed on 27 March 2003.

Bakhtin, M. (1981). *The dialogic imagination: Four essays*. Austin: University of Texas.

Ball, M. (2003). Outback oasis – Journey through an ancient land – Below the timeless Gulf. *Sunday Telegraph* (Sydney) 20.04.03.

Balme, C. B. (1998). Staging the Pacific: Framing authenticity in performances for tourists at the Polynesian Cultural Center. *Theatre Journal, 50*(1), 53–71.

Bandy, J. (1996). Managing the other of nature-sustainability, spectacles, and global regimes of capital ecotourism. *Public Culture, 8*(3), 539–566.

Barabe, A. (1995). Tourism and sustainable development. *Society and Leisure, 18*(2), 395–414.

Barker, C. (2000). *Cultural studies – theory and practice.* London: Sage.

Barlow, C. (1994). *Tikanga Whakaaro: Key Concepts in Maori Culture.* Auckland: Oxford University Press.

Barnett, S. (1997). Maori tourism. *Tourism Management, 18*(7), 471–473.

Barr, N. (2002). Social trajectories for rural landscaping connections – farm, food and resource issues. Retrieved from the world wide web: http://www.agribusiness.asn.au/Connection7Autumn2002/barr.htm.

Bartolome, L., & Macedo, D. (1997). Dancing with bigotry: The poisoning of racial and ethnic identities. *Harvard Educational Review, 67.*

Baruah, B. (1998). *Sustainable development of rural aboriginal communities of Northern British Columbia: A case study of the Tl'azt'en nation.* Unpublished Masters thesis, University of Northern British Columbia, Prince George.

Bass, J., & Nepal, S. (2002). Resource recreation and tourism — Annotated bibliography. A Report for the "First Nations and Ecotourism: Building Indigenous Capacity in Planning, Developing, and Managing Ecotourism in Traditional Territories. The Tl'azt'en Nation." Research Project Report — Appendix 2, submitted to the Forest Renewal British Columbia (FRBC), Canada.

Bauer, R. (1997). *Transculturations in colonial space: Creole identities and the ethnographic imagination in early British and Spanish American writing.* Michigan State University: Ann Arbour.

Bauman, Z. (2000). Tourists and vagabonds: Or, living in postmodern times. In: J. E. Davis (Ed.), *Identity and Social Change* (pp. 13–26). New Brunswick, NJ: Transaction Publishers.

Beard, J. G., & Ragheb, M. G. (1980). The leisure satisfaction measure. *Journal of Leisure Research, 12*(1), 20–33.

Beard, J. G., & Ragheb, M. G. (1982). Measuring leisure attitude. *Journal of Leisure Research, 14*(2), 155–167.

Beard, J., & Ragheb, M. G. (1983). Measuring leisure motivation. *Journal of Leisure Research, 15*(3), 219–228.

Bee, R. (1982). *The politics of American Indian policy.* Cambridge, MA: Schenkman Publishing Company.

Beeho, A. J., & Prentice, R. C. (1997). Conceptualising the experiences of heritage tourists. A case study of New Lanark World Heritage Village. *Tourism Management, 18*(2), 75–87.

Bell, D. (1998). *Ngarrindjeri wurruwarrin: A world that is, was and will be.* Melbourne: Spinifex.

Bell, D. (2001). The politics of surviving. *Off our backs,* March, 6 and 18.

Beltran, J. (Ed.) (2000). *Indigenous and traditional peoples and protected areas.* Principles, guidelines and case studies. Gland: IUCN/WWF and Cambridge, UK.

Benner, P. (1994). The tradition and skill of interpretive phenomenology in studying health, illness and caring practices. In: P. Benner (Ed.), *Interpretive phenomenology: Embodiment, caring and ethics in health and illness.* Thousand Oaks, CA: Sage.

Bent, R., De Ferranti, J., Dore, L., Murphy, P., & Sims, W. (1999). Human resource practices in remote places: A regional tourism project of LaTrobe University. In: J. Molloy, & J. Davies (Eds), *Tourism and hospitality: Delighting the senses* (p. 233). Part One, Proceedings of the 1999 9th Australian Tourism and Hospitality Research Conference, 10–13 February, Adelaide.

Berke, P., & Kartez, J. (1995). *Sustainable development as a guide to community land use policy.* Lincoln Institute of Land Policy Research Papers.

Bird, A., Osland, J., Mendenhall, M., & Schneider, S. (1999). Adapting and adjusting to other cultures: What we know but don't always tell. *Journal of Management Inquiry, 8*(2), 152.

Blamey, R. K. (1998). *Profiles and Motivations of Nature-Based Tourists Visiting Australia.* Occasional Paper Number 25, Canberra, Bureau of Tourism Research, Commonwealth of Australia.

Blangy, S., & Nielsen, T. (1993). Ecotourism and minimum impact policy. *Annals of Tourism Research, 20*(2), 357–360.

Blundell, V. (1993). Aboriginal empowerment and souvenir trade in Canada. *Annals of Tourism Research, 20*(1), 64–87.

Boggs, L. P. (2002). *Community Based Natural Resource Management in the Okavango Delta.* Unpublished Paper, Maun, 16pp.

Boissevain, J. (1977). Tourism and development in Malta. *Development and Change, 8*(4), 528–538.

Boissevain, J. (1997). *Friends of Friends: Networks, Manipulators and Coalitions.* Oxford: Basil Blackwell.

Boniface, P. (1998). Tourism culture. *Annals of Tourism Research, 25*(3), 746–749.

Boo, E. (1990). *Ecotourism: The potentials and pitfalls.* Washington, DC: World Wildlife Fund.

Booth, A. (1990). Tourism boom in Indonesia. *Bulletin of Indonesian Economic Studies, 26*(3), 45–73.

Booth, A. (2000). *Linking forestry and community in the tl'azt'en nation: Lessons for aboriginal forestry.* Unpublished research Paper, University of Northern British Columbia, Prince George.

Bourdieu, P. (1977). Outline of theory of practice. Cambridge: Cambridge University Press.

Bowry, C. (2003). *Backpackers – could they be the new money-makers of the tourism industry in Australia?* Unpublished Minor Thesis at the International College of Tourism and Hotel Management, Manly, Australia.

Boyd, S., & Butler, R. (1996). Managing ecotourism: An opportunity spectrum approach. *Tourism Management, 17*(8), 557–566.

Boyle, A. (2001). Australian indigenous tourism research strategy scoping study. Workshop Discussion Paper, May 2001, Research Gap Literature Review.

Brandon, K. (1993). Basic steps towards encouraging local participation in nature tourism projects. In: K. Lindberg, & D. Hawkins (Eds), *Ecotourism: A guide for planners and managers* (pp. 134–152). North Bennington, VT: Ecotourism Society.

Bras, K. (2000). *Image building and guiding on Lombok: The social construction of a tourist destination.* Ph.D. Thesis, Katholieke Universiteit Brabant.

Brim, W. (1993). *Tjapukai – The impact of success.* Proceedings of the Indigenous Australians and Tourism Conference, Darwin, June 1993, Goanna Print, Canberra.

Briton, B. (2001). Hindmarsh Island decision: Ngarrindjeri people yet to see justice. *The guardian,* August 29, available at: http://www.zip.com.au/~cpa/garchve4/1060hind.html.

Brodie, V. (2001). A Divisive Bridge. Interview in *The Koori Mail,* 21 March: 4.

Brohman, J. (1996). New directions in tourism for third world development. *Annals of Tourism Research, 23*(1), 48–70.

Brooks, G. (1999). *Note on the charter revision process: The 8th draft of the international cultural tourism charter.* Adopted by ICOMOS at the 12th General Assembly, October 1999. Guadalajara, Mexico: ICOMOS.

Brosnan, D. (1996). Indian policy, Indian gaming and the future of tribal economic development. *American Review of Public Administration, 26*(2), 213–225.

Brown, N. (1992). Beachboys as culture brokers in Bakau Town, The Gambia. *Community Development Journal, 27*(4), 361–370.

Bruner, E. M. (1988). Of cannibals, tourists and ethnographers. *Cultural Anthropology, 4,* 438–445.

Bruner, E. M. (1991). Transformation of self in tourism. *Annals of Tourism Research, 18*(2), 238–250.

Bruner, E. M. (1994). Abraham Lincoln as authentic reproduction: A critique of post-modernism. *American Anthropologist, 96*(2), 397–415.

Bruner, E. M. (1995). The ethnographer/tourist in Indonesia. In: M.-F. Lanfant, J. B. Allcock, & E. M. Bruner (Eds), *International tourism: Identity and change* (pp. 224–241). London: Sage.

Bruner, E. M. (1996). Tourism in the Balinese Borderzone. In: S. Lavie, & T. Swedenburg (Eds), *Displacement, diaspora, and geographies of identity* (pp. 157–180). Durham and London: Duke University Press.

Bruner, E. M. (2001). The Maasai and the Lion King. *American Ethnologist, 28*(4), 881–908.

Buchsbaum, H. (1995). Culture clashes: Sacred sites. *Scholastic Update, 127*(9), 12–13.

Burton, L. (1991). *American indian water rights and the limits of law.* Lawrence, KS: University Press of Kansas.

Butler, R. W. (1993a). Pre and post-impact assessment of tourism development. In: D. Pearce, & R. Butler (Eds), *Tourism research: Critiques and challenges* (pp. 135–155). New York, NY: Routledge.

Butler, R. W. (1993b). Tourism: An evolutionary perspective. In: *Tourism and sustainable development: Monitoring, planning, managing* (pp. 27–44). Waterloo: University of Waterloo.

Butler, R., & Hinch, T., (Eds) (1996). *Tourism and indigenous peoples.* London: International Thomson Press.

Calas, M., & Smircich, L. (1999). Past postmodernism? Reflections and tentative directions. *Academy of Management Review, 24*(4), 649–671.

Calmels, P. (1996). Non-standard activity management: The role of the tour guide-courier in Terres d'Aventure. *Cahiers Espaces 1996, 48*, 25–27.

Caputo, J., & Yount, M. (1993). Institutions, normalization and power. In: J. Caputo, & M. Yount (Eds), *Foucault and the critique of institutions* (pp. 3–23). University Park, Pennsylvania: University of Pennsylvania Press.

Carmichael, B. (1998). Casinos, communities, and sustainable economic development. Paper presentation at Annual Association of American Geographers Conference.

Casidy, L., Good, K., Mazonde, I., & Rivers, R. (2001). *Assessment of the status of the san in botswana.* Regional Assessment of the Status of the San in Southern Africa, Report Series, Legal Assistance Centre, Windhoek.

Cassidy, L. (2001). Improving women's participation in CBRNM in Botswana. CBNRM Support Programme, Occasional Paper No. 5. Gaborone, IUCN/SNV CBNRM Support Programme.

Cassidy, L., Good, K., Mazonde, I., & Rivers, R. (2001). *Assessment of the Status of the San in Botswana.* Regional Assessment of the Status of the San in Southern Africa, Report Series, Legal Assistance Centre, Windhoek.

Cater, E. (1995). Environmental contradictions in sustainable tourism. *The Geographical Journal, 161*(1), 21–28.

Cave, J. (2001). Culture and heritage definition study: Report of the Working Party to define a new culture and heritage facility for Tauranga and the Western Bay of Plenty. Tauranga: Community Services Division, Tauranga District Council.

Cave, J. (2002). *At the margins of paradise, community tourism in action: The development potential of a Pacific Island business and cultural centre.* Unpublished manuscript, Istanbul, Turkey.

Cave, J., Ryan, C., & Panakera, C. (2004). Cultural Tourism Product: Pacific Island Migrant Perspectives in New Zealand. Paper submitted to *Journal of Travel Research.*

Ceballos-Lascurain, H. (1993). Ecotourism as a world-wide phenomenon. In: K. Lindberg, & D. Hawkins (Eds), *Ecotourism: A guide for planners and managers* (pp. 12–14). North Bennington, VT: Ecotourism Society.

Ceballos-Lascurain, H. (1996). *Tourism, ecotourism and protected areas: The state of nature-based tourism around the world and guidelines for its development.* Gland and Cambridge: IUCN.

Central Statistic Office, CSO (2002). *National population and housing census*. Ministry of Finance and Development Planning, Gaborone.

Cheek, L. (1996). *Sante Fe*. Oakland, CA: Fodor's Travel Publications.

Cherokees. (1998). *Eastern Band of Cherokees*. Internet URL: http://www.hanksville.com.

Chhabra, D., Healy, R., & Sills, E. (2003). Staged authenticity and heritage tourism. *Annals of Tourism Research, 30*, 702–719.

Christou, E., & Sigala, M. (2002). Conceptualising the measurement of service quality and TQM performance for hotels: The HOSTQUAL model. *Acta Turistica, 14*(2), 140–169.

Cleary, P., & Murphy, C. (2002). Census mirrors real Australia. *Australian financial review*, 18.06.02.

Clendinnen, I. (1999a). *Pilgrims, saints and sacred places*. Lecture Two of the Radio National's 'The Boyer Lectures', Australian Broadcasting Corporation.

Clendinnen, I. (1999b). *Inside the contact zone: Part two*. Radio National's 'The Boyer Lectures', Australian Broadcasting Corporation.

Cocteau, J. (2003). After the Kuta bombing: In search of the Balinese soul. *Antropologi Indonesia, 25*(70), 41–59.

Cohen, E. (1972). Toward a sociology of international tourism. *Social Research, 39*, 164–182.

Cohen, E. (1974). Who is a tourist? A conceptual clarification. *The Sociological Review, 22*, 527–555.

Cohen, E. (1979a). Rethinking the sociology of tourism. *Annals of Tourism Research, 6*, 18–35.

Cohen, E. (1979b). A Phenomenology of touristic experiences. *Sociology, 13*(2), 179–201.

Cohen, E. (1983, Pt. II.). The dynamics of commercialised arts: The Mao and Yao of Northern Thailand. *Journal of National Research Council of Thailand, 15*(1), 1–34.

Cohen, E. (1984). The sociology of tourism: Approaches, issues, and findings. *Annual Reviews of Sociology, 10*, 373–392.

Cohen, E. (1985). The tourist guide: The origins, structure and dynamics of a role. *Annals of Tourism Research, 12*(1), 5–29.

Cohen, E. (1988). Authenticity and commoditization in tourism. *Annals of Tourism Research, 15*, 371–386.

Cohen, E. (1993a). The study of tourist images of native people. In: R. Butler, & D. Pearce (Eds), *Tourism research: Critiques and challenges* (pp. 59–83). New York, NY: Routledge.

Cohen, E. (1993b). The hetrogeneization of a tourist art. *Annals of Tourism Research, 20*(1), 138–163.

Cole, S. (2003). Appropriated meanings: Megaliths and tourism in Eastern Indonesia. *Indonesia and the Malay World, 31*(89), 140–150.

Collins, R. E. (1993). Indigenous Cultures as a Tourism Attraction: An International Perspective. *Indigenous Australians and Tourism: A Focus on the Northern Territory*. Proceedings of the Indigenous Australians and Tourism Conference, June, ATSIC, 32–37.

Commonwealth Department of Tourism (1994). *A Talent for Tourism*. Commonwealth of Australia, Canberra, ACT.

Cornell, S., & Kalt, J. (Eds) (1992). *What can tribes do?: Strategies and institutions in American Indian economic development*. Los Angeles, CA: American Indian Studies Center.

Cornell, S., & Kalt, J. P. (1990). Pathways from poverty: Economic development and institution-building on American Indian reservations. *American Indian Culture and Research Journal, 14*(1), 89–125.

Costa, J., & Livio, F. (1998). *Sociocultural perspectives on tourism planning and development*. Virtual Conference Centre, MCB Press. Retrieved January 1998, from the World Wide Web: <http://www.mcb.co.uk/services/conferenc/jan98/eit/paper4-3.htm>.

Council for Aboriginal Reconciliation (2000). Accessed on 10 November 2002, at: http://www.austlii.edu.au/au/other/IndigLRes/car/2000/16/appendices05.htm.

Cowden, R. (1996). *The economics of reservations*. Hearing before the U.S. Senate Committee on Indian Affairs. Washington, DC: U.S. Government Printing Office.

Cozzatto, D. (1995). The economic and social implications of Indian gaming: The case of Minnesota. *American Indian Culture and Research Journal, 19*(1), 119–131.

Craik, J. (2001). Cultural Tourism. In: N. Douglas, N. Douglas, & R. Derrett (Eds), *Special interest tourism: Context and cases* (pp. 113–139). Brisbane, Australia: John Wiley & Sons.

Cronin, L. (1990). A Strategy for tourism and sustainable developments. *World Leisure and Recreation, 32*(3), 12–17.

Crotty, M. (1996). *Phenomenology and nursing research*. South Melbourne: Churchill Livingstone.

Csikszentmihalyi, M. (1975). *Beyond boredom and anxiety*. San Francisco, CA: Jossey-Bass.

Csikszentmihalyi, M. (1990). *Flow – The psychology of optimal experience*. New York: Harper & Row.

Daniel, Y. P. (1996). Tourism dance performances: Authenticity and creativity. *Annals of Tourism Research, 23*(4), 780–797.

Dann, G. (1999). Writing out the tourist in space and time. *Annals of Tourism Research, 26*(1), 159–187.

Darkoh, M. B. K., & Mbaiwa, J. E. (2001). Sustainable development and resource conflicts in Botswana. In: M. A. M. Salih, T. Ditez, & A. G. M. Ahmed (Eds), *African pastoralism: Conflicts, institutions and government* (pp. 39–55). London: Pluto Press.

Dearden, P., & Harron, S. (1994). Alternative tourism and adaptive change. *Annals of Tourism Research, 2*, 81–102.

de Beauvoir, S. (1997). *The second sex*. Harmondsworth: Penguin.

de Bruyn, E. (2003). Alfaville, or the utopics of Mel Bochner. *Grey Room 10, 10*(Winter), 76–111.

Deloria, V., Jr. (1985). The evolution of federal Indian policy making. In: V. Deloria, Jr. (Ed.), *American Indian policy in the twentieth century* (pp. 239–256). Norman, OK: University of Oklahoma Press.

Department of Industry, Tourism and Resources (2003). A medium to long term strategy for tourism, green paper, http://www.industry.gov.au/assets/documents/itrinternet/Tourism_Green_Paper20030908110117.pdf?CFID=224439&CFTOKEN=49692842.

Department of Wildlife and National Parks, DWNP (1999). *Joint venture guidelines*. Department of Wildlife and National Parks, Gaborone.

Department of Wildlife and National Parks, DWNP (2000). *CBNRM progress report for 2000*. Department of Wildlife and National Parks, Gaborone.

Devenish, S. (2002). A phenomenological explication method. *Indo-Pacific Journal of Phenomenology 3*. On-line journal http://ipjp.org. Site visited May 10, 2002.

D'Hauteserre, A.-M. (1998). Foxwoods casino resort: An unusual experiment in economic development. *Economic Geography*, AAG Special Issue, 112–121.

Dhume, S. (2002). Jurassic showdown. *Far eastern economic review* (May 16).

Dinas Pariwisata (Tourism Board), & Pemerintah Kabupaten Daerah Tingkat II Manggarai (1999). *Rencana Induk Pariwisata Daerah Kabupaten Daerah Tingkat II Manggarai, Laporan Akhir, Ruteng*.

Douglas, N., & Douglas, N. (1996). Social and cultural impact of tourism in the South Pacific. In: C. M. Hall, & S. Page (Eds), *Tourism in the pacific: Issues and cases*. London: International Thomson Business Press.

Dow, C. (1999). In search of the picturesque: Aborigines and tourists in 19th century Gippsland. *Tourism, Culture and Communication, 2*(2), 111–122.

Doxey, G. V. (1976). A causation theory of visitor-resident irritants: Methodology and research inferences. Paper Presented at the The Impact of Tourism Proceedings, 6th Annual Conference of Travel Research Association, San Diego.

Drake, S. P. (1991). Local participation in ecotourism projects. In: T. Whelan (Ed.), *Nature tourism: Managing for the environment* (pp. 132–163). Washington, DC: Island Press.

Drdácký, M. F. (2002). *Impact and Risks of Tourism in Cultural Heritage Environment.* Conference Proceedings of the Scientific Conference: Preservation, Development and Monitoring of Historic Cities in 21st Century, April 18–20, 2002. Athens: ICOMOS.

Duggan, B. J. (1997). Tourism, cultural authenticity, and the native crafts cooperative: The Eastern Cherokee experience. In: E. Chambers (Ed.), *Tourism and culture* (pp. 31–57). Albany, NY: State University of New York Press.

Duke, C. R., & Persia, M. A. (1996). Performance-importance analysis of escorted tour evaluations. *Journal of Travel and Tourism Marketing, 5*(3), 207–222.

DuMars, C. T. (1984). *Pueblo indian water rights: struggle for a precious resource.* Tucson: University of Arizona.

Dunlevy, M. (2002). Property wave rolls on. *The Weekend Australian* (23 November), Local, 5.

Durie, M. (1998). *Te mana te kawanatanga, The politics of maori self-determination.* Auckland: Oxford University Press.

Dyer, P., Aberdeen, L., & Schuler, S. (2003). Tourism impacts on an Australian indigenous community: A Djabugay case study. *Tourism Management, 24*(1), 83–95.

Eco, U. (1987). *Vad kostar ett mästerverk*? Stockholm: Brombergs.

Eco-tourism Coup. (2001). *The advertiser* (28 October), 8.

Edwards, G. (1993). *Stepping into the magic: A new approach to everyday life.* London: Piatkus.

Edwards, S. (2001). Phenomenology as intervention. *Indo-Pacific Journal of Phenomenology, 2.* On-line journal http://ipjp.org. Site visited October 15, 2001.

Erb, M. (1997). Contested time and place: Constructions of history in Todo, Manggarai (Western Flores, Indonesia). *Journal of Southeast Asian Studies, 28,* 47–77.

Erb, M. (2000). Understanding tourists: Interpretations from Indonesia. *Annals of Tourism Research, 27*(3), 709–736.

Erb, M. (2001a). Eco-tourism and environmental conservation in Western Flores: Who benefits? *Antropologi Indonesia, 66,* 72–88.

Erb, M. (2001b). Le Tourisme et la Quête de la Culture a Manggarai. *Anthropologie et Sociétés, 25,* 93–108.

Erb, M. (2003). Uniting the bodies and cleansing the village: Conflicts over local heritage in a globalizing world. *Indonesia and the Malay World, 31*(89), 129–139.

Erisman, M. H. (1983). Tourism and cultural dependency in the West Indies. *Annals of Tourism Research, 10*(3), 337–361.

Eyles, J., & Smith, S. J. (Eds) (1988). *Qualitative methods in human geography.* Cambridge: Polity Press.

Fawcett, C., & Cormack, P. (2001). Guarding authenticity at literary tourism sites. *Annals of Tourism Research, 28,* 686–704.

Feifer, M. (1985). *Going places.* London: Maximillan.

Fennell, D. (1999). *Ecotourism: An introduction.* London: Routledge.

Fidzani, B., Mlenga, W. S., Atlhopheng, M., & Shatera, M. M. (1999). *Socio-economic effects of CBPP in Ngamiland.* Division of Agricultural Planning and Statistics, Ministry of Agriculture.

Filion, S. (1993). Defining the concepts of ecotourism. In: K. Lindberg, & D. Hawkins (Eds), *Ecotourism: A guide for planners and managers* (pp. 1–12). North Bennington, VT: Ecotourism Society.

Finlayson, J. (1991). *Australian Aborigines and cultural tourism: Case studies of Aboriginal involvement in the tourist industries.* Working papers on multiculturalism, No. 15, Center for Multicultural Studies, University of Wollongong, Wollongong, Australia.

Finlayson, J. (1992). Issues in Aboriginal cultural tourism: Possibilities for a sustainable industry. In: B. Weiler (Ed.), *Ecotourism incorporating the global classroom* (pp. 66–69). Bureau of Tourism Research, Canberra.

Finlayson, J. (1995). *Aboriginal employment, native title and regionalism*. CAEPR Discussion Paper No. 87, Center for Aboriginal Economic Policy Research, Australian National University, Canberra.

Finlayson, J., & Madden, R. (1995). Regional tourism case studies: Indigenous participation in tourism in Victoria. In: Bureau of Tourism Research (Ed.), *Tourism research and education in Australia* (pp. 269–275). Proceedings from the Tourism and Education Conferences, Queensland, BTR, Canberra.

Fiszbein, A. (1997). Lessons from Columbia. *World Development, 25*(7), 1029–1043.

Fitzgerald, T. K. (1998). Metaphors, media and social change: Second generation Cook Islanders in New Zealand. In: J. Wassmann (Ed.), *Pacific answers to western Hegemony: Cultural practice of identity construction* (pp. 253–268). Oxford: Berg.

Fixico, D. (1996). The struggle for our homes. In: J. Weaver (Ed.), *Defending mother earth* (pp. 29–46). Maryknoll, NY: Orbis Books.

Follow the Flame (2000). *Direct broadcast from Sydney Olympic Games 2000 opening cermonies*. Seven Network, 15.09.00.

Foucault, M. (1979). *Discipline and punish: The birth of the prison*. Translated from the French by Alan Sheridan, New York: Vintage Books.

Foxall, G. (1990). *Consumer psychology in behavioral perspective*. London: Routledge.

Friberg, S. (2003). Kulturministern. *Västra Nyland*. 06.05.03.

Frow, J. (1997). *Time and commodity culture: Essays in cultural theory and postmodernity*. Oxford: Clarend Press.

Fullagar, S. (2001). Encountering otherness: Embodied affect in Alphonso Lingis's travel writing. *Tourist Studies, 1*(2), 171–183.

Galbraith, J. K. (1992). *The culture of contentment*. London: Sinclair-Stevenson.

Gao, F. (Ed.) (2001). *Research on ethnic villages in Yunnan: The Naxis in Huangshan, Lijiang*. Kunming: Yunnan University Press.

Gelder, K., & Jacobs, J. (1997). Promiscuous sacred sites: Reflections on secrecy and scepticism in the Hindmarsh Island Affair. *Australian humanities review*, accessed: http://www.lib.latrobe.edu.au/AHR/archive/Issue-June-1997/gelder.html, Downloaded on 19 September 2000.

Gendall, P., Esslemont, D., & Day, D. (1991). A comparison of two versions of the Juster Scale using self completion questionnaires. *Journal of the Market Research Society, 33*(3), 257–264.

Getz, D. (1991). *Festivals, special events and tourism*. New York: Van Nostrand Reinhold.

Getz, D. (1997). *Event management and event tourism*. New York: Cognizant Communication Corporation.

Gewertz, D., & Errington, F. (1989). Tourism and Anthropology in a Post-Modern World. *Oceania, 60*, 37–54.

Gillespie, D. (1988). Tourism in Kakadu National Park. In: D. Wade-Marshall, & P. Loveday (Eds), *Northern Australia: Progress and Prospects, contemporary issues in development* (Vol. 1, pp. 224–250). North Australia Research Unit, Darwin.

Gillette, J. B. (1994). Sweetgrass saga. *Historic preservation, 46*(5), 28–32, 90–92.

Giorgi, A. (1997). The theory, practice and evaluation of the phenomenological method as a qualitative research procedure. *Journal of Phenomenological Psychology, 28*(2), 235–260.

Glass, K. (1993). Sinkyone: An intertribal Indian park. *Earth Island Journal, 8*(1), 26–27.

Glasson, J., Godfrey, K., & Goodey, B. (1995). *Towards visitor impact management: Visitor impacts, carrying capacity and management responses in Europe's historic towns and cities*. Avebury, England.

Glick, D. (1991). Tourism in Greater Yellowstone: Maximizing the good, minimizing the bad, eliminating the ugly. In: T. Whelan (Ed.), *Nature tourism: Managing for the environment* (pp. 58–74). Washington, DC: Island Press.

Go, F. M., & Zhang, W. (1997). Applying importance-performance analysis to Beijing as an international meeting destination. *Journal of Travel Research, 35*(4), 42–49.

Gollan, N. (2002). Personal communication, 23rd June, Cultural Museum of Camp Coorong, Meningie, South Australia.

Gonzalez, E. (2003). IMAX film shines light on the real 'Australia'. *Rocky mountains news*, 30.05.03.

Goodall, B. (1995). Environmental auditing: A tool for assessing the environmental performance of tourism firms. *The Geographical Journal, 161*(1), 29–37.

Goodwin, H. (1996). In pursuit of ecotourism. *Biodiversity and Conservation, 5*(3), 277–291.

Gorter, P. (1997). The social and political aspirations of a new stratum of industrialists: Local politics on a large industrial estate in West India. In: Rutten & Upadhaya (Eds), *Small business entrepreneurs in Asia and Europe*. New Deli, Thousand Oaks, London: Sage.

Government of Botswana (1997). National Development Plan VIII 1997–2003. Government Printer, Gaborone, 509 pp.

Government of South Australia: Small Business Development Corporation (2000). website: www.text.sacentral.sa.gov.au.

Graburn, N. (Ed.) (1976). *Ethnic and tourist arts. Cultural expressions from the fourth world*. Berkeley: University of California Press.

Green, K. (2002). The other as another other. *Hypatia, 17*(4), 1–15.

Greenwood, D. J. (2004). Culture by the pound: An anthropological perspective on tourism as cultural commodization. In: S. B. Gmelch (Ed.), *Tourists and tourism: A reader* (pp. 157–169). Long Grove, IL: Waveland Press.

Grekin, J., & Milne, S. (1996). Toward sustainable tourism development: The case of pond inlet, NWT. In: R. Butler, & T. Hinch (Eds), *Tourism and indigenous peoples* (pp. 76–106). London: Routledge.

Grinde, D., & Johansen, B. (1995). *Ecocide of native America*. Sante Fe, NM: Clear Light Publishers.

Gruber, A. (1970). Purchase intent and purchase probability. *Journal of Advertising Research, 10*(1), 23–27.

Gujadhur, T. (2000). Organisation and their approaches in community based natural resources management in Botswana, Namibia, Zambia and Zimbabwe. CBNRM Support Programme, Occasional Paper No. 6, IUCN/SNV CBNRM Support Programme, Gaborone.

Gujadhur, T. (2001). Joint venture options for communities and Safari operators in Botswana. CBNRM Support Programme, Occasional Paper No 6, IUCN/SNV CBNRM Support Programme, Gaborone.

Guo, D. (Ed.) (1999). *General survey of the naxi culture*. Kunming: Nationalities Publishing House of Yunnan.

Gurian, E. H. (2002). Issues for museums 2002 — Te Papa National Services — Seminar series. February 2002. Wellington: Te Papa.

Hailey, J. M. (1987). *Entrepreneurs and indigenous business in the pacific*. Hawaii: East West Center, University of Hawaii Press.

Hall, C. M. (1992). *Hallmark tourist events: Impacts, management and planning*. London: Belhaven Press.

Hall, C. M., & McArthur, S. (1998). *Integrated heritage management: Principles and practice*. London: Stationary Office.

Hamilton, A. (1984). Spoon-feeding the lizards: Culture and conflict in Central Australia. *Meanjin, 43*(3), 362–378.

Harawira, W. (1997). *Te kawa o te marae. A guide for all marae visitors.* Auckland: Reed Childrens Books.

Harkin, M. (1995). Modernist anthropology and tourism of the authentic. *Annals of Tourism Research,* *22*(3), 650–670.

Harris, C. (2002). *Making native space: Colonialism, resistance, and reserves in British Columbia.* Vancouver: UBC Press.

Harris, R. G. B., & Nakamura, G. (1995). Tribal self-governance and forest management at the Hoopa Valley Indian Reservation, Humboldt County, California. *American Indian Culture and Research Journal, 19*(1), 1–38.

Havitz, M. E., & Dimanche, F. (1999). Leisure involvement revisited: Drive properties and paradoxes. *Journal of Leisure Research, 31,* 122–149.

Haynes, V. D. (1997). U.S. culture clash: Native Americans vs. park tourists. *Chicago Tribune, 6*(15), 1.

He, Z. (Ed.) (2000). *Lijiang culture assembly.* Beijing: Religious Culture Press.

Heimerson, S. (2000). *Vanligt hyggligt folk.* Stockholm: Wahlström & Widstrand.

Henderson, M. (1992). American Indian reservations: Controlling separate space, creating separate environments. In: L. Dilsaver, & C. E. Colten (Eds), *The American environment: Interpretations of past geographies* (pp. 115–134). Lanham, MD: Rowman and Littlefield Publishers.

Hetherington, K. (1996). The utopics of social ordering — Stonehenge as a museum without walls. In: S. MacDonald, & S. Fyfe (Eds), *Theorising museums: Representing identity and diversity in a changing world* (pp. 153–177). Oxford: Blackwell.

Hetherington, K. (1997). *The badlands of modernity: Heterotopia and social ordering.* London: Routledge.

Higginbottom, K., Muloin, S., & Zeppel, H. (1999, 1–3 December). *Indigenous wildlife tourism project.* Paper presented at the 14th Australasian Wildlife Management Conference, Northern Territory University.

Higgins-Desbiolles, F. (2002). Looking for the noble savage and booking that cannibal tour: Tourism, racism and indigenous peoples. Paper presented to *Sharing the Space* conference of the International Australian Studies Association, Flinders University, July 11–13. Publication forthcoming.

Higgins-Desbiolles, F. (2003a). Globalisation and indigenous tourism: Sites of engagement and resistance. In: M. Shanahan, & G. Treuren (Eds), *Regional perspectives on globalisation* (pp. 240–262). Adelaide, Wakefield Press.

Higgins-Desbiolles, F. (2003b). Reconciliation tourism: Tourism healing divided societies? *Tourism Recreation Research, 28*(3), 35–44.

Hill, B. (1992). Sustainable tourism. *Parks and Recreation, 23*(8), 84–90.

Hinch, T. (2003). Tourism in Canada's Northern Periphery: The arctic winter games as a cultural attraction. Paper presented at the IGU-conference Perspectives on Tourism in Nordic and other Peripheral Areas, 21–24 August 2003, Umeå: Department of Social and Economic Geography.

Hinch, T. D., & Delamere, T. A. (1993). Native festivals as tourism attractions: A community challenge. *Journal of Applied Recreation Research, 18*(2), 131–142.

Hitchcock, M. (1998). Tourism, Taman Mini, and national identity. *Indonesia and the Malay World, 26*(75), 124–135.

Hitchcock, R. K. (1996). *Kalahari communities: Bushmen and the politics of the environment in Southern Africa.* IWGIA Document No. 79, Copenhagen.

Hitchcock, R. K., & Holm, J. D. (1993). Bureaucratic domination of African hunter-gatherer societies: A study of the San in Botswana. *Development and Change, 24*(1), 1–35.

Hoare, T., Robinson, M., & Levy, C. (1993). Participatory action research in native communities: Cultural opportunities and legal implications. *The Canadian Journal of Native Studies*, *8*(1), 43–68.

Hoffman, T. (1997). Moving beyond dualism: A dialogue with Western European and American Indian views of spirituality, nature, and science. *The Social Sciences Journal*, *34*(4), 447–460.

Hollinshead, K. (1998). Tourism, Hybridity and Ambiguity: The Relevance of Bhabha's 'Third Space' Cultures. *Journal of Leisure Research*, *30*(1).

Hollinshead, K. (1999a). Surveillance and the worlds of tourism: Foucault and the eye of power. *Tourism Management*, *20*(1), 7–24.

Hollinshead, K. (1999b). Disney and commodity aesthetics: A critique of Fjellman's analysis of 'distory' and 'historicide' of the past. *Current Issues in Tourism*, *1*(1), 119–580.

Holroyd, C. (2001). Phenomenological research method, design and procedure: A phenomenological investigation of the phenomenon of being-in-community. *Indo-Pacific Journal of Phenomenology*, *2*. On-line journal http://ipjp.org. Site visited October 14, 2002.

Hoolihan, C. (2002). *Outback not our sole blessing. Townsville Bulletin*, 26.02.02.

Hough, J. (1991). The Grand Canyon National Park and the Havasupai People: Cooperation and conflict. In: P. C. West, & S. R. Brechin (Eds), *Resident peoples and national parks: Social dilemmas and strategies in international conservation* (pp. 215–230). Tucson: University of Arizona Press.

Howe, J., McMahon, E., & Propst, L. (1997). *Balancing nature and commerce in gateway communities*. Washington, DC: Island Press.

Hudson, S. (1993). *The role of the Australian tourist commission in the marketing and development of indigenous tourism, indigenous Australians and Tourism: A focus on Northern Australia*: Darwin: Office of Northern Development.

Hudson, S., & Shephard, G. W. H. (1998). Measuring service quality at tourist destinations: An application of importance-performance analysis to an Alpine ski resort. *Journal of Travel and Tourism Marketing*, *7*(3), 61–77.

Hughes, G. (1995). Authenticity in tourism. *Annals of Tourism Research*, *22*(4), 781–803.

Hunter, C., & Green, H. (1995). *Tourism and the environment: A sustainable relationship?* London: Routledge Publishers.

Ingram, G. (2001). *Farm tourism in the south west tapestry region, Western Australia. experiences of hosts and guests*. Unpublished Masters thesis. Edith Cowan University, Bunbury, Western Australia.

Ingram, G. (2002). Motivations of farm tourism hosts and guests in the south west tapestry region, Western Australia. A phenomenological study. *Indo-Pacific journal of phenomenology*, *3*. On-line journal http://ipjp.org. Site visited October 14, 2002.

Ingram, P. T. (1990). *Indigenous entrepreneurship and tourism development in the Cook Islands and Fiji*. Doctoral dissertation, Massey University, New Zealand, Palmerston North, New Zealand.

Irigary, L. (1991). Equal or different? In: M. Whitford (Ed.), *The Irigary Reader*. Oxford: Basil Blackwell.

Ivy, M. (1995). *Discourses of the vanishing: Modernity, Phantasm, Japan*. Chicago: University of Chicago Press.

Jacobs, J., & Gale, F. (1994). *Tourism and the protection of Aboriginal cultural sites* (No. 10). Canberra: Australian Heritage Commission.

Jafari, J., & Way, W. (1994). Multicultural strategies in tourism. *The Cornell Hotel and Administration Quarterly*, *35*(6), 72–80.

Jamal, T., & Hill, S. (2002). The home and the world: (post)touristic spaces of (in)authenticity? In: G. M. S. Dann (Ed.), *The tourist as a metaphor of the social world* (pp. 77–107). Wallingford: CABI Publishing.

Janiskee, R. L., & Drews, P. L. (1998). Rural festivals and community reimaging. In: R. Butler, C. M. Hall, & J. Jenkins (Eds), *Tourism and recreation in rural areas* (pp. 157–175). Chichester: Wiley.

Jansen-Verbeke (1998). Tourismification and historical cities. *Annals of Tourism Research, 25*(3), 739–741.

Jenkin, G. (1979). *Conquest of the Ngarrindjeri.* Point McLeay, SA: Raukkan Publishers.

Jenks, C. (1993). *Culture/Chris Jenks.* London and New York: Routledge.

Jett, S. (1990). Culture and tourism in Navajo Country. *Cultural Geography, 11*(1), 85–107.

John, D., Nepal, S., Nepal, S. K., & Zeiger, J. (2002). *Recreation resource assessment in the Tl'azt'en Territory: Selected sites.* A Report for the "First Nations and Ecotourism: Building Indigenous Capacity in Planning, Developing, and Managing Ecotourism in Traditional Territories. The Tl'azt'en Nation." Research Project Report No. 3, submitted to the Forest Renewal British Columbia (FRBC), Canada.

Johnston, A. (2001). Oh Canada, your home on native land. *Native Americas* (Fall/Winter), 74–79.

Johnston, B. R. (1994). Breaking out of the tourist trap. *Cultural Survival Quarterly, 14*(1), 2–4.

Joseph, V., Nepal, S., & Zeiger, J. (2002) *Community visions for ecotourism: tl'azt'en nation —* Results from the Workshops Conducted in Tache, May 25, 2001 and July 4, 2001. A Report for the "First Nations and Ecotourism: Building Indigenous Capacity in Planning, Developing, and Managing Ecotourism in Traditional Territories. The Tl'azt'en Nation." Research Project Report No. 2, submitted to the Forest Renewal British Columbia (FRBC), Canada.

Jostad, P. M., McAvoy, L., & McDonald, D. (1996). Native American land ethics: Implications for natural resource management. *Society and Natural Resources, 9*, 565–581.

Juster, F. T. (1966). Consumer buying intentions and purchase probability. Occasional Paper 99, National Bureau of Economic Research, Columbia University Press.

Kalt, J. (1996). *Economic development on Indian reservations.* Hearing before the United States Senate Committee on Indian Affairs. Washington, DC: U.S. Government Printing Office.

Kearns, R. A., & Joseph, A. E. (1997). Restructuring health and rural communities in New Zealand. *Progress in Human Geography, 21*, 18–32.

Keelen, N. (1996). Maori Heritage. Visitor Management and Interpretation. In: C. M. Hall, & S. McArthur (Eds), *Heritage management in Australia and New Zealand: The human dimension* (pp. 195–201). Oxford: Oxford University Press.

Kgathi, D. L., Mbaiwa, J. E., & Motsholapheko, M. (2002). *Local institutions and natural resource management in Ngamiland.* Harry Oppenheimer Okavango Research Centre, University of Botswana, Maun.

Kickingbird, K. (1973). *One million acres.* New York, NY: MacMillan.

Kinsley, M. (1994). Sustainable development. *Public Management, 79*(10), 6–10.

Kirshenblatt-Gimblett, B. (1998). *Destination culture: Tourism, museums, and heritage.* Berkeley, LA, CA: University of California Press.

Klaic, D. (1991). *The plot of the future: Utopia and dystopia in modern drama.* Ann Arbor: University of Michigan Press.

Koori Business Network: Victorian Department of Industry, Innovation and Regional Development. www.sbv.vic.gov.au.

Lacy, M. G. (1985). The U.S. and American Indians: Political relations. In: V. Deloria, Jr. (Ed.), *American Indian policy in the twentieth century* (pp. 83–104). Norman, OK: University of Oklahoma Press.

LaDuke, W. (1994). Native environmentalism. *Cultural Survival Quarterly, 14*(1), 46–48.

Lantto, P. (2000). Time begins anew: An analysis of the ethnopolitical mobilization among the Sami in Sweden 1900–1950. *Kulturens frontlinjer, 32*, Umeå Universitet.

Latour, B. (1987). *Science in action.* Harvard University Press.

Lawrence, T., & Wickens, D. (1997). Managing legitimacy in ecotourism. *Tourism Management*, *18*(5), 307–316.

Laxson, J. (1991). How "we" see "them": Tourism and Native Americans. *Annals of Tourism Research*, *18*(3), 365–391.

Lee, R. B. (1976). Introduction. In: R. B. Lee, & I. Devore (Eds), *Kalahari hunter-gatherers: Studies of the !kung san and their Neighbours*. Cambridge: Cambridge University Press.

Lego, R., & Shaw, R. N. (1992). Convergent validity in tourism research: An empirical analysis. *Tourism Management*, *13*(4), December, 387–393.

Leiper, N. (1990). Tourism systems. Department of Mangement Systems, Occasional Paper 2. Palmerston North: Massey University.

Leiper, N. (1995). *Tourism Management*. Collingwood, Vic.: TAFE Publications.

Lengkeek, J. (2001). Leisure experience and imagination. Rethinking Cohen's modes of tourist experience. *International Sociology*, *16*(2), 173–184.

Lester, A. (1998). 'Otherness' and the frontiers of empire: The Eastern Cape Colony 1806–c.1850. *Journal of Historical Geography*, *24*(1), 2–19.

Lew, A. (1996). Tourism management on American Indian lands in the USA. *Tourism Management*, *17*(5), 355–365.

Lew, A., & Van Otten, G. (1998). *Tourism and gaming on American Indian Lands*. Elmsford, NY: Cognizant.

Lewis, D. R. (1993). Still native: The significance of Native Americans in the history of the twentieth century American West. *Western Historical Quarterly*, *24*, 203–227.

Lewis, D. R. (1994). Native American environmental issues. In: M. B. Davis (Ed.), *Native America in the Twentieth Century*. New York, NY: Garland Publishers.

Lewis, J. (2002). *Cultural studies – The basics*. London: Sage.

Li, X., & Li, L. (Eds) (1998). *The Dongba culture of the Naxi*. Guangzhou: Ling Nan Art Publishing House.

Ling, J. (1995). The role of environmental management in sustainable growth: We need action. *Vital Speeches*, *61*(10), 306–314.

Little, J. (1999). Otherness, representation and the cultural construction of rurality. *Progress in Human Geography*, *23*(3), 437–442.

Lonely Planet *New South Wales* 3rd ed. (2000). Footscray: Lonely Planet Publications.

Lowenthal, D. (1985). *The past is a foreign country*. Cambridge: Cambridge University Press.

MacCannell, D. (1973). Staged Authenticity: Arrangements of Social Space in Tourist Settings. *American Journal of Sociology*, *79*(3), 589–603.

MacCannell, D. (1976). *The tourist: A new theory for the leisure class*. New York: Schocken.

MacCannell, D. (1990). Cannibal tours. *Society for Visual Anthropology Review* (Fall), 14–23.

MacCannell, D. (1992). *Empty meeting grounds – The tourist papers*. London: Routledge.

MacCannell, D. (1999). *The tourist – A new theory of the leisure class*. Berkley and Los Angeles: University of California Press.

Macdonald, G. F., & Alsford, S. (1989). *Museum for the global village: The Canadian Museum of Civilisation*. Hull, Canada: Canadian Musuem of Civilisation.

MacDougall, J. M. (2003). From Puiq (Silencing) to Politik: Transformations in political action and cultural exclusion from late-1990s. *Antropologi Indonesia*, *27*(70), 60–76.

Maori Tourism Taskforce Report (1992). *Maori tourism taskforce report*. Wellington: Te Puni Kokiri.

Masberg, B. A., & Silverman, L. H. (1996). Visitor experiences at heritage sites: A phenomenological approach. *Journal of Travel Research* (Spring), 20–25.

Masilo-Rakgoasi, R. (2002). An assessment of the community-based natural resource management approach in Botswana: Case study of Xaixai and Gudigwa communities. M.A. Thesis, Department of Sociology, University of Botswana, Gaborone.

Mathieson, A., & Wall, G. (1982). *Tourism economic, physical and social impacts*. New York: Longman.

Maynard, R. (2003). The other side of Sydney. *Courier-Mail* (Brisbane), 12.04.03.

Mbaiwa, J. E. (1999). *Prospects for sustainable wildlife resource utilisation and management in Botswana: A case study of East Ngamiland District*. Unpublished M.Sc. Thesis, Department of Environmental Science, University of Botswana, Gaborone.

Mbaiwa, J. E. (2001). The people of the Okavango River Basin: The case of Angola, Namibia and Botswana. *Co-management of the okavango river Basin*. Proceedings of a Workshop Organised by Kalahari Conservation Society to initiate the process of Basin-wide Stakeholder Participation in Co-management of the Okavango River Basin, 16th – 18th October 2001, Sedie Hotel, Maun, Botswana, Kalahari Conservation Society, Gaborone, Botswana, 13–20.

Mbaiwa, J. E. (2002a). *The socio-economic and environmental impacts of tourism development in the Okavango Delta, Botswana: A baseline study*. Harry Oppenheimer Okavango Research Centre, University of Botswana, Maun.

Mbaiwa, J. E. (2002b). The sustainable use of wildlife resources among the Basarwa of Khwai and Mababe in Ngamiland District, Botswana: The past and present perspectives. *Pula: Botswana Journal of African Studies*, *16*(2), 110–122.

Mbaiwa, J. E. (2003a). Community-based tourism in Ngamiland District, Botswana: Development, impacts and challenges. In: M. B. K. Darkoh, & A. Rwomire (Eds), *The human impact on the environment and sustainable Development in Africa* (pp. 379–402). Ashgate, Oxford.

Mbaiwa, J. E. (2003b). The socio-economic and environmental impacts of tourism in the Okavango Delta, Northwestern Botswana. *Journal of Arid Environments*, *54*(2), 447–468.

Mbaiwa, J. E. (2003c). Culture considered. *The tourists: Botswana's premier tourism magazine*. Okavano/Chobe, Can the Wilderness get any Wider (May–September 2003), 28.

Mbaiwa, J. E. (2003d). The socio-economic sustainability of tourism development in the Okavango Delta, Botswana. In: T. Bernard, K. Mosepele, & L. Ramberg (Eds), *Environmental monitoring of tropical wetlands* (pp. 495–519). Proceedings of a Conference in Maun, Botswana, December 4–8, 2002, Harry Oppenheimer Okavango Research Centre, University of Botswana and H. T. Odum Centre for Wetlands, University of Florida.

McCormick, P. J. (2002). Being ourselves for you: The global display of cultures by Nick Stanley. *The International Journal of Tourism Research*, *4*(3), 266–268.

McIntosh, A. J. (1998). Mixing methods: Putting the tourist at the forefront of tourism research. *Tourism Analysis*, *3*(2), 121–127.

McIntosh, A. J. (2004). Tourists' appreciation of Maori culture in New Zealand. *Tourism Management*, *25*(1), 1–15.

McIntosh, A. J., Hinch, T., & Ingram, T. (2002). Cultural Identity and Tourism. *International Journal of Arts Management*, *4*(2), 39–49.

McIntosh, A. J., & Prentice, R. C. (1999). Affirming authenticity: Consuming cultural heritage. *Annals of Tourism Research*, *26*(3), 589–612.

McIntosh, A. J., Zygadlo, F. K., & Matunga, H. (2004). Rethinking Maori Tourism. *Asia Pacific Journal of Tourism Research*, *9*(4), 331–351.

McKercher, B. (1993). Some fundamental truths about tourism: Understanding tourism's social and environmental impacts. *Journal of Sustainable Tourism*, *1*(1), 7–15.

McKercher, M., & Chow, B. S. M. (2001). Cultural distance and cultural tourism participation. *Pacific Tourism Review*, *5*(1/2), 21–30.

McKercher, B., & du Cros, H. (1998). *I climbed to the top of Ayres Rock but still couldn't see Uluru: The challenge of reinventing a tourist destination*. In: B. Faulkner, C. Tidswell, & D. Weaver (Eds), (pp. 376–386). Proceedings of the 8th Australian National Tourism and Hospitality Research Conference, Part 1, 11–14 February, Gold Coast, Griffith University.

McKercher, B., & du Cros, H. (2002). *Cultural tourism – The partnership between tourism and cultural heritage management*. New York: Haworth Hospitality Press.

McLauren, R. D. (1999). History of indigenous people and tourism. *Cultural Survival Quarterly*, (Summer), 27–30.

McLeod, S., Perrott, A., & Thomson, A. (2002, July). Take skills home, islanders urged. *The New Zealand Herald* http://www.nzherald.co.nz/storydisplay.cfm?thesection=news&thesubsection=&storyID=2098267.

Meredith and Associates. (2000). *Fort St. James LRMP – Forest recreation and tourism opportunities study* (Main Report and Appendices). Ministry of Small Business, Tourism and Culture, British Columbia, Canada.

Metoyer-Duran, C. (1995). Economic development on American Indian reservations: A citation analysis. *Library and Information Sciences Research*, *17*(1), 49–85.

Mihesuah, D. (1996). *American Indian stereotypes and realities*. Atlanta, GA: Clarity Press.

Milne, S., Grekin, J., & Woodley, S. (1998). Tourism and the construction of place in Canada's Eastern Arctic. In: G. Ringer (Ed.), *Destinations: Cultural landscapes of tourism* (pp. 101–120). London: Routledge.

Mitchell, V. M., & Greatorex, M. (1990). Consumer purchasing in foreign countries: A perceived risk perspective. *International Journal of Advertising*, *9*, 295–307.

Molale, E. (2001). *Management of funds realised from the community based natural resources management project*. Savingram No. LG 3/6/2/1 IV (46) of 30th January 2001. Ministry of Local Governments, Gaborone.

More, M. (2003). *Principles of extropy version 3.11*. Extropy Institute. Sourced from http://www.extropy.org/.

Morgan, M. (1995). *Mutant message down under*. New York: Harper Collins.

Morris, M. (1995). Life as a tourist object in Australia. In: M. F. Lanfant, J. Allcock, & E. Bruner (Eds), *International tourism – identity and change* (pp. 177–191). London: Sage.

Morris, P. (1999). *History of the establishment of tree farm license 42*. Unpublished report from the "Linking Forestry and Community in the Tl'azt'en Nation: Lessons for Aboriginal Foresty" project. University of Northern British Columbia, Prince George.

Morris, P., & Fondahl, G. (2002). Negotiating the production of space in Tl'azt'en territory, Northern British Columbia. *The Canadian Geographer*, *46*(2), 108–125.

Moscardo, G. (1996). Mindful visitors: Heritage and tourism. *Annals of Tourism Research*, *23*, 376–397.

Moscardo, G., & Pearce, P. L. (1989). Ethnic tourism: Understanding the tourists' perspective. In: *Travel Research: Globalization, the Pacific Rim and Beyond* (pp. 387–394). Salt Lake City: University of Utah.

Moscardo, G., & Pearce, P. L. (1999). Understanding ethnic tourists. *Annals of Tourism Research*, *26*(2), 416–434.

Moscovi, C. (2001). Hybridity and ethics in Chateaubriand's Atala. *Nineteenth-Century French Studies*, *29* (Nos. 3 and 4 Spring-Summer 2001), 197–216.

Moustakas, C. (1994). *Phenomenological research methods*. Thousand Oaks, CA: Sage.

Mowforth, M., & Munt, I. (1998). *Tourism and sustainability: New tourism in the third world*. London and New York: Routledge.

MPAC (1999a). *Pacific vision strategy – Pacific directions report. A report to government on a possible pathway for achieving Pacific people's aspirations*. Wellington, NZ: Ministry of Pacific Island Affairs.

MPAC (1999b). *The social and economic status of pacific peoples in New Zealand*. Wellington, NZ: Ministry of Pacific Island.

Mphinyane, S. T. (2002). Power and powerless: When support becomes overbearing – The case of outsider activism in the resettlement issue of the Basarwa of the Central Kalahari Game Reserve. *Pula: Botswana Journal of African Studies, 16*(2), 75–84.

Müller, D. K., & Pettersson, R. (2001). Access to Sami tourism in Northern Sweden. *Scandinavian Journal of Hospitality and Tourism, 1*(1), 5–18.

Munasinghe, M., & McNeely, J. (1995). Key concepts and terminology of sustainable development. In: M. Munasinghe, & W. Shearer (Eds), *Defining and measuring sustainability: The biological foundations* (pp. 19–46). The International Bank for Reconstruction and Development/The World Bank, Washington.

Murphy, P. (1985). *Tourism – A community approach.* London: Routledge.

Murray, D. (2000). Haka fracas? The dialetics of identity in discussions of a contemporary Maori dance. *The Australian Journal of Anthropology, 11*(3), 345–357.

Mwenya, A. N., Lewis, D. M., Kaweche, G. B. (1991). *Policy, background and future: National parks and wildlife services, new administrative management design for game management areas.* USAID, Lusaka.

National CBNRM Forum. (2001). *Proceedings of the second national CBNRM conference in Botswana,* 14th–16th November 2001, Gaborone, IUCN/SNV CBNRM Support Programme.

Navajoland (1998). *Explore the navajo nation.* Internet URL: http://www.navajoland.primenet.com.

Nelson, J. (1994). The spread of ecotourism: Some planning implications. *Environmental Conservation, 21*(3), 248–255.

Nepal, S. K. (1997). Sustainable tourism, protected areas, and livelihood needs of local communities in developing countries. *International Journal of Sustainable Development and World Ecology, 4,* 123–135.

Nepal, S. K. (2000). National parks, conservation areas, tourism and local communities in the Nepalese Himalaya. In: R. W. Butler, & S. Boyd (Eds), *Tourism and national parks – issues and implications* (pp. 73–94). Guildford: Wiley.

Nepal, S. K. (2002). Involving indigenous peoples in protected area management: Comparative perspectives from Nepal, Thailand and China. *Environmental Management, 30*(6), 748–763.

Nepal, S., & Zeiger, J. (2002). *Ecotourism in the Tl'azt'en nations territory: Community perspectives.* Report for the "*First Nations and Ecotourism: Building Indigenous Capacity in Planning, Developing, and Managing Ecotourism in Traditional Territories. The Tl'azt'en Nation.*" Research Project Report No. 5, submitted to the Forest Renewal British Columbia (FRBC), Canada.

*Ngurunderi: A Ngarrindjeri Dreaming* (1987). Director Max Pepper. Executive Producer John Dick. Pepper Studios for the South Australian Film Corporation and the South Australian Museum with the assistance of the Ngarrindjeri Community. Kent Town, SA.

Nicholson, H. (1997). Collusion, collision or challenge? Indigenous tourism and cultural experience in British Columbia, Canada. In: P. E. Murphy (Ed.), *Quality management in urban tourism* (pp. 115–136). Toronto: Wiley.

Norris, R. (2001). Australian indigenous employment disadvantage: What, why and where to from here? *Journal of Economic Social Policy, 5*(2), 13–42.

Northern Territory Government & Department of Industries and Northern Territory Tourist Commission (2000). *A guide to tourism.* February 2000. Produced by Northern Territory Government. Darwin, NT.

Northern Territory Tourist Commission (1999). Territory tourism – Selected statistics 1997/1998, http://nttc.com.au/aboutnttc/stats/.

Northern Territory Tourist Commission (2000). Territory tourism – Selected statistics 1998/1999, http://nttc.com.au/aboutnttc/stats/.

Northern Territory Tourist Commission and Office of Aboriginal Development (2001). *Experience aboriginal culture*. Northern Territory Tourist Commission. Darwin, NT.

North West District CBNRM Forum (2001). *Minutes of the 5th North West District CBNRM Forum*, March 29, 2001, Maun.

North West District Council, NWDC (2003). *District development plan six 2003/2004–2008/2009*. North West District Council, Maun.

Norusis, M. J. (1990). *SPSS/PC+ ™ 4.0 advanced statistics for the IMB/XT/AT and PS/2*. Chicago: SPSS.

Notzke, C. (1999). Indigenous tourism development in the Arctic. *Annals of Tourism Research*, 26(1), 55–76.

Novatorov, E. V. (1997). An importance-performance approach to evaluating internal marketing in a recreation center. *Managing Leisure*, 2(1), 1–16.

NPWSA (1990). *Coorong national park management plan*. Adelaide, Australia.

NPWSA (1999). *Coorong national park tourism and recreation plan*. Adelaide, Australia.

Oakes, T. S. (1997). Ethnic tourism in rural Guizhou: Sense of place and the commerce of authenticity. In: M. Picard, & R. Wood (Eds), *Tourism, ethnicity and the state in southeast Asia and the Pacific* (pp. 35–70). Honolulu: University of Hawaii Press.

O'Brien, S. (1985). Federal Indian policies and the international protection of human rights. In: V. Deloria, Jr. (Ed.), *American Indian policy in the twentieth century* (pp. 35–61). Norman, OK: University of Oklahoma Press.

Office of Aboriginal Economic Development (2001). *The enterprise solutions initiative, business and management expertise initiative, strategic financial investment and the integrated services provision*. WA Department of Industry & Technology. Office of Aboriginal Enterprise Development website: www.indtech.wa.gov.au.

Office of National Tourism (1996). *A Talent for Tourism*. Available at: http://www.sport.gov. au/publications/talent/campcoorong.html. Accessed 7 March 2001.

Office of National Tourism (1998). *Aboriginal and Torres Strait Islander Tourism*. Tourism Facts No. 11. Canberra: Commonwealth of Australia.

Office of the UNESCO Regional Advisor for Culture in Asia Pacific (2000). *A heritage protection and tourism development: Case study of Lijiang ancient town China*. Paper for A UNESCO conference/workshop in Bhaktapur, Nepal, 8–16 April 2000. Bangkok, UNESCO Asia and Pacific Regional Bureau.

Oppermann, M. (1993). Tourism space in developing countries. *Annals of Tourism Research*, 20(3), 535–556.

Orams, M. (1995). Towards a more desirable form of ecotourism. *Tourism Management*, 16(1), 3–8.

Ostrom, R. (2000). Bali's tourism interests: Local responses to Suharto's globalization policies. *Southeast Asian Journal of Social Science*, 28(2), 111–130.

Oussoren, K., Nepal, S., & Zeiger, J. (2002). *Ecotourism planning: Tl'azt'en nation*. A Report for the "First Nations and Ecotourism: Building Indigenous Capacity in Planning, Developing, and Managing Ecotourism in Traditional Territories. The Tl'azt'en Nation." Research Project Report No. 1, submitted to the Forest Renewal British Columbia (FRBC), Canada.

Oxford Advanced Learner's Dictionary 5th edition (1995). Oxford: Oxford University Press.

Palmer, L. (1998, October 13). *Land rights, land ethics and the 'tourist interest' in Kakadu National Park*. Paper Presented in the CINCRM Seminar series.

Palmer, L. (1999). *Safari hunting and indigenous peoples*. Paper presented at the 14th Australasian Wildlife Management Conference, Northern Territory University, 1–3 December. Cooperative Research Center for Sustainable Tourism, Griffiths University, Queensland, Australia.

Panakera, C. (2003). *Pacific island entrepreneurs*. Unpublished manuscript. Department of Tourism Management. The University of Waikato Management School, Hamilton, New Zealand.

Parasuraman, A., Zeithaml, V. A., & Berry, L. L. (1988). SERVQUAL: A multiple-item scale for measuring consumer perceptions of service quality. *Journal of Retailing*, *64*, 12–37.

Parasuraman, A., Zeithaml, V. A., & Berry, L. L. (1991). Refinement and reassessment of the SERVQUAL scale. *Journal of Retailing*, *67*, 420–450.

Parasuraman, A., Zeithaml, V. A., & Berry, L. L. (1994a). Alternative scales for measuring service quality: A comparative assessment based on psychometric and diagnostic criteria. *Journal of Retailing*, *70*(3), 201–230.

Parasuraman, A., Zeithaml, V. A., & Berry, L. L. (1994b). *Moving forward in service quality research: Measuring different customer-expectation levels, comparing alternative scales, and examining the performance-behavioral intentions link*. Marketing Science Institute Working Paper, Report No. 94–114, September 1994.

Parasuraman, A., Zeithaml, V. A., & Berry, L. L. (1994c). Reassessment of expectations as a comparison standard in measuring service quality: Implications for further research. *Journal of Marketing*, *58*(January), 111–124.

Parminter, T. G., Thorrold, B. S., Perkins, A. M. L., McGowan, A., Quinn, J., Collier, K., Moore, P., Hill, S., Iti, R., & Richards, A. (1999). *A participatory approach for involving communities in catchment management*. Multiple Objective Decision Support Society.

Parminter, T. G. L., Wedderburn, I., Tarbotton, G., Lauder, A. Donnison, & Cave, J. (2003). *Building resilience in rural communities and enhancing their capacity for sustainable future development*. Unpublished manuscript. Hamilton.

Patton, M. Q. (1990). *Qualitative evaluation and research methods* (2nd ed.). London: Sage.

Pearce, D. G. (1993). Comparative studies in tourism research. In: D. G. Pearce, & R. W. Butler (Eds), *Tourism research: Critiques and challenges* (pp. 20–35). London: Routledge.

Pearce, P. L. (1988). *The Ulysses Factor: Evaluating visitors in tourist settings*. New York: Springer Verlag.

Pearce, D., Markandya, A., & Barbier, E. B. (1989). *Blueprint for a green economy*. Earthscan, London.

Peart, K. (1995). First Americans. *Scholastic update* (February), 4–5.

Pemberton, J. (1994). Recollections from 'beautiful Indonesia': Somewhere beyond the postmodern. *Public Culture*, *6*, 241–262.

Perdue, R., Long, P., & Allen, L. (1992). Resident support for tourism development. *Annals of Tourism Research*, *17*(4), 586–599.

Pettersson, R. (2001). *Sami tourism – Supply and demand: Two essays on indigenous peoples and tourism*. ETOUR scientific book series 2001:8. Östersund: ETOUR.

Pettersson, R. (2003). Indigenous cultural events: The development of a Sami winter festival in Northern Sweden. *Tourism*, *51*(3), 319–332.

Pfister, R. E. (2000). Mountain culture as a tourism resource: Aboriginal views of the privileges of storytelling. In: Godde, P., Price, M. F., & Zimmermann, M. F. (Eds), *Tourism and development in mountain regions*. Oxon: CABI Publishing.

Picard, M. (1990, Summer). Kebalian Orang Bali: Tourism and the uses of "Balinese culture" in New Order Indonesia. *Review of Indonesian and Malaysian Affairs*, *24*(1), 1–38.

Picard, M. (1995). Cultural heritage and tourist capital: Cultural tourism in Bali. In: M.-F. Lanfant, J. B. Allcock, & E. M. Bruner (Eds), *International tourism: Identity and change* (pp. 44–66). London: Sage.

Picard, M. (1997). Cultural tourism, nation-building and regional culture: The making of a Balinese identity. In: M. Picard, & R. E. Wood (Eds), *Tourism, ethnicity and the state in Asian and Pacific societies* (pp. 181–214). Honolulu: University of Hawaii Press.

Pierce, D. (1993). Edu-tourism and immersion in American Indian culture. *Winds of Change* (Spring), 62–65.

Pierce, D. (1995). Edu-tourism in Montana's Indian Country. *Winds of Change* (Spring), 68–73.

Pitcher, M. (1997, April). *Preliminary analysis of 1995 and 1996 tourist questionnaires – Manyallaluk Aboriginal cultural tours.* Unpublished Paper, Northern Territory University.

Pitcher, M., van Oosterzee, P., & Palmer, L. (1999). *Choice and control: The development of indigenous tourism in Australia.* Darwin, Northern Territory University and Cooperative Research Centre for Sustainable Tourism.

Pitterlee, S. (1999). *International visitors' interest and experience with indigenous tourism products,* workshop for Northern Territory tourist operators. Northern Territory Tourist Commission, Darwin.

Place, S. (1995). Ecotourism for sustainable development: Oxymoron or plausible strategy? *GeoJornal, 35*(2), 161–173.

Plog, S. C. (1977). Why destinations rise and fall in popularity. In: E. M. Kelly (Ed.), *Domestic and international tourism* (pp. 26–28). Wellesley, MA: Institute of Certified Travel Agents.

Prentice, R. C., Witt, S. F., & Wydenbach, E. G. (1994). The endearment behaviour of tourists through their interaction with the host community. *Tourism Management, 15*(2), 117–125.

Quinn, B. (2003). Symbols, practices and myth-making: Cultural perspectives on the Wexford Festival Opera. *Tourism Geographies, 5*(3), 329–349.

Reed, K. (1999). *Aboriginal peoples: Building for the future.* Don Mills, ON: Oxford University Press.

Rehn, A. (2003). The 'old people' return home. *The advertiser* (May 6), 8.

Reynolds, T., & Gutman, J. (1988). Laddering theory, method, analysis and interpretation. *Journal of Advertising Research* (February/March), 11–29.

Richards, P., & Ryan, C. (2004). The Aotearoa traditional Maori performing arts festival 1972–2000. *Journal of Tourism and Cultural Change, 2*(2), 94–117.

Rideout, D. (2000, December). Inuit culture, the secret to arctic tourism growth. Nunatsiaq News. (www.nuatsiaq.com/archives/nunavut001231/nut2101_10html) Accessed February 22, 2002.

Riegner, H. (1992). New concepts in tourism development. *Business America, 113*(24), 2–6.

Rigney, M. (2002). Chairman of Ngarrindjeri Native Title Committee, personal communication, 25th January, Camp Coorong, Meningie, South Australia.

Rihoy, E. (1995). From state control of wildlife to co-management of natural resources – the evolution of community management in Southern Africa. In: E. Rihoy (Ed.), *The commons without tragedy? Strategies for community-based natural resources management in Southern Africa* (pp. 1–36). Proceedings of the Regional Natural Resources Management Programme Annual Conference: SADC Wildlife Technical Co-ordinating Unit, Kasane.

Rihoy, E., Jones, B., Anstey, S., & Rolfes, M. T. (1999). *Tenure in transition: A stakeholder guide to natural resource tenure in Southern Africa-community-based natural resource management.* Africa Resources Trust, SADC Natural Resources Management Project, Gaborone.

Robinson, G. (1997). Community-based planning: Canada's Atlantic coastal action program (ACAP). *The Geographical Journal, 163*(1), 25–37.

Robinson, M. (1999). Collaboration and cultural consent: Refocussing sustainable tourism. *Journal of Sustainable Tourism, 7*(3/4), 379–397.

Robinson, M. (2002). Boating playground: Hindmarsh Island, South Australia. *Club Marine, 18*(1), 140–143.

Rogers-Martinez, D. (1992). The Sinkyone Intertribal Park Project. *Restoration and Management Notes, 10*(1), 64–69.

Rojek, C., & Urry, J. (1997). *Touring cultures – transformations of travel and theory.* London: Routledge.

Rothert, S. (1997). Which way the Okavango. In: KCS and DWNP (Eds), *Conservation and management of wildlife in botswana – strategies for 21st century* (pp. 158–162). Proceedings of

Conference hosted by the Department of Wildlife and National Parks and Kalahari Conservation Society, Gaborone.

Rowse, T. (1999). *The collector as outsider – T. G. H. Strehlow as 'public intellectual'*. Occasional Paper, No. 2. Alice Springs: Strehlow Research Centre.

Rozemeijer, N., & Van der Jagt, C. (2000). Community based natural resource management in Botswana: How community based is community based natural resource management in Botswana. Occasional Paper Series, IUCN/SNV CBNRM Support Programme, Gaborone.

Rudner, R. (1994). Sacred geographies. *Wilderness, 58*(2), 11–28.

Ruppert, D. (1996). Intellectual property rights and environmental planning. *Landscape and Urban Planning, 36*, 117–123.

Russell, S. (2002). Aboriginals focus of tours down under. *The Toronto Star*, 09.03.02.

Rutten, M. (1997). Cooperation and differentiation. Social history of iron founders in Central Java. In: M. R. C. Upadhya (Ed.), *Small business entrepreneurs in asia and europe –Towards a comparative perspective* (Vol. 39). New Delhi, Thousand Oaks and London: Sage.

Ryan, C. (1997a). Review of tourism and indigenous peoples by R Butler and T Hinch. *Tourism Management, 18*(7), 479–480.

Ryan, C. (1997b). Maori and tourism – a relationship of history, constitutions and rites. *Journal of Sustainable Tourism, 5*(4), 257–279.

Ryan, C. (1998). Dolphins, Marae and canoes – eco-tourism in New Zealand. In: E. Laws, G. Moscardo, & B. Faulkner (Eds), *Embracing and managing change in tourism – International case studies* (pp. 285–306). London: Routledge.

Ryan, C. (1999a). Some dimensions of Maori involvement in Tourism. In: M. Robinson, & P. Boniface (Eds), *Tourism and cultural conflicts* (pp. 229–246). Wallingford: CABI Publishing.

Ryan, C. (1999b). From the psychometrics of SERVQUAL to sex – measurements of tourist satisfaction. In: A. Pizam, & Y. Mansfeld (Eds), *Consumer behavior in travel & tourism* (pp 267–286). Binghamtom, NY: Haworth Press.

Ryan, C. (2000a). Indigenous peoples and tourism. In: C. Ryan, & S. J. Page (Eds), *Tourism management: Towards the new millennium* (pp. 421–430). Pergamon: Oxford.

Ryan, C. (2000b). Tourists' experiences, phenomenographic analysis, post-positivism and neural network software. *International Journal of Tourism Research (Formerly Progress in Tourism and Hospitality Research), 2*(2), 119–131.

Ryan, C. (2002a). Tourism and cultural proximity: Examples from New Zealand. *Annals of Tourism Research, 29*(4), 952–971.

Ryan, C. (2002b). *The tourist experience*. London: Continuum.

Ryan, C. (2002c). Equity, power sharing and sustainability — issues of the "New Tourism". *Tourism Management, 23*(1), 17–26.

Ryan, C. (2004). Ethics in tourism research – objectivities and personal perspectives. In: B. W. Ritchie, P. Burns, & C. Palmer (Eds), *Tourism research methods: Integrating theory and practice* (pp. 9–19). Wallingford, Oxon: CAB International.

Ryan, C. (2005). Indigenous tourism and the visitor experience. Paper submitted to *Annals of tourism research*.

Ryan, C., & Cave, J. B. Y. (2004, February). Letting the visitor speak: An analysis of destination image through the use of neural network software and power point presentation. Paper presented at the Creating Tourism Knowledge: Cauthe 2004, Brisbane, Australia.

Ryan, C., & Crotts, J. (1997). Carving and tourism: A Maori perspective. *Annals of Tourism Research, 24*(4), 898–918.

Ryan, C., Hughes, K., & Chirgwin, S. (2000). The gaze, spectacle and ecotourism. *Annals of Tourism Research, 27*(1), 148–163.

Ryan, C., & Huyton, J. (1998). Dispositions to buy postcards at Uluru-Kata Tjuta National Park. *Journal of Sustainable Tourism, 6*(3), 254–259.

Ryan, C., & Huyton, J. (2000a). Aboriginal tourism – a linear structural relations analysis of domestic and international tourist demand. *International Journal of Tourism Research, 2*(1), 15–29.

Ryan, C., & Huyton, J. (2000b). Who is interested in Aboriginal tourism in the Northern Territory, Australia? A cluster analysis. *Journal of Sustainable Tourism, 8*(1), 53–88.

Ryan, C., & Huyton, J. (2002). Tourists and Aboriginal people. *Annals of Tourism Research, 29*(3), 631–647.

Ryan, C., & Martin, A. (2001). Tourists and strippers: Liminal theater. *Annals of Tourism Research, 28*(1), 140–163.

Ryan, C., & Trauer, B. (2004). Involvement in adventure tourism: Toward implementing a fuzzy set. *Tourism Review International, 7*(3/4), 143–152.

Ryan, C., Trauer, B., & Pendergast, D. (2004). Darling Harbour – site of the carnivalesque? Paper Presented at *Tourism – The State of the Art II*. The Scottish Hotel School, The University of Strathclyde, Glasgow.

Said, E. W. (1975). *Beginnings: Intention and method*. New York: Basic Books.

Said, E. W. (1978). *Orientalism*. London: Penguin Books.

Sametinget, T. (2003). *Samisk näringsutveckling och kultur. Underlag för tillväxtprogrammen i Norrbotten, Västerbotten och Jämtland 2004–2007*. Kiruna: Sametinget.

Schalcher, S. (2001). *Report to LIPI on research in Moni, Eastern Flores* 19 pages, author's files.

Schanzel, H., & McIntosh, A. J. (2000). An insight into the personal and emotive context of wildlife viewing at the Penguin Place, Otago Peninsula, New Zealand. *Journal of Sustainable Tourism, 8*(1), 36–52.

Scheyvens, R. (2002). Backpacker tourism and Third World development. *Annuals of Tourism Research, 29*(1), 144–164.

Schmiechen, J. (1993, August). Paper on Camp Coorong in Ecotourism: An Aboriginal Perspective. South Australian Eco-tourism Forum, Adelaide.

Schuler, S. (1999). *Tourism impacts on an Australian indigenous community: A Djabugay case study*. Unpublished MA thesis, Environmental and Planning Studies, Faculty of Arts, University of the Sunshine Coast.

Schwaller, C. (1992). *'As others see us': The role of cultural awareness in European tourism*. Paper presented at the Tourism in Europe: The 1992 conference, 8–10 July, Durham, UK.

Schweitzer, R. (1998a). *Philosophical foundations of phenomenology*. Paper presented at a Phenomenology Seminar for Edith Cowan University, Bunbury, Western Australia.

Schweitzer, R. (1998b, May). Phenomenology and qualitative research method in psychology. Seminar presented at Edith Cowan University, Western Australia.

Sears, J., Nepal, S., & Zeiger, J. (2002). *Tl'azt'en ecotourism survey in the Fort St. James region: Data set and general description of tourism entrepreneurs attitudes towards ecotourism, and participation of first nations in ecotourism*. A Report for the "First Nations and Ecotourism: Building Indigenous Capacity in Planning, Developing, and Managing Ecotourism in Traditional Territories. The Tl'azt'en Nation." Research Project Report No. 4, submitted to the Forest Renewal British Columbia (FRBC), Canada.

Seton, K. (1999). *Fourth world nations in the era of globalisation*. From the Center for World Indigenous Studies, accessed 27/3/01 on line: http://www.cwis.org/fwj/41/fworld.html.

Shapiro, K. (1985). *Bodily reflective modes, a phenomenological method for psychology*. Durham: Duke University Press.

Sheehan, N. (2002, August 16–18). Speaking notes Pacific Economic Symposium, Manukau Auckland.

Shenev-Keller, S. (1993). The Israeli souvenir: Its text and context. *Annals of Tourism Research*, *20*(1), 182–196.

Sheppard, B. H., Hartwick, J., & Warshaw, P. R. (1988, December). The theory of reasoned action: A meta-analysis of past research with recommendations for modifications and future research. *Journal of Consumer Research*, *15*(1), 325–343.

Sheridan, D. (1999). Making sense of Detroit. *Michigan Quarterly Review*, *38*(3), 321–353.

Sherwood, P. (2001). Client experience in psychotherapy. What heals and what harms? *Indo-Pacific Journal of Phenomenology*, *1*(2). On-line journal http://ipjp.org. Site visited October 15 2001.

Siegel, P., & Jakus, P. (1996). Tourism as a sustainable rural development strategy: Building consensus in resident attitudes. *Southern Journal of Rural Sociology*, *11*(1), 17–41.

Simons, M. (2003). *The meeting of the waters*. Sydney, Hodder.

Sims, W. (1997). *Labour turnover at Yulara resort complex*. Unpublished Paper. Department of Tourism, La Trobe University.

Sissons, J. (1993). The systematisation of tradition: Maori culture as a strategic resource. *Oceania*, *64*(2), 97–116.

Sissons, J. (1998). The traditionalisation of the Maori meeting house. *Oceania*, *69*(1), 36–46.

Sklair, L. (2002). *Globalization, capitalism and its alternatives* (3rd ed.). Oxford: Oxford University Press.

Smiles, R. (2002). Cultural immersion. *Black Issues in Higher Education*, *19*(13), 22.

Smith, C., Burke, H., & Ward, G. K. (2000). Globalisation and indigenous peoples: Threat or empowerment? In: C. Smith, & G. K. Ward (Eds), *Indigenous cultures in an interconnected world*. St. Leonards, NSW, Allen and Unwin.

Smith, C., & Ward G. K. (2000). *Indigenous cultures in an interconnected world*. Vancouver: UBC Press.

Smith, D. H. (1994a). The issue of compatibility between cultural integrity and economic development among Native American tribes. *American Indian Culture and Research Journal*, *18*(2), 177–205.

Smith, D. H. (1994b). Native American economic development: A modern approach. *Review of Regional Studies*, *24*(1), 87–103.

Smith, V. L. (1996). Indigenous tourism: The four Hs. In: R. Butler, & T. Hinch (Eds), *Tourism and indigenous peoples* (pp. 283–307). London: International Thomson.

Smith, V. L. (2001). The culture brokers. In: M. Brent (Ed.), *Hosts and guests revisited: Tourism issues of the 21st century* (pp. 275–282). Elmsford: Cognizant Communication Corporation.

Snipp, M. (1986). American Indians and natural resource development. *American Journal of Economics and Sociology*, *45*(4), 457–474.

Snipp, M. (1991). The Indian wars, again? *The Rural sociologist* (Winter), 11–16.

Sobecki, S. (2002). Mandeville's thought of the limit: The discourse of similarity and difference in The Travels of Sir John Mandeville. *The Review of English Studies*, *53*(211), 329–343.

Sofield, T. H. B. (1995). Indonesia's national tourism development plan. *Annals of Tourism Research*, *22*(3), 690–694.

Soja, E. (1995). Heterotopologies: A remembrance of other spaces in the citadel – LA. In: K. Gibson (Ed.), *Postmodern city spaces*. Oxford: Blackwell.

Solomon, M. R., Suprenant, C., Czepiel, J., & Gutman, E. (1985). A role theory perspective on dyadic interactions: The service encounter. *Journal of Marketing*, *49*(Winter), 99–111.

Song-Hyung Sop, Stubbles, R. L., & Song, H. S. (1998). Residents' attitudes and importance-performance evaluation toward the impacts of tourism in the Black Hills, USA. *Journal of Korean Forestry Society*, *87*(2), 179–187.

SOU 2001:101 (2001). *En ny rennäringspolitik – öppna samebyar och samverkan med andra markanvändare*. Reports of the Government Commissions, SOU-series. Stockholm: Fritzes.

South Australian Tourism Commission (1996). *Aboriginal tourism strategy* (August). Adelaide, SA.

South Australian Tourism Commission (1998). *Guidelines for tourism joint ventures between Aboriginal and non-Aboriginal partners.* Coopers & Lybrand Consultants and Quoin Technology. Printing House: South Australia.

South Australian Tourism Commission (2000). *Discover the secrets of South Australia.* Media Kit, Adelaide.

South Australian Tourism Commission (2001). *Marketing South Australia: An operators guide 2001/2002.* Designed and produced by SATC. Adelaide, SA.

South Australian Tourism Commission in conjunction with National Parks & Wildlife South Australia, Aboriginal Partnership (2001). *South Australian aboriginal cultural experiences.* Adelaide, SA.

State & Regional Development (2001). *Victorian small business counselling services and the regional assistance program.* SRD website: www.sbcs.org.au.

Statistics, N. Z. (2001). *2001 census snapshot 6: Pacific peoples.* Statistics New Zealand 18 April 2002. Accessed through http://www.statistics.govt.nz. Retrieved 2002, from the World Wide Web.

Statistics, N. Z. (2002). *2002 Pacific Island peoples.* www.stats.govt.nz. Retrieved, from the World Wide Web.

Steiner, A., & Rihoy, E. (1995). *The commons without tragedy? Strategies for community-based natural resources management in Southern Africa* (pp. 1–36). Proceedings of the Regional Natural Resources Management Programme Annual Conference: SADC Wildlife Technical Co-odinating Unit, Kasane.

St. John, G. (2001). Alternative cultural heterotopia and the liminoid body: Beyond Turner at ConFest. *Australian Journal of Anthropology, 12*(1), 47–67.

Stott, M. A. (1978). Tourism in Mykonos: Some social and cultural responses. *Mediterrean Studies, 1*(2), 72–90.

Suasta, P., & O'Connor, L. (1999). Democratic mobilization and political authoritarianism: Tourism developments in Bali. In: R. Rubenstein, & L. H. Connor (Eds), *Staying local in the global village: Bali in the twentieth century* (pp. 91–122). Honolulu: University of Hawaii Press.

Sutton, I. (1991). The political geography of Indian Country. *American Indian Culture and Research Journal, 15*(2), 1–2.

Sweet, J. D. (1991). Let 'em loose: Pueblo Indian management of tourism. *American Indian Culture and Research Journal, 15*(4), 59–74.

Sweet, J. D. (1994). The portals of tradition: Tourism in the American Southwest. *Cultural Survival Quarterly, 14*(2), 2–8.

Szynklarz, R., & Firth, T. (2004), *The challenges of conducting tourism research into Aboriginal communities* (pp. 341–345). Proceedings of the 14th Conference of the Council of Australian Universities in Tourism and Hospitality Education, University of Queensland, Brisbane.

Tahana, N., & Oppermann, M. (1998). Maori cultural performances and tourism. *Tourism Recreation Research, 23*(1), 23–30.

Taiga Rescue Network (2003). *Aboriginal experiences in Canada – Parks and protected areas.* Jokkmokk, Sweden: Taiga Rescue Network.

Tanoi, E. (1993). *A process evaluation of the business workshop programme of the Pacific Islands employment development board.* Hamilton, NZ: Waikato University.

Tau, T. (2000). J. Cooksen, & G. Dunstall (Eds), *Southern capital Christchurch: Towards a city biography 1850–2000.* Christchurch: Canterbury University Press.

Taubman, A. (2002). Protecting Aboriginal sacred sites: The aftermath of the Hindmarsh Island dispute. *Environmental and Planning Law Journal, 19*(2), 140–158.

Tauroa, H., & Tauroa, P. (1986). *Te Marae: A guide to customs and practices.* Auckland: Reed Methuan Publishers.

Taylor, J. (2001). Authenticity and sincerity in tourism. *Annals of Tourism Research, 28*(1), 7–26.

Taylor, J., & Altman, J. (1997). *The job ahead: Escalating economic costs of indigenous employment disparity.* ATSIC, Canberra.

Taylor, M. (2000). *Life, land and power, contesting development in northern Botswana.* PhD Thesis, University of Edinburgh.

Taylor, M. (2001). *Whose agendas? Reassessing the role of CBNRM in Botswana.* National Museum of Botswana, Gaborone.

Taylor, S. A. (1997). Assessing regression-based importance weights for quality perceptions and satisfaction judgments in the presence of higher order and/or interaction effects. *Journal of Retailing, 73*(1), 135–159.

Taylor, S. A., & Baker, T. L. (1994). An assessment of the relationship between service quality and customer satisfaction in the formation of consumers' purchase intentions. *Journal of Retailing, 70*(2), 163–178.

Te Awekotuku, N. (1981). *The socio-cultural impacts of tourism on the Te Arawa people of Rotorua.* Unpublished Ph.D. Thesis, University of Waikato, Hamilton, New Zealand.

Thakadu, O. T. (1997). *Indigenous wildlife knowledge systems and their role in facilitating community-based wildlife management projects in Botswana.* M.Sc. Thesis, School of Environment and Development, University of Natal, Pietermaritzburg.

Thaman, K. (2002). Shifting sights: The cultural challenge of sustainability. *International Journal of sustainability in Higher Education, Bradford, 3*(3), 233–243.

The Ecotourism Society (1991). *Ecotourism guidelines for nature-based tour operators.* Vermont, USA: Ecotourism Society.

The Ecotourism Society (1997). Internet URL: http://www.ets.org.

The Navajo Crisis (1997). Internet URL: http://www.primenet.com/~dineh/news.html.

The Southwest Indian Foundation (1998). *A Native American perspective.* Autumn.

The Vancouver Sun (2001, October 27). *BC first nations – Creating new opportunities for economic development* (pp. E1–E8). Special Advertising Feature, Saturday.

Thistlewait, B., & Davis, D. (1996). *Pacific 2000 – A sustainable future for Melanesia.* Canberra: National Centre for Development Studies, Australian National University.

Thomsen, D. A. (2001). *Care or control? Ngarrindjeri participation in natural resource planning.* Unpublished Honours Thesis, University of Adelaide.

Timothy, D. J., & Boyd, S. W. (2003). *Heritage tourism.* Harlow: Prentice-Hall.

Tjapukai Aboriginal Cultural Park (1997). *Tjapukai aboriginal partners newsletter,* 1 (June).

Tlou, T. (1985). *History of Ngamiland: 1750–1906. The formation of an African State.* Gaborone: Macmillan.

Tourism Concern (2002). IYE: Southern perspectives (Campaigns Insert).

Tourism NSW (2001). Brochure: NSW Indigenous Cultural Experience. Sydney.

Tourism NSW, & Victoria (2001). Brochure, Murray Ontbact Aboriginal Cultural Trial. Sydney.

Tourism Queensland (2000). Special interest unit – *New product research – A research report.* Brisbane: Tourism Queensland.

Tourism Queensland (2001). *The tourism assistance database.* Tourism Queensland website: www.tq.webcentral.com.au/tad.default.asp.

Tourism Training Australia (1996). Brochure: *Tourism our way.* Sydney.

Tourism Training Australia & Commonwealth Department of Education, Training & Youth Affairs (2000). Information folder/kit: *Pathways.* DETYA. Sydney.

Trauer, B., & Ryan, C. (2004). Romance in tourism – an application of intimacy theory to the tourist experience. Paper presented at the Creating Tourism Knowledge: Cauthe 2004, Brisbane, Australia.

Trauer, B., & Ryan, C. (2005). Romance in tourism – an application of intimacy theory to the tourist experience. Accepted for publication in *Tourism Management*.

Trilling, L. (1972). *Sincerity and authenticity*. London: Oxford University Press.

Trosper, R. (1995). Traditional American Indian economic policy. *American Indian Culture and Research Journal, 19*(1), 65–95.

Tsing, A. L., Brosius, J. P., & Zerner, C. (1999). Assessing community-based natural resource management. *Ambio, 28*, 197–198.

Tucak, L. (2001). Artist not skimping on real Australia. *The Australian*, 28.08.01.

Turner, L., & Ash, J. (1975). *The golden hordes: International tourism and the pleasure periphery*. London: Constable.

Turner, V. (1982). Social dramas and stories about them. In: V. Turner (Ed.), *From ritual to theatre: The human seriousness of play* (pp. 61–88). New York: Performing Arts Journal Publications.

Twyman, C. (2000). Participatory conservation? Community-based natural resource management in Botswana. *The Geographical Journal, 166*(4), 323–335.

United Nations Development Program (2004). About indigenous peoples – definition. http://www.undp.org/csopp/CSO/NewFiles/ipaboutdef.html.

Urry, J. (1990). *The tourist gaze: Leisure and travel in contemporary societies*. London: Sage.

Urry, J. (1995). *Consuming places*. London: Routledge.

Uys, C. (1994). *Schmidtsdrift: Where next?* Diploma in African Studies, University of Cape Town, Cape Town.

Van Manen, M. (1990). *Researching lived experience. Human science for an action sensitive pedagogy*. Ontario, Canada: University of Western Ontario.

Venbrux, E. (2000). Tales of Tiwiness: Tourism and self-determination in an Australian Aboriginal society. *Pacific Tourism Review, 4*, 137–147.

Viken, A. (1997). Sameland tilpasset turistblikket. In: J. K. S. Jacobsen, & A. Viken (Eds), *Turisme: Fenomen og næring* (pp. 174–180). Oslo: Universitetsforlaget.

Viken, A. (2002). Turismens Sameland: Tradisjoner i transformasjon. Web-journal *Utmark* 2002:1, www.utmark.org.

Vinje, D. L. (1985). Cultural values and economic development on reservations. In: V. Deloria, Jr. (Ed.), *American Indian policy in the twentieth century* (pp. 155–176). Norman, OK: University of Oklahoma Press.

Vogt, W. P. (1993). *Dictionary of statistics and methodology: A nontechnical guide for the social sciences*. Newbury Park, NY: Sage.

Waitt, G. (1997). Selling paradise and adventure: Representation of landscape in the tourist advertising of Australia. *Australian Geographic Studies, 35*(1, March), 47–61.

Walker, S. (1997). Perceived impacts of ecotourism development. *Annals of Tourism Research, 24*(3), 743–745.

Wall, G. (1997). Is ecotourism sustainable? *Environmental Management, 21*(4), 483–491.

Walpole, M. J., & Goodwin, H. J. (2000). Local economic impacts of dragon tourism in Indonesia. *Annals of Tourism Research, 23*(3), 559–576.

Walsh, B. (1996). Authenticity and cultural representation. A case study of Maori tourism operators. In: C. M. Hall, & S. McArthur (Eds), *Heritage tourism management in Australia and New Zealand* (pp. 202–207). Auckland: Oxford University Press.

Wang, N. (1999). Rethinking authenticity in tourism experience. *Annals of Tourism Research, 26*(2), 349–370.

Wang, N. (2000). *Tourism and modernity: A sociological analysis*. Oxford: Pergamon Press.

Warren, C. (1998a). Tanah Lot: The cultural and environmental politics of resort development in Bali. In: P. Hirsch, & C. Warren (Eds), *Reclaiming resources: The Political economy of environment in Southeast Asia* (pp. 229–261). London: Routledge.

Warren, C. (1998b). Whose tourism? Balinese fight back. *Inside Indonesia*, *54*(April/June), 24–25.

Wasko, J., & Meehan, E. (Eds) (2001). *Dazzled by Disney? The global Disney audiences project*. Leicester: Leicester University Press.

Wassmann, J. (Ed.) (1998). *Pacific answers to western hegemony: Cultural practices of identity construction*. Oxford, New York: Berg.

Watson, G. L., & Kopachevsky, J. P. (1994). Interpretations of tourism as commodity. *Annals of Tourism Research*, *21*(3), 643–660.

Weaver, D. (1995). Alternative tourism in Montserrat. *Tourism Management*, *16*(8), 593–604.

Weaver, D. (2001). *The encyclopedia of ecotourism*. Oxford: CABI Publishing.

Welcome to Tjapukai (n.d.). Tjapukai cultural park. Available on-line: http://www.tjapukai.com.au/. Accessed on June 28th 2003.

West, P. C., & Brechin S. R. (Eds) (1991). *Resident peoples and national parks: Social dilemmas and strategies in international conservation*. Tucson: University of Arizona Press.

Western Australian Tourism Commission (2002). *Marketing guide*. Tourism Industry Development Division brochure. Perth, WA.

White, D. (1993). Tourism as economic development for native people living in the shadow of a protected area: A North American case study. *Society and Natural Resources*, *6*(4), 339–345.

White, H. (1993). The homecoming of the Kagga Kamma Bushmen. *Cultural Survival Quarterly*, *17*(2), 61–63.

Whitford, M., Bell, B., & Watkins, M. (2001). Indigenous tourism policy in Australia: 25 Years of Rhetoric and Economic Rationalism. *Current Issues in Tourism*, *4*(2–4), 151–181.

Wickaksono, A. (1996). Participatory planning strategy for Komodo National Park. A consultancy report submitted to The Nature Conservancy Indonesia Program.

Wickens, E., & Harrison, A. (1996). *Staging modernity: The consumption of hybrid playful experiences in Chalkidiki – Northern Greece, culture as the tourist product*. Sunderland: Centre for Travel and Tourism.

Wight, P. (1997). Ecotourism accommodation spectrum: Does supply match demand? *Tourism Management*, *4*(2), 209–220.

Williams, P. W., & Richter, C. (2002). Developing and supporting European tour operator distribution channels for Canadian Aboriginal tourism development. *Journal of Travel Research*, *40*, 404–415.

Williams, T. (2002). Bone find triggers apology on bridge. *The Advertiser*, *8* (October), 3.

Wilson, J., & Udall, L. (1982). *Folk festivals: A handbook for organisation and management*. Knoxville: University of Tennessee Press.

World Commission on Environment and Development (WCED) (1987). *Our common future: The Brundtland report*. London: Oxford University Press.

World Tourism Organisation (1998). *Tourism highlights 1997*. Madrid: WTO.

Xie, P. F., & Wall, G. (2002). Visitors' perceptions of authenticity at cultural attractions in Hainan, China. *The International Journal of Tourism Research*, *4*(5), 353–366.

Xu, J. (Ed.) (2000). Yunnan "Tu-Dian" illustrated book: Lijiang. Kunming, Yunnan People's Publishing House.

Yamamura, T. (2002). The process of social transformation associated with tourism development in the world-heritage city, Lijiang, China. In: K. W. Wöber (Ed.), *City tourism 2002* (pp. 123–132). Wien: Springer-Verlag.

Yamamura, T., Kidokoro, T., & Onishi, T. (2001). The actual situation of the tourism industry based on the world heritage and its problems. *Papers on City Planning, November 2001, City Planning Review Special Issue*, *36*, 247–252.

Yang, Z., & Zhang, F. (Eds) (2000). *Ancient Lijiang town*. Kunming: Art Publishing House of Yunnan.

Yothu Yindi Foundation (1999). Garma festival of traditional culture. *Yothu Yindi Foundation Newsletter*, 2(1), 4.

Zaichkowsky, J. (1985). Measuring the involvement construct. *Journal of Consumer Research, 12*, 341–352.

Zeppel, H. (1995). Authenticity and Iban Longhouse tourism. *Borneo Review*, 6(2), 109–125.

Zeppel, H. (1997a). Touring the dreamtime: Marketing Aboriginal culture in Australian tourism. In: D. Rowe, & P. Brown (Eds), *Proceedings ANZALS conference 1997* (pp. 218–224). Newcastle: Department of Leisure and Tourism Studies, University of Newcastle.

Zeppel, H. (1997b). Maori tourism in New Zealand. *Tourism Management, 18*(7), 475–478.

Zeppel, H. (1997c). Meeting "wild people": Iban culture & longhouse tourism in Sarawak. In: S. Yamashita, & J. S. Eades (Eds), *Tourism and cultural development in Asia and Oceania* (pp. 119–140). Bangi: Penerbit Universiti Kebangsaan.

Zeppel, H. (1998a). Come share our culture: Marketing Aboriginal tourism in Australia. *Pacific Tourism Review, 2*(1), 67–82.

Zeppel, H. (1998b). *Tourist dreamings: The national aboriginal cultural center, Sydney*. Paper Presented at Inter-Cultural Studies 1998, Conference, The University of Newcastle, Unpublished Paper.

Zeppel, H. (1998c). Selling the dreamtime: Aboriginal culture in Australian tourism. In: D. Rowe, & G. Lawrence (Eds), *Tourism, leisure, sport, critical perspectives* (pp. 23–28). Sydney, Hodder Headline.

Zeppel, H. (1998d). Issues in Maori tourism. *Pacific Tourism Review, 1*(4), 363–370.

Zeppel, H. (1999a). Touring Aboriginal cultures: Encounters with Aboriginal people in Australian travelogues. *Tourism, Culture and Communication, 2*(2), 123–141.

Zeppel, H. (1999b). *Aboriginal tourism in Australia: A research bibliography*. CRC Tourism Research Report Series: Report 2, Co-operative Research Center for Sustainable Tourism, Griffith University, Gold Coast, Queensland.

Zeppel, H. (2000). *Indigenous heritage tourism and its economic value in Australia*. Conference Proceedings of 2000 Heritage Economics: Challenges for Heritage Conservation and Sustainable Development in the 21st Century. Available at: http://www.ahc.gov.au/infores/publications/generalpubs/economics/pubs/economics72.pdf.

Zeppel, H. (2001). Aboriginal cultures and indigenous tourism. In: N. Douglas, N. Douglas, & R. Derrett (Eds), *Special interest tourism: Context and cases* (pp. 232–259). Melbourne: Wiley.

Zeppel, H. (2002). Cultural tourism at the Cowichan Native Village, British Columbia. *Journal of Travel Research, 41*, 92–100.

# Author Index

# Subject Index